The Land of the Fanns
and its history

To Bob and Sharon
Wishing you happy times exploring our local history
Sue

The Land of the Fanns
and its history

Compiled and written by

Sue Smith
Dip TP MRTPI Grad.Dipl.Cons(AA) IHBC

The Land of the Fanns and its history

First published by Sue Smith, March 2022
35 Woodman Road, Warley, Brentwood, Essex CM14 5BG

© Susan J. Smith, 2022

ISBN 978-1-3999-2011-7

Further copies of this book are available from
Thames Chase Forest Centre, Pike Lane, Upminster, Essex RM14 3NS
or via the Thames Chase website www.thameschase.org.uk

All rights reserved. No part of this publication may be reproduced or transmitted in any form or by any means, electronic or mechanical, including photocopying, recording, or by any information storage and retrieval system, without the prior written permission of the publisher, with the exception of reproduction for use in an educational environment.

The author and publisher gratefully acknowledge the permission granted to reproduce the copyright material in this book. Every effort has been made to obtain the permission for the use of copyright material. The publisher apologises for any errors or omissions and would be grateful if notified of any corrections that should be incorporated into future reprints of this book.

British Library Cataloguing in Publication Data
A catalogue record for this book is available from the British Library

Printed by Lavenham Press Ltd
Water Street, Lavenham, Suffolk CO10 9RN

Cover artwork © D. Ian Smith
Line drawings and artwork, unless otherwise indicated, © D. Ian Smith

This Book is dedicated to all students of the
Land of the Fanns
long may this precious landscape be enjoyed by all

'The view from the summit is admitted to be one of the finest in the kingdom.
It stretches over the Vale of the Thames from London to Southend, a distance of nearly 40 miles, with the hills of Kent as a background, and to the North it extends over a large tract of beautiful country to the well-wooded uplands of Brentwood and Billericay, and beyond.'
Artware Fine Art

Upper Langdon by John Louis Petit FSA in pencil & watercolour 1831

Rev. John Louis Petit FSA (1801-1868) was an architectural historian and watercolourist who is known for recording his subject faithfully yet also conveying the emotional impact of the scene. From 1828-34 he was a curate at Mistley in Essex and this painting by him was likely produced during that period in 1831. He argued against the Victorian restorers and was a forerunner of the Society for the Protection of Ancient Buildings (SPAB) and a founder member of the British Archaeological Institute.

Preface

My ancestors travelled up from Dorset in the 18th century to settle in the East End of London where I also was born, a Cockney within the sound of Bow Bells. But I was brought up in Old Dagenham and Rainham, educated in Hornchurch, Thurrock, Chelmsford and London, becoming a Chartered Planner specialising in historic building conservation. I settled in Brentwood 50 years ago and have worked in Thurrock and for over 30 years as Havering's Conservation Officer/Coordinator. I now work for the family Architectural Practice across all the boroughs local to this area and continue to specialise in Planning and Built Heritage matters. I am a local girl and value our rich local heritage, so it has been a privilege to have been asked to draw together the myriad historic events in which this area has played its part and to tell its story.

This work has been enabled through the **Land of the Fanns** (LotF) Landscape Partnership Scheme, which is a history and natural heritage restoration and celebration project funded by the National Lottery Heritage Fund and others. Within the considerable partnership programme of projects and events, this book draws together the history stories of the local area for the pleasure and education of all those interested in its past to be able to better enjoy, value and respect this hard-pressed landscape for the future.

The Land of the Fanns and its Borough environs centres on the Thames Chase Community Forest (coloured green) that extends across much of the LotF

General Introduction

The vision for the book is for it to enable quick, clear and easy access to an understanding of local history right across this landscape. In this way the area may become better recognised as a connected and cohesive place where its heritage is loved and understood by local people and visitors, students and their teachers alike.

The aim is to reveal the heritage of this landscape in terms of its pre-history, history and natural heritage so that readers are better informed in understanding the landscape and their attachment to it and are thereby better able to celebrate and connect with the landscape.

The book is designed as a reference point and guide to all audiences for future research. It is written for students of all ages and abilities including children and their teachers at junior schools; pupils in secondary education and at GCSE level; students at sixth form college and in Further Education; those undertaking private study or for general interest; for post-graduate study and those amongst the University of the 3rd Age and is guided by the Key Stages for Education – KS1 history and geography; KS2 history and geography; KS3 history; KS4 humanities; KS5 humanities.

In that context 'A high-quality history education will help pupils gain a coherent knowledge and understanding of Britain's past and that of the wider world. It should inspire pupils' curiosity to know more about the past. Teaching should equip pupils to ask perceptive questions, think critically, weigh evidence, sift arguments, and develop perspective and judgement. History helps pupils to understand the complexity of people's lives, the process of change, the diversity of societies and relationships between different groups, as well as their own identity and the challenges of their time.', the National Curriculum in England, Key Stages 1 and 2 History.

SECTION A of the book is about Landscape, it covers geography and natural heritage and geology, and sets the basis for the later Sections. As landscape scale is over vast time periods so timescales are given as million years ago (mya) or thousand years ago (kya) and Marine Isotope Stage (MIS) dating is also indicated.

SECTION B is about prehistory, the archaeological periods of the Stone Age, the Bronze Age and the Iron Age and the terminology used is of the established BC 'Before Christ' running backwards from 1BC.

SECTION C is about the history periods from the Romans to the 20th century and the term AD 'Anno Domini' (in Latin 'the year of our Lord') running forwards from AD1 is used. Dates are not definitive.

There are also four themes which reoccur throughout this book as identified by *TellTale* and local people working together through the auspices of LotF in 2018. These are the **surprise** facts and stories that are invariably found in each area and over each period of history and pre-history; the **migration** of both people and of plant and animal species ever criss-crossing this landscape; the landscape that is all about **the relationship of the land and the water;** and the productive nature of this landscape for **agriculture, trade, commerce and industry** as well as for national defence and for innovation.

'This unique landscape covered by the Land of the Fanns Partnership Scheme has, over time, been fragmented and eroded by many industrial, economic and lifestyle changes. Crisscrossed by boundaries and access routes to and from London and bounded by the busy River Thames, the natural and built heritage of the area has been lost or misunderstood. The Land of the Fanns Partnership Scheme has sort to draw together the stories of the built and natural heritage of this area to celebrate its historic roots and identity. This important book is a framework on which the rich physical and social history of this evolving landscape hangs and endeavours to aid exploration, understanding and pride in the landscape that is Thames Chase Community Forest.' **Thames Chase Trust**

'The phrase 'The Land that Fanns' was first coined in Leslie Thompson's local history study in 1957 which celebrates a more unified landscape. 'Fanns' is derived from the Saxon word for fen which meant 'low marshy land' and perfectly describes much of this lost watery landscape. Although the Land of the Fanns Landscape Partnership Scheme have used this phrase to cover an area encompassing more than just historic fenland, the wider landscape owes so much of it's character to a marshy origin. By adopting the historic name for our area, the 'Land of the Fanns' captures the essence of our ambition: to reunifiy our landscape and spark renewed attachment to it.' **Land of the Fanns Landscape Partnership**

Through its auspices, the LotF Partnership Scheme has produced a companion volume to this book of the stories and reminisces of local people over the turn of the 21st century. Called *Fens, Forests and Fields* the Introductory essay is by the acclaimed writer and social historian Ken Worpole. The book of local memories across the LotF is also lavishly illustrated with artwork produced in a Community Mapping project based on 100 stories gathered through walks and writing workshops led by outdoor arts organisation Kinetika, and concludes with conversations with local workers and volunteers on the subject the 'Future of the Fanns'.

A note from the author: As Dame Hilary Mantel remarked about writers during her Reith lectures on the BBC in July 2020, 'you only write about one tenth of what you know'. This may be a fulsome tome but the *Land of the Fanns* has so much more to tell and to reward students of this landscape...

Contents

Preface i
General Introduction ii

Section A: Landscape Introduction 1
Chapter 1   The 'Land of the Fanns' 3
Chapter 2   Geography: landscape, people and natural heritage 6
Chapter 3   Geology and development of this Landscape 38

Section B: Prehistory & Archaeology Introduction 59
Chapter 4   Stone Age *c.2.6 million years ago – c.2,500 BC* 63
Chapter 5   Bronze Age *c.2,550 BC – c.750 BC* 74
Chapter 6   Iron Age *c.750 BC – c.AD 50* 87

Section C: History Introduction 99
Chapter 7   Romans *AD 43 – 5th century AD* 103
Chapter 8   Saxons & Danes *5th – 11th centuries* 113
Chapter 9   Norman & Plantagenet *11th – 15th centuries* 126
Chapter 10 Tudor & Stuart *15th – 17th centuries* 144
Chapter 11 Georgian *18th century* 164
Chapter 12 Victorian *19th century* 188
Chapter 13 Edwardian era *Early 20th century* 209
Chapter 14 House of Windsor *Mid 20th century* 233

Legacy 252

Appendix
Abbreviations used in the text and references 254
Acknowledgements 256

Throughout the book 💡 introduces bright ideas and projects for kids.

💡 Do you know this area well enough – can you unravel the meanings of this Land of the Fanns landscape illustrated in the different parts of the cover picture? Answers at the end of the book.

Section A
Landscape Introduction

A whole cavalcade of history has paraded across this landscape over the millennia and continues to today - either east/west along the route of the Roman Road or via that great maritime highway the river Thames diverted here during the Ice Age; or north/south via the river valleys of prehistoric trade routes or the low hills of medieval pilgrimage trails. This has led to a legacy of tangible cultural heritage including buildings, landscape, monuments, books, works of art and artefacts and also intangible culture such as folklore, traditions, language and knowledge as well as natural heritage including biodiversity. So that the landscape heritage here of built, archaeological, natural and cultural components in many ways spreads over a far wider area than its immediate boundaries and informs and influences far wider audiences. Indeed, its local role very often plays a far greater part in the regional, national and at times the international story of heritage and culture, which is certainly worth investing in and exploring.

Constant movement of people across this landscape over the centuries leaves little opportunity for communities to either understand or to contribute towards the local and cultural heritage. By bringing the history of the area together in a comprehensive way and encouraging physical and intellectual access for all, the richness of our inheritance can become clearer, encouraging understanding and appreciation for mutual benefit.

In the distant past this area has enjoyed successive identities as part of wider, independent countries with resilient peoples, but now as a part of historic south-west Essex merging into north-east London the local identity is less clear. Although visually this landscape retains its own distinctive character and local people still instinctively feel allied to the landscape, its form is no-longer easily understood, and the heritage and its linkages cannot be readily accessed in a comprehensive way. These difficulties do not just apply to local people, it is especially difficult for visitors and enquiring students because the heritage is hard to interpret as research is complex due to the ancient dividing north-south administrative boundary along the Ingrebourne Valley – a role that now largely falls to the **M25 motorway corridor**. Today that boundary largely splits both the stories and the demographics of the area between Greater London to the west and the modern Essex County to the east so that even local residents find that they are puzzled about their heritage.

By bringing back together the history and stories of this surviving London fanns and marshes area of southwest Essex and drawing out the various historical themes and tales imbuing the landscape to explain and aid its interpretation the reader can better understand the landscape and their attachment to it. It becomes easier to celebrate, restore and reconnect the landscape and through strengthening a *sense of place* the area becomes a better place to live, work and visit. The Book is intended to act as a spring board for further specific and more detailed research as may be required and an ideas base for school projects or for art, design and other craft work for individuals or clubs and societies.

Looking south as the M25 motorway marks the separation of the Essex part of the LotF landscape to the east (left) from the London area on the west (right). Here Thames Chase Visitor Centre is in the middle ground. (Photograph courtesy of Malcolm Fish)

An understanding of the heritage of this landscape can be restored by drawing together the details of its natural formation through its geological evolution and the resultant geography; and the prehistory story of human impact and influence on the landscape told through the archaeology of the area and the historical events that have all come naturally out of its geological origins; and by considering the pressures and current trends and their amelioration. So that whether by getting out and about or through further study, local people and visitors can all enjoy and benefit from a clearer understanding of this place, its rich past and future promise.

Chapter 1
The 'Land of the Fanns'

Here, as East London crosses into south-west Essex, this landscape of high ridges, lowland, river valleys and marshes along with the Thameside quarry townscape tells a distinctive heritage story of people, wildlife and culture that has evolved over the millennia retaining its sense of identity and place although peoples have come and gone. It has witnessed, and often given rise to so much of the nation's heritage story and played its part, moulding and yielding and sometimes rebelling in response.

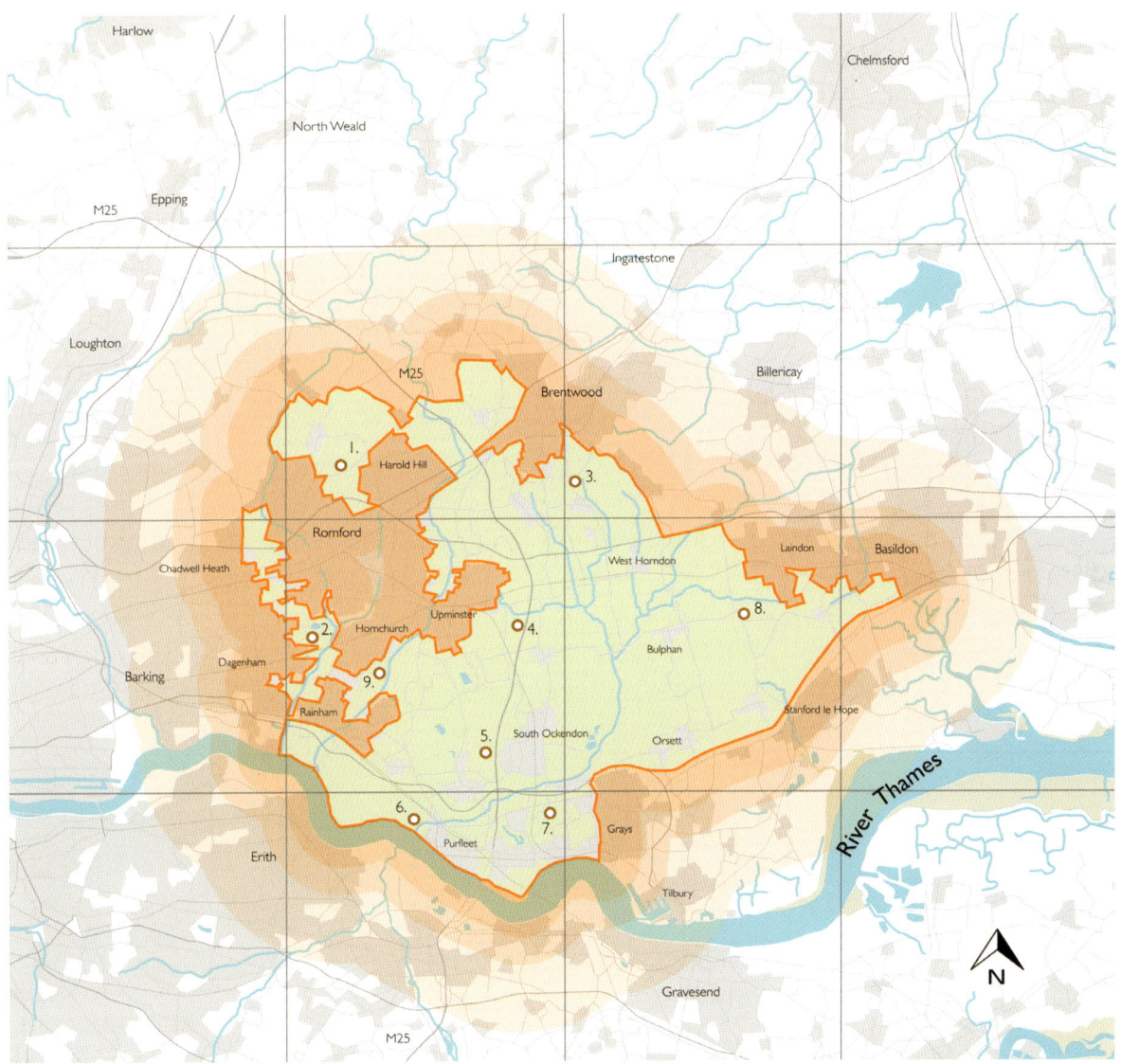

Map of the Land of the Fanns, the Thames Chase Community Forest at its heart, together with its immediate area of influence and the wider environs (courtesy LotF). © Crown copyright 2021 OS LICENCE no. 100064852. Visitor Centres are indicated at Points 1-9: Bedfords Park; Eastbrookend Country Park Discovery Centre; Thorndon Park South; Thames Chase Visitor Centre; Belhus Woods Country Park Visitor Centre; RSPB Rainham Marshes, Purfleet Chafford Gorges Nature Park (Visitor Centre itself closed 2021); Langdon Visitor Centre; Hornchurch Country Park

This is a landscape busy with industry and trade along Thameside and with a quiet and desirable hinterland accessible to the sea and London. As pressure for the outward expansion of London developed, aided by improvements to transport systems for people and goods, north-east London relentlessly expanded into historic south-west Essex. That pressure would quite naturally present opportunity for being inventive and for developing social awareness, and it has done so over time bringing new scientific, cultural and business ideas and as a result over the centuries of the many notable people born, residing, visiting, working or taking their inspiration locally, some in particular have affected this landscape, its people, their character and culture.

The busiest and most populated areas are those closer to the London conurbation in the west; those to the south along Thameside closest to the busy modern commercial Thames wharfs and ferries and the Thames Crossing; and in the desirable higher land to the north around Brentwood that was found in 2016 to be amongst 'the top 12 places to live in Britain' (as reported in *The Times* newspaper), and significantly it is this area that features primarily in the reality television production *The Only Way is Essex*. Whilst although in 2012 the southern lowland area was recorded as part of a broader district having low levels of life satisfaction (Mail Online: *Govt. 'happiness survey'*); but interestingly only three years later the same district had redeemed itself and was found to be 'one of the top 20 locations Londoners have relocated to in the past year. And its appeal includes its green space.' (*Evening Standard,* 3 Feb. 2015). All three active and highly populated areas turn to the heart of this landscape for a contrasting break from their pace of life.

Thames Chase Community Forest is not just at the core of this landscape and its community as in fact it stretches tendril-like reaching right out to local town centres to include Romford, Hornchurch, Upminster, Brentwood, Grays and Basildon, bringing large populations and transportation links into close proximity with the heritage of this landscape (Photograph courtesy of Malcolm Fish)

Here, in and around the Thames Chase Community Forest[1] people find the peace and quiet of the countryside as well as the outdoor recreational and learning opportunities that are found both in the transformed post-industrial and post-military landscapes, as well as along its natural river valleys and marshes, across its hillsides and broad lowland plane that are still dotted reassuringly with historic Essex vernacular buildings, aged specimen trees and supporting local wildlife conservation.

United this landscape has a very real job to do in providing ready and sustainable access to outdoor relief for its huge audience not only of local people but those from neighbouring areas as well as visitors, whilst sustaining precious and essential wildlife corridors and at the same time accommodating huge competing national pressures for all manner of development and service corridors and with vast numbers of people daily passing through. The very real need now is to work together to improve physical and intellectual accessibility to the landscape so as to be best equipped to sustain the best of what we have, be effective in ameliorating inherited problems and inform future decision making.

---

[1] Thames Chase Community Forest is said to be 'The biggest park in Greater London,' (*Eat, Sleep London* online) covering some 98.4 sq. km (38 sq. miles) [and compares for example to Epping forest at 24.8 sq. km (9.6 sq. miles) and West London's Richmond Park at only 9.6 sq. km (3.7 sq. miles)]. It was set up in 1990 as one of ten (now eleven) Community Forests across the country for environmental regeneration, bringing woodlands back into use and providing opportunities for leisure, recreation and cultural activities. Now over 2 million trees have been planted here, and new areas of meadowlands and wetlands created with access by footpaths, cycle and bridleways transforming the landscape and helping to create 'healthy, inspiring resilient places' for people and nature to live, side by side (Community Forest Trust).

Chapter 2
Geography: landscape, people and natural heritage

NATIONAL CURRICULUM Hints

This is a diverse geographical landscape that reaches from the Brentwood Heights to Thameside and from Dagenham to the Langdon Hills and encompasses an intriguing broad plain of fanns[1] and fens. The landscape has directly influenced both the indigenous people and the coming of migrations over the millennia. Its underlying geological makeup, before and throughout the Ice Age Stages has been dramatic and has only recently come to be more properly understood[2] and is deserving of a curiosity and fascination about the place.

For students, a study of the varied geography of this landscape and its dramatic underlying geological story provides for a deepened 'understanding of the interaction between physical and human processes and the formation and use of landscapes and environments'. It teaches about 'diverse places, people, resources and natural and human environments' on both land and sea, through spatial variation and change over time (Key Stages 1 and 2).

SURPRISE *'The Land of the Fanns is an intricate landscape, full of surprises and 'hidden gems' and rewards exploring.'* **(TellTale working with the public 2018)**

This is a landscape of surprises, so much of which is about the views:

- the unexpected and spectacular view from all highpoints across this landscape down over the sweeping plain of the Thames Valley to the Kentish Hills
- the sudden and dramatic views over the sea wall of the broad river Thames as it begins to near its estuary and is dominated by huge commercial shipping with occasional Thames barges and other small craft on pleasure trips or world-wide curtesy calls like the historic Tall Ships on their way to the Port of London
- the bright lights of London that can be seen both from the high ridges and along the river Thames
- fine views of the Queen Elizabeth II Bridge from along Thameside
- dramatic sunsets over London in the distance

---

[1] *Fanns* is a Saxon word for marsh and gave rise here to the fann men working this marshy landscape during the 17th and 18th centuries as identified in *The Land that Fanns* by Leslie Thompson, pub. Tindal Press 1957.
[2] Ian and Ros Mercer (2022) *Essex Rock – Geology beneath the Landscape* ISBN 9781784272791

Sunset over distant London from Purfleet-on-Thames

LANDFORM *'The Land of the Fanns is about land and water and the often shifting relationship between them.'* **(TellTale working with the public 2018)**

This landscape crosses the border of the North Thames Basin National Character Area (NCA) 111 and the Inner London NCA 112 and is characterised as being '…on a broad flood plain which rises in gentle terraces, providing panoramic views of London's skyline from the clay plateaux and ridges in the north'.

We can see this fine view for ourselves both in the early 19th century frontispiece artwork (see dedication page) by John Louis Petit FSA and in the beautiful landscape views that we still have today:

Langdon Hills view (Photograph courtesy of Debbie Brady, Heritage Engagement Officer LotF, 2017)

The geography of this landscape is the product of the cumulative effect of the Ice Age Stages on this area that was on the margins of the ice, resulting in an unexpected and remarkable landscape with a ridge of higher land overlooking the Thames river plain that spreads out in a fan-like fashion and is formed of wetlands and marshes, intersected by local river valleys and interspersed by a low hilly landscape.

A study of the significance of the geography of this exceptional range of landscapes as a whole and its relationship with its people and with the natural environment can reveal the value and special contribution of this area to the nation's history.

The natural arrangement of this landscape was created as successive ice sheets pushed the great river Thames ever southwards, from its original outlet at the Norfolk Wash to its present location forming the southern boundary of this area (see Geology Chapter). As the Thames is tidal here a major settlement was inevitably created at the river's lowest bridging point west of this area on exceptional agricultural land, eventually becoming London the country's capital city; whilst to the east the North Sea coastal boundary is moderately close. In addition, there are two natural east-west travel arteries bordering this landscape – the Thames in the south and the northern ridge of higher land above the marshes; while the north-south movement was naturally formed by local river tributaries of the Thames and their river valleys.

Today this landscape plays host to a wide variety of natural and built heritage sites of interest for local people and visitors alike. For example, in addition to the Visitor Centres (see map in Chapter 1) there are DiscoverMe sites (see Chapter 14 – Legacy) at: Rainham Hall and Gardens; The Old Chapel, Upminster; Havering Museum; Eastbury Manor House; Davy Down; Upminster Windmill; Thames Chase Forest Centre; Queen Elizabeth's Hunting Lodge; Ilford Hospital Chapel; Tilbury Fort; Coal House Fort and Park; Valentines Mansion and Park; Thurrock Museum and Valence House Museum.

The geography of this landscape became of essential importance to the story of the nation's history through the Thames delivering international access straight to the capital city by water or directionally by air. In doing so this landscape immediately became relevant to the defence of London and the country throughout the millennia; it also enabled the inevitable development of industry along Thameside making an essential contribution to the national economy; and, with its proximity and ease of access to the capital, the area was also always bound to be essential for its agricultural contribution to the London market.

MIGRATION *'This is a cross roads landscape: because of its location on the Thames ...*
people have always travelled into, through and away from this area.'
(TellTale working with the public 2018)

In respect of the **natural environment**, in his book *A History of Essex* in 1958 A.C. Edwards concluded from a study of the details included in the Domesday Survey of 1086, that the Essex hinterland bore the most heavily wooded areas, as compared to the coastline and the northern bank of the Thames. The less wooded area here spans from Barking in the west to Horndon-on-the-Hill in the east and from the Thames in the south, northwards to the Brentwood Heights. Falling naturally outside the Great Forest of Essex, it determines a distinctive landscape loop here, more in common with the Thames riverside and Essex coastline than the county's interior.

This area hosts a well beloved and unusual variety of niche landscapes of considerable variation over fairly short distances which provide the relief of open green space for communities around the East London fringe, all in the original spirit of the nation-wide Community Forests that here are centered on the Thames Chase Community Forest. This exceptional range of landscapes is one of the last ancient landscapes in London and translates into an intriguing diversity of habitats and species of plants and animals including some of national importance. Human intervention has had a significant impact on the development and maintenance of those habitats, which in combination has resulted in a surprising and unique **biodiversity**[3] so close to London.

Nevertheless there is a relatively high proportion of **'ancient woodlands'** in the landscape, which refers to those woodlands having existed continuously since 1600, even if cut down and replanted over time since then. Before that date it was unusual for woodlands to have been purposefully planted. These woods have a long history of being managed through coppicing and pollarding 'which has allowed rich ground flora to develop and also supports rare mosses and deadwood invertebrates' (NCA profile for the Northern Thames Basin). This together with evidence of early assorted field boundaries suggests the close relationship of woodland to the settlement of people over time.

However the long history of human intervention upon this landscape continues apace leading to tensions existing between development pressures and biodiversity. Loss of woodlands and hedgerows is a contributor to climate change, soil erosion and habitat fragmentation. It is also a loss to the local character of the wooded hills and farmlands, also the ancient hedgerows are valuable biodiversity and antiquity indicators. The NCA has identified that 'climate regulation: soils, woodland and hedgerows are likely to be significant stores of organic carbon across this area' also 'The restoration of hedgerows across the landscape can reduce the scale of wind erosion.'

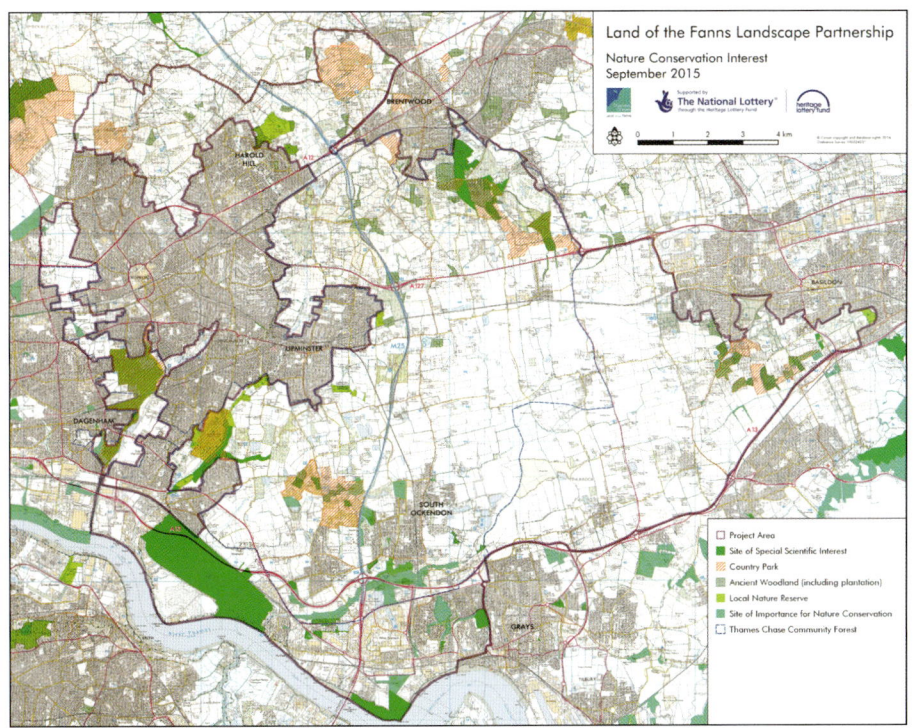

Areas of Nature Conservation Interest within the LotF (Courtesy LotF and Alison Farmer Associates 'Land of the Fanns Assessment Report') © Crown copyright 2021 OS LICENCE no.100064852

The map above shows the distribution of **natural heritage** interest and designations across the landscape. Although much of the area is managed for agriculture, there are still important habitats

---

[3] biodiversity refers to the variety of life, their communities and habitats including the evolutionary, ecological and cultural processes that sustain life.

interspersed within this productive land including a high density of ponds for great crested newts and other aquatic life and a scattering of ditches and small reed beds across the Thames floodplain. Hedgerows and other linear natural features such as railway lineside and roadside verges are wildlife corridors when they are properly managed and maintained.

Rewarding connectivity for people with wildlife can be achieved as suitable habitats are established, managed and protected. Already for example wild orchids and wild bluebells can be found in the area and species of deer roam freely in the north and anecdotally wild boar, and the Ingrebourne river supports kingfishers even close to residential estates, also a heronry and great numbers of duck breeds are present on a popular fishing lake nearby, here barn owls have been known to fly even in daytime view of the Ingrebourne Valley Nature Discovery Centre.

The lack of nature conservation designations towards the central lowland is notable and reflects the area's importance as farmland. Nevertheless, the ditches that drain this landscape, whilst undesignated, perform an important role as wildlife corridors. Elsewhere, unimproved meadows, ponds and heaths comprise part of the agricultural landscape mosaic. Many of the hedgerows are mature and thick, providing important habitats and supporting a range of species.

ECONOMY *'This area is justly famous for trade, commerce and industry: these have been important here for many centuries.'* (TellTale working with the public 2018)

Here is an **historic environment** landscape of higher land, unusual in Essex, that embraces a lowland plain interspersed by low hills and ridges and otherwise comprised of fens and fanns and crossed by three rivers, their marshes and their tributaries that contribute to low-lying damp and dank conditions susceptible to water logging and flood and that feed into the river Thames along the southern boundary.

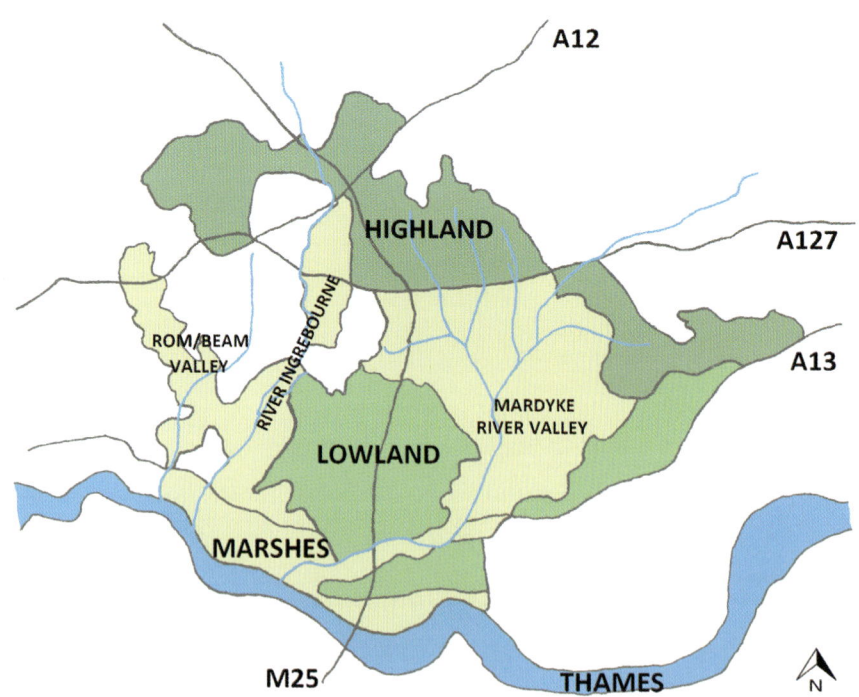

Basic geography of the area showing higher land in dark green; lower land in light green; valleys and marshes in light brown and indicating rivers and major roads

As well as its nature conservation interest and contribution this is also an area of diverse built heritage interest, including many sites and events of national importance and connections to the national story. Through its location and form this landscape has naturally been witness to so much of the nation's prehistory and historical events, as Havering's Local Studies Librarian, Simon Donoghue has put it 'as national history passes across this landscape it leaves a little of itself attached here', and collectively those events influence the landscape, its people and its sense of place.

The basic landscape forms comprising the higher land; lowland; river valleys and marshes and an urban quarry townscape, are made up of:

The Higher Land The rural higher land of **Havering Ridge, Brentwood Heights, and Langdon Hills** are amongst the highest spots in Essex, and frame the north and eastern fringes of this high value landscape. It has a strong historic character, time depth and a feeling of remoteness combined with wildlife interest with roaming deer herds, nature reserves, country parks, tree-lined rural lanes, woodland and farmland. The Parkland and Plotlands[4] sites from Hainault to Langdon Hills are notable for ancient woodland and species rich grassland and woodland pasture occasionally as mosaics. Interspersed are villages and hamlets typical of medieval Essex in form and layout with historic buildings, and there are strong intangible heritage assets with a history rich with historical connections and fables and important archaeological potential and ancient monuments.

The great elevation and expansive views of the ridge from Marks Gate continues eastwards to make the countryside special as it skirts Brentwood town round to Langdon Hills where local people have remarked on the: 'Great walking area', the 'Bluebell walks', and the 'Amazing views towards London and the Thames' (*Landscape Conservation Action Plan 2016,* LotF Project). The scenic quality derives from the topography, visual variety and quality of its views and landform, land use patterns and textures, historic parkland with old specimen trees as well as wood pasture, an important habitat resource of unimproved grassland interspersed with woodland and veteran trees, also commons, and countryside recreational opportunities and Visitor Centres, a Countryside Conservation Area and a designated Living Landscape. The landscape is an important resource for a significant urban population nearby but is sensitive to change and suffers from the pressures of its location on the edge of an urban area.

The distinctive native British bluebells on Shenfield Common (Photograph courtesy of Aisling Woodhead)

[4] for Plotlands see 20th century Chapter 13.

Chapter 2 Geography: landscape, people and natural heritage

Havering Ridge is an Area of Special Character (a local Planning designation), from here there are excellent views of London and down to the Thames and even northwards with extensive countryside views, which local people have described in particular the 'Views across into London' and the 'Views over Romford and London show off the Essex ridge and plateau – a geology of landscape', and 'Breathtaking space in Harold Hill' (LotF 2016), all contribute to making this area special but so far such views remain unprotected. The area focuses on the attractive historic village of **Havering-atte-Bower**, now both a conservation area and an Archaeological Priority Area (APA), with numerous listed and local heritage buildings and structures, also common land, public footpaths and bridleways supporting the strong horsey-culture, farmland and a retained parkland character and with significant areas of ancient woodland such as Bower Wood, Foxburrow Wood and Trench Pond Plantation that reflect historic management practices such as coppicing. The pebble gravel at the top of the ridge naturally favours the growth of birch trees, gorse shrubs and bracken, while further south the London Clay better supports the growth of oak and hornbeam trees and brambles. The Ridge favours a different mix of breeding birds, wildflower meadows and grassland sites in early summer.

Havering Council's Heritage Walk circumnavigates Havering village, which is on the London Outer Orbital Path (London Loop sections 20 westwards to Chigwell, and 21 southwards via the densely populated Harold Hill post Second World War Housing Neighbourhood (see Mid 20th century Chapter) and Harold Wood dormitory suburb). In the village the listed parish church is believed to mark the position of the now lost Saxon royal hunting lodge and later royal Palace of Havering popular with British kings and queens for 600 years and the reason for the area's rich archaeological potential. Here within Havering Country Park is the second largest avenue of Wellingtonia trees (Sequoiadendron giganteum or Giant Redwoods) in England and one of the first of such plantations in the country. It marks Havering Ridge as it points into central London and is said to guide today's royal fly-pasts to Buckingham Palace.

Havering Country Park avenue of Giant Redwood trees (Photograph courtesy LotF)

To the south the extensive **Bedfords Park** is a metropolitan Site of Importance for Nature Conservation (SINC), once a privately owned estate where the mansion has gone but the parkland survives and is now a Local Nature Reserve (LNR) with an Essex Wildlife Trust (EWT) Visitor Centre and a Walled

Garden with Friends Group. A Victorian owner planted a bank of larch trees that screen off the historic Charles Bridgeman's (see Georgian Chapter) woodland that adjoins the site, and on a small, flat hill-top plateau planted a woodland of specimen trees creating a woodland walk next to the house. A herd of captive red deer are a popular attraction at Bedfords Park, and with summer grazing of cows for grassland conservation.

Hedge layering at Bedfords Park (Photograph courtesy LotF)

The parkland also affords panoramic views to the Thames and to London and from here continuous pedestrian links through local parks and public gardens in Havering (the philanthropic inspiration of local trader and Councillor Tommy England during the 1930s) make the countryside directly accessible from Romford town centre that retains a sense of London's old East End.

Moving eastwards, **Noak Hill** is a hamlet of numerous listed[5] and local heritage buildings,[6] including a church and cottages originally for farm workers employed at the adjacent Dagnams Estate. The successive mansions at Dagnams are now lost but **Dagnam Park** survives, originally landscaped by Humphry Repton (see Georgian Chapter) it is part of the EWT initiative, it now has a Friends Group and is a LNR with the surrounding farmland having been managed for a time as 'set aside'. Here, an apparent network of overgrown medieval roads around Dagnams and approaching Manor Farm remain visible and Cockerels Moated Site is a Scheduled Ancient Monument (SAM). Dagnam Park together with Hatters Wood is a metropolitan SINC; the adjacent Duck Wood was once part of the extensive Forest of Waltham and is a Borough SINC. Here also is the start of the Ingrebourne Way Sustrans[7] Connect2 route 136 for walking and cycling to the Thames at Rainham.

• • • • • • • • • • • •

[5,6] For definitions of a listed building and local heritage building see the Tudor Chapter.

[7] Sustrans (Sustainable Transport) is a UK charity for walking and cycling and is custodian of the National Cycle Network.

To the east the ridge continues as the **Brentwood Heights** and a cattle tunnel provides pedestrian access beneath the M25 motorway through historic settlements at **St. Vincent's Hamlet** and **South Weald** village. This is a picturesque conservation area of many listed and historic buildings and stands at the high point with adjoining **Weald Country Park** (grade II Registered Parks & Garden) an EWT initiative and a countryside area covering the slopes down the hill to the north and west. Here the deer park was established in the 11th century but today wild deer roam free across the northern ridge with signs of them gradually extending their range southwards. Increasing unmanaged wild deer populations result in over grazing and browsing of veteran and young trees and loss of undergrowth habitat. Deer are commonly seen in Dagnam Park and roaming local residential streets on Harold Hill and crossing rural lanes. These narrow lanes can also experience heavy volumes of traffic with roadside verge erosion and, although the main road network is not generally visible here, traffic noise can be intrusive.

Fallow Deer at Dagnam Park LNR (Photograph courtesy of Don Tait)

Adjacent to the Park, South Weald village is known for its drifts of bluebells around the village in springtime and during June the events associated with the celebrated annual South Weald Flower Festival bring together the parish church and village school with the local community. This landscape has significant areas of ancient woodland but, as elsewhere in this area there is also a loss of veteran trees due to diseases such as Sudden Oak Death, a legacy Dutch Elm disease and Ash Dieback.

Once again there are distant views from the Brentwood Heights that continue the ridge eastwards and swings round to the south-east dropping down to cross the head of the Ingrebourne Valley at the old hamlet of **Brook Street** beside the M25 motorway junction and outside the highly populated **Brentwood Cathedral Town**. Wooded farmland surrounds Brentwood Town including the eastern slopes of Weald and the southern slopes of Great and Little Warley, Ingrave and Herongate (Chris Blandford Associates, 2006). The countryside encompasses Brook Street where it crosses the old Roman Road (A12) from Colchester to London. The hillside continues past the town of Brentwood via **Warley Country Park** on former farmland, with views back over to South Weald it was opened by Brentwood Borough Council in 2001.

As the ridge turns further to the east and to the south at Brentwood's outskirts the old garrison town of Warley with its sense of history and historical events is an intangible heritage asset as it spreads south into **Great Warley** village that at 116 m (380 ft.) is one of the highest points in Essex with extensive views across farmland and leads further eastwards down over **Warley Gap** to Thorndon. Brentwood Borough Council have produced a Walk through the attractive little valley that skirts the village on its eastern side to **Great Warley Common** that lies north-east of the village.

From Warley Road looking south past Great Warley village towards the valley of the Mardyke (Photograph courtesy of Debbie Brady, Heritage Engagement Officer LotF, 2017)

Great Warley is an historic village in a rural setting. This is a long linear village, reflecting the shape of local parishes in this area, each taking a share of the higher land, lower slopes and the marshes. Dark Lane is a Protected Lane and enters Great Warley village on The Green. Here is the entrance to **Warley Place Nature Reserve** (grade II registered with additional local authority Planning protection). This was originally laid out as gardens that were the life-time's passion of Ellen Willmott (d. 1934), the famous horticulturalist and writer (see Victorian Chapter). Further south in Warley village there are more listed and other historic buildings including a grade I, Art Nouveau[8] church. This exceptional church and the access to Warley Place Nature Reserve direct from the village centre make this a tourist hot-spot, outside the busy rush hour of Brentwood commuter traffic.

The historic Warley Common reaches right into Brentwood town via Brentwood Council's Donkey Lane Plantation, Hartswood Ancient Woodland, Kent's Wood and King Georges Playing Field to Shenfield Common. These woodlands and open spaces also link via Hartswood Access Trails and Little Warley Common, along the ridge beyond Warley Barracks site (see Chapter 13) to **Thorndon Country Park**.

The Country Park is divided into two distinct but linked areas, North and South. This is a Registered Park & Garden of national significance in a green belt landscape and a Special Landscape Area containing Sites of Special Scientific Interest (SSSI) that include the 15th century deer park, and Local

---

[8] Art Nouveau is an ornamental, decorative, flowing and floral artistic style.

Wildlife Sites (LWS), SAMs and listed buildings (see Tudor Chapter for definition) and is important for geological interpretation (see Geology Chapter). Thorndon contains wood pasture habitats and ancient woodland and the presence of Birch-Sessile Oak and Pendunculate Oak-Hornbeam woods support an outstanding assemblage of beetles (Coleoptera). In Springtime the Park is known for woodland flowers and birdsong, and for autumn colour and fungi on the woodland floor (Tony Gunton). Thorndon Park North has the Visitors EWT Nature Discovery Centre and woodlands hosting the *Gruffalo Trail* and with views of the imposing Georgian Palladian Thorndon Hall by James Paine, now subdivided into residential units (see Georgian Chapter). Thorndon Park South has mainly open parkland with wonderful views of the landscape and to Canary Wharf.

The backdrop to the Park along its eastern boundary, is Herongate another village conservation area with numerous vernacular listed buildings alongside the A128 road. This route south from Brentwood to the Thames passenger crossing at Tilbury follows the junction between the clay plateau out of the area to the east and the hilly ground of variable geology to the west. The long linear hamlets of **Little Warley** and **Childerditch** lie on the southern slopes of Thorndon Park between the Park and Great Warley. They each maintain a sense of rural isolation with their historic and vernacular buildings. The local popularity for horses means that passing horse riders and others with ponies and traps are fairly common and riders like to meet occasionally on places like Little Warley Common where the animals can graze while they can take refreshment at an adjacent hostelry, such as the historic Greyhound Inn.

• • • • • • • • • • • •

Langdon Hills rises to some 116 m. (381 ft.) comparable to Great Warley, and was first named by the Saxons literally as the 'Lang dun' the 'long hill'. This tall, hilly countryside range would have been a clear geographical vantage point for these people. Even in the 19th century one view was captured in an engraving by B.A. Branfill of Upminster Hall, captioned *View from Langdon Hills looking South-west* and used as the frontispiece by local historian T. L. Wilson in his *History and Topography of Upminster* in 1880/1. Such views that so impressed Victorian and Georgian people before them, remain today as illustrated below:

View from Langdon Hills (Photograph courtesy LotF)

The ridge that continues to provide a wonderful and surprising view interestingly seems to *fan out* before you, from all vantage points along this ridge of hills, particularly from the Langdon Hills Country Park here, and the village of Havering-atte-Bower and from the site of the Old Thorndon Hall at Herongate, and daily provides a spectacular view for thousands of south-bound M25 motorway travellers as they come off the ridge at Brentwood (Junc. 28) with a surprise and delight in the sudden view of this great fan-shaped plain spreading out from west to east as the road drops down towards the river Thames and Fobbing marshes and with the backdrop of the Kent Hills beyond.

Here is an area of 'Living Landscapes', established in 2012 and part of a nationwide Wildlife Trusts strategy that seeks to take a landscape scale approach to connecting and developing habitats. It provides opportunity to conserve and enhance the qualities of the area and includes many recreational sites. It extends along the ridge from Dunton in the north to Vange in the south. There is a high concentration of LNR here, the **Langdon Nature Reserve** of 210 ha. (519 acres) is managed by EWT with a Visitor Centre at Dunton Plotlands, and includes Lincewood, Willow Park and Marks Hill, while Vange Hill LNR is managed by Basildon Council. The 162 ha. (400 acres) of **Langdon Hills Country Park,** managed by Thurrock Council, includes Westley Heights and One Tree Hill as well as golf courses. The SSSI at Basildon Meadows is valued for its unimproved and herb rich grassland and wild orchids grow. There are a significant number of protected ancient woodlands including Hall, Coombe, Great Sutton, Northlands and Martinhole Woods including oak and coppiced hazel or sweet chestnut that act as a unifying element. Patches of acid soils support areas of bracken, birch and beech woodland which adds texture and variety to the area along with remnant commons and grazed parkland.

Here the landscape maintains a sense of separateness from urban areas such as nearby Basildon town which is served by this countryside area, although the town does have some visual impact, while any unchecked growth of woodland vegetation results in the loss of some key views. There is also a proliferation of horse grazing resulting in visual clutter and changes to enclosure patterns. There is some erosion of country lanes due to high traffic volume and parking and the popularity of the area for open-air recreation. Gradual improved footpath and cycleway connections to the wider landscape to the west would help to alleviate this pressure. However this is a high quality landscape derived from the topography, woodlands and views and the perception is of a deeply tranquil, rural landscape crossed by green lanes with a strong character and time depth.

<u>Places to visit nearby:</u>

- Havering Country Park
- Havering-atte-Bower & Havering Country Park Heritage Walk
- Bedfords Park, Essex Wildlife Trust Visitor and Nature Discovery Centre and Friends of Bedfords Park
- Weald Park Conservation Area is a surviving parkland landscape originally a planned Georgian Parkland and has a Visitor Centre and adjoins the South Weald Conservation Area which is an historic, rural, hilltop hamlet of mainly Georgian and Victorian buildings
- Warley Country Park
- EWT at Warley Place, Warley Place Nature Conservation Area and Nature Reserve, which also adjoins the Great Warley Conservation Area, which is an attractive, historic, hilltop village
- Thorndon Country Park and Thorndon Park Nature Discovery Centre, Thorndon Park Gruffalo Walk and Thames Chase Circular Walk 4

- Langdon Hills Country Park, Visitor Centre and Nature Discovery Park including One Tree Hill and Westley Heights, the largest inland EWT reserve comprising 461 acres of woodland, meadows, lakes, and former plotland gardens, on some of the highest land in Essex, with a wildlife garden as well as over 350 wild flowering plants including seven species of wild orchid, some 30 butterfly species, also badgers, foxes and weasels and visited by turtle doves, nightingales and woodcock.
- Thames Chase Destination Walk D5 is from Noak Hill to Upminster rail station via Dagnam Park, Harold Court and Pages Wood
- Ingrebourne Way Sustrans route 136 and Thames Chase Walk 11 in Harold Hill
- Wild Essex Walks (*Walk Wild Essex: 50 Wildlife Walks in Essex and East London* by Tony Gunton, pub. Lopinga Books ISBN 978-0-9530362-9-5) include:
    - Bedfords Park Walk from Romford Station
    - Weald & Navestock from Weald Country Park
    - Tylers Common & Great Warley
    - Brentwood Station to Thorndon Park circuit
    - Laindon station to Langdon Hills circuit
- Thames Chase Circular Walks 7 and 9 Great Warley, Harold Court and Pages Wood
- Sections 20, 21, of the London Loop cross this area from Chigwell to Havering-atte-Bower and on to Harold Wood

Ideas for further projects:

- Encourage children to make 'picture frames' out of card or with their thumbs and index fingers (turned sideways) to look through the frame to find and study a view – consider whether the view is accidental and natural or planned as living art, what makes it attractive? Then draw the view and write on it what is so good about the view (Framing the View Key Stage 1-4)
- Encourage the designation of the Noak Hill conservation area for its history and surviving heritage contribution
- Encourage the designation of the Dagnams (the Manor) Country Park (for history see *Harold Hill & Noak Hill: A History* by Simon Donoghue & Don Tait ISBN 0956327249, 9780956327246)
- Working with local people promote a village plan for the protection of Havering-atte-Bower with a well organised visitor attraction e.g. facilities including parking, WC, teas and by linking existing visitor attractors and seek the improvement of public transport links and protect the views, both from and to London and Kent
- Seek opportunity to locate the lost site of Havering Palace – archaeology project taking advice from the Greater London Archaeological Advisory Service (GLAAS)
- A study of the various types of wild deer herds particularly across Havering and Brentwood's wooded hills and country parks at Warley and South Weald and deer expansion patterns further across this landscape, in order to inform any other related studies, problems or opportunities
- Further research into, and seeking opportunity to protect key views of this inspirational landscape. Distant views will include those from the range of Wooded Hills across to London and over the lowland fen and the river Thames west to the London skyline including Canary Wharf and The Shard and east to the QEII Bridge. Also views across the

Thames including the mariners' historic sight-line across the Thames from the Erith bank north via Rainham to Hornchurch and the view from Lesnes Abbey at Abbey Wood in Kent to the Water Tower on the skyline atop Havering Wooded Hills.

Further Reading:

- Ballard, E.G. (Ted) (1987). *Our Old Romford & District pub.* Swan Libraries. ISBN 0 9503151 2 5
- Cobbett, Ray for Essex Wildlife Trust *Guide to Warley Place*
- Donoghue, Simon & Tait, Don (2013). *Harold Hill & Noak Hill: A History* pub. LBH ISBN 9780956327246
- Essex Wildlife Trust Brentwood & Billericay Group (2001 rev. 2005) *Warley Place*
- Gilby, Wally – see Laindon & District Community Archive online *A Journey from Langdon Hills to Corringham and Back*
- Harper, George (1984). *Warley Magna to Great Warley* pub. The Dickens Publishing Co. Ltd. ISBN 9780946204663
- Smith, Harold (1925). *A History of the Parish of Havering-atte-Bower, Essex* re.pub. LBH 1990
- Terry, George (1880). *Memories of Old Romford* pub. Straker Bros. & Co.

The Lowland The central lowland comprises on the western side of a raised plateau of mainly quarried farmland around **Aveley, Belhus and the Ockendons,** and from where London's tallest buildings and lights can be seen at night. To the east is the reclaimed fen land around **Bulphan and Horndon** lying along the southern boundary of the Brentwood ridge and the beauty of the views back across this lowland plain to the ridges of the higher land also remain today. Running parallel to the ridge is the mainline railway from London to the coast and calling here at Upminster, West Horndon and Basildon. A slightly higher range of hilly farmland or downs around **Stifford and Orsett** further to the south are bounded by the major A13 road from London to the Thames Estuary at Shoeburyness.

Fen Lane, Bulphan looking north to Thorndon (Photograph courtesy of Ian and Ros Mercer)

The flat, open and exposed central fenland of history is cut by an ancient grid-iron pattern of straight country roads, causeway lanes, dykes and drainage ditches reflecting the early enclosure of fenland and marsh. An east/west Iron Age route is thought to pass through here and possibly a network of Saxon routes to Chafford Heath (see below). Here are open expansive views and a feeling of remoteness where local communities have remarked on the 'Lovely drive through flat landscape', that is 'Remote', and with 'Big skies' (LotF Project 2016). Here too are dispersed farms and valuable arable farmland and wildlife corridors together with hidden historic villages at higher spots or fenland edges at **Little Warley, Bulphan and West and East Horndon** with historic buildings and SAM.

Fen lane from Harrow Bridge as it crosses a tributary of the Mardyke

The intangible assets are in the history of the fens and marshes, the fann lands and its people, and the resilience of successful farming practices over the centuries here, together with the historic pilgrims' route crossing these marshes. With its strong but surprising sense of place the area retains an air of mystery and vulnerability. This remains a lowland watery area with numerous field ponds and with an historic vulnerability to flooding and is the origin of the Mardyke River in a network of streams and ditches across the fens. These watery conditions are recalled in history and in local and nearby place names such as the historic Fanns Farmhouse and Farm, also Fangate Farm, Rabbetts Fan, Fann Rise, Marsh Way, Fen Covert, Fen Gate, Fen Lane and Fen Close, Childerditch Fen, Stringcock Fen, Orsett Fen and Bulphan Fen – originally *Bulgenen* meaning 'marshland by a fortified place'.

Orsett fen and farmland looking north towards Thorndon hills

• • • • • • • • • • • •

Central to this gently rolling countryside farming landscape is the **Thames Chase Community Forest**, designated in 1990, that through partnership working seeks to reverse the trend of loss of woodland to development and through natural events such as storms and disease that had led to a decrease in the distinctive woodland character of the landscape. Newly planted mixed woodlands such as Cely Woods, Belhus Chase, and Kennington Park reflect these efforts. Here is the Thames Chase Forest Centre with its historic farm buildings at Broadfields Farm and the **Broadfields Tree Trail** of native species covers an area immediately to the south of the Visitor Centre with new and existing plantings.[9] 💡 The maturing woodland and grassland mosaics, in particular those forming large blocks, are key points of nature heritage importance as Thames Chase Trust seeks to connect, restore and conserve the landscape elements and its biodiversity.

Tree planting at Thames Chase (Photograph courtesy LotF)

Although sited in open countryside the Visitor Centre lies close to the well populated district of Upminster, Cranham and Corbets Tey, and numerous information leaflets have been produced including Walks of natural and built heritage interest from the Forest Centre that link to the wider landscape network of paths and bridleways and popular cycle routes. The built heritage story accessed through these local Walks relates very much to the effect of the national heritage story on this area. Thames Chase Walk No. 2 leads visitors through Cranham Nature Reserve, an important survival of the marshland habitat, and Walk No. 3 from the Forest Centre is a Circular walk to the historic Cranham Brickfields (see Victorian Chapter). However this wider fenland area is vulnerable to urbanisation bringing visual intrusion and changes to the fens drainage threatening to change the nature, special value and appeal of this landscape.

• • • • • • • • • • • •

💡 [9] The Broadfields Tree Trail forms a basis that could be used as a starting point for learning about when exotic tree species were being introduced from abroad.

Chapter 2 Geography: landscape, people and natural heritage

The western raised plateau between 10m and 20m contours (33 and 66 ft.) with high spots at **Aveley and North Ockendon**, is a highly pressurised and threatened urban fringe landscape, fragmented and with loss of hedgerows and native elm trees for example and much pressed in upon by development, that has all resulted in a 'downtrodden', low to moderate landscape quality. It is bisected by the M25 motorway with associated traffic congestion, and the local Upminster to Grays railway line and is crisscrossed by narrow lanes at times spoiled by fly tipping and frequent lorry movements. Farms and farming are under pressure and the area has long been badly affected by quarrying for aggregate and landfill activity with mixed restoration success some returned to agriculture, other areas with recent tree planting associated with landfill sites. In all it has become fragmented and exhibits a *used* character and is consequently unsettling in places. However there is a concentration of often hidden but publicly accessible lakes created from former quarry sites such as at **Stubbers Outdoor Pursuits Centre**.

There are also precious intangible assets including potential for archaeology, and with possible remnant Saxon routes linking to the Chafford Hundred Saxon Gathering ground (meeting place) at Chafford Heath from surrounding areas such as Fen Lane via North Ockendon church. Ancient woodland survives around Belhus Park and narrow stream valleys are associated with corridors of meadow/reed beds, and fields are defined by elm hedges. Here **South Ockendon** historic village lies hard against extensive post war housing estates and Aveley village is close by. The settlement pattern of historic villages on high spots at Cranham, Corbets Tey and North Ockendon with ancient manors, parklands, country parks, and the natural heritage of geology, drainage, the flora and fauna including the Thames terrace flower-rich grasslands with rich invertebrate assemblages, all aid in making this area special.

The fenland remnants of **Cranham Nature Reserve** feeds the fish pond and parkland associated with **Gaynes Park** (now substantially built over) at **Corbets Tey**. The mansion, long demolished was designed by the famous architect James Paine (see Georgian Chapter). Locally called 'Cranham Brook' it flows onwards to the Water Vole sanctuary in Bonnets Wood, and then to Berwick Pond and the Ingrebourne Marshes SSSI. Our communities in particular have identified that this 'Was a barren area – much better now', and that the 'Thames Chase Forest Centre is wonderful and a much-needed facility' (LotF Project 2016). South of the Thames Chase Forest Visitor Centre and Cranham village lies **Belhus Woods Country Park** (see Georgian Chapter). There are a number of important ancient woodland sites some famed for their native bluebells. Running Water Brook and Common Watercourse from Belhus to Wennington has potential to become a significant wildlife corridor, and in South Ockendon a reclaimed gravel pit now forms the basis for **Grangewaters Outdoor Education Centre** with managed and natural woodland, open grassland and lakes.[10]

• • • • • • • • • • • •

To the south, the area of low hills between 15m and 35m (50 and 115 ft.) around Orsett is special for its historic landscape pattern of mixed arable and pastureland use in small to medium fields with mature hedges, trees and blocks of woodland and fenland views and for connecting woodland,

---

[10] Grangewaters offers water-based and outdoor activities catering for all ages and abilities. For Y5 children (9 - 10 year olds) 'The Centre is particularly good for water based activities' Woodside Academy.

heath and fen. Despite the loss of field patterns through hedgerow removal and loss of orchards here it remains an attractive, rolling, lowland farming area where it meets the 'Langdon Living Landscape' as it crosses over from Langdon Hills, and again isolated villages are hidden from view but there is pressure for housing growth associated with the settlements. Here is a sense of a long history and intangible heritage in the historic north/south commercial route to the Thames, and in local traditions such as 'hanging of the bun' in **Horndon-on-the-Hill** village, an unspoiled conservation area full of historic buildings. Here is a strong local vernacular and a visible reminder of the area's long history and considerable time depth.

Parkers Farm Road, Orsett looking east to Horndon Hill
(Photograph courtesy of Ian and Ros Mercer)

The historic **Orsett** village is a nucleated fen edge settlement, also a conservation area with many listed buildings. Immediately on the west side of the village is the old hamlet of **Baker Street** and two large areas of SAM's. Our communities remark on the 'Glimpses of Baker Street windmill from the A13' and say that there is 'Lots of green space still here', but also that the area is 'Threatened by Lower Thames Crossing' (LotF Project 2016). This landscape is bisected by the **Lower Thames Crossing** proposals that exit the M25 motorway between North and South Ockendon, and cross **Orsett Fen** and pass between Orsett village and Baker Street and onwards to the river Thames. The potential effect on the landscape, the historic settlement pattern and listed buildings in this area, and the nearby SAM's would need to be carefully understood and considered to avoid or mitigate adverse impact of the proposed Crossing alignment in the area.

As a whole this green belt hinterland has become a highly pressurised urban fringe landscape testing farmers, visitors and local communities alike. In doing so it has become a forgotten landscape that has lost its sense of identity so that, in particular over the last century, development decisions have necessarily been taken against this backdrop with a weakness in information locally about the markedness of the area and its sense and meaning. Today major decision-makers, visitors and local people all deserve access to a good understanding of the identity and significance of an area in order for balanced decisions to be made with informed mitigating solutions wherever necessary.

Also opportunity can be taken to invite visitors in by developing the host of often isolated, visitor attractions and revealing their significance and story, their offer and their physical and historical links and by re-establishing linkages, restoring physical structure to this landscape, appropriate tree planting with hedgerow and woodland management, restoring corridors of natural habitat and returning a sense of place to this historic landscape.

Places to visit nearby:

- Belhus Woods Country Park, and Little Belhus Country Park (currently being restored from former landfill by Rural Arisings), South Ockendon
- Kennington Park, Aveley
- Horndon Meadow Nature Reserve, South Hill, Horndon-on-the-Hill
- Stubbers Adventure Centre, Upminster
- Grangewaters Outdoor Education Centre, South Ockendon
- Cranham Marsh Nature Reserve comprising 32 acres of the once extensive fenland of southern Essex, with a variety of habitats including one of the best surviving sedge fens in Essex as well as marsh and ancient woodland; generally peaks in numbers of butterflies, dragonflies and other insects during July to August
- Thames Chase Community Forest Centre, Cranham and the 40 sq. miles of Thames Chase Community Forest is one of 12 such forests set up in England. Its network of 47 sites stretches across Barking & Dagenham, Havering, Brentwood and Thurrock and with the Forestry Commission owning and managing 10 community woodlands within the area
- Thames Chase Forest Centre Walks (1, 2, 3, 5, 6a, 6b, and Broadfields Tree Trail) have linkages to its historic Broadfields Farm with its distinctive modern Visitor Centre. Walks introduce both the geography and something of the built and natural history of the area and for example, bring visitors into contact with many native species of trees and exotic species introduced into landscaped Parks and Gardens as specimen trees.
- Thames Chase Circular Walk 12 (Belhus Country Park)
- *Walk Wild Essex* by Tony Gunton (see below) includes an Upminster Circuit from Upminster Bridge Station

Ideas for further projects:

- A study of the planned landscapes here such as by Charles Bridgeman, Lancelot 'Capability' Brown, Richards Woods or Humphry Repton
- Learn about historic tree plantings and study what is happening to trees today and the habitats and species that the hedgerows, trees and woodlands support
- Opportunity for the study of the historical import of new tree species to Britain in this area via the nearby ports, to note that contribution and apply the information to our knowledge of past histories of both this landscape and its part in the nation's story
- There is an opportunity and need here to identify the ancient hedgerows, and ancient tree species including Wild Service trees and Mulberry trees in order to better interpret the heritage
- Investigating opportunity for restoring fenland

Further Reading:

- Ballard, E.G. (Ted) (1981). *Our Old Upminster & District* pub. Swan Libraries. ISBN 0 9503151 1 7
- Crabtree, Margaret (1996). *Growing Up in North Ockendon* pub. Ian Henry Publications. ISBN 0 869025 475 5
- Drury, John (1986). *A History of Upminster & Cranham* pub. Ian Henry Publications. ISBN 0 86025 405 4
- Everson, Gordon R. (2001). *East & West Horndon Today and Yesterday*
- Pyke, Cecelia (2014). *Voices of North & South Ockendon* pub. The History Press
- Wilson, T.L. (1880-1). *History & Topography of Upminster* pub. Wilson & Whitworth

---

River Valleys & Marshes The NPPF[11] defines open space as 'All open space of public value, including not just land, but also areas of water (such as rivers, canals, lakes and reservoirs) which offer important opportunities for sport and recreation and can act as a visual amenity.' As open space, bodies of water are an important resource in the Land of the Fanns, it has a watery southern boundary and three other river valleys, as well as numerous lakes and ponds and water-filled clay pits.

The three main river valleys of the Dagenham Corridor, the Ingrebourne Valley, and the Mardyke Valley together with their feeder rivers, tributaries and marshes cut across this landscape and the Thames marshes, feeding into the river Thames itself. The valleys each provide essential green 'lungs' for nearby communities and vital open corridors that are important for wildlife and people alike with each playing host to a range of important habitats, including wet meadows, carr woodland and reed swamps. Along with the waterways they provide important diversity not only as wildlife habitats but also as recreational resources for surrounding communities and provide countryside access into town centres and access to the London Loop for long distance walkers. The river valleys are also vital routes through the urban area for migrating bird species, who use them to navigate the landscape to and from the marshes along the River Thames and the local river banks support aquatic invertebrates and one of the densest water vole populations in the country and are important for ecosystem services.

• • • • • • • • • • • •

The **Dagenham Corridor** comprises the north/south valley of the Rom and Beam rivers and their tributaries and is traversed by the east/west road and rail routes linking London to the coast with numerous intermediate rail destinations and frequent access by busses. The Corridor marks the boundary between the London Boroughs of Barking & Dagenham and Havering and it provides an invaluable rural landscape break between those two large urban conurbations helping to meet a heavy demand for recreational facilities through its open space.

---

[11] The National Planning Policy Framework sets out government's planning policies for England and how these are expected to be applied.

The Corridor is within the Metropolitan Green Belt (MGB) and is identified in the East London Green Grid (later incorporated into the London Plan)[12] as a strategic open space opportunity. It is made up of a continuous link of country parks, sports grounds and parks, Nature Reserves including a metropolitan SINC, and riverside walks such as the Collier Row Green Link. This important strategic green Corridor is the first relief of open space for anyone heading east out of London and provides immediate access to open-air recreational space for thousands of local people in town centres and the residential areas of Chadwell Heath, Collier Row, Rush Green, Hornchurch, Elm Park, South Hornchurch, Dagenham and Romford – an historic market town with something of the 'feel' of London's old East End. The popular country parks in the Corridor offer facilities and Visitor Centres but financially local authorities now seem to struggle in maintaining the offer.

The Corridor runs from Havering Ridge, Havering Country Park and the London Loop in the north to Dagenham and Hornchurch Thameside marshes in the south. The heavy clays in the northern section of the Dagenham Corridor support remnants of the old Hainault Forest, once part of the Forest of Waltham that stretched from Bow Bridge in London to Colchester, and contrasts sharply with the marsh and gravels familiar in the south of the Corridor.

At the highest point in the north of the corridor on reasonably level ground on the hill and with an open aspect overlooking the Thames Valley, is a rare, surviving WW2 anti-aircraft double gun site complex (see 20th century Chapter). From the site are clear views of Romford, the Queen Elizabeth II Bridge at the Dartford Crossing and across to Canary Wharf to the west and it is a protected view in the vicinity of the gun site looking in a south-easterly direction towards the Thames Valley. There are listed and locally listed buildings across the Corridor including at Marks Warren Farm in the north at Marks Gate where there is also an unscheduled moated site of Marks Manor and three of the listed Forest Boundary Stones of 1642 relating to the limits of the Forest and its laws at that time.

Southwards the open nature of the Corridor continues through the historic Crown Farm, across playing fields and a golf course and sports ground and via the listed Dagenham Civic Centre to Central Park where the *Timberland Trail* begins a route through Eastbrookend Country Park in Dagenham with the visitors Discovery Centre, and on to The Chase LNR. Nearby in the central area an arm of the Corridor follows the river Rom past the listed Rom Skateboard Park and pushes between residential areas towards Romford town.

Beyond The Chase LNR and across the river Beam, the Bretons Outdoor Recreation Centre in Havering is based around a fine cluster of Georgian buildings on a medieval site set in old farmland now parkland and sports pitches (see Georgian and Victorian Chapters). This open landscape site is complemented west of the river by Dagenham's Beam Valley Country Park that was formerly derelict land following gravel extraction but most of which are now LNRs, accessible from Dagenham East rail station (Thames Chase Walk D1); south-east of the river by the Beam Bridge the land was used in parts for horse grazing after the Second World War.

The Country Park also links to the more formal urban Old Dagenham Park and close by is the old Dagenham Village conservation area with its cluster of grade II, II* and locally listed buildings.

---

[12] The London Plan 2021 is the Spatial Development Strategy for Greater London and sets out a framework for how London will develop over the next 20-25 years.

Traditionally based on the medieval street plan the village retains its historic inn and parish church of St. Peter and St. Paul, the churchyard is also a LNR, and the village is much valued by local people (see Tudor Chapter). As the Saxon Daeccanham or Daecca's home, on the Wantz Stream a tributary of the river Beam, old Dagenham village is thought to be one of the earliest Saxon settlements in Essex. It was built on the low gravels running along the northern edge of the Thameside marshes that continue via Rainham and Wennington villages to originally provide a main route from London to Tilbury via crossing places on the Beam (now Beam Bridge) and Ingrebourne rivers (at Dovers Corner).

Historical features within the valley include areas of archaeological significance recommended as Archaeological Priority Areas (APA), plus items such as tank traps, and pill boxes and a section of the old Romford Canal and despite the urban fringe nature of the Corridor such relics support an intangible sense of history particularly in the northern and southern areas. The things that make this area special are the urban growth and recreation opportunity and demand and in particular nature conservation. The Beam river valley includes several rare mature black poplars at one of the very few native London sites for this UK and London Biodiversity Action Plan (BAP) priority species, and a juxtaposition of wetlands and drier acid grasslands makes this landscape important for a wide variety of birds and invertebrates.

Our communities say about this area that: 'Bretons is beautiful and peaceful', and 'Horses running free at the Chase', the 'Lovely green spaces but needs promoting', and that it is a 'Joy to walk and see wildlife' (LotF Project 2016).

• • • • • • • • • • •

Like the Dagenham Corridor, the **Ingrebourne River Valley** runs north/south through this landscape and provides a virtually continuous open space link for people throughout its length and with good accessibility for pedestrians, long distance walking, jogging and recreational cycle routes. It is a highly valued amenity resource in close proximity to urban areas although its narrowness and nature conservation interest make it sensitive to change.

The Ingrebourne is an intact, natural river with a sinuous course, its special features include its ecological value, ancient alder carr woodland, the floodplain grassland and reed beds, its recreational opportunities and social history. The valley has country parks, wildlife and distant views, Forestry England (a division of the Forestry Commission that manages the nation's forests) woodlands and Common land, listed buildings and archaeological heritage. Its intangible assets include a sense of remoteness and a Bronze Age landscape along the valley with settlements and possibly a long distance trade route (see the Bronze Age Chapter). At Hacton, the deep-sided road to Hacton bridge may be a clue to an early fording point of the river accessing the royal manor of Havering.

The Valley provides essential and popular access to open space for local people in nearby residential areas including Harold Park, Harold Wood and Emmerson Park, Upminster Bridge, Hacton, Elm Park, South Hornchurch, Rainham and in Upminster town and district. However, as a whole over time the valley has been effective in administratively separating the western part (Greater London) from the eastern (Essex) part of this area. This has led to fragmented access to information and understanding of the significance of this historic landscape as a single entity and an unusual area so that its heritage and the many parts it has played over the millennia in the wider regional and national stories and events becomes lost and forgotten.

The Forestry England woodlands in the northern part of the Valley are accessible and linked by the public rights of way network and horse riders are welcome. Havering's **Tylers Common** is important for the large blocks of maturing woodland and grassland forming mosaics around the Common, and is linked by bridleway to **Tylers Wood** (Forestry England) with its wonderful views over East London to Canary Wharf. Amongst other woodlands in this northern part of the Valley since 2000 Forestry England have also planted three other community woodlands at **Folks Lane Woodland, Harold Court Woods and Pages Wood** – which is the largest Forestry England site in Thames Chase Community Forest containing a range of valuable habitats.

However, today the Ingrebourne Valley narrows where the river channel has been straightened and over-deepened in the centre area through Upminster and it struggles across the heavily built up district of Upminster Bridge. The adjacent urban areas and roadside lighting reduces the sense of tranquillity in places but urban proximity itself brings public transport links and opportunities for walkers to take refreshments and even here it provides vital access to the meandering riverside **Suttons, Hacton and Gaynes Parkways** where surprisingly kingfishers and heron thrive despite living cheek-by-jowl with residential estates. Our communities tell us: 'I saw a kingfisher as a bright blue flash by on my walk today' (LotF Project 2016). The old Suttons Farm/Suttons Airfield/RAF Hornchurch (see 20th century Chapter) in the Ingrebourne Valley is now the Hornchurch Country Park and a LNR and has a nicely established Visitor Centre with wildlife and local Royal Air Force (RAF) history on display and with an emerging RAF Hornchurch Museum nearby.

The **Ingrebourne Marshes** SSSI is the largest single area of floodplain grassland and continuous reed bed in Greater London and supports an important population of water voles. However, phosphates, agricultural and urban runoff as well as discharge from sewage works significantly affect the water quality and the Ingrebourne has had poor ecological status, failing for invertebrates, water plants, algae and fish. Invasive plant species require continued management and reduce the diversity of native species. Increased flooding events reduce accessibility at times and there is loss of traditional valley meadows and pasture with some areas under grazed and overgrown with scrub plants giving an unkempt and unmanaged appearance.

The London Loop towards Rainham takes visitors on from Thames Chase Walk no. 5 through **Rainham Village** before continuing on to Rainham's Thameside marshes. This little gem of a Conservation Area bursts with listed buildings and focusses on the exceptional Norman Church built in 1170 and is associated with penance made in relation to the murder of St. Thomas Beckett (see Norman & Plantagenet Chapter). Next to the church is the National Trust's Rainham Hall, the house and gardens have been welcomingly restored and re-opened to the public attracting visitors to the area. In this southern area of the Valley in 2003 Forestry England planted **Bonnets Wood** and **Berwick Glades** linking Hornchurch Country Park through to Parklands Open Space on the borders of Upminster and Corbets Tey.

• • • • • • • • • • •

The **Mardyke River** is a memory of an earlier position of the Thames and survives as an ancient meander of that great river (see Geology Chapter). The special features of this area include the river corridor, nature conservation and traditional land uses and recreational opportunities. The river valley landscape is a peaceful and atmospheric combination of ancient woodlands, the Roman and Dutch fens and the marshes and areas of reed beds.

At Bulphan, the river gathers the network of streams and ditches as it drains across the fens down to the reclaimed Orsett fen. This low-lying Bulphan and Orsett fens area is a remote agricultural landscape with an ancient system of small scale, managed valley bottom pastures enclosed by ditches and has a strong intact character with arable land use on the upper slopes.

Downstream the valley is fairly steep sided in places as far as Stifford Bridge. Woodland has been an important resource and some of the woodland in the area is particularly old. Above the north bank of the Mardyke between Stifford Bridge and the M25, Forestry England woodlands at **Low Well Wood, Millard's Garden and Brannett's Wood** cushion the edge between the riverside and the South Ockendon housing estate from which they are easily accessed. The woods were individually separated by medieval wood banks - tree-topped earth mounds, but together as **Mardyke Woods** they are thought to predate the arrival of the Romans and are now designated as Ancient Semi Natural Woodland. In particular, Brannets Wood was first recorded in 1339 and is the oldest recorded woodland in south east Essex and likely to have been well established when the Romans arrived in 54BC. Opposite, on the south bank of the river are **Brickbarn Wood** ancient woodlands, and **Combe Wood. Watts Wood** along the Arterial Road and **Hangmans Woods** in Stifford Road are also ancient woodlands.

Tree work at Mardyke Woods (Photograph courtesy LotF)

Davy Down had also been a farming area and then used for market gardening until road works divided the landholding and made its agricultural use uneconomic. Today the **Davy Down Urban Riverside Park** is the gateway to the river Mardyke valley for visitors to explore with both the ancient woodland and a valley habitat that suits species adapted to still or slow moving water environments as well as floodplain and water-meadow loving species and includes water voles, marsh frog and kingfishers. In places there are sculptures of local wildlife by the artist Ptolemy Elrington as well as the Stifford Pumping Station (see Edwardian Chapter) to see and the impressive 10m (33 ft.) high, Victorian Stifford Railway Viaduct.

From Davy Down the 12 km (7.5 mile) long **Mardyke Way** riverside walk (Thames Chase Circular Walk 10) can be joined at Stifford Bridge partway along between Ship Lane in Aveley village to Bulphan and Thames Chase Walk D2 links to West Horndon Station. Alongside the river below North Stifford village, runs the 'Field of Peace' (gifted to Thurrock Borough Council), a tranquil area memorial commemorating the end of WWI. In particular, local communities have commented they: 'Rambled from Davy Down along the Mardyke River – beautiful area and enjoyed by all of us', 'Love the railway viaduct', 'Is a hidden gem' (LotF Project 2016).

The local rail line crosses the Mardyke viaduct passing the little village of **North Stifford** with its limited dispersed farms contrasting sharply with the dense populations in the southern part of the West Thurrock and Grays area. The village overlooks the Mardyke Valley, and with many attractive listed, historic and often thatched buildings adds to local character and, despite excessive through traffic it retains a sense of peace and calm.

Major infrastructure crosses the valley carrying the M25 motorway, A13 major road and the main railway line with its attendant visual intrusion. However, the extensive views down over the Mardyke valley for travellers on the M25 motorway is surprising and quite spectacular and changes with flood conditions as the valley broadens to a more open floodplain until it finally enters the Thames at Purfleet through the Mardyke Canal lock.[13]

• • • • • • • • • • • •

The **Thameside marshes of Rainham, Wennington, Aveley and West Thurrock** together form a vast, ancient, wild and atmospheric wetland landscape essential for wildlife and for bird migration and significant for nature conservation and with one of the densest water vole population in the country. Much is designated as the **Inner Thames Marshes SSSI** important for its grazing marsh, and part of the **Greater Thames Marshes Nature Improvement Area** (NIA)[14] it is also attractive to visitors particularly for its sense of remoteness, history and breath-taking riverside views.

The marshes continue with an open aspect as far as Purfleet where they narrow as the Mardyke enters the Thames then re-emerge later as **West Thurrock Lagoon and Marshes SSSI** at Stone Ness. However this is also a scarred landscape as a result of its geographical position and geology and remains under threat in modern times. In places the Thameside area has been ravaged by rich mineral workings and the development of valuable Thameside industry, although all borne out of

---

 [13] Investigate how the Mardyke river and its valley changes as it moves from the source to the mouth; then carryout a desk-top exercise to plan and write an informative programme for a canoe trip down the Mardyke to highlight how the river and valley changes (Curriculum link to Geography – river valleys).

[14] NIA's are 'inter-connected networks of wildlife habitats intended to re-establish thriving wildlife populations and help species respond to the challenges of climate change.' NPPF (12 areas across the country were announced in 2012 – see Natural England for details).

expediency and necessity at the time, the landscape is pressed in upon by industry, container ferries and national service corridors including the Channel Tunnel Rail Link (CTRL).

The marshes combine to form a mosaic of habitats including salt marsh, saline lagoons, medieval grazing marsh and grasslands and with an abundance of birds and other wildlife. From prehistoric times the marshes were managed for fishing and fowling, then as reed beds and for sheep and cattle grazing – the latter now reintroduced by a local farmer on the Royal Society for the Protection of Birds (RSPB) site on Rainham marshes as part of a wider land management programme.

The things that make this area special are the nature processes and nature conservation, and its role in produce and trade. Intangibles include the sense of remoteness, archaeology and history in the area like the relics of historic defence and military activity. Historic churches on the inland fringes of the marsh act as local landmarks and the historic aid to shipping of the view north from Coldharbour Point via Rainham church to Hornchurch church is a further intangible heritage asset that deserves protection. Our communities particularly value the wide-open spaces and especially the 'Views over the Thames', and 'The birds at RSPB Rainham Marshes' (LotF Project 2016).

The modern A13 road is partially diverted across these marshes but from the high vantage point of this road travellers pass over the whole range of history and change that the Thameside marshes have undergone. Modern wind turbines dot the horizon and north of the road a major network of electricity pylons march across the marsh landscape and the C2C and Eurostar rail lines together line the low gravel ridge from Dagenham and Rainham that continues past South Hall bridge and the historic South Hall Farm, reminders of the Norman manor of South Hall, and on past the tiny Wennington village with its medieval church. Here like Rainham, Wennington once had its own commercial wharf and, although now silted Wennington Brook ran into the Thames that no doubt like the other 'drains' across this marsh, were once a haven for smugglers.

In Rainham, Ferry Lane is an ancient route running alongside the Rainham Creek section of the lower river Ingrebourne and defines a western edge to the marshes as industry and commercial activity are held back exploiting the Hornchurch and Dagenham marshland and masking their marsh origin and continuity of history. New local pedestrian routes and cycleways exit the village and cut across the marsh through the old Rainham Rifle Ranges built in 1915, and converge with Section 24 of the London Loop as the Thames Riverside Path that continues across the marshes from Rainham to Purfleet shadowing Rainham Creek to Thameside where there is a sudden glorious view of the Thames, the City skyline and the Queen Elizabeth II Dartford Bridge.

The path is supported in several locations with visitors car parks and with points of visitor attractions that include the moored **concrete barges** used as supply back-up for the D-Day Normandy landings (see 20th century Chapter) that have themselves created an area within the bay that is of significant importance for biodiversity and wildlife. The path continues eastwards towards Coldharbour Point (that may indicate a Roman staging post, see Roman Chapter), around an adjacent artificial hill with expansive views across the Thames to the Kentish hills and north along the Ingrebourne Valley.

Eastwards is the Rainham Local Nature Reserve, a part of **Rainham Wildspace** linking to **Wildspace Thurrock**. This is a medieval marshes landscape that is a haven for wildlife including water voles and dragonflies. Since the start of the 21st century, much of this land has been managed for nature conservation by the RSPB and the London Borough of Havering with access for visitors and Visitor Centre with its own impressive and unexpected view of the river. This internationally significant **RSPB Rainham Marshes Nature Reserve** combines the habitats created by human intervention and by the geological and fluvial character of the area and brings these together as a resource managed for both nature conservation and recreation. Here is one of the largest reed beds in London and the marshes along the banks of the River Thames are important wetland habitats for a range of bird species, including wintering ducks, breeding wading birds, birds of prey and species such as Avocet, Ringed Plover, Little Egret and Lapwing.

Along the riverside walkers are able to look down on either side of the path both over the marshes of the Reserve and to the Thames, with its medieval sea walls and its foreshore. Here along the foreshore, visible at low tide, are both areas of prehistoric peat and the **Purfleet prehistoric forest** (see Geology Chapter). From medieval times attempts have been made to defend London from inundations from the Thames. There are at least three ever higher sea walls along this north Thameside area with further **flood defences** as the various creeks enter the main river now all backed up by the Thames Barrier with evidently more and greater London flood defenses to come. Rarely have the defences failed in the area although there have been famous inundations at Dagenham Breach on the South Hornchurch marshes (see Tudor & Stuart Chapter) and at Purfleet and Canvey Island (see 20th century Chapter). Also numerous legal efforts were necessary in previous centuries to compel local people to carry out their responsibilities in those days for ditch clearance and flood defence measures. At Rainham village the river Ingrebourne becomes Rainham Creek where, until the modern Thames flood defence works were carried out, the river was tidal and served Rainham Wharf in Rainham village until the mid 20th century.

West Thurrock Lagoon and Marshes SSSI is a particularly striking example of a brownfield site now significant for biodiversity that was once grazing marsh, the site saw a power station constructed after World War 2 with large areas covered with associated fly ash waste over the following decades. Following demolition of the power station in the 1990s, wildlife began to recolonise the site and it is now one of the richest and most biodiverse sites in the country with over 1,200 species of invertebrate, bird and reptile. Some species are extremely rare and endangered such as the Distinguished jumping spider (Sitticus distinguendus). The efforts in 2014 of Buglife (The Invertebrate Conservation Trust) in the High Court to save this SSSI illustrate the tension between development pressure and brownfield biodiversity in this part of the landscape.

Places to visit nearby:

- The Discovery Centre and Eastbrookend Country Park
- The Chase Local Nature Reserve
- The Beam Valley Country Park
- Walk the 'Timberland Trail' from Central Park and the Beam Valley Path, Dagenham
- Beam Parklands wetlands
- Bretons Outdoor Recreation Centre
- EWT Ingrebourne Valley Visitor Centre, Nature Discovery Centre and Hornchurch Country Park and Friends of Ingrebourne Valley
- RSPB Rainham Marshes Nature Reserve

- Thames Chase Destination Walks: D1 and D4 are between Dagenham, Rainham and Purfleet rail stations while D3 runs south along the Ingrebourne Valley between Upminster and Rainham stations, and D5 runs north along the valley from Upminster station to Noak Hill
- Sections 22, 23 and 24 of the London Loop cover the Ingrebourne Valley from Harold Wood to Rainham via Upminster Bridge and then on to Purfleet
- Sustrans Connect 2 walking and cycling path 136 extends along the length of the Ingrebourne valley
- Thames Chase local Walks 5 and 6a connect to the long-distance national routes providing additional linkages for people to ever extensive areas of open space and both routes include Berwick Glades (Forestry Commission) in Rainham with its excellent views of the Ingrebourne Valley especially towards Hornchurch and Elm Park.
- Davy Down Riverside Park

Ideas for further projects:

- Restoration of water meadows and pasture in river valleys
- A study of the often accidental import or migration of plants and animals via the numerous local wharfs and ports on the Thames and its tributaries and any resultant surprising and unique biodiversity so close to London
- A study of the human impact, such as quarrying, on the geography of this landscape
- A study of the ways that the geography of this area influenced prehistoric and historic routes over the millennia and how they have come down to us today surviving the test of time and consider their value in informing local, strategic and regional decision making today
- Geological investigation in Hornchurch in relation to the internationally important SSSI at Hornchurch Railway Cutting, in conjunction with Essex Rock & Mineral Society
- Investigate ways to control/combat increasing pressures for land drainage and hard surfacing in built-up areas and improve river management in order to aid in mitigating the increasing risk of winter floods and summer droughts that adversely impact on wildlife and people alike
- Investigate and seek the means to address the excessive richness of nutrients or eutrophication on bodies of water from farmland runoff and airborne nitrates from vehicles and by phosphates from domestic waste, which accelerate the development of woodland succession with the loss of plant diversity that in turn adversely impacts on invertebrates and then on up the food chain

Further Reading:

- Astbury, A.K. (1980). *'Estuary – Land & Water in the lower Thames basin'* The Carnforth Press. ISBN 0 9507246-0-2
- Evans, Brian (1992). *Bygone Dagenham and Rainham* pub. Phillimore. ISBN 0 85033 831 X
- Cowin, Jan & Clifford (2012). *'The Idyll in the Middyl': North Stifford Village: The idyll hidden in the middle of urban sprawl'* email book@northstiffordvillage.co.uk www.northstiffordvillage.co.uk/book.htm

- Lewis, Frank (1966). *A History of Rainham - with Wennington & South Hornchurch* pub. Peter R. Davis
- O'Leary, John Gerard, FSA, FLA (1964). *'The Book of Dagenham – a History'* pub Benham & Co.
- Morgan, Glyn H. (1951 re-pub. 2008). *Forgotten Thameside* Havering Museum Ltd. ISBN 978 0 86025 934 3
- Neale, Kenneth (1969). *Discovering Essex in London* pub. Essex Countryside, (re-pub. 1986) Ian Henry Publications Ltd. ISBN-13 9780860254065
- Perfect, Charles Thomas (1917). *Ye Olde Village of Hornchurch* pub. Ian Henry Publications (1982). ISBN 0 86025 801 7
- Phillips, Rita and Peter (2015). *The illustrated guide to Thames Sailing Barges* pub. Phillips Design Publishing. ISBN 978-0-9563059-8-5
- West, Jack (1993). *Personal Memories of Dagenham Village - 1920 onward* pub. Arthur H. Stockwell Ltd. ISBN 0 7223 2725-0

Thameside Urban Quarry Townscape This is a low-lying urban landscape corridor from Purfleet to Grays between the A13 major road and the Essex Thameside railway that run from London to the coast. This was once an area of significant chalk quarrying and of brick earth, the pits having now been reclaimed for retail and residential use and with some old villages now subsumed amongst surrounding development. Now, on the face of it this is a highly populated area of domestic, commerce, industry and regional retail uses and is busily criss-crossed by major road and rail arteries, heavily used long distance routes and local and commuter rail accessibility. While the people here are resilient, there is an understandable sense of resentment and being put upon over generations. However, the developments overlay and surround important wildlife havens, unexpected historic sites with villages, conservation areas, listed and historic buildings, ancient monuments, nationally important geology and access to Country Parks and Nature Parks. The key points of nature heritage interest are the Thames terrace grassland and the brownfield sites, open space and natural elements associated with the former quarry pits including lakes used for recreation and the grassland and woods at **Chafford Gorges Nature Park** that has opportunity to disseminate information about the landscape, places to visit and access.

Within this southern urban area, chalk quarrying and deindustrialisation has created a legacy of brownfield sites that have become significant for biodiversity together with striking chalk gorges and cliffs also with their distinctive biodiversity value. This area is now the Chafford Gorges Nature Park (see Geology Chapter), a 200 ha (81 ac.) EWT nature reserve based around old chalk quarries where the chalky soil supports many varieties of alkaline loving plants, the sand and gravel areas support many unusual insects, and the lakes, woodlands and chalk cliffs are habitats for great crested newts, several species of bats, great crested grebes and sand martins for example. Warren Gorge is the largest, with meadows and lakes with ideal conditions for the chalk loving plants including orchids and for kingfishers and house martins. Grays Thurrock Chalk Pit is a SSSI for its biological interest containing nine species of orchid and wildflowers, and is home to adders, slow worms and grass snakes as well as birds, butterflies, bees and beetle species. Lion Gorge includes the 19th century Lion Pit Tramway Cutting SSSI for its geological interest, animal fossils and evidence of early man 200,000 years ago.

This area is special for its geological and archaeological interest, its industrial heritage and regeneration. In particular the community says that: 'Warren and Lion Gorge – very quiet and peaceful', and that 'Lion Gorge is a wonderful place' (LotF Project 2016). All this within the **Chafford Hundred housing estate**, one of the largest housing developments of the 1990s. From here a high-level pedestrian walkway links the Chafford Hundred residential estate and the Lakeside regional shopping centre to the Lakeside rail station on the Upminster to Grays line. From Grays the first stop westwards is at Purfleet with access to the river Thames and Rainham Marshes Nature Reserve and also to High House Production Park an international centre of excellence for creative industries. While on the Upminster rail link the first stop is at South Ockendon and makes ready access for residents and visitors to the newly emerging Little Belhus Country Park and Belhus Woods Country Park beyond.

Places to visit nearby:

- EWT Chafford Gorges Nature Discovery Park for its geological and wildlife interest across grassland, meadow, pond and woodland habitats
- Grays Chalk Quarry Nature Reserve, a biological SSSI and wildlife haven with fine views, geological chalk exposures and sarsen stones
- *Walk Wild Essex* by Tony Gunton (see below): include Walks from either Chafford Hundred station or Grays station to Chafford Gorges circuit

Ideas for further projects:

- A study across this landscape of influence from Barking Creek to Mucking of the part the north Thames marshes played in history and its role today including the national wildlife scene

Further Reading:

- Benton, Tony (1991). *Boldly from the marshes – A history of Little Thurrock and its people* pub. The author with Thurrock Museum ISBN 0-9506141-3-0
- Leyin, Alan in partnership with Thurrock Council (1997). *Thurrock's Past – Echoes from a Place* pub. Lejins Publishing ISBN 0 9528789 0 9

Summary Today we get that same wonderful and surprising view that our Georgian predecessors valued so much, that interestingly seems to fan out before us, both on the Langdon Hills and from all vantage points along the ridge of hills, particularly from the village of Havering-atte-Bower and from the site of the Old Thorndon Hall at Herongate, and daily provides a spectacular view for thousands of south-bound M25 motorway travellers as they come off the ridge at Brentwood (junc. 28) with a surprise and delight in the sudden view of this great fan-shaped plain spreading out from west to east as the road drops down towards the river Thames and with the backdrop of the Kentish Hills beyond.

The beauty of the landscape and views across it are crucial as are the wildlife corridors and access for people to countryside pursuits for physical and mental health and relief. The future of this landscape may be considered fragile as it remains under constant competing pressures from the needs of people, nature, wildlife and commerce. Through its visitor hubs, this landscape provides opportunity to secure open air activities and facilities for families seeking safe places to walk, to run and to roam, to explore and to picnic, for children to have adventures and to learn the Country Code, its meaning and intent; for retirees, of all ages and abilities, wanting to take exercise, to sit and reflect; also for dog walkers and for horse riders; for commuters and local workers seeking morning, evening or lunchtime open air exercise and walking for health, cycling or running; providing education opportunities for school parties and others wanting to learn about the heritage of the landscape's inter-relationship with London the capital city and the heritage of the countryside, its plants, animals and insects; for bird watching or for wildlife and scenic photography; or for mums wanting safe play for kiddies with coffee and companionable chat at the Visitor Centres.

Understanding the significance of the area makes it possible for local people to get involved in important local decision-making in an informed way and for regional and national agencies to make informed decisions and enable communities to agree positive solutions to meet the demands of continued dynamic change.

Places to visit further afield:
- Fobbing Marsh Nature Reserve, off Marsh Lane, Fobbing
- Stanford Warren Nature Reserve, Mucking Wharf Road, Stanford-le-Hope
- Thameside Nature Discovery Park, Enovert Community Trust Visitor Centre, Mucking Wharf Road
- The Thames Estuary Path 1, 2, 3, 4 and 5 from Tilbury Town taking in Tilbury Fort and Coalhouse Fort, carry on to East Tilbury and Stanford-le-Hope, Pitsea and Benfleet to Leigh-on-Sea
- Natural History Museum
- Royal Botanic Gardens, Kew includes the papers of many botanists, gardeners and others
- Writtle University College specialises in agriculture and environment and land-based industries. It offers Further Education and Higher Education programmes, undergraduate and postgraduate degrees as well as research, apprenticeships, part-time study and short courses and Certificates of Competence, it serves adult learners and can lead to new career opportunities, and offers week-end work

Ideas for further projects:
- Collect fallen leaves, twigs and similar items for arts and crafts projects making a picture or a map of the landscape, perhaps in different seasons, with different items to represent the landscape elements (Curriculum link to Art - developing techniques, creativity and experimentation)
- For ideas for active outdoor interest and wildlife interest in general see:
  - *365 Days Wild* by Lucy McRobert for a 'random act of wildness for every day of the year'. ISBN: 97800088292423; ISBN10: 0008292426. Imprint William Collins 2019

- *Wild Essex: A guide to the nature reserves and country parks of Essex and east London* Tony Gunton ed. Pub. Lopinga Books, 2000. ISBN 0-9530362-2-7/ ISBN 0-9530362-3-5
- *Explore Wild Essex: A guide to the nature reserves and country parks of Essex and east London (Nature of Essex S.)* by Tony Gunton pub. Lopinga Books, 2008. ISBN: 10: 095303626X ISBN 13: 9780953036264
- *Walk Wild Essex: 50 Wildlife Walks in Essex & East London (Nature of Essex)* by Tony Gunton. ISBN: 9780953036295

- Investigate the possibility to establish/maintain effective corridors for wildlife so that plants and animals can easily migrate. This is to aid both in combatting the fragmentation of habitat by major roads and other national and regional service corridors that create barriers to wildlife movement, and also addresses the adverse effects of climate change as conditions for animals and plants becomes unsuitable
- Support for improved equestrian access may be sought through the British Horse Society (BHS) and the Forestry Commission East Anglia British Horse Society (BHS). At present there are some 12 riding schools and livery yards across just Havering Borough providing for an estimated 400 horses, with more establishments in Brentwood Borough, also in the Dagenham Corridor and around Orsett.

References for further research:

- Alison Farmer Associates in association with Countryscape, (Feb. 2016) *Land of the Fanns Landscape Character Assessment – Final Report* Unpub. (LotF/Thames Chase Trust)
- Basildon Natural History Society
- Essex Historic Environment Record (EHER) is a database of all known archaeological sites and monuments, historic buildings, parks and gardens in Essex
- Historic England *Register of Parks & Gardens of Special Historic Interest in England*
- Individual Local Authority *Conservation Area Appraisals & Management Plans*
- LotF *Landscape Conservation Action Plan*, Unpub.
- LotF and The Gardens Trust (2020) online. *Fifty Fabulous Features* Statements of Significance for fifty Features of Historic Designed Landscapes within the LotF
- Mayor of London (2008). *East London Green Grid Framework, Supplementary Planning Guidance*
- Natural England (2013). *National Character Area Profile: 111 Northern Thames Basin (NE466)*
- Rackham, Oliver (1995). *The History of the Countryside* pub. Weidenfeld & Nicolson. ISBN 0 297 81622 5
- Scappler & Gowan (April 2016). *The Land of the Fanns Historic Landscape Report*, Unpub. (LotF /Thames Chase Trust)
- Unlocking Essex Past (UEP). provides online access to the Essex Historic Environment Record

Chapter 3
Geology and development of this Landscape

NATIONAL CURRICULUM Hints

Geology is the primary Earth Science, it is about the Earth, the rocks that make up the Earth, how they change over time and the processes that affect them. It is about finite raw materials, they supply minerals, filter our water and produce non-renewable energy sources, produce soils, affect habitats and in turn local wildlife species. The study of geology helps us to mitigate natural hazards, it defines and influences what happens in the landscape, where and how we build and the creation of our 'sense of place'. It is the only means we have to understand the record of the earliest history of the planet and what we can learn from this about further changes that are likely to come.

Here, the geology of this local landscape is of significant interest to the wider emerging geological story of southern Britain across the immensity of geological time. It could be said to begin when Essex was part of 'Dinosaur Island' during the Jurassic period 180 million years ago (mya) and continue to the Ice Age with its cold glacial and warmer interglacial stages that we are in now.

Evidence is revealed here in the landform of the ridges, hills and marshes, together with remains of ancient life such as the fossils in the Chalk 100 million years old, to the Neolithic (New Stone Age) submerged fossilised forest from 10 thousand years ago (kya). Information comes through the geological study of local pits, deep cuttings and cliff faces and opportune archaeological sites and includes the analysis of pollen and fossil plant and animal remains as well as the sediments themselves.

Assembling this evidence shows the gradual movement of the Thames across this landscape as just one significant feature. The value of this information is also in helping visitors appreciate the basis of wildlife habitats as well as the record of climate change. It is important therefore to value and protect this evidence and take up opportunities that it affords to plan for the future.

The Landscape Our local landscape crosses over from northeast London to southwest Essex and lies along the north bank of the river Thames in the Lower Thames Valley, where the river is joined by its major tributaries from along both its north and south banks. Today the Thames Chase Community Forest lies central to this landscape, the 'Land of the Fanns' that encompasses a great bowl of low-lying fens landscape that comprises the Mardyke river valley with the ditches and rivulets of the fens draining into the main dyke that itself flows into the Thames as the Mardyke river.

At times local people wonder about this strange, often misty, damp landscape with its mysterious *feel* and intangible heritage that they have identified (LotF project with local people led by TellTale) as being a surprising place, a place of migration, with an important interplay of land and water that is valuable for commerce, trade and industry. It is the geological processes over the last 450,000 years of the Ice Age up to the present that created this curious landscape. It is the form of this landscape that then influenced the pre-history development of the area and also affected the pattern of historical events that took place here and still influences the present landscape and how it is managed today. This fascinating and somewhat forgotten area of southern Essex provides a wonderful story in which geology and topography reveal how past climates have left a strange landscape 'hidden in plain sight'.

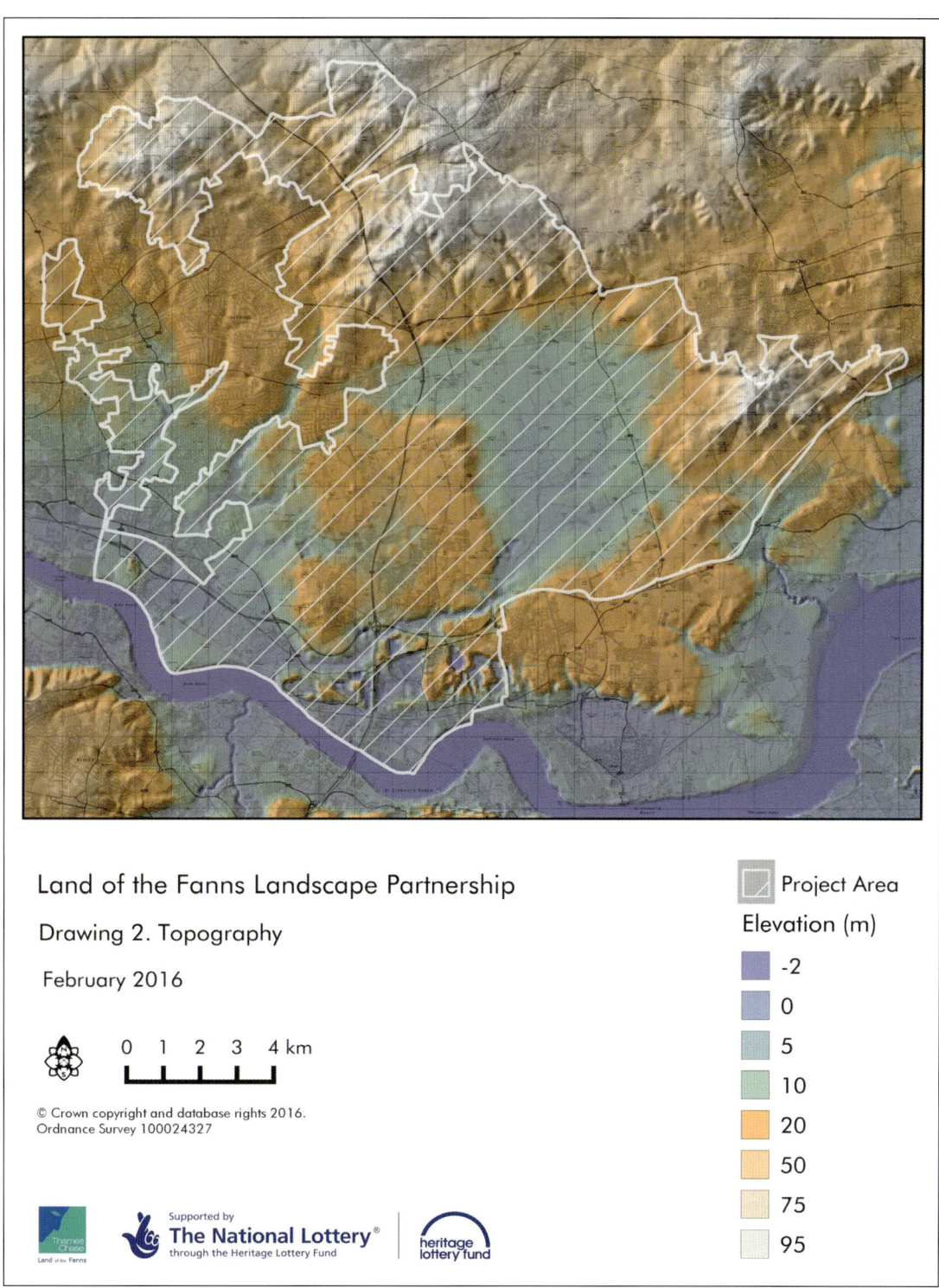

Topographic map of the Land of the Fanns shows the low-lying bowl shaped area central to this landscape (Courtesy LotF and Alison Farmer Associates 'Land of the Fanns Assessment Report')
© Crown copyright 2021 OS LICENCE no. 100064852

Chapter 3 Geology and development of this landscape

SURPRISE *The Land of the Fanns is an intricate landscape, full of surprises and 'hidden gems' and rewards exploring.'* **(TellTale working with the public 2018)**

The Geology This was once an area covered by a **warm shallow sea** and we know this through the evidence in the geology. The oldest rock revealed in the landscape is the **Chalk,** which forms the foundation of the London Basin. This soft, pure white limestone was deposited towards the end of the 'Age of the Dinosaurs' 100 million years ago. Before this Essex had been part of a balmy, tropical 'Dinosaur Island' with Jurassic marine reptiles such as ichthyosaurs and pliosaurs, together with ammonites in the surrounding sea, and dinosaurs on the island itself.

• • • • • • • • • • •

Then the sea rose to an exceptionally high level and flooded the land to form a vast, clear **tropical sea** across most of England and northern Europe. All trace of the dinosaurs here were swept away. The climate was very warm and there was no polar ice. Over time the fragmented shells of microscopic algae formed layers of limy mud at the bottom of this sea that eventually became the thick **Chalk** we see around Purfleet. We can see the Chalk here because, as the continents of Africa and Europe slowly collided and the Alpine mountain range was pushed up around 15 million years ago the outward ripples left an arch-shaped fold in the rocks called the Purfleet Anticline. Erosion of this feature has exposed the Chalk at the surface in the south of our area along the river Thames at Purfleet, Thurrock and Grays.

The 'White Cliffs of Purfleet', once visible from the river, have long been quarried away and outlines of the former workings can be seen on the topographic maps. At Purfleet Greenlands Quarry (sometimes called Dolphin Pit) and three other adjacent disused quarries - Bluelands Quarry, Botany Pit and Esso Pit - together make up the Purfleet Pits Site of Special Scientific Interest (SSSI) for their geological importance and is a Geological Conservation Review Site indicating its national or international importance. Adjacent to this, west of the M25 motorway is the West Thurrock Dolphin Chalk Quarry (formerly the Metropolitan Works Quarry), where the quarrying has left a 20 metre (65 ft.) high Chalk wall face.

While east of the M25 the West Thurrock Chalk pits have been reclaimed for mainly retail and residential use including the regional Lakeside Shopping Centre, the Retail Park and the Cliffside Trading Park on the floor of the former Tunnel Cement Works Chalk Quarry (Motherwell Way Quarry) where the vertical Chalk quarry face can still be seen, and also the Chafford Hundred housing estate that winds its way around the open spaces and wildlife areas of **Chafford Gorges Nature Park**. This is said to be the finest area for geology in south Essex.

The Park is managed by Essex Wildlife Trust (EWT) and various points of access are available locally. Here the extensive Chalk deposits provide important evidence for an understanding of the most ancient geological development of the wider landscape. There are three notable chalk pits here – Warren Gorge, Lion Gorge (Lion Pit and Tramway Cutting geological SSSI) and Grays Gorge (previously called Grays Chalk Quarry and Titan Pit and now the Grays Thurrock Chalk Pit biological SSSI). After analysis the high-quality water present in the bottom of this quarry was used to supply drinking water and led to the origin of the South Essex Waterworks Company (Essex & Suffolk Water). Additionally Woodham Chalk Cliff provides a breath-taking view over Lion Gorge, Mill Wood Sand Cliff is an area of ancient woodland and has excellent views over the Thames Estuary and together with Sandmartin Cliff reveals sections through the sands that overlie the Chalk.

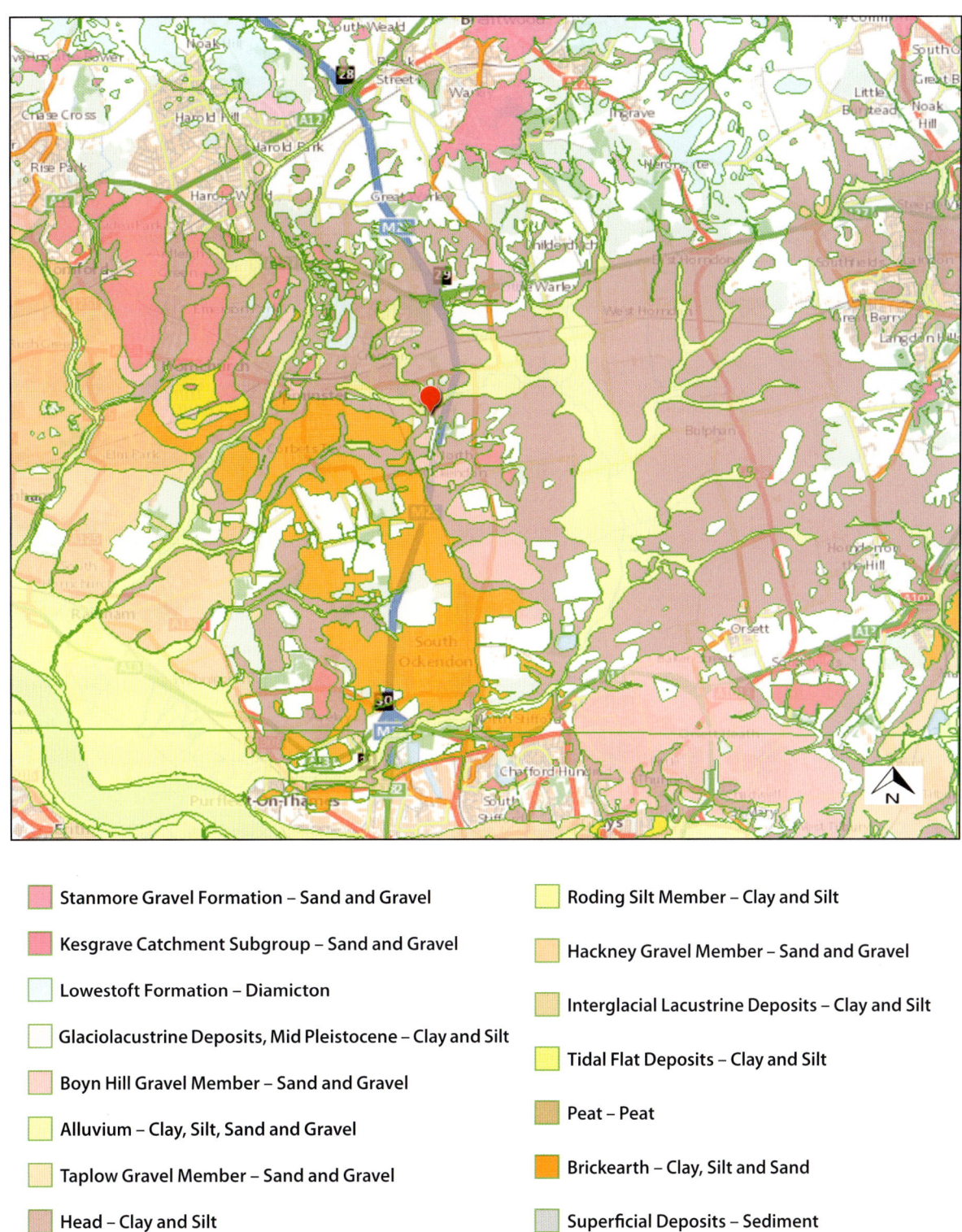

▇	Stanmore Gravel Formation – Sand and Gravel	▇	Roding Silt Member – Clay and Silt
▇	Kesgrave Catchment Subgroup – Sand and Gravel	▇	Hackney Gravel Member – Sand and Gravel
▇	Lowestoft Formation – Diamicton	▇	Interglacial Lacustrine Deposits – Clay and Silt
▇	Glaciolacustrine Deposits, Mid Pleistocene – Clay and Silt	▇	Tidal Flat Deposits – Clay and Silt
▇	Boyn Hill Gravel Member – Sand and Gravel	▇	Peat – Peat
▇	Alluvium – Clay, Silt, Sand and Gravel	▇	Brickearth – Clay, Silt and Sand
▇	Taplow Gravel Member – Sand and Gravel	▇	Superficial Deposits – Sediment
▇	Head – Clay and Silt		

Superficial (youngest) Deposits Geological map of the Land of the Fanns area
(The red coloured dot locates Thames Chase Visitor Centre central to this landscape)
Contains British Geological Survey Data © UKRI 2021. Base mapping is provided by ESRI.
Available from https://www.bgs.ac.uk/map-viewers/geology-of-britain-viewer and released under the
Open government Licence (http://www.nationalarchives.gov.uk/doc/open-government-licence/version/3/)
© Crown copyright 2021 OS LICENCE no. 100064852

Chapter 3 Geology and development of this landscape

Lion Gorge chalk cliff (Photograph courtesy LotF)

Fossil finds from the Chalk help to reconstruct past environments and they can be a useful guide to the age of rocks. Fossils found locally include giant clams, sharks teeth, sea urchins and molluscs as well as a specimen of a tooth 5 centimetres (2 inches) long from a fearsome mosasaur, a giant marine reptile over 10 metres long (30 feet). The chalk here also contains layers of flint, which is a durable rock made of silica from glass sponges (animals with a framework made of silica) that lived in profusion on the bed of the Chalk Sea. The flint formed as infills of burrows made by creatures such as sea urchins, lobsters and worms in the sea bed, which explains the often odd and contorted shapes of flint nodules. The regularly-spaced bands of flints within the chalk may provide evidence for cycles of climate change (Milankovitch cycles) some 80 million years ago. Flint can be broken into very sharp pieces and was used by early people as tools and weapons and to start fires, later it was also used in pottery manufacture and for gunflints, occasionally as gems for decoration and as a building material – a local example are a pair of flint-faced cottages in Warley Hill.

• • • • • • • • • • • •

Then, about 66 million years ago a worldwide catastrophic event occurred caused by a meteor impact. Dinosaurs and many other species across the world became extinct (**Cretaceous-Paleogene extinction event**) as the 'Age of the Dinosaurs' gave way to the 'Age of Mammals'. There was a period of uplift and erosion as the British Isles were tilted up from the west by the opening of the Atlantic, and the North Sea area continued to subside. The Essex area was along a shoreline and the sea came and went from the east, rounding the flint pebbles eroded from the Chalk and depositing alternate layers of sand and mud and pebbles during that early Palaeogene period. That included a layer of flints, called the **Bullhead Bed** after their strange horned shapes, that was left behind as the softer chalk was eroded.

Above this lie the **Thanet Sands** that surprisingly contain much material brought down by coastal currents from erosion of the mountains in Scotland. The sands were deposited some 58 million years ago in relatively shallow water, filling solution hollows or pipes earlier dissolved in the Chalk surface, probably by seeping ground water. The Thanet Sands are found at the top of the chalk in many of the quarries in Thurrock and at the Purfleet Chalk Ridge there are 'Sandy pipes penetrating into the chalk at Botany Pit' (Essex Field Club) and at the Wouldham Cliff. Further across London where it is present fine Thanet Sand is an important construction consideration for tunnelling in large engineering projects as reported such as Crossrail Ltd (the Elizabeth Line).

The Thanet Sands were followed by the **Lambeth Group** deposits of sands and clays 56-55 million years ago that have been exposed in one or two of the Thurrock pits such as the disused Buckingham Hill Sand Quarry near Linford. At the Orsett Depot Quarry, a cross section through the sea floor of about 55 million years ago could once be seen including fossilised burrows of marine animals such as shrimps, revealing that the quarry site was close to a shore line. The variability and the particular hazards associated with these thin, but inconsistent deposits are of concern to engineers engaged in tunnelling projects such as the Lower Thames Crossing.

• • • • • • • • • • • •

Gradually the sea level began to rise again and about 54 million years ago a wide, deep **subtropical sea** had become established. This sea was fed by muddy rivers from as far north as Yorkshire that brought in sediments that would become the thick, sticky, impermeable **London Clay**.

During the construction of a deep cutting for the M25 motorway at the foot of the Brentwood Heights an abundance of marine fossils were revealed including bivalve molluscs (scallops and clams), gastropods (snails) and the pearly nautilus.

Artist impression　　　　　　　　　　　**Cross section**

The pearly nautilus mollusc is a distant cousin of the octopus, squid and cuttlefish

Chapter 3 Geology and development of this landscape

Photograph of pearly nautilus fossil uncovered nearby (Courtesy of Ian & Ros Mercer)

Flora and fauna continued to evolve including primates and bats and there is a rich fossil record from the London Clay of many species of plants that show the land had tropical vegetation including palms and cinnamon trees and mangrove swamps. A large number of logs together with fruits and seeds were found in the Aveley Clay Pits at Sandy Lane and the pits yielded thousands of other fossils including many types of molluscs, corals, sea lilies, turtle bones, fish, lobster, crabs and sharks teeth.

Over time the sea reduced in size and depth and beds of clay mixed with silt and fine sand called the **Claygate Beds**, were formed above the London Clay. These are visible at Thorndon Country Park where streams have cut through the Claygate Beds to expose the older London Clay beneath (see *Thorndon Country Park Pebble Walk*, pub. Essex Rock & Mineral Society).

Eventually the river deltas along the shoreline extended across Essex and their sands were reworked by offshore currents to form the fine-grained beds of **Bagshot Sand**. These sands are evident locally at Harts Wood in Brentwood and south of Stony Hills Farm, Great Warley, at Langdon Hills and Lincewood Hill (part of Langdon Nature Reserve), High Beech in Epping Forest and at Billericay. At the old Brentwood Brickworks off London Road the Claygate Beds, Bagshot Sand and London Clay beneath have yielded many fossils including mammals, bird bone, many mollusc species and three shark species as well as crab and lobster.

From the geological map it can be seen that the London Clay floors the bowl-shaped depression that forms the central feature of the Land of the Fanns – the fen itself. This area was not protected by later pebble deposits and so the soft clay was easily scoured out. The clay takes in water, but does not let it through so the ground easily becomes waterlogged, thus creating this extensive low-lying marshy area of the fen.

MIGRATION *'This is a cross roads landscape: because of its location on the Thames ... people have always travelled into, through and away from this area.'*
(TellTale working with the public 2018)

The Ice Age Over the last million years or so the effects of the Ice Age, together with the migration of the ancient River Thames, have had a profound impact on the shape and peculiarities of the local landscape. The geology and archaeology of the 'Land of the Fanns' tell the story of a land that has shaped both our history and society today.

The origins of the River Thames occurred long before ice affected this area. It flowed from the mountains in the west of the British Isles probably since Palaeogene times over 50 million years ago. The **Ice Age Thames** was a huge, wild river system with many water channels, a braided river, that flowed from North Wales. The river cut through the chalk hills of the Chilterns at Goring, then along the Vale of St. Albans and across mid Essex to join the River Rhine where the North Sea is now. River systems such as these would act as convenient inland routes for animals and for early humans who visited Britain at various times during the last million years of the 'Age of Humans'. During this time, Britain was periodically connected to mainland Europe whenever sea levels fell. This happened when sea water was bound up in the developing ice caps each time the climate cooled. People settled across the exposed bed of the North Sea, in Doggerland, and many artefacts together with mammal bones have been dredged up from the modern sea bed.

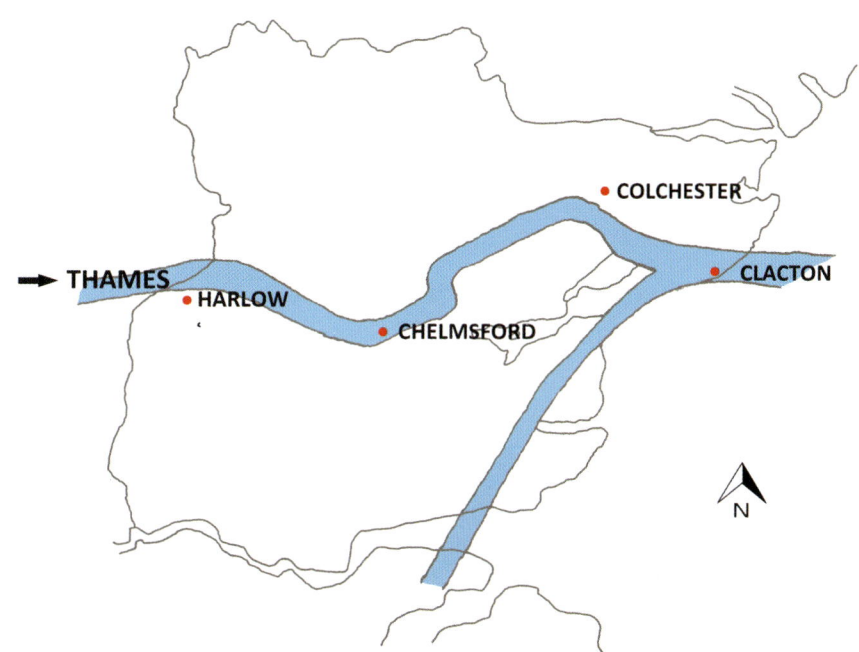

The Thames route across Essex via Harlow, Chelmsford and Colchester c.500 kya

Tributary rivers to this early Thames flowed northwards from Kent across southern Essex leaving beds of gravel that now top the highest areas of south Essex following uplift and the subsequent erosion of surrounding areas. These are known as 'High Level Gravels' or sometimes 'Stanmore Gravel'.

The gravel-topped hills of Havering at Bedfords Park (a London Geodiversity Partnership recommended Regionally Important Geological Site (RIGS), Great Warley, Holden's Wood at Brentwood, South Weald,

Langdon Hills, High Beech in Epping and at Norsey Wood Nature Reserve near Billericay, are prominent examples where the resistant gravel has protected the underlying soft sediments along the courses of these ancient rivers. The unprotected surrounding clay areas were vulnerable to erosion as the land gradually rose by about 120 metres (400 feet) since the time the rivers were flowing, leaving the gravel as toppings on the elongated elevated areas. The low hills followed by the road through North and South Ockendon (the Saxon 'Wocca's Hill') may similarly be the eroded-down remnants of previously gravel-topped uplands.

• • • • • • • • • • •

During the **Anglian Glacial Stage** of 450,000 years ago, an ice sheet extended south across the British Isles as far as north London. In places lobes of the ice sheet stretched southwards – the Hornchurch lobe reached further south than any other part of the ice sheet. The edge of the ice reached The Dell off Hornchurch High Street. 'St. Andrew's church Hornchurch is the furthest location reached by a Pleistocene ice sheet in Britain.' (The Essex Field Club *'Geology Site Account, The Dell'*).

Evidence of the ice sheet was first observed in the nearby Hornchurch railway cutting when the Upminster to Romford railway line was dug in the 1890s. Here material called 'till' that travelled in the base of the ice sheet was seen underneath river gravels. The till contains abundant evidence of rocks and fossils carried in the ice sheet from the Midlands including a vertebra from a plesiosaur, a huge marine reptile from the Jurassic Period. This is considered to be: 'one of the most important Ice Age sites in Britain' being 'of considerable significance for the correlation of the internationally important Thames terrace sequence with the glacial stratigraphy of southern Britain' (The Essex Field Club) and is protected as an SSSI.

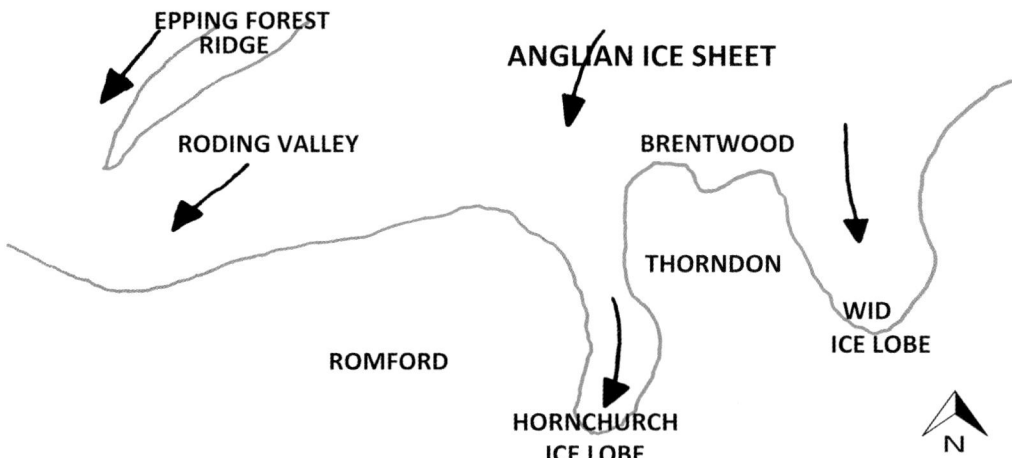

The Hornchurch and river Wid ice lobes that greatly influenced the landscape here as the warmer interglacial led to the ice melt down from Thorndon over the Mardyke area

West of here there were two more **ice lobes** that determined the rerouting of the River Thames southwards, these were at Finchley in North London and St. Albans in Hertfordshire. Because of these two great lobes of ice, the Thames became ponded up creating huge lakes that eventually spilled over to the south east. In this way the River Thames became diverted to the south beyond the ice sheet and away from central Essex. As a result the diverted Thames now joined the river Medway near Southend to flow north towards Clacton.

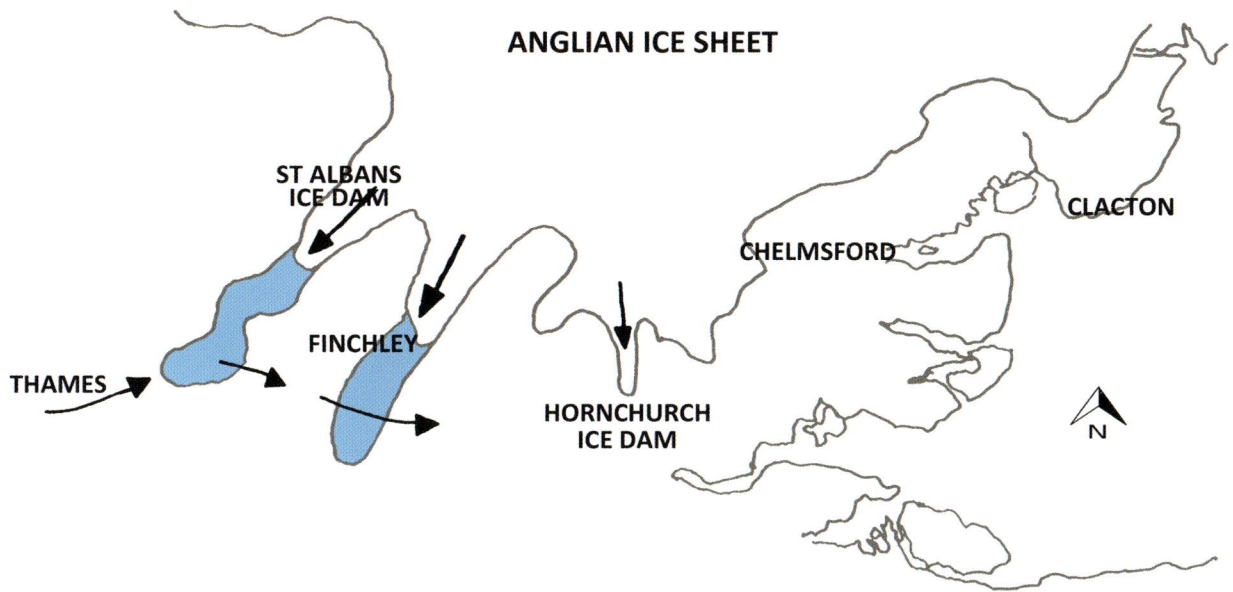

Map of the ice lobes (original source: Bridgland 1995) with Finchley and St. Albans ice dams effect on the route of the Thames

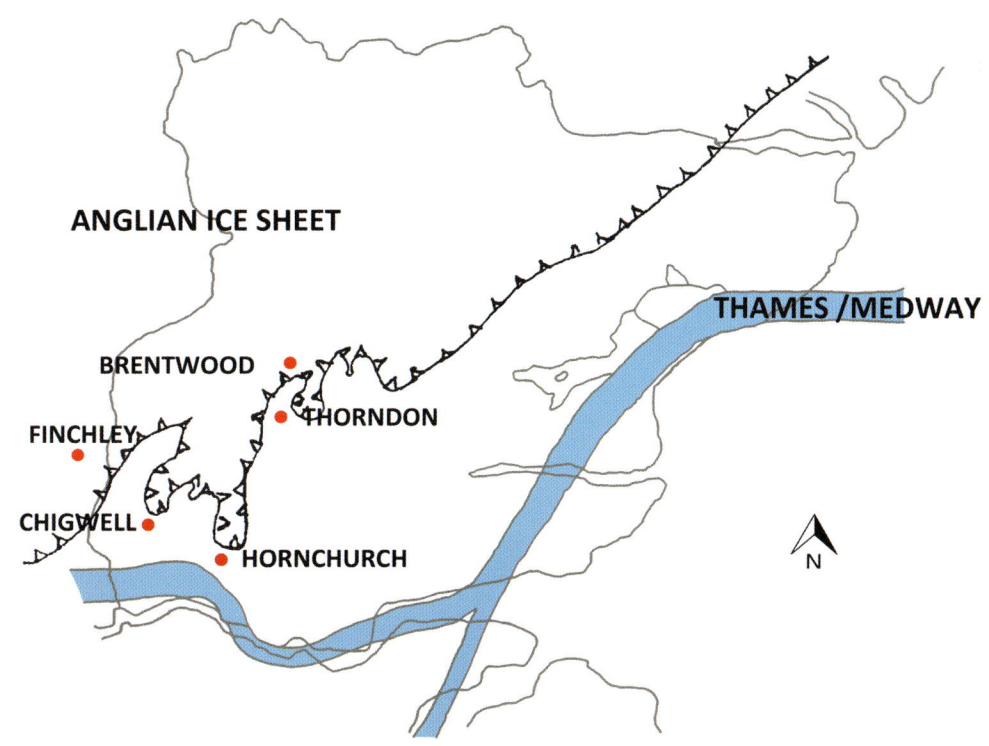

Map of the maximum extent of the Anglian Ice Sheet at Hornchurch and the movement of the Thames river to its subsequent position

The glacial deposits include **large erratic (non-local) boulders** that are occasionally found in the northern part of our area. On farmland north of Collier Row and close to Havering Country Park, there is a very large **sarsen stone** (sandstone) beneath a large oak tree. The stone is close to a patch of boulder clay (till) which suggests that the stone is a glacially-transported boulder, brought to this spot by the ice sheet from the chalk hills of north Essex where sarsen stones are relatively abundant.

Another erratic boulder was discovered at Marks Warren Farm Quarry, near Chadwell Heath. This is made of an igneous rock called dolerite. The nearest match to this rock is the Whin Sill in Northumberland, which suggests that it has been transported south 450 km (300 miles) by the ice sheet. It was then carried in the diverted River Thames and incorporated into the river gravels where it was found. It is now on display at the Bedford's Park Visitor Centre. This shows that the track of the ice sheet can be traced using erratics in the glacial deposits.

The Bedfords Park 'erratic' - a dolerite boulder on display at Bedford's Park, Havering-atte-Bower (Photograph courtesy of Ian & Ros Mercer)

When the Anglian ice sheet reached its limit and stopped, the ice-front was occasionally surrounded by **glacial outwash torrents** from melting ice, as seen in Iceland today. At Brentwood Heights large spreads of outwash sediment were recycled from the ancient High Level Gravel river beds across the Warley and Brentwood hills as the icy waters flowed out to the south. The waters with their sediment load joined the huge diverted River Thames as it swept across the areas now occupied by Ockendon and Orsett. Some of this outwash sand and gravel is still to be seen in the lowest bed of the cut section at Thorndon Country Park.

Examining the outwash sand and gravel at the section in Thorndon Country Park (Photograph courtesy of Ian and Ros Mercer)

EPOCH	STAGES	CLIMATE	M.I.S.	YEARS AGO	DEPOSITS LOCALLY
HOLOCENE	Flandrian Stage	Temperate	1	10,000	Present Interglacial
PLEISTOCENE	Devensian Glacial Stage	Glacial	2.5d	50,000	
	Ipswichian Interglacial	Temperate	5a	125,000	
	Unnamed cold stage	Cold	6	150,000	
	Aveley Interglacial	Temperate	7	200,000	Mucking Gravel
	Unnamed cold stage	Cold	8	250,000	
	Purfleet Interglacial	Temperate	9	300,000	Corbets Tey Gravel
	Unnamed cold stage	Glacial	10	350,000	
	Hoxnian Interglacial	Temperate	11	400,000	Orset Heath Gravel
	Anglian Glacial Stage	Glacial	12	450,000	Thames diverted by ice

Timescale of the last 450,000 years of the Quaternary Period (Ice Age) in Britain; we are now in the Flandrian Stage of the Holocene epoch

In the warming climate that came with the following Hoxnian Interglacial around 400,000 years ago, the ice and permafrost melted and water flowed in colossal torrents southwards carrying large quantities of sand and gravel to the diverted Thames. The first new course of the Thames went over the Purfleet Chalk Ridge where its river gravels may now be seen on top of the Chalk. At Orsett these sandy riverbed gravels form the barren land of Orsett Heath.

There followed several more glacial and interglacial stages in the fluctuating climate of the Ice Age. During glacial periods the ice sheets did not extend this far south again, but the landscape would have been permafrost tundra, almost devoid of vegetation. At these times most of the erosion of material from the higher ground would take place and the snow-melt torrent rivers would carry huge amounts of sand and gravel. The landscape of Thorndon Country Park reveals that during the next cold period 300,000 years ago, snow-melt torrents would have again flowed down across the area, gradually eroding the previous outwash gravels and the underlying sandy clay sediment (Claygate Beds), eventually right down into the London Clay beneath. The land had risen over the previous 100,000 years and deep valleys were carved into these soft sediments, lining them with gravel.

• • • • • • • • • • •

Meanwhile, the course of the Thames at this time cut down lower and could not go over the Purfleet Ridge. Instead the river flowed south east from the Hornchurch area towards Ockendon, went round the ridge in a loop to flow westwards as far as Purfleet, where it turned back to complete a great **backwards 'S' shape** to then continue on its eastwards course towards the coast.

Chapter 3 Geology and development of this landscape

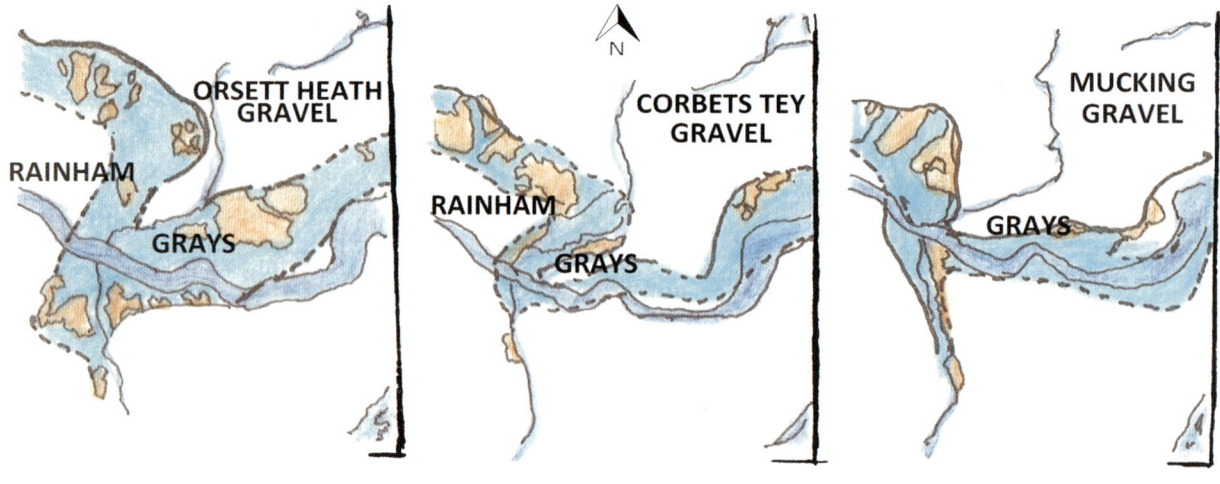

Maps of successive routes of the Thames (shown in light blue) 400 kya, 300 kya and 200 kya through what is now Thurrock during deposition of the Orsett Heath Gravel, the Corbets Tey Gravel and the Mucking Gravel (maps extracted from Bridgland 1994); the brown areas are what is left of the gravels now; the modern Thames is shown in dark blue colour

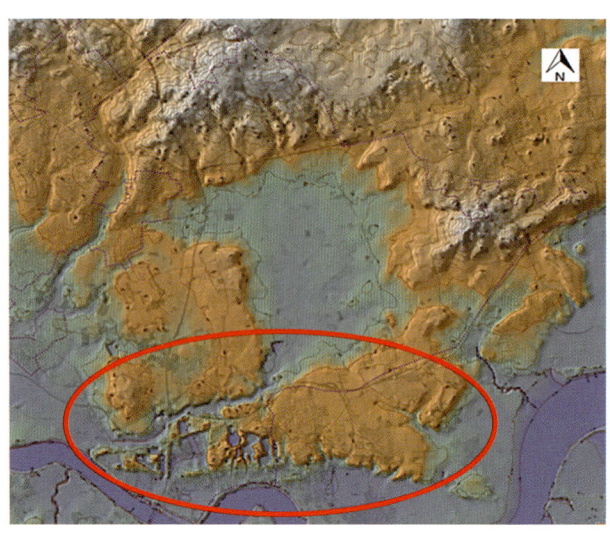

Extract from the Topographic map above showing the central fen area of the Mardyke; the square cut-out areas within the red outline are old quarries in the Chalk and various Sands.

(Courtesy LotF and Alison Farmer Associates 'Land of the Fanns Assessment Report')
© Crown copyright 2021 OS LICENCE no. 100064852

The Purfleet Ridge blocked the gravel laden torrents coming down from Thorndon and these became ponded-up in the great clay-lined bowl that is the beginnings of the heart of the Land of the Fanns. Subsequent cold-stage torrents would have deepened the incised valleys in the higher ground of Thorndon in the north, flowing into the flat area around Bulphan. Unable to escape through the rising ground of the surrounding gravel and clay hills, the icy waters would have been trapped in the fen area depositing riverbed sand and gravels. Eventually the water found its way around the chalk ridge by following the old Thames course, incising a wide, flat-bottomed wadi-like valley: the Mar Dyke and soils and marshes formed across the bowl that is floored by impermeable London Clay, through which the Mardyke river now flows. The present river Mardyke rises in Holden's Wood between Great and Little Warley, with tributaries from Upminster, Childerditch, Thorndon Country Park and Dunton Plotlands on Langdon Hills but it is just a small trickle within the valley previously occupied by the huge torrents of water during each cold period.

• • • • • • • • • • • •

At the end of each glacial stage the Thames cut down through its floodplain to deposit successive **new terraces** of gravels at lower levels. The land's uplift and tilting pushed the Thames further south each time, leaving the terraces of the earlier river floodplains across southern Essex, high above the present course of the Thames. The highest terraces are the oldest with the youngest at and even below modern river level. The Boyn Hill Terrace/Orsett Heath Gravel is the highest of the diverted Thames terraces, deposited some 400,000 years ago. This gravel is also found in the Hornchurch Railway Cutting and at other sites such as Socketts Heath Gravel Pit at Piggs Corner, Grays and at Fairlop Waters, now a landscaped area of former gravel pits. At Gun Hill/Broom Hill, West Tilbury the gravel lies some 25 metres (80 feet) above what is now the level of the river Thames. More of this gravel is found near Aveley (just east of the Sandy Land Clay Pit), where Kennington Park in Romford Road was created during the 1990s from the old gravel pits that were restored as fishing lakes, with areas of gravel exposed as low 2 m (6ft) cliffs along the path on the northern edge of the Park (Essex Field Club).

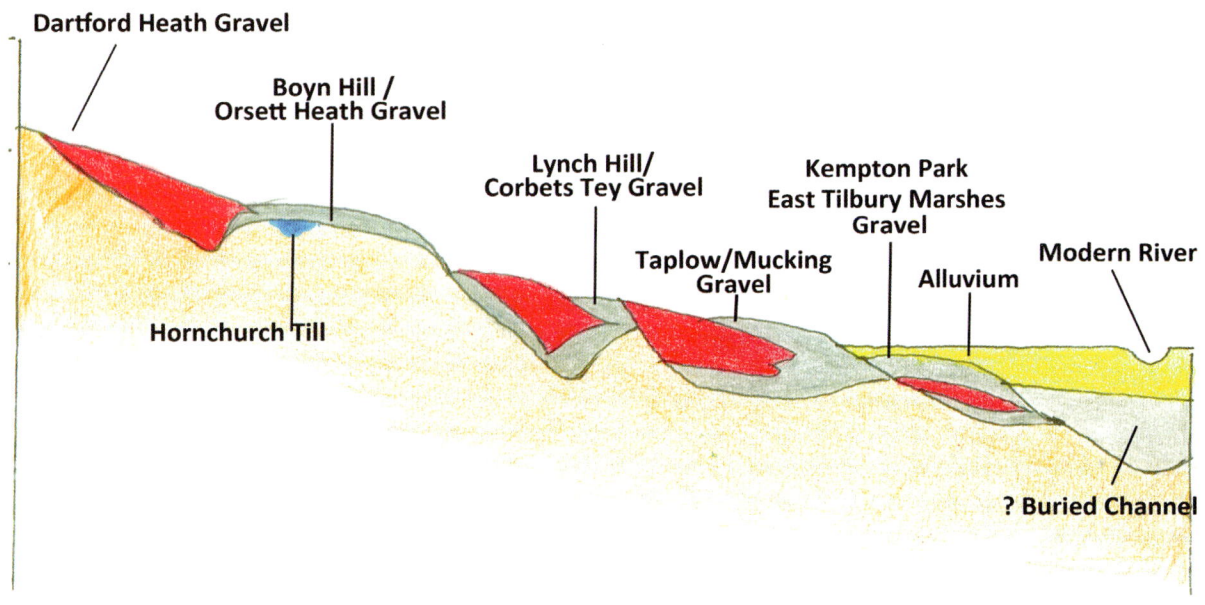

Diagrammatic cross section of The Lower Thames Valley terraces with cold climate gravels, areas coloured red indicate interglacial 'Mammalian Assemblage Zones' (MAZ) deposits i.e. collections of fossil bones of mammals (Original source: Schreve, 2004)

Pollen and other fossil evidence for the **'Purfleet' Interglacial** around 300,000 years ago, found at Belhus Park M25 cutting, near Aveley indicates a broad river channel with clear moving water and rush lined banks with dogwood, alder and Scots pine trees and red squirrel, water chestnut and freshwater fish and pond tortoise. At Greenlands Quarry one bank of the then river Thames is exposed and is cut into ice-shattered chalk called 'coombe rock' formed during the previous glacial period. The river channel is filled with layers of silt and sand with shell beds together with many flint artefacts made by early humans who lived beside the river. Excavations for the M25 motorway at Belhus Park evidenced the width of the river here and where in the opposite river bank a large flint hand axe 22 centimetres (9 inches) long was discovered and is now in the British Museum. Fossil evidence of animals had been found at Greenlands Quarry and three other adjacent disused quarries – Bluelands Quarry, Esso Pit and Botany Chalk Pit. Research based on the geology and archaeology of these deposits paints a picture of an episode in the story of the ancient River Thames, where people made their hunting gear from flints along this loop of the river, with the chalk ridge above making an excellent look-out.

View across the Thames terraces from Bedfords Park southwards down and across towards the Kentish hills (Photograph courtesy of Ian and Ros Mercer)

During the following glacial stage 250,000 years ago, the meander loop of the Thames became cut off and the river resumed a more direct route eastwards that is familiar to us today. Sediments at the Lion Pit Tramway Cutting SSSI (Lion Gorge) in South Stifford span the time from one glacial period to the next, with the **'Aveley' Interglacial** deposits sandwiched between from around 200,000 years ago when Neanderthals were living in Britain. This interglacial is recognised in the Aveley A13 Road cutting SSSI, from where its proposed name was derived, and which produced important and interesting finds of animal bones, including the famous 'Aveley Elephant' (see Stone Age Chapter) and other creatures and plant remains.

Another cold stage followed and then the warm **Ipswichian interglacial** stage of 100,000 years ago with evidence locally at the pits across Thurrock at Aveley, at West Thurrock and at East Tilbury Marshes. Many large mammals now roamed the forested landscape but mysteriously no traces of people have been found anywhere in Britain during this time.

From around 50,000 years ago a patterned ground of ice wedge polygons from the **Devensian glacial stage** were revealed in crop marks at Whalebone Lane, Romford and also near Harlow, both photographed from the air during the exceptional dry summer of 1976. At Thorndon Country Park the Devensian stage is recognised where 'in the top half of the cliff several long pebbles are in a near vertical position due to constant freezing and thawing of the ground.' (GeoEssex and Essex Rock & Mineral Society).

Finally, the current **Flandrian interglacial** began around 12,000 years ago signalling the end of the Old Stone Age (Palaeolithic) and the emergence of the Middle Stone Age (Mesolithic) and the arrival of modern humans through to the New Stone Age (Neolithic) with the development of new technologies.

• • • • • • • • • • • •

There are many more large sarsen stones found in the Land of the Fanns area. Due to permafrost 'freeze-thaw' action, most of these have gradually been 'let-down' from their original level within the Lambeth Group rock layers that have been eroded from above the Chalk, so they have not been transported very far. The south bank of the Mardyke river at Brickbarn Wood and Combe Wood is said to be deserving of SSSI status for its rare collection of some 30 - 40 sarsen stones, partially buried in the spoil from old gravel workings, many are over 2m (6ft) long and with good examples of smoothly rounded knobbly 'mamillated' surface and rootlet holes (these woods are also a Local Wildlife site). Nearby another large sarsen stone, said to be the finest in Essex, has been moved a short distance to the Davy Down Riverside Park from its previous location near to Brannett's Wood, others are found at Grays Gorge that is also a biological SSSI and part of Chafford Gorges Nature Park, and also at Socketts Heath and at Globe Pit (previously Globe Works), Grays. Sarsen stones at Moor Hall Farm near Aveley are thought to have also been deliberately moved to their present location – perhaps as ancient boundary markers.

LANDFORM *'The Land of the Fanns is about land and water and the often shifting relationship between them'* **(TellTale working with the public 2018)**

With all the tens of millions of years of geological activity of shifting seas, the raising and tilting of land, a spreading ice sheet and massive and repeated climate changes, the landscape we experience here today is a particular and rare pattern of hills, lowland, rivers and marshes that continues to serve people well locally and nationally as a strategically important location alongside the river Thames.

Modern settlements across the Land of the Fanns and its environs

As described, the landscape bedrock beneath the Land of the Fanns is of layers within the London Basin, with the Chalk ridge at Purfleet, the thick London Clay and finally the superficial Ice Age deposits. Sediments left by the varying courses of the River Thames in its old riverbeds and material laid down by the ice sheet provide invaluable evidence for the work of geologists, geographers, archaeologists and climatologists.

The dominant feature of the landscape is made up of the central fens or fanns around Bulphan. The fens are fed by the upper reaches of the Mardyke river and its tributaries that over time have laid down sediments forming such alluvial deposits across the London Clay bedrock. The fens are surrounded by low hilly farmland to the west around Belhus and low hills around Orsett to the south east that are formed by the Lambeth Group of clays, silts, sands and gravels. In the west the London Clay, the brickearths and the sands and gravels have typically been quarried in the past, where important sites remain: the A13 Road Cutting SSSI providing evidence of the Aveley Interglacial for example. The Mardyke river meanders across the fen until it approaches the Purfleet ridge. It then flows westwards in a straight channel along a wide, steep sided valley following a previous course of the Thames, before it finally joins the present River Thames at Purfleet. In its lower course it is a 'miss-fit' stream flowing through a valley that is much larger than its present flow could have carved. In past historical times the Mardyke formed the Saxon boundary ditch, from which it may have derived its name between Chafford Hundred and Barstable Hundred, and the fanns or marshes were tamed as fens and worked by the fann men for generations. This great enigmatic bowl of low-lying landscape is the heart of the Land of the Fanns encompassed by the Thames Chase Community Forest.

To the north the higher ground from the Lea Valley, across Hainault Forest and High Beach eastwards that forms the geographical northern boundary of the Land of the Fanns is along the southern edge of the Essex Plateau and is known locally as Havering Ridge and Brentwood Heights and it extends south-east to Langdon Hills. This higher land provides distant views south and west across the river valleys and the fenland bowl to the Thames with views back to the wooded horizons in the north and east. The heights are made up of London Clay overlain by the sandy clay of the Claygate Beds and the overlying Bagshot Sands topped with the gravels associated with the north flowing tributaries of the ancient Thames. Springs occasionally emerge at the junction of the clay and sands, such as at Bedfords Park in Havering-atte-Bower. At Jury Hill, Childerditch the southern and western slopes have suffered from successive landslips since the retreat of the ice (Essex Field Club) and again at St. Michael's Hill, Pitsea the old Thames cliff line is a land slipped area.

As well as the Mardyke, the wider landscape is dissected by two other river valleys forming from west to east the Rom/Beam Valley in the Dagenham Corridor and the Ingrebourne Valley where both rivers flow directly south to join the River Thames. The Ingrebourne is another "mis-fit" stream that meanders intricately within the wide, flat-bottomed valley carved by a lobe of the Anglian ice sheet, and Cranham Marsh Nature Reserve in Havering is a relic of fen land that drains into the Ingrebourne. Alongside the Thames are marshes at Dagenham, Hornchurch, Rainham and Wennington, Aveley, Purfleet and West Thurrock. These Thameside marshes are formed on the Chalk and London Clay bedrock overlain with alluvium deposited by the present day river. The marshes are edged by a low gravel ridge between Dagenham and Rainham that continues eastwards past South Hall Farm by South Hall bridge and Wennington village. Further east the landscape of West Thurrock is now largely an urban townscape characterised by abandoned chalk quarries that have now been repurposed for warehousing, retail centres and housing developments. Features of significance include the importance for study of the geological exposures in the SSSI's along the Purfleet ridge at Purfleet Chalk Pits, at Chafford Gorges Nature Park and at Globe Pit in Grays.

ECONOMY *'This area is justly famous for trade, commerce and industry: these have been important here for many centuries.' (TellTale working with the public 2018)*

The strategic location of this landscape beside the River Thames lends itself to excellent provision for local, national and international trade, commerce and industry as well as its particular suitability for homes, recreation and transport links. Additional to this are the quality of the soils for agriculture, and the underlying geology for mineral extraction.

• • • • • • • • • • •

Ice Age geological deposits from both cold and warm stages are important to the development of **soils** as a habitat for organisms and enabling plant growth and supporting animal and human populations. Soil is a major component of the Earth's ecosystem and may be essentially sandy, clay, chalky or peaty depending on their differing composition, each may be found in this area and are suitable for **differing forms of agriculture.** Ancient farming crop marks often appear in the southern area in particular and give clues to past settlements and agricultural and industrial practices, all useful information for archaeologists and historians for example. The marshes have been used for sheep and cattle grazing from the Iron Age, while farming in the area around Bulphan and the bowl-shaped valley of the Mardyke is affected by high water tables in the winter. The lighter soils on the Thames river terraces for example suit crop growing and allowed market gardening, salad crops and orchards to flourish here.

In 1876 James Thorne published his *Handbook of the Environs of London* where he described (North) Stifford as 'A quiet, secluded, agricultural village', and at Little Thurrock 'The occupations are agricultural; there are considerable arable farms; the marshes afford pasture; and vegetables, and especially peas, are largely grown for the London market. There are also extensive brick and chalk pits…' he also goes on to describe the medieval Dene Holes chalk mines nearby. At Wennington he again describes the occupations as agricultural and 'Large quantities of peas are grown for the London market'. Nearby Rainham is described as 'the centre and port of an extensive district of market gardens, and a considerable trade is done in carrying potatoes and the like by lighters to London and bringing back coal and manure'. However the development of agriculture here has also been in response to wider pressures and demands and agriculture within the semi-urban nature of this landscape is itself a story of marvellous resilience.

• • • • • • • • • • •

During the 20th century extensive **mineral extraction** of sand, gravel, chalk and clay led to the development of large quarries. These included gravel quarries in the northern area between Barkingside and Romford and very large chalk and sand quarries in the southern area along Thameside. Here the chalk was quarried for more than two centuries for many uses such as quick lime for agriculture and for chemical use including whiting for paint and putty. Huge quantities were quarried in the 1950s -1970s for making cement. Clay was also used extensively in cement manufacture and for brickmaking, and sand and gravels are necessary in the construction industry.

However, quarrying degraded and blighted areas of this landscape for a considerable period and with extraction still ongoing in places such as Wennington. However extensive efforts continue to be made to turn this situation to advantage including proactively protecting important geological evidence for future study and opening up areas to visitors for interest, educational purposes and research. Other areas are transformed into wildlife and nature parks or leisure areas with lakes for fishing and sports activities. A lead is also shown in agricultural land reclamation and in waste management with completed landfill areas opened as low vantage point hills as at Rainham riverside, or areas planted with new Forestry Commission woodland walks as part of the Thames Chase Community Forest.

Places to visit near and far:

- Essex Wildlife Trust Chafford Gorges Nature Park chalk pits for the geology trail (leaflet guide may be available by enquiry online)
- Davy Down Riverside Park for the scattered river deposits of large boulders called sarsens by the banks of the Mardyke river
- RSPB Visitor Centre, Purfleet for the petrified tree on display from the landscape covered in yew forest 5,000-6,000 years ago
- Thorndon North Country Park: an Ice Age gravel wall and a 'Pebble Walk' leaflet by Essex Rock & Mineral Society
- Cudmore Grove Country Park, Mersea Island is one of the most important geological sites in Essex with important geological exposures for Pleistocene studies at East Mersea including those associated with the Thames/Medway river system 300 thousand years ago. The 'Mersea Flats' are extensive deposits of London Clay on the Eocene foreshore dating to c.50 million years ago
- The Essex Field Club, Green Centre, Wat Tyler Country Park, Pitsea Hall Lane, Pitsea, Basildon SS16 4UH. Houses collections from the old Passmore Edwards Museum in Stratford accumulated over the Club's long history since 1880. Public displays and activities. (Centre Opening Information: www.essexfieldclub.org.uk)
- Swanscombe Heritage Park, SSSI and NNR

Ideas for further projects:

- Undertake essential clearance and continued maintenance of a narrow swathe of rock clear at Chafford Gorges
- Further investigate the origins of the pebble gravel deposits atop Havering Ridge the Brentwood Heights, Langdon Hills range of highland
- Further investigate the route of the Thames meander across this landscape
- A study at the Grangewaters Outdoor Education Centre for its quarry origins and earlier fen landscape and comparing and informing the Lower Thames Crossing proposals

- Geological investigation in Hornchurch in relation to the internationally important SSSI at Hornchurch Railway Cutting, in conjunction with Essex Rock & Mineral Society
- A study of the wooded banks and the sarsen stones at Davy Down Riverside Park and along the Mardyke river, also the erratics at Moor Hall and Havering Country Park, and the possibility of the past use of some as wayside markers
- In the interests of preserving the geological and fossil records in respect of informing an understanding of climate change and for geological engineering investigations for strategic projects, support investigation, protection and presentation of the West Thurrock Gorges in Grays and Purfleet and coordinate public accessibility between sites of interest (see the National Character Area profile for the Northern Thames Basin: 'The sedimentary deposits and the fossils contained within them represent an important context for our understanding of and insights into the potential impacts of future climate change on our landscapes. Several sites also preserve important evidence for early human occupation of the area dating back around 300,000 years.')

References for further research:
- Geologist's Association
- Rockwatch, UK Nationwide Geology Club for Children
- The Geological Society
- Young Zoologists Club, Museum of Zoology, Cambridge
- Museum of London (MOL)
- Historic England Greater London Archaeology Advisory Service (GLAAS)
- The Council for British Archaeology (CBA) and its London Branch (CBA-L)
- The Heritage Gateway is a single online access to many of England's local and national historic environment records
- London Geodiversity Partnership
- British Geological Survey online; also Onshore GeoIndex viewer with GeoScenic photographs and other data
- Cunliffe, Barry (2008) 'Europe between the Oceans 9,000 BC- AD 1,000' Yale University Press ISBN 978-0-500-17086-3 (pbk)

Further Reading:
- Alison Farmer Associates in association with Countryscape (Feb. 2016) *Land of the Fanns Landscape Character Assessment – Final Report*
- Bridgland, David & Schreve, Danielle (2004) *Quaternary lithostratigraphy and mammalian biostratigraphy of the Lower Thames terrace system, South-East England*
- Clements, Diana compiled *The Geology of London: Geologists' Association Guide No. 68* includes Itinerary no. 5 Purfleet to Chafford Hundred
- Crane, Nicholas (2017) *The Making of the British Landscape* pub. Weidenfeld & Nicolson ISBN 978 0 7538 2667 6

- Dartnell, Lewis (2018) *Origins – How the Earth made us* pub. The Bodley Head ISBN 9781847924353
- Essex Rock & Mineral Society informative booklets and leaflets including *Essex Rocks, Fossils in Essex* and *Pebbles in Essex*
- Lucy, Gerald for Essex Rock & Mineral Society (1997) *Brentwood rock – A Geological Trail of Brentwood High Street*
- Mercer, Ian and Mercer, Ros (2022) *Essex Rock* ISBN 9781784272791 Pelagic Publishing

Definitions:

Eon The primary defined divisions of time, currently the Phanerozoic. Eons are divided into Eras.

Era One or more geological Periods, currently the Cenozoic Era.

Period The basic unit of geological time, currently the Quaternary Period.

Epoch A variable length of time that is shorter than a Period, currently the Holocene Epoch.

MIS Marine Isotope Stages are numbered from 1 the most recent, to 104 some 6 mya (and may go back even further). MIS 1-12 are alternating warm and cold stages back to the Anglian Glacial Stage, the even numbers relate to the cold glacial stages, the odd numbers relate to the warm, interglacial intervals, the present being MIS 1.

LGS Local Geological Sites (formerly RIGS – Regionally Important Geological and Geomorphological Site).

Revised and edited by: Ros Mercer BSc FGS & Ian Mercer BSc FGA, Essex Rock & Mineral Society

Section B
Prehistory & Archaeology Introduction

Prehistory This is about the time before written records generally existed and dates backwards from the year 1BC. The prehistory story of the development of human technology comes out of the geology and formation of the landscape, its geography and the archaeological evidence it holds. In addition to its built and natural form, the culture of the landscape includes its peoples and traditions and diversity, as well as the arts, and intellectual activity and achievement.

The prehistoric Early Stone Age (the Pleistocene) coincided with the several cold Stages of the Ice Age and the warmer Interglacials. The present post-glacial (or interglacial) began around 10,000 years BC, this was the beginning of the geological Holocene epoch when people were able to populate Asia and Europe as the glaciers and ice sheets receded and melted. Those early peoples progressed through the Middle Stone Age (the Mesolithic) and the New Stone Age (Neolithic) refining Stone Age life, their tools and techniques.

Knowledge and skills further developed as the Stone Age eventually gave way to the Bronze Age as the ability to used bronze and other soft metals was developed during 2,000 – 2,400 years BC and later around 750 years BC with the development of the use of iron. These three main periods of division that tell the story are the **Stone Age** (Old, Middle and New); the **Bronze Age** (includes the Ages of Copper and Tin) and the **Iron Age** and these form the chapters for this section of the book.

Archaeology Much of the prehistory information relies on archaeological evidence, but archaeology also reveals evidence for the historic periods too leading up to modern day and supplements the written records that are more often available for the historic periods.

The nature of the particular geology of this landscape has resulted in important evidence found here that is significant to the story of the London basin during early prehistory. By its location and form this landscape has naturally been witness to so much of the nation's prehistory and historical events that have inevitably passed across it, each leaving something of itself and collectively influencing the landscape, its people and its sense of place.

Nationally the story of the hunter-gatherers gradually settling the landscape is becoming much better understood and here this countryside landscape retains wonderful opportunity through local archaeological work to reveal much more detail about the prehistory activity in the London Basin because in comparison to London, this landscape is relatively undeveloped and the archaeology of the wider landscape more likely to have survived. This is borne out in particular by a substantial part of the western area of the landscape in Havering and Dagenham that is identified as of archaeological importance and many sites are individual Archaeological Priority Areas (APA's) or within an Archaeological Priority Zone (APZ) or are otherwise similarly designated, and also from finds sites in the southern area in Thurrock, as well as from archaeological information about the development of the landscape and its peoples as it is gradually revealed. Here is still the rare surviving archaeological landscape of Britain's capital city before the growth and expansion of outer London – in the words of the Museum of London in their exhibition largely based on this area that is: 'London before London'.

Much of the archaeological importance or interest of this area is for the information it can reveal, if less so for rich pickings of artefacts – although it does have its moments of glorious finds as national, regional and local museums can attest. Nationally important find sites in this area include the 'Aveley Elephant'; in the Ingrebourne Valley over recent years work has identified a Bronze Age landscape including three sites with rare continuous-occupation from the Bronze Age through to Saxon near Dovers corner and in Berwick Pond Road, Rainham and may be a clue to Bronze Age trade routes with the story now supplemented by the fabulous Wennington hoard; also the magnificent pair of glass drinking horns excavated from a pagan Saxon cemetery at Gerpins Pit, Rainham and now held by the British Museum with more of the objects held locally at Valence House Museum, Dagenham. There are also many Scheduled Ancient Monuments (SAM's) in the landscape and many more unscheduled Ancient Monuments (AM's). As an example, many moated sites remain as AM's but are not comprehensively recorded, and some have potential to be taken forward for Scheduling. In Havering alone every part of the area that was not fen or marsh supported a medieval moated house site and this pattern is seen across this landscape around places like Bulphan.

Leaflets produced by the Thames Chase Community Forest have information on various Walks of natural and built heritage interest from the Forest Centre in Cranham. The heritage story accessed through these local Walks relates very much to the relationship of the national heritage story with this area. However past information remains split firmly east and west of the East London administrative boundary with modern Essex, with collation and interpretation still a complex matter. Moreover, from the mid 1980s access to archaeological and museum advice and activity had invariably become patchy and hard to access in the western part of the area. This situation was monitored at the time by establishing the Standing Conference on London's Archaeology (SCOLA) and in recent years that organisation has re-emerged as the Council for British Archaeology London branch (CBA-L) that sensibly includes Essex representation. Also, more recently museum responsibility for the north-east London area has passed to the Museum of London (MOL) allowing it to become more active across this area, and with local area museums provision through popular demand, such as Havering Museum. The CBA (and SCOLA previously) has a local feeder organisation the London Archaeology Forum (LAF) and also operates its Young Archaeologists Club (YAC) outside of this area, and the MOL organises local groups such as the Thames Mudlarks closer to London.

Greater continuity across this landscape would help to clarify its archaeological story and its place within the wider pre-history story of southern Britain and may encourage and enable support for local people interested in archaeology here and give opportunity for them to become actively involved in archaeology. This landscape has a very real job to do in providing ready and sustainable access to outdoor opportunity for its huge audience of local people and those from neighbouring areas, and archaeology has such an important role here in providing informed access and staying ahead of development decision making.

Places to visit near and far:

- Local Museums:
    - Valance House Museum, Becontree Avenue, Dagenham;
    - Havering Museum, High Street, Romford;
    - Thurrock Museum, Thameside Complex, Grays
    - Brentwood Museum, Lorne Road off Warley Hill, Brentwood
    - Chelmsford Museum, Oaklands Park, Moulsham Street, Chelmsford
- National museums:
    - Museum of London (MOL) and MOL Docklands
      - See their schools programmes and also ideas for fun learning at home
    - British Museum, Great Russell Street, London
      - Use their Image Bank and notes for teachers
    - Natural History Museum, South Kensington, London
- English Heritage care for over 400 historic buildings, monuments and sites countrywide including prehistoric sites, medieval castles, Roman forts and a Cold War bunker

Ideas for further archaeological projects:

- Investigate and action means to record all unscheduled sites across the landscape such as moated sites and mills, and seek to have the statutory list of Scheduled Monuments updated in order to more accurately inform the Historic Environment Record across the landscape
- Get involved with the Upminster Windmill archaeological group
- Get involved with local museums like the Upminster Hall 'Tithe' Barn Museum of Nostalgia
- A study to locate the various sites and purposes of Thames ferries
- A study of the role of the Thames in the defence of the realm across this landscape
- Explore any possibility for some restoration or recording of Botany Way gardens at Purfleet
- Study and record the history and the site of Warley Barracks heritage survivals for example the practice trenches, bawl alley and so on

References for further research:

- Council for British Archaeology (CBA) and its London branch (CBA-L) and CBA East and the Young Archaeologists Club (YAC). The CBA is a National Amenity Society and a charity founded for the 'safeguarding of all kinds of archaeological material and the strengthening of existing measures for the care of ancient and historic buildings, monuments, and antiquities' and to improve public education about archaeology
- West Essex Archaeology Group (WEAG)
- Museum of London Docklands: Thames Mudlarks
- London Archaeology Forum (LAF)
- Birkbeck College and Anglia University for archaeology courses
- Historic England Greater London Archaeology Advisory Service (GLAAS) at Historic England

- The Heritage Gateway is a single online access to many of England's local and national historic environment records
- Essex Historic Environment Record (EHER) is a database of all known archaeological sites and monuments, historic buildings, parks and gardens in Essex
- Unlocking Essex Past (UEP) provides online access to the Essex Historic Environment Record
- Cunliffe, Barry (2008) *Europe between the Oceans 9,000 BC - AD 1,000* Yale University Press ISBN 978-0-500-17086-3 (pbk)

Further Reading:

- Brown, Nigel & Massey-Ryan, Roger (2004) *The Finest Prospect in All England – the Archaeology of South Essex, UK* pub ECC, ISBN 185281 245 1
- Greenwood, Pamela; Perring, Dominic & Rowsome, Peter (2006) *From Ice Age to Essex – a history of the people and landscape of East London* gives guidance on the archaeology of this landscape in relation to the wider archaeological story pub MOL ISBN 1-901992-61-6
- *London Archaeologist* Quarterly Magazine pub. by The London Archaeologist Association
- *The Essex Journal* published twice yearly by the Essex Society for Archaeology and History (ESAH)

Chapter 4
Stone Age
c.2.6 million years ago – c.2,500 BC

NATIONAL CURRICULUM Key stages 1 and 2 hints

The Stone Age is a long time of prehistory when people used stone such as flint to make tools and weapons like hand axes with wood and other natural materials such as bone, shells, leather and with string and netting made from plant fibres. The Stone Age continues until the Bronze Age with the innovation in the use of bronze for making implements. This time is divided into the **Old Stone Age** (Palaeolithic), followed by the **Middle Stone Age** (Mesolithic) and then the **New Stone Age** (Neolithic), and this story of human development coincides with the most recent geological Period called the Quaternary.

SURPRISE *'The Land of the Fanns is an intricate landscape, full of surprises and 'hidden gems' and rewards exploring.'* **(TellTale working with the public 2018)**

During the 'Age of Humans' that began about 2.6 million years ago (mya) there have been five really inhospitable Glacial Stages of the Ice Age each with artic conditions, but each is separated by warmer Interglacial Stages at least as warm as today when plants and animals could flourish. About 2.5 mya at a time at the beginning of the Old Stone Age the North Sea covered much of eastern England and Britain was connected to the continent by a land bridge called **Doggerland**[1], although at times as the climate warmed and sea levels rose Britain would become an island cut off from the rest of the continent. During this time large braided rivers (interconnecting river channels) were flowing into the North Sea including the early ancestral river Thames north of here (Bytham River, see Geology Chapter).

The major river systems were like great super highways for animals and for early humans at times to make their way into the interior of the country. Now and again archaeologists find evidence of these visitors, their environment and how they were living. Here much later after the Thames had settled into the present Thames Valley, evidence has been found along its banks of plants and animals and early human hunter-gatherers living here and travelling by during those warm Interglacials –

- on the Becontree Housing Estate in Dagenham, at Rainham, Corbets Tey, Belhus Woods Country Park and at Aveley and South Ockendon, Purfleet, South Stifford and between West Thurrock and Little Thurrock during the Old Stone Age,
- at Marks Warren Farm in Chadwell Heath (Tier 1 Archaeological Priority Area - APA) and at Dagenham, Rainham and Orsett during the Middle Stone Age,
- at Rainham, Orsett, Dagenham and Marks Warren Farm during the New Stone Age.

---

[1] Doggerland is a submerged land mass beneath the southern North Sea around the area of Dogger Bank that formerly connected Britain to mainland Europe.

Extent of the Anglian ice sheet indicating Stonehenge and Hornchurch, also the location of Doggerland (now under the North Sea)

By the New Stone Age in the south the damp grasslands around the junction of the rivers Beam and Wantz in Dagenham (Tier 1 APA) had willow trees growing with pine trees and dwarf birches on higher ground around. The much higher land at Marks Warren was a wooded area with streams where trees were being cleared so that by the later period it seems there were people living here and beginning to farm the land.

MIGRATION *'This is a cross roads landscape: because of its location on the Thames ... people have always travelled into, through and away from this area.'* **(TellTale working with the public 2018)**

Old Stone Age (Palaeolithic) c.2.6 million years - c.10,000 BC During the Glacial Stages this area was an icy wasteland or tundra where the land is frozen during the coldest months and only warms in summer to become treeless wetlands of bogs and marshes with typically restricted plant growth such as dwarf shrubs, sedges, grasses, moss and lichens. However between the cold Stages during the warmer Interglacial Stages the climate made it more inviting for animals and for early humans to migrate into this area. Coming via the land bridge from the continent of Europe and using the river systems as convenient inland routes visitors began arriving in Britain many thousands of years ago. In fact a set of early human footprints were discovered in Thames river mud (Bytham River) at Happisburgh from c.900 thousand years ago (kya) when the Thames flowed across Norfolk (see Geology Chapter) (*Our Human Story* by Louise Humphrey & Chris Stringer, pub. Natural History Museum 2019 ISBN 978 0 565 093914).

During the **warm Interglacials** the earliest evidence of early humans found in Essex is a worked flint flake from some 600 kya found at Westcliff-on-Sea at a time of hunter-gathers before people had learned the use of fire. By about 500 kya Britain had a Mediterranean climate and the Thames was flowing north of here across mid-Essex via Harlow, Chelmsford, Braintree, Colchester and Clacton.

• • • • • • • • • • • •

However, the glacial **Anglian Ice Stage** arrived c.478 kya (Marine Isotope Stage 12)[2] and the ice sheet extended as far south as Hornchurch, further south than any other. This ice sheet diverted the river Thames south-eastwards towards its present position so that the river now flowed through the Thames Valley with the Upper Thames around Oxford, the Middle Thames from Reading to central London and the Lower Thames crossing this area on the east London/southwest Essex borders as it continued on its way out to the North Sea. Animals roaming here during the Old Stone Age included wild boar, wolf, lion and woolly rhinoceros. Nomadic hunter-gathers visited in pursuit of the big game and the famous Clacton yew spear was discovered in an early channel of the Thames. Remarkably it is dated to some 450 kya when the cold climate and short daylight hours would have limited time for hunting, which some have suggested may have encouraged the development of tools of this sort.

• • • • • • • • • • • •

The Anglian Ice Stage was followed by the warm **Hoxnian Interglacial** c.424 kya–c.374 kya (MIS 11) with a temperate climate. The huge volumes of melt water from the ice sheet would have been released over the wider landscape, modifying it over time by carving down the gravel topped hills of London Clay and depositing its glacial outwash sediments of gravel, sand and mud widely across this landscape and over the Thames Valley and is evidenced at Thorndon and at Scrub Hill on Little Warley Common and across the top of the hill over the chalk at Chafford Gorges.

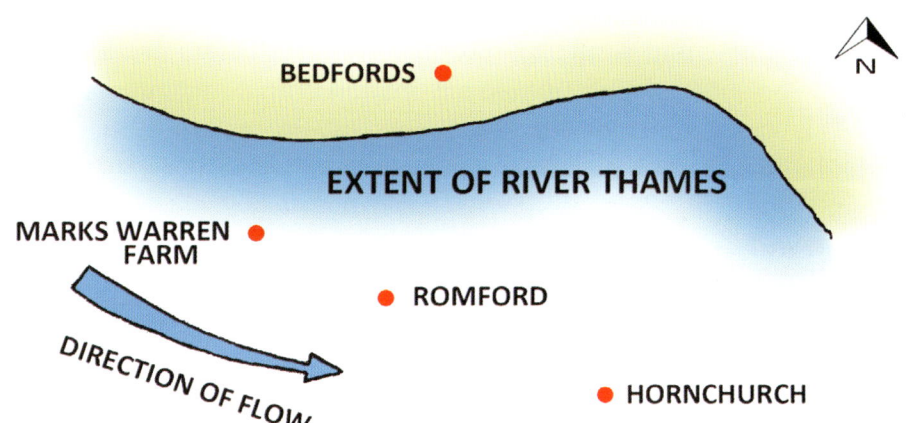

Indication of the extent of the river Thames to the north across this landscape 400 kya

Having being realigned to this area the Thames shifted its width and course through the Thames Valley over time, and some detail about the position and width of the Thames over later time periods has been recorded for example by archaeologists examining the marsh edge during investigations in 1993 at the Brookway allotment site between Wennington and Rainham.

The river also repeatedly cut down into the valley contributing significantly to the landscape by forming gravel terraces like a staircase that are locally referred to as **'The Romford Steps'**, but they actually extend across the whole length of the Thames Valley through London to Reading. This process continued until stopped by rising global sea levels from melting glacial water towards the end of the last Ice Stage. Each terrace name is followed by the name of the local gravel deposits.

---

[2] MIS is a geological temperature record of changing temperatures and counts backwards from the present MIS 1.

The oldest and therefore the highest of these, is an Anglian Stage melt water outwash that created the **Boyn Hill/Orsett Heath gravel terrace** about 380 kya (MIS 12-10). During this time there is evidence of early humans not so far from the Land of the Fanns. The Clacton Cliffs and Foreshore Site of Special Scientific Interest (SSSI) bears the site of 'a simple flint-working industry' evidence for early humans in Essex, an ancestor of the Neanderthals, some 400 kya. Also, the skull of an early Neanderthal woman was found from c.380 kya in the same river Thames Boyn Hill/Orsett Heath gravel terrace at Swanscombe in Kent, where there were also flint tools, molluscs and animal bones.

• • • • • • • • • • • •

There followed another Glacial Ice Stage c.350 kya (MIS 10) where the ice sheet did not come as far as Essex but evidence is found locally at Greenlands Quarry, Purfleet, at Belhus Woods Country Park, Aveley, at Orsett Heath and at Globe Pit, Grays (a SSSI for its interrelationship of geology with archaeology) where many flint tools comprising more refined flint flakes and the cores they were cut from, rather than hand axes, were found in the gravel from the Old Stone Age and a rare supply of small vertebrate fossil mammals from a time when the Thames flowed through here.

• • • • • • • • • • • •

That Ice Age Stage was followed by a previously unknown warm Stage c.335-280 kya (MIS 9) named the **'Purfleet' Interglacial** with evidence for it found at the Purfleet Chalk Pits SSSI that is used for geological research so important in unravelling the complicated history of the climate. It contains a record of three separate episodes of early human occupation from a cold interval to a warm time and back to cold again. This site also includes fossil evidence of a hyena and bones of monkey, beaver, deer, bison and straight-tusked elephant and indicates a mixed woodland environment.

Pollen and other fossil evidence for this time at Belhus Woods Country Park M25 cutting near Aveley, indicates a broad, deep river channel about 1 km (0.6 miles) wide with clear, slow moving water and rush lined banks with water chestnut, freshwater fish and pond tortoise and Scots pine trees, alder, dogwood and red squirrel. The Tunnel Cement Works and Thurrock Chalk Quarry, Motherwell Way, West Thurrock yielded many mammal bones including woolly rhinoceros and elephant and what was described as 'a mass of elephant tusks' and also beds of mollusc shells. At Grays, Brickearth extends for some 5.5 km (4 miles) from West Thurrock to Little Thurrock most of it having been quarried away but with many fossils found from this Interglacial including lion, wolf, brown bear, rhinoceros and wild boar, and cut marks from some bones is evidence of early humans living in the area.

At this time people hunted and butchered animals such as antelope and woolly mammoths and some of their flint tools and waste flint flakes and cores survive for archaeologists to discover today. This is the **Lynch Hill /Corbets Tey Gravel terrace** and as well as the large hand axe found in the ancient Thames river bank (at Belhus Woods/M25 road excavation) examples of flint hand axes for this Stage have been found in South Ockendon, at Gerpins Pit in Rainham and at Corbets Tey. At the same terrace level on the river Roding a flint hand axe and flint stone tools were found in a slip road cutting for the M11 motorway in Woodford, and possibly 'one of the earliest sites to provide evidence of the uses of fire in Britain' (the Essex Field Club).

• • • • • • • • • • • •

During the next cold Stage c.300kya (MIS 8) the ice sheet extended as far south as Peterborough in Cambridgeshire, but even so early humans were here on the bleak tundra and making flint tools like hand axes.

Around 200 kya (MIS 7) the **Aveley Interglacial Stage** began, named after the local area where it was first recognised. Neanderthals were living in Britain and this area was more like the African savannah with wide grassy plains, abundant vegetation and animal herds. Now once again brown bear, bison, rhinoceros, straight-tusked elephant and mammoth were roaming the area. Evidence for the **Taplow /Mucking Gravel Terrace** (MIS 8, 7, & 6) is present in Corbets Tey and at Belhus Park, Aveley and at Greenlands Quarry, Purfleet. At the Botany Pit quarry site in Purfleet some fossil bones were found including horse and red deer and deposits were very rich in Old Stone Age stone tools with hundreds of flint flakes and cores and some hand-axes indicating an early flint industry, two hand-axes went to Thurrock Museum, Grays and the other finds were sent to the British Museum in London.

Along what were the banks of the Thames at the Purfleet Road, Aveley A13 Road Cutting SSSI, plant and pollen remains, insects, vertebrates and molluscs were found along with more of the animal bones and also including wolf, giant deer, a very large lion and a marsh-dwelling jungle cat the first to be uncovered in Britain. From the Aveley site it seems that at first during this warm phase this was a woodland area that later became open grassland with horses and mammoth roaming. At Sandy Lane Clay Pit flint hand axes were recovered and also the famous straight-tusked 'Aveley Elephant' and a young mammoth uncovered in 1964 and sent to the Natural History Museum in London for display at the time. At the Lion Pit Tramway Cutting SSSI In South Stifford early humans were collecting flints and manufacturing stone tools by flint knapping on the gravel beach at the base of an ancient Thames riverside chalk cliff rich in more of the mammal fossils.

From this same Interglacial Stage Eastbrookend Country Park in Dagenham is situated on the junction of the **Lynch Hill/Corbets Tey Terrace and the Taplow/Mucking Terrace** north and south of the District Railway line respectively. Six hand axes and other flint tools were discovered here and likely date to c.200 kya, the hand axes were deposited in the British Museum. On the same terrace junction by Ilford town centre a site covering about 2 km (over a mile) extends from the river Roding and Uphall (Camp) in the west to Severn Kings in the east. Victorian excavations revealed more of the same animals and included at least 100 mammoths and 77 rhinoceroses and the southern sites included the 'Ilford steppe-Mammoth', unique to its timeframe (MIS 7). A copy of the catalogue of the collection published by Sir Antonio Brady in 1874, is held at the Essex Records Office (Essex Field Club).

• • • • • • • • • • • •

An inhospitable long, severe cold Stage followed 150 kya (MIS 6) with no evidence of humans in Essex. The warmer **Ipswichian Interglacial** began between around 130 kya and 100 kya (MIS 5e) and corresponds with the later part of the Middle Old Stone Age and the temperature was a little higher than today this being the warmest of the Interglacial Stages. By c.120 kya the Thames as a tributary of the river Rhine, together with other major rivers such as the Seine joined the English Channel, which at that time was a river flowing west out to the Atlantic ocean and was all that now separated Britain from the Continent and something that people were able to cross.

At first during the cooler period the landscape was of birch and pine forests with shrubs and grasses, then eventually deciduous oak woodland and maples, hazel and later elms and hornbeam trees became common. Now there were spotted hyena, brown bear, lion, steppe bison, Merck's rhinoceros, narrow-nosed rhinoceros, straight-tusked elephant, woolly mammoth, auroch (wild ox from which cattle are probably descended) together with some species common to us today such as horse, red deer and fallow deer while, under Trafalgar Square in London and by the coast at Mersea Island rare hippopotamus were also discovered. Humans were absent from Britain during this time when c.110 kya sea levels were relatively high with Britain likely cut off as an island (Jon Cotton, MOL 2016). However people were not so far away - this was a period during which stone tools of early humans have been discovered at various sites throughout Europe, North Africa and the Near East.

• • • • • • • • • • • •

Eventually Britain's forests gave way to pine and birch trees once again as the climate became colder and the **Devensian Ice Stage** became established around 115,000 - 11,700 years ago (MIS 5d-MIS 2) with the glacial sheet advancing and retreating over time. This was the most recent of the Ice Age Stages and extended as far south as north Norfolk when Cambridge was covered by a huge glacial lake and with treeless tundra returning to this area and there is evidence for reindeer and artic plants as well as mammoth, woolly rhinoceros, reindeer and artic wolf found near the river Lea to the west of here.

When this Ice Stage was at its maximum sea levels were much lower and Britain was again connected to Jutland, Germany and the Netherlands in northern Europe by Doggerland with its dry land of hills and valleys, marshes and swampy lagoons across what is now part of the North Sea. Doggerland was populated for over 9,000 years by Stone Age people making good use of that fertile place for foraging, hunting and fishing. However, in around 10,000 BC with the end of this Ice Stage and the beginning of the next Interglacial came the end of the Old Stone Age (the Palaeolithic) and the beginnings of the Middle Stone Age (the Mesolithic).

<u>LANDFORM</u> *'The Land of the Fanns is about land and water and the often shifting relationship between them.'* **(TellTale working with the public 2018)**

<u>Middle Stone Age (Mesolithic) c.10,000-4,500 BC</u> The **Flandrian Interglacial** began in c.10,000 BC (MIS 1) and continues to the present. The ice retreated and the climate warmed and became dryer and lush birch and pine forests began to expand and the Middle Stone Age of development began to emerge.

Flint hand axes of Neanderthal people living at East Tilbury at this time have been found, but by this Interglacial time early humans were being displaced and modern humans (Homo sapiens) had begun to arrive and settle in Britain. This area was on the edge of the Doggerland plain land bridge that was occupied by light-eyed, dark-haired, olive-skinned Mediterranean-looking people from the Continent, indigenous Middle Stone Age hunter-gathers who trailed after wild animals like deer and wild horses, ate fish and water fowl and foraged for wild plants, fruits and berries.

Over time flint tools became more refined, smaller and finer arrow and spear heads and as well as flint, bone and antler tools people were also using shells, animal teeth and mammoth ivory for jewellery, and they had hollowed out log boats and at this time dogs were the first animals to be domesticated and were kept for hunting, security and comfort. Evidence of hunting camps have been found at Dagenham Heathway in a mixed forest area of oak and elm, lime and alder trees, also scatters of worked flints were found where the Beam and Wantz rivers meet (Tier 1 APA) south of the Beam Bridge between Dagenham and Havering. Some of the smaller flint blades typical of the Middle Stone Age were found at the Brookway site in Rainham and large flint adzes of the time were dredged from the Thames at Grays.

• • • • • • • • • • • •

People moving westwards across Doggerland would arrive at the Thames, which gave travellers access inland on an east/west route past here and via the river Kennet to Britain's heartland the 775 sq. km (300 sq. miles) Salisbury Plain (Nicholas Crane, 2016, *'The Making of the British Landscape'* pub. Weidenfeld & Nicolson ISBN 978 0 7538 2667 6). Many theories have been put forward as to why Salisbury Plain should have been chosen for the development of a great monument, **Stonehenge**. English Heritage have suggested that the open landscape nature of that chalk downland may have been unusual and attractive to people at a time when most of southern England was covered by woodland. Today Stonehenge is a UNESCO World Heritage site but English Heritage tell us that in the Middle Stone Age the earliest evidence for structures at the site are four or five pits of which three seem to have held 'large pine totem-like posts erected between 8,500 and 7,000 BC' but it is not known in what way those posts might have related to the later stone megaliths of the monument or what clues it might give us to similar practices elsewhere in the country at that time and how it may have influenced our local area.

• • • • • • • • • • •

However, in around 4,500-4,200 BC with the continued melting of the ice sheet and sea levels rising, a **tsunami** flooded the North Sea, so Doggerland flooded and the English Channel was formed and people were forced either side onto the higher land of Britain and the Netherlands as the Channel separated Britain from the rest of the Continent. Some five thousand or so people are estimated to have been stranded in the British Isles at the time. As the landform changed so the Thames was cut off from the great river Rhine as the land had been overtaken by the flooded North Sea. In this area there is evidence for this time in river meanders and modern river alluvium and the peat beds at Tilbury and Rainham. The landscape here running alongside the river Thames would have been full of interconnecting river channels prone to flooding within a more marshland landscape with high spots of dry land and islands (eyots) between its channels. Today the modern A1306 road runs approximately along much of the boundary between the dryer gravels and the marshes.

People could settle on the dryer land and on higher areas within the marshes and at Orsett the hilly landform across to Langdon Hills is within an ancient landscape that is a multi-period Area of Archaeological Significance from the Middle Stone Age through to the New Stone Age with finds including Middle Stone Age flint tools and heating stones.

ECONOMY *'This area is justly famous for trade, commerce and industry: these have been important here for many centuries.'* **(TellTale working with the public 2018)**

New Stone Age (Neolithic) from c.4,500 BC to c.2,500 BC In c.4,000 BC people began to cross the Channel into south-east England and further westwards into the Irish Sea. They brought agriculture, crops, animals and new technologies with them and around this time chambered tombs (**long barrows**) began to be constructed in Britain. The people came from the Mediterranean and originally from Turkey. Generally they had lighter skin and brown eyes and seem to have replaced the earlier hunter-gathers, and with their new ideas they hailed the emergence of the New Stone Age (the Neolithic).

Now the quite intense woodland cover began to be cleared and cattle and sheep were being domesticated providing a ready supply of meat, leather, milk and wool. People here were also eating pork and drinking ale, and later their diet is found to also include hazelnuts, sloes and crab apples. They were also cultivating barley and wheat and harvested grains needed to be stored encouraging the development of a more settled way of life in farming communities and with trading developing. People also continued to hunt and catch wild fowl and fish. A polished basalt (lava) hand axe from the late New Stone Age or early Bronze Age was found in the Barking marshes and archaeologist discovered an early New Stone Age **causewayed site**[3] at Southall Farm in Rainham and nearby a **ring ditch**[4] was discovered at Launders Lane, indicating either a burial site or a later roundhouse.

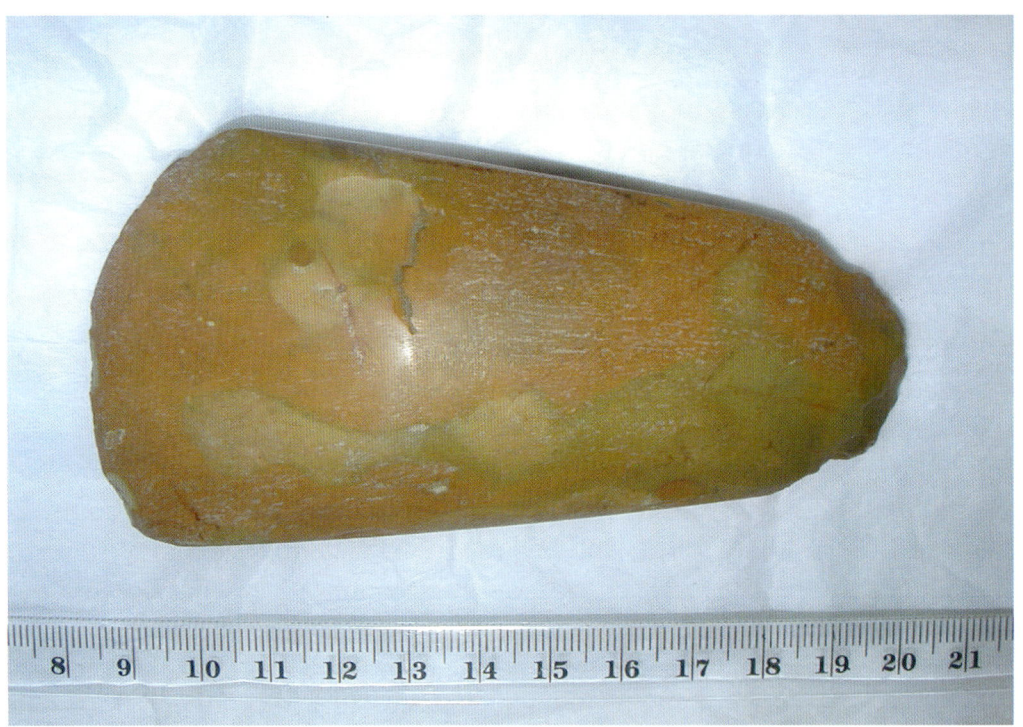

Ceremonial polished flint hand axe 11.5 cm (4.5 inches) long, found by a groundsman at Corbets Tey Crematorium (photograph courtesy Havering Libraries – Local Studies)

• • • • • • • • • • • •

---

[3] The earliest known types of enclosed open space, called causewayed enclosures after their distinctive form of earth works defining the perimeter broken ditch and earth bank.
[4] Circular fortified enclosure with bank and external ditch, from the 11th to 8th centuries BC (EH).

Along Thameside a **submerged forest** of fossilised fallen tree trunks that flourished on the mud flats of the Thames floodplain from between 4,000 and 3,000 BC during temporary falls in sea levels, is visible today at low tide along the marshes at Rainham, Purfleet and Tilbury and in Newham and on the Kent side. These are mainly yew trees but include ash, alder and other trees (*The Archaeology of the Essex Coast, Vol. 1* by T.L. Wilkinson and P.L. Murphy, pub. ECC Archaeology Section 1995).

In 1665 Samuel Pepys recorded that Dr. Johnson had made a similar discovery of the trees further into London at Blackwall; they were also studied locally by Dr. Derham of Upminster and recorded by him in 1712 and they were visible during the Dagenham Breach in 1771. This is an important area of Thames riverside for the study of changes in sea level since the last Ice Stage and the Royal Society for the Protection of Birds (RSPB) have placed a large fossilised tree-trunk specimen for closer display outside their Visitor Centre at Purfleet.

Photographs of the fossilised tree at the RSPB Visitor Centre, Purfleet

• • • • • • • • • • • •

There may have been early connections between local areas and the distant **Stonehenge**, perhaps in ideas and certainly in the style of pottery, that during the Bronze Age became important throughout the country. In the West Country for hundreds of years around 3,500 BC Stonehenge continued to be developed for various purposes, not all of which are clear even today and comprising several large open areas of earthworks (cursus and a causewayed enclosure) and with long barrows constructed. The stone monument itself was built in stages from c.3,000 BC perhaps first as a solar temple for religious ceremonies as it is aligned on the mid-winter and mid-summer solstices and appears to have a processional route. For several hundred years around this time it was used as a cremation cemetery with a circular earthwork enclosure of 'blue' stones transported from Wales and set into the ground (known as 'Aubrey Holes') (Univ. of Southampton 2019).

While locally at Orsett a large and important causewayed enclosure (see Bronze Age Chapter) for a larger number of people was revealed that may also indicate the beginnings of groups of people working together and is an important indicator for the transition towards wider social and political units. Settled communities could become larger and with people having differing roles or specialist occupations such as making pottery bowls as well as crafting tools and quarrying for stone, constructing their thatch roofed longhouses of timber wattles and clay daub, and ceremonial sites and long barrows for burials. From c.2,900 - c.2,100 BC people were making grooved-ware pots that were used by the early builders at Stonehenge and across Britain including more locally with a style found in East Anglia and the Thames Valley including at Mucking and at Lyon Point, Jaywick near Clacton (Evans, Christopher; Appleby, Grahame and Lucy, Sam, 2015, *Lives in Land Mucking excavations: Vol 1* pub Oxbow Books).

By the end of the New Stone Age copper metallurgy was being developed, people found that by mixing copper with tin the harder and therefore more useful metal bronze is produced and so the Age began to transition to the Bronze Age.

Places to visit near and far:

- RSPB Visitor Centre, Purfleet for the petrified tree on display from the landscape covered in yew forest 5,000-6,000 years ago
- S.E. London Green Chain Walk: *Time trail Erith Riverside submerged forest* London Geodiversity Partnership
- Swanscombe Heritage Park, SSSI and National Nature Reserve
- Butser Ancient Farm, Hampshire is an experimental archaeology site in the South Downs National Park, with reconstructions of ancient buildings from the Stone Age, Iron Age, Roman Britain and the Anglo-Saxon period.
- English Heritage maintain the World Heritage Site of Stonehenge, Wiltshire
- Long barrows in the Cotswold area in the care of English Heritage such as Uley Long Barrow
- Star Carr is a prehistoric lakeside settlement site just outside Scarborough in North Yorkshire. Dating to the Middle Stone Age close to the end of the last Ice Age c.9,000 BC. The story of Star Carr is told at Yorkshire Museum with site exhibits; other materials from Star Carr are held at the Museum of Archaeology and Anthropology, Cambridge
- Skara Brae is a New Stone Age village, in the West Mainland parish of Sandwick, Orkney, a UNESCO World Heritage Site (Neolithic c.3180 BC – c.2,500 BC)
- Creswell Crags Museum & Heritage Centre, Welbeck Road, Worksop, Nottinghamshire S80 3LH plus online talks and 'Life on the Edge' challenge for young peoples uniformed groups

Ideas for further projects:

- In the interests of preserving the geological and fossil records in respect of informing an understanding of climate change, support investigation, protection and presentation of the Country Parks and West Thurrock Gorges in Grays and Purfleet and coordinate public accessibility between sites of interest (see the National Character Area profile for the Northern Thames Basin - 'The sedimentary deposits and the fossils contained within them represent an important context for our understanding of and insights into the potential impacts of future climate change on our landscapes. Several sites also preserve important evidence for early human occupation of the area dating back around 300,000 years.').
- A more coordinated look at the archaeology across this area may provide some key information on Britain's pre-history. Eg a more comprehensive study would be helpful of the movement of Neolithic mammoth hunter-gathers from their prehistoric landscape called Doggerland, which connected the British Isles to continental Europe who would inevitably pass across this area westwards following the edge of the Ice Sheets and the river Thames. Their trekking south-westwards would presumably have led to the rare geological site with strange springs said to have inspired spiritual and ritualistic activity leading to development of the wood henge that eventually became Stonehenge, and the subsequent relationship of this area to Stonehenge that was most readily accessed via the Thames.
- Some comprehensive research on the Thames foreshore of this area for its prehistoric peat, charting earlier meanders and successive extents of the width of the Thames as revealed in the Brookway Allotment archaeological dig for example (see Havering Libraries-Local Studies)

References for further research:

- See Section B: Prehistory & Archaeology Introduction, p. 59

Further Reading:

- Crane, Nicholas (2017) *The Making of the British Landscape* pub. Weidenfeld & Nicolson. ISBN 978 0 7538 2667 6
- Howell, Isca J.; Swift, Dan; Watson, Bruce (2011) *Archaeological landscapes of east London: six sites excavated in advance of gravel quarrying in the London Borough of Havering* pub. MOLA ISBN 978-1-907586
- Humphrey, Louise & Stringer, Chris (2019) *Our Human Story* pub. Natural History Museum. ISBN 978 0 565 09391 4

Definitions:

MIS Marine Isotope Stage, MIS1 is the current warm period.

Geological Period A subdivision of geological time. Eons and Eras can be divided into Periods and Periods can themselves be divided into Epochs and Ages.

Quaternary The most recent of the three Periods of the Cenozoic Era.

mya Million years ago.

kya Thousand years ago.

SSSI Site of Special Scientific Interest.

APA Archaeological Priority Area. Divided into tiers 1-4, with Tier 1 being the most important.

APZ Archaeological Priority Zone, these are being phased out in favour of APA tiers.

Chapter 5
Bronze Age
c.2,550 BC – 750 BC

NATIONAL CURRICULUM Hints

After the long period of the Stone Age when life only changed gradually as more refined Stone Age tools and weapons were developed and an awareness of spirituality evolved and so on, now eventually life began to change more quickly with the development of metalworking skills such as in tin, copper, bronze and gold. This was speeded by the arrival of new people like the Beaker culture, from the Continent of Europe with their new skills and cultural ideas in around 2,500 BC, and by 2,100 BC metals were being mined in Britain and trading was taking place with the Continent. Now people were using metal as well as stone tools and settling down to farming as well as hunting and gathering foods growing wild.

SURPRISE *'The Land of the Fanns is an intricate landscape, full of surprises and 'hidden gems' and rewards exploring.' (TellTale working with the public 2018)*

Early Bronze Age c.2,550 BC – 1,500 BC After Britain was finally cut off from the Continent by the formation of the English Channel in c.4,500-4,200 BC, gradually at this late Neolithic /early Bronze Age time people began supplementing their hunting and gathering lifestyle by beginning to settle and take up farming, here for example especially on the lighter soils in the southern part of this landscape. They were cultivating crops like cereals with barley and emmer wheat for bread and raising sheep, pigs and cattle. Their stone tools became ever better refined and they built small settlements cut out of the woodland.

In the east of London, although there is sparse evidence for this period places like Goresbrook in Dagenham 'indicates a general movement of settlement from Earlier Neolithic riverside locations out to the gravel terraces of the Thames and its tributaries.' (Catherine Douglas Excavation Report, London Archaeologist Spring 2017). Also at Goresbrook evidence was found of wild clematis that is thought to have been woven into a wreath or basket together with Spring-flowering plants, fruit and tubers and used for a ritual or symbolic act, the clematis was radio carbon dated to 2,571-2,302 BC.

• • • • • • • • • • • •

During the early Bronze Age stone circles were still important to people and they continued with construction work as they had been during the Neolithic Age as that Age gradually merged into the next. The largest and most impressive of the stone circles is **Stonehenge** in Wiltshire, that had already gone through two known phases of development during the late Neolithic Age, and that perhaps surprisingly became important throughout the country including to this area.

However, in c.2,400 BC a period of great change began with newcomers arriving from across the channel bringing their new ideas and abilities and coinciding with, or perhaps instigating, a third phase of work taking place at Stonehenge. Now sarsen sandstone slabs were quarried mostly from some 40 km (25 miles) north of Salisbury Plain and brought to the site. They were erected in an upright position and arranged into an inner horseshoe-shaped structure of five trilithons graduated in height - each has two vertical stones with its own horizontal lintel, and also an outer circle was erected of 30 stones capped with continuous stone lintels.

The monument was at its peak use in around 1,900 BC and during the following thousand years of the Bronze Age as many alterations continued to be made its original uses also appear to have changed during that time. Also, through the period 1,800-1,500 BC many more monumental tombs and ritual pits were built in the landscape around Stonehenge so that it became one of the greatest concentrations of Early Bronze Age barrows in Britain, and it seems that many were located to overlook Stonehenge. *From Ice Age to Essex: A history of the people and landscape of East London* (by Pamela Greenwood, Dominic Perring and Peter Rowsome, 2006, pub MOL) comments that 'Powerful individuals dominated the agricultural communities and, through monuments like Stonehenge, chartered the seasons that determined the success of their crops.'

In around 1,750-1,500 BC, 115 images of mostly life-size Bronze Age metal axe heads and three Bronze Age daggers were carved into 5 of the stones (English Heritage, 2012, *Stonehenge Laser Scan: Archaeological analysis Report* ISSN 2046-9799 (Print) ISSN 2046-9802 (Online)), in relation to charting the seasons perhaps this was in an effort to appease a storm deity and protect crops or it may have been in connection with funerary reasons. Even locally in this landscape such markings were produced where a cremation burial of an adult and child at Muckingford Road, East Tilbury contained part of a reused saddle quern stone slab with markings on the underside '… which could be said to resemble a handled knife or dagger and a hand-shield…' *Thurrock's Deeper Past* (by Tripp, Christopher John, 2018).

Of Stonehenge itself, altogether it does appear that it had at one time stood completed, at some point attempts were made to demolish it, it has also been damaged by visitors through the ages and over time some stones are now damaged, graffitied, fallen, or missing.

MIGRATION *'This is a cross roads landscape: because of its location on the Thames … people have always travelled into, through and away from this area.'*
(TellTale working with the public 2018)

Beaker People 2,500-1,500 BC By a little before 2,000 BC the long, timber plank-built boats rowed by oarsmen were able to withstand heavy winds and would carry trade goods such as animals, worked metals, weapons, pots and jewellery as well as people. The newcomers were settlers from Western Europe who began to cross the Channel defying its dangerous currents and bringing with them new ideas and abilities, these were the 'Beaker People'. These settlers may have spoken an early form of Celtic, they lived in small family groups and were farmers growing crops such as wheat. They were also metalworkers and came here for trade, for example south-west England was rich in tin, which was a rare metal elsewhere and essential in Bronze-making.

These people also brought new cultural ideas and had their own distinctive pottery. Although their name is unknown to us, they are called 'Beaker' people after their pottery that was used for example for the storage of grain, as large drinking vessels used in feasting and for cremation burials. The name 'All-over Corded Beakers' is given to the beaker style where cord is impressed into the wet clay and was made by northern Europeans and people from further east and was traded with Britain. People from the south-west corner of Europe produced a 'Bell Beaker' style shaped like upside-down bells and decorated with zig-gags and horizontal lines. These people made tools and weapons in bronze and introduced the improved barbed, flat arrowheads, they also used bronze and the softer copper for ornamental or ceremonial weapons like copper knives and they made small ornamental things in gold.

From c.2,000 BC across the Essex hinterland 'great oak forests spread over the Essex Claylands, making it difficult for all later invaders from the Continent to move inland from their settlements on the coast and then north side of the Thames... The only ways open to them were the corridors formed by river valleys, and here they were able to make their homes on the waterside terraces of well-drained gravel.' (Edwards, A.C., 2000, *A History of Essex*). Here the settlers developed this landscape along Thameside and across the bowl of fenlands formed in the valley of the river Mardyke and its tributaries. They transformed the landscape by clearing local woodlands and creating rectangular ditched fields for farming that continued through the centuries until c.800 BC.

The incomers appear to have settled in Britain without warfare although the pre-existing population became decimated at the time, possibly through disease or their way of life may already have been failing but they left only a fraction, perhaps just ten percent of the original British New Stone Age people, so it is unsurprising that the new ideas overtook those that had been long established here. The newcomers lived in **round houses**, they built earth and timber monuments and stone circles were important to them for holding ritual ceremonies. The earlier communal long barrow burials were now abandoned in favour of individual, perhaps elite, **round barrows** often with a distinctive Beaker pot buried alongside the body together with other grave goods. These burials were often clustered together and high spots were favoured such as at Lesnes Abbey on the south side of the Thames opposite Rainham that would have provided views over the Thames and across to Essex.

Beaker burials are not common in Essex and it is thought that barrows may have been ploughed away and lost in modern times, however –

- eight Early Bronze Age barrows were found at Mucking in east Thurrock;
- another was recorded at Marks Warren Farm, Chadwell Heath 'on a prominent position giving prominence to the monument, the deceased and the community';
- there is an Early Bronze Age Beaker burial near the Orsett Cock in Thurrock with 2 beakers and one bowl of East Anglian style and indicating a date of 2,500-2,000 BC;
- a barrow is thought to be likely at Passingford Bridge on the river Roding in a low watery location, but one that would still have been impressively visible to those using the main means of travel by river (The M25 excavation from Junction 27/Passingford Bridge to Junction 30/Dartford Tunnel in 2015).

• • • • • • • • • • • •

At this time people would travel from all over Britain, even from as far as York, and the Scottish Highlands bringing their animals with them to work and celebrate at Stonehenge during the winter and the summer solstice with perhaps as many as 4,000 people taking part ('Stonehenge Without

Borders' Mike Pitts 2018) – and people from this area would have been no different so that despite its distance away Stonehenge would have been of great importance to people of this landscape.

It is at Stonehenge that the rich burial of the famous **Amesbury Archer** was discovered and nearby the grave of a young man, thought to be his son. They were very early settlers, the older man arrived in around 2,300 BC and came from the Alps region of Europe probably Switzerland. In the grave 'He had the accoutrements of a hunter and symbols of status……..he had everything that a person would need to survive – clothing, tools, weapons, pottery and spare flints to make new tools.' (Wessex Archaeology) and included two gold hair tresses or clips from c.2,400 BC, which is the oldest dated gold found in Britain. It is not known who he was but he could have been an archer, he may have been a coppersmith, at Stonehenge he may have been a pilgrim seeking healing for an inherited illness father and son both had, or he may have been the architect of work taking place at the monument. His burial is that of a high status person and this idea of a powerful elite would have been new to a society that in the Stone Age had been one of relative equality (Wessex Archaeology). It is from his grave that a great deal of information about the Beaker people and life at the time is now understood.

• • • • • • • • • • •

People were still hunter-gatherers at this time but they were becoming more settled, they were loom weavers and were domesticating animals including horses and oxen, they were farmers and raising livestock and locally they were constructing wooden trackways to move cattle out into the Thames marshes that have been discovered along the Thames foreshore from Rainham to Newham as well as across the river in Erith. In South Dagenham a wide, Middle Bronze Age causeway of gravel, burnt flint and sand was discovered. It was probably used for herding cattle from a wooded area down to richer summer pastures, and was found immediately east of the rare and important **Dagenham Idol** revealed in peaty soil in the Thames marshes. The idol was made of Scots pine wood and dates from around 2,250 BC and is one of the oldest human representations found in Europe, it is now on loan at Valence House Museum.

The Dagenham Idol on display to visitors (Image by kind permission of LBBD/Valence House Museum)

Chapter 5 Bronze Age

For a millennia from c.2,000 BC there was a considerable economic expansion in southern England together with a major shift in regional power and wealth towards the lowlands of eastern England but, despite the Amesbury Archer the 'Beaker Culture seems to have made little impact to the west of London' (*From Ice Age to Essex* Greenwood *et al.*). Important to expansion was the development of mixed farming with well organised large scale livestock farming with 'droveways, stock proof fencing, watering holes, cow pens, sheep races and gateways for stock handling' (Yates, David T., 2007, *Land, Power and Prestige*):

- at South Hornchurch the land was organised in this way with cultivated land and with pastures and paddocks arranged in a grid pattern of banks with hedges and fences; this was an area of 'small farms and hamlets regularly affected by flooding';
- just to the south across the Ingrebourne river at Bridge Road, Rainham, the reedy marsh area was transforming over time with a dominant alder carr woodland and with oak, linden, hazel and some birch, elm and ash trees on the dry land (London Archaeologist Vol. 6.9), people had been working this area for generations and have continued to do so on the gravel outcrop that would become Rainham village;
- early Bronze Age Beaker pottery were revealed in pits at the former Rainham Football Ground;
- Beaker sherds were found at Launders Lane, Rainham in 1963 and at Great Arnolds Field in Launders Lane an early Neolithic ring ditch had 'a central pit containing Beaker pottery (c.2,400-1,700 BC) implying that the monument remained in use for over a millennium;
- contemporary with that central pit were a group of features at Moor Hall Farm, Aveley, which also contained Beaker pottery' (MOL 2013);
- excavations at Gerpins Lane, Rainham located another Beaker vessel (Sites & Monuments Record, SMR 060051);
- a single early Bronze Age flint tool was found at Brookway allotments, Rainham (Greenwood and Maloney 1993);
- at High House, Purfleet the earliest find is Beaker, and horse bones there confirm that horses were reintroduced to Britain by the Early Bronze Age;
- at New Road, Rainham an Early Bronze Age (c.2200-c.1800 BC) domestic Beaker site was excavated finding Beaker pottery and some Middle Iron Age features and Roman activity. 'This is a site on a minor promontory at the edge of the river gravel terrace above the wide alluvial floodplain of the Thames (Rainham Marsh) and between the Beam river and the Ingrebourne river.' The Beaker finds here are non-funerary and therefore are of 'clear regional significance especially when looked at in the context of an apparent focus of Beaker use and deposition around Rainham at sites like Great Arnolds Field.'.

(Except where otherwise identified information here is extracted from the Transactions of the Essex Society for Archaeology & History).

ECONOMY *'This area is justly famous for trade, commerce and industry: these have been important here for many centuries.'* **(TellTale working with the public 2018)**

Middle Bronze Age c.1,500-1,000 BC Effectively it was the innovation of heating (smelting) mineral-bearing rock (ore) to extract its metal that caused the Stone Age to give way to the Bronze Age. However the first metals were tin and copper, which have relatively low melting points, low enough for smelting in the Neolithic pottery kilns but it was carried out on a small scale in Britain. Later it was found that by adding tin to copper bronze was produced, which was a harder and stronger metal. Whilst iron has a high melting point and so did not come into common use until nearly 1,000 BC. The transitional period between the Neolithic and the Bronze Age is called the Copper Age and in Britain was between c.2,500 – 2,200 BC.

Navigation skills improved during this Age together with greater knowledge of mathematics and astronomy and also the invention of the wheel that would all aid in the growth of trade. Gradually in around 2,000 BC people began working in copper and gold, and later on bronze tools and ornaments. As metalworking continued to develop the earliest evidence of metal axe use in England found locally is on the Rainham/Dagenham boarders. Other early evidence is from the **Seahenge** site (Tripp, Christopher John, 2018, *Thurrock's Deeper Past: A Confluence of Time*) built by the Beaker people near Old Hunstanton, Norfolk–some 2,050 BC. Following conservation the Seahenge timbers are now held at Lynn Museum, Norfolk.

Sketch of a Bronze Age axe – much harder than stone, longer lasting and with a sharper edge. An innovation to reduce impact damage to the handle was to secure the wooden handle through a ring in the axe head. This was followed by the development of the bronze plough, an improvement over the earlier stone ploughs that shattered and wood ploughs that quickly wore down

By about 1,600 BC there was a booming trade in British tin exports to the Continent and copper was being mined in North Wales in the Middle Bronze Age. It is thought that trade abroad led to a development of Celtic languages in the Late Bronze Age. By this same time an early metalworking building in Somerset is dated to c.1,200 BC, and huge concentrations of broken metalwork objects have been found in the Thames upstream of Woolwich, in the river Lea and in Barking Creek, these together with 'votive' offerings indicates a strength of interest in beliefs, and urns were being used for cremations and it was a time of disposable wealth, possibly from agricultural surplus (*From Ice Age to Essex*, Greenwood *et al.*). By the Late Bronze Age at Mucking and at South Hornchurch and at High House, Purfleet the economy of high status sites was based on metalworking and salt production from the nearby marshes which had also now begun.

Around this time the climate worsened becoming wetter and colder so that less communal effort went into the construction of ceremonial monuments on exposed hilltop sites and monuments became abandoned in preference to putting effort into more sheltered valley sites and creating fields and developing large livestock farms. This generated economic growth and led to more forest clearances

Chapter 5 Bronze Age

that transformed the landscape from c.1,500 BC when sites at Mardyke and Mucking had been cleared and were being farmed. The creation of a network of ditched fields and a settlement at Whitehall Wood (Greenwood 1986) and elsewhere such as Bridge Road, Rainham (Bruck, Joanna ed. *Bronze Age Landscapes: Tradition and Transformation*), have been discovered and this agricultural landscape continued for centuries in one form or another. The pollen record of fewer trees and more grass and cereal types at sites along the A1306 and at the former Rainham Football Ground demonstrates an increase in settlement, woodland clearance and agricultural activity during the Middle Bronze Age.

There were signs of agricultural intensification at High House at Purfleet during the Late Bronze Age/Early Iron Age when it 'appears to be an unenclosed settlement at the highest point overlooking the Thames to the south'. It was the 'focus of later Bronze Age activity' that 'can be seen as evidence for sporadic land-use throughout the Middle-Late Bronze Age/Early Iron Age' with 'Mixed husbandry strategies for milk and meat as well as for wool and use as draught animals ... and indicates rather small animals' (Channel Tunnel Rail Link archaeology work), and here there is thought to be a possible Middle Bronze Age animal droveway. Grains of emmer wheat and chaff, barley grains and possibly spelt wheat have been found at High House. 'The small number and dominance of seeds of larger seeded species seen at many of the prehistoric sites in the region would suggest that crops were brought to, and stored at the settlement in a relatively clean state. This storage would occur after they had been threshed, winnowed and sieved and most of the smaller, lighter seeds removed, following harvest in mid to late summer.' (Except where otherwise identified information here is extracted from the Transactions of the Essex Society for Archaeology & History).

LANDFORM *'The Land of the Fanns is about land and water and the often shifting relationship between them.'* **(TellTale working with the public 2018)**

Later Bronze Age c.1,000-700 BC A later group of Beaker people who reached the Thames between 1,000 and 750 BC were lakeside dwellers from the Alps and one of their crannogs or pile dwellings has been found at Southend-on-Sea (Edwards, A.C. *A History of Essex*); also a West Alpine group reached Basildon where a bronze founder's hoard[1] was discovered (Payne, Jessie K., 1987, *When Basildon was farms and fields* Ian Henry Publications ISBN 0-86025-416-X). In c.1,000 BC, this local area itself became a place of elite importance to the Bronze Age people. In the Essex area Beaker people settled on the north bank of the Thames around Clacton and westwards across this area so that by the Late Bronze Age there were two main concentrations of land management in this area – one focussed between the river Ingrebourne at South Hornchurch and Mucking in east Thurrock and the other on the Southend-on-Sea peninsula (Bruck, Joanna ed., 2001, *Bronze Age Landscapes: Tradition and Transformation* pub Oxbow Books).

During the Late Bronze and Early Iron Age people were still making good use of the wetland areas on the edge of the dryer gravel terraces. Here they were able to exploit the natural resources of two distinctive landscapes. Along with farming they were fishing and fowling and using reed beds for sheep and cattle grazing and their brushwood trackways and causeways for access have been found in such areas in Rainham and Dagenham, where scatters of flint were also found along the river Beam, and beyond in Barking and in the Roding Valley – where Uphill Camp has been dated

---

[1] A 'founder's hoard' is a collection of tools, equipment and the stock-in-trade of a bronze-worker buried and probably with the intention of being recovered later.

back to a Late Bronze Age origin - together with many finds of metal and other objects. (*London Archaeologist* Winter 2019 Vol 15 no.7 – ref.: Stafford, E., *2000-2003, Landscape & prehistory of the east London wetlands Investigation along the A13 Road Scheme, Tower Hamlets, Newham and Barking and Dagenham*). Cattle grazing on the marshes has now been reintroduced on the RSPB Rainham marsh and in the Ingrebourne Valley Country Park as important contributors once again to managing the marshes for the benefit of food, farming and wildlife.

During c 1500-c 800 BC an unenclosed Late Bronze Age/Early Iron Age settlement including 3 or 4 round houses were constructed at Hunt's Hill Farm, Upminster together with other finds 'indicating that this part of the site is near the main focus of settlement' (*Essex Archaeology & History*, 1996), and a series of ringworks were established in the locality including two at Mucking and probably another example at Hacton (MOL 2013). At Mucking the Late Bronze Age ringwork of bank and external ditch enclosing dwellings and bronze metalworking activity and storage buildings were discovered dating from c.1,100 – 800 BC. The Mucking site with its excellent vantage point at the head of the Thames estuary in east Thurrock is of particular importance, remains survive from a period of 3,000 years from the Neolithic to the Middle Ages but it is the Bronze Age and Anglo-Saxon features that are of particular importance and the site archive is held by the British Museum.

Defensive ringforts are rare and mainly in eastern England and there is a concentration around Springfield Lyons, Chelmsford. They seem to be associated with metalworking and fine pottery and may be high status centres (Historic England 2018: *Enclosed Prehistoric Settlements*). Indeed, high status prime agricultural sites were chosen along the coast and the Thames estuary for example and along major river valleys with sites locally in:

- Church Lane, Church Street in Dagenham (Late Bronze Age pottery);
- Dagenham Heathway (Late Bronze Age/Early Iron Age);
- Bridge Road in Rainham;
- South Hornchurch;
- Whitehall Woods (Late Bronze Age/Early Iron Age field system);
- William Edwards School site at Stifford Clays;
- An open settlement at Baker Street at Orsett (two Scheduled Ancient Monuments 'SAM');
- A Late Bronze Age field system at Gun Hill in West Tilbury;
- Late Bronze Age ditches at Linford;
- Sites along the line of the Horndon to Barking natural gas pipeline (*Land, Power and Prestige* by David T. Yates 2007);
- A possible early hillfort[2] at Marks Warren Farm, Chadwell Heath.

During the Bronze Age Britain appears to have developed with chiefdoms based upon an agricultural economy carrying out trade between themselves and with Europe (Time Team 2002). Sea and river trade routes using flat bottomed boats became well established and the river Thames would have been essential to this. On land **droveways** could be used by animal-drawn vehicles and with roadside holding pounds they are local clues to trade routes with the Continent via the Channel and the North Sea.

---

[2] Similar to ringworks, in prominent locations and possibly communal gathering places or ceremonial centres from the 13th century – 9th century BC (EH).

The extensive Late Bronze Age ringwork with a contemporary field system and settlement discovered on a 2.5 ha (6 acre) site in South Hornchurch (*Proceedings of the Prehistoric Society* 2014) includes a 'droveway heading south-west toward the Thames' (Yates, David T. *Land, Power and Prestige*). This is presumably via the droveway identified close by at Bridge Road and Coldharbour Point on Thameside at Rainham, Essex, which lies opposite the Kent side where Coldharbour Road in Gravesend, Kent was a cattle and sheep track heading towards the Thames 3 km (1.8 miles) away (Yates, *Land, Power and Prestige*) and may be a clue to a long distance route operating in this area in the valley of the river Ingrebourne during the Late Bronze Age and 'may reflect the importance of the Thames as an artery for transport to and from Europe ... The hoards found in London probably form part of a wider distribution which runs along both sides of the Thames to the mouth of the estuary,' (*The Archaeology of Greater London* MOL 2000) and also 'A few Middle Bronze Age metal hoards have also been found in the London region, those in east London possibly being part of a wider distribution of such deposits across south Essex.' (MOL 2000).

The Ingrebourne Valley has an important archaeological heritage, it seems to have been a distinctive and accessible north/south trade route during the Bronze Age with a Bronze Age hoard reportedly found at Hornchurch and with similar hoards further north out of the area. These together indicate that the Valley may have been part of a Bronze Age trade route from Barking on the Thames north to the ancient cross-country Ridgeway track and Icknield Way providing an access route between The Wash in Norfolk to the south-west coast of England via the area of Salisbury Plain and Stonehenge. The Ingrebourne Valley certainly appears to be a Bronze Age landscape with four settlements identified in the southern section from Rainham to Hacton with a major trackway running north-west to south-east, three of the settlements sites having rare continuous occupation through to Saxon. A Bronze Age beaker was found on the east side of the valley at Gerpins Farm, and recorded by the British Museum but later stolen (The Antiquaries Journal *Archaeologia,* vol. 96 1955). A socketed axe head and a copper ingot fragment were recovered in the Valley at an Upminster farm held at Barking Museum accession number 1958.165.

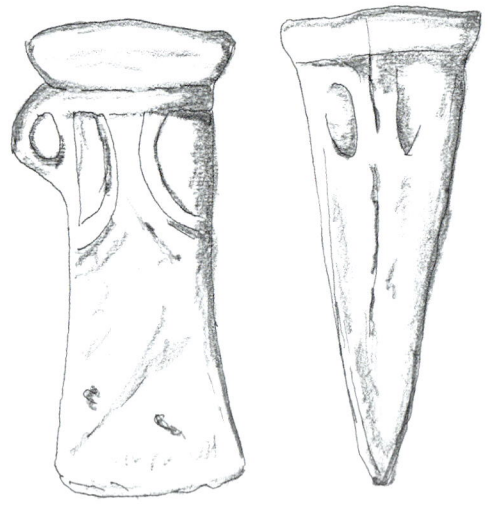

Illustration of axe head from an Upminster farm in 1957

Bronze axe head c. 14 cm long (5.5 inches) discovered in landfill at Harold Hill (Photograph courtesy Havering Libraries - Local Studies)

North of Ingrebourne Valley at Harold Hill a metal axe head from the period was found amongst fill at Harold Hill, which is thought to have arrived amongst rubble from nearby and is now in Havering Museum, Romford. Other Late Bronze Age sites in the valley include well represented human activity in the vicinity of the former Rainham Squash & Snooker club, Ferry Lane/Wennington Road, however 'The majority of the later Bronze Age to Middle Iron Age settlements in the vicinity of the site occupy land higher up the gravel terrace,' such as at:

- Scott and Albyns Farm' c.900m (0.5 miles) to the north where a large Late Bronze Age settlement was recorded ;
- more features c.2.3 km (1.4 miles) to the east in Berwick Pond Road;
- at Maybank Ave (Greater London Sites & Monuments Record GLSMR) c.3.35km (2 miles) north;
- around 1km (0.6 miles) to the east a causewayed site at South Hall Farm (GLSMR);
- at Launders Lane (GLSMR) c.2.2km (1.4miles) east ;
- at Hunts Hill Farm (GLSMR) c.3.9 km (2.4 miles) east north-east, there is evidence of permanent settlement with roundhouses and associated pits and ditches;
- there is also evidence for small scale occupation near Moor Hall, Aveley (MOLAS 2000).

The easiest means of travelling inland was by boat along the rivers for transporting heavy goods, and the Ingrebourne river remained navigable as far as Hornchurch until at least the 13th century when a hythe is recorded. However people had also learned to tame horses for travelling cross-country and were making wheels and using carts pulled by oxen or horses by around 1000 BC. By the end of the Bronze Age people were building horse drawn war chariots driven by standing riders.

The rare, native Exmoor ponies are an ancient breed, small, strong, hardy and stocky, they look very much like horses of the Bronze and Iron Age; their brown, bay and dun colouring helps them blend in amongst surroundings of bracken, gorse, rushes and grasses

Havering Hoard Perhaps the most interesting site of all is the rich Bronze Age discovery made at a gravel extraction site at Wennington (*Current Archaeology* 2020) in 2018 on the site of a Late Bronze Age enclosure ditch overlooking the river Thames. This is the largest Bronze Age hoard to be discovered in London, although other small hoards are known in Havering and Grays for example, and 'The area around Rainham and South Hornchurch is believed to have been well-inhabited around 3,000 years ago. In the 1990s, a large number of Bronze Age artefacts were discovered, dated to between 1,000 and 800 BC.' (Roy Stephenson MOL 2019).

This latest hoard of mostly damaged and mostly copper alloy objects was carefully deposited in four aligned pits with weapons and tools including axe heads, spearheads, fragments of swords, daggers and knives, woodworking tools, sickles, razors and copper ingots possibly from the Alps, alongside some other unusual objects rarely found in the United Kingdom make up a total of 453 bronze objects dating between c.900 and c.800 BC (MOL). The Guardian newspaper reported in February 2020 that the finds included 'copper ingots possibly originating from the Alps' also 'a bracelet believed to be from what is now north-west France' and 'what are believed to be a pair of terret rings used to prevent the reins tangling on horse-drawn carts. Bronze age examples have been found before in France but not in the UK.' Kate Sumnall, curator of archaeology at MOL reported that 'These objects give clues about how this wasn't an isolated community but rather one that fitted into a much larger cultural group with connections along the Thames Valley and across the continent.'

The reason for depositing such hoards may become clearer by comparing with the hoard found in East Anglia at Isleham in Cambridgeshire of more than 6,500 bronze pieces from the Late Bronze Age c.1,000 -700 BC broken up and ready for melting in a crucible 'The hoard must surely represent the stock of a group of bronzesmiths who travelled around East Anglia, but whose principle workshop was at Isleham. A subsidiary workshop was found at Wilburton in 1882 with 163 objects found in that hoard … probably indicates a wealthy, flamboyant and warlike aristocracy in East Anglia at the beginning of the late Bronze Age.' Moyse's Hall Museum, Bury St. Edmunds.³

Regionally there was a gradual increase in land exploitation from the Early Iron Age when possessing and using land seems to have become more important than ownership of bronze metal (MOL 2000) and 'characterised by small-scale settlements, surrounded by fields used for a mixture of pastoral and arable farming.'

- at Fairlop Quarry, Aldborough Hall Farm, Romford, Bronze Age/Iron Age evidence indicates 'a Late Bronze Age barrow (Archaeological Solutions Ltd Unpub. 2016) and 'small scale pastoral and agricultural activity.' (Arch in Essex 2008/9);
- in 2015 the M25 excavation from Junction 27 to Junction 30 (Ex Soc. for Arch. & Hist. Occasional Papers, New Series No. 3) found that at Passingford Bridge during the Middle Bronze Age and the Late Bronze Age there was 'permanent Bronze Age occupation of the area … settlers were using pottery, possibly for storage and consumption, and making flint tools … crops grown nearby.' ;
- at Upminster pottery was found of the Late Bronze Age or Early Iron Age and Middle Bronze Age-Late Bronze Age burials with other Late Bronze Age burials along the route of the motorway;
- at Junction 29, Hobbs Hole there was a 'Low-level later Bronze Age or Early Iron Age settlement activity' and similar was found at West Thurrock;
- Orsett revealed a Late Bronze Age or Early Iron Age site 'crammed with flint-tempered pottery' (Wilkinson 1988) implying nearby domestic activity similar to the Mucking site;
- also pottery sherds dating to the Late Bronze /Early Iron Age period were found at Stifford County Primary School, Grays (Essex Archaeology & History, 1996);

---

 ³ Why do you think that the Havering bronze hoard was hidden and why in four lots?

- Late Bronze Age occupation at the former Manser Works, 137-139 New Road, Rainham, was identified;
- a Late Bronze Age settlement at Scott and Albyns Farm in the Ingrebourne Valley;
- at Whitehall Woods, Upminster, features date to the Late Bronze Age/Early Iron Age 'with some similarities to Moor Hall Farm, Rainham'.

(Except where otherwise identified information here is extracted from the Transactions of the Essex Society for Archaeology & History).

Smiths also became skilled in making gold jewellery and ornamentation and 'As the bronze-based prestige goods economy collapsed and new inter-regional exchange networks were established, the Late Bronze Age/Earliest Iron Age ringworks and the highly regulated formal landscapes in Southern England went out of use.' (Yates, D.T. 2007, *Land, Power and Prestige*). Now at Mucking for example, which was in a controlling position for trade on Thameside, there were 'new fortified farmsteads that would develop into hillfort monuments during this period and into the Iron Age' (Tripp, C.J. *Thurrock's Deeper Past,*).

Places to visit near and far:

- Norsey Woods Local Nature Reserve, Outwood Common Road, Billericay - SSSI for its special nature conservation interest and Ancient Monument with a Bronze Age round barrow or tumulus excavated in 1865 containing three Middle Bronze Age clay cremation urns (a second barrow was destroyed for housing development but contained seven urns, one with cremated remains).
- Following conservation some of the 'Seahenge' or 'Holme 1' timbers are now on display at Lynn Museum, Norfolk
- British Museum for the Mucking site archive – in storage
- Great Orme Bronze Age opencast Copper Mine, Great Orme Country Park, Llandudno, North Wales, a Special Area of Conservation, SSSI and Heritage Coast

Ideas for further projects:

- Additional information would be beneficial about Bronze Age trade routes, identified by numerous hoard finds alongside the Thames at Barking then along the river Ingrebourne at Hornchurch, the limit of its navigability, connected with previous find sites north of the Ingrebourne Valley to the Ridgeway ancient long-distance route that connected the Wash in Norfolk to the south-west coast of Britain.
- Investigate possible trade route linkages between the Ingrebourne Valley, Coldharbour Point in Rainham, Essex and Coldharbour Lane in Gravesend, Kent
- The Bronze Age settlements in the more extensive Bronze Age landscape of the Ingrebourne Valley may benefit from further study

References for further research:

- See Section B: Prehistory & Archaeology Introduction, p. 59
- Ancient Monuments Society (AMS) now Historic Buildings & Places, is the National Amenity Society for 'the study and conservation of ancient monuments, historic buildings and fine old craftsmanship'

Further Reading:

- *Archaeologia* – various volumes Antiquaries Journal
- Bruck, Joanna ed. *Bronze Age Landscapes: Tradition and Transformation*
- Edwards, A.C. (2000) *A History of Essex* ISBN 1860771564 ISBN 13: 9781860771569 pub. Phillimore & Co. Ltd.
- Tripp, Christopher John (2018) *Thurrock's Deeper Past: A Confluence of Time* pub Archaeopress, ISBN 978-1-78969-111-5, ISBN 978-1-78969-112-2 (ePdf)
- Yates, David T. (2007) *Land, Power and Prestige: Bronze Age Field Systems in Southern England* pub. Oxbow Books ISBN 9781782974246

Chapter 6
Iron Age
c.750 BC – AD 50

NATIONAL CURRICULUM Hints

The interesting thread through the prehistoric periods is an understanding of both change and continuity of human development from the enormously long evolution of the Stone Age, through to the development of metalworking in the Bronze Age until the end of the Iron Age and the coming of written histories.

SURPRISE *'The Land of the Fanns is an intricate landscape, full of surprises and 'hidden gems' and rewards exploring.'* **(TellTale working with the public 2018)**

During the Iron Age, although the many different peoples in western Europe did not write down their own histories they did have similar languages, art form and culture and they seem to have had good trading links, together they were referred to by the writers of ancient Greece and Rome as 'Celts'. Surprisingly, although it's more than two millennia since Iron Age people were living here, the name of our local tribe is known to us, they were the **Trinovantes** (or Trinobantes) people. We also know the names of some of their leaders and where their main settlements were and we know something of how they lived and who their enemies were.

Arriving here, the Trinovantes were seaborne settlers, probably an ancient tribe of Celts called the Belgae from the North Sea or the Baltics. Via the east coast of Britain they settled this area with their lands extending from the coast to the London area and included what would become all Essex and up into south Suffolk. Their name translates as 'newcomers' or 'very vigorous people' and later to the Romans they were the 'people living by the broad water' (ref. e.g. *'Excursions in the County of Essex'* by Thomas Cromwell 1792-1870) that was the river Thames.

MIGRATION *'This is a cross roads landscape: because of its location on the Thames ... people have always travelled into, through and away from this area.'* **(TellTale working with the public 2018)**

Centuries before it had been discovered on the Continent that iron is a metal tougher than bronze, and it was a material readily available and easier to work and to shape into harder and sharper objects that would make better and more durable tools. Being kept secret at first, gradually the use of iron spread from Turkey across the Eastern Mediterranean and from there to Central Europe and by 750 BC Iron Age Celtic people began to expand towards Gaul in modern France, and from c.500 BC Britain itself gradually came under Celtic influence from the Continent and the Celts began to cross into Britain in waves of new societies that vied one another for territory.

These people brought trade, economics and technology, they had religious beliefs in common and their religious leaders were the elusive druids. Today the languages of these people survive as Gaelic, Welsh, Irish and Breton. The first of the newcomers assimilated seemingly without war or major battles and although the second wave of Iron Age people to arrive in Britain were more warlike they did not penetrate inland so far as this area.

This area along the north bank of the Thames at that time was mainly marshland with other inland areas heavily wooded with oak and hornbeam and other trees like hawthorn, blackthorn, hazel and elder, when it became occupied in c.400 BC by a third wave of Celts, the Trinovantes tribe who settled here. Evidence from this early time is recorded at Hornchurch Aerodrome (Priddy 1984) in the Ingrebourne Valley, and at Manor Farm part of a settlement and defensive enclosure were identified (P. Greenwood and Mike Stone 1984) but abandoned apparently during this time (MOL 2011).

Eventually other Celtic tribes settled across Britain, with the northern neighbours of the Trinovantes being the **Iceni tribe,** south of the Thames were the **Cantiaci**, to the west of London came the **Catuvellauni** people and beyond them the **Atrebates** settled, with other tribes occupying lands beyond. Although alike, each tribe would have their own recognisable customs, pottery, jewellery and textile decorations for example, identifying themselves and the region they controlled.

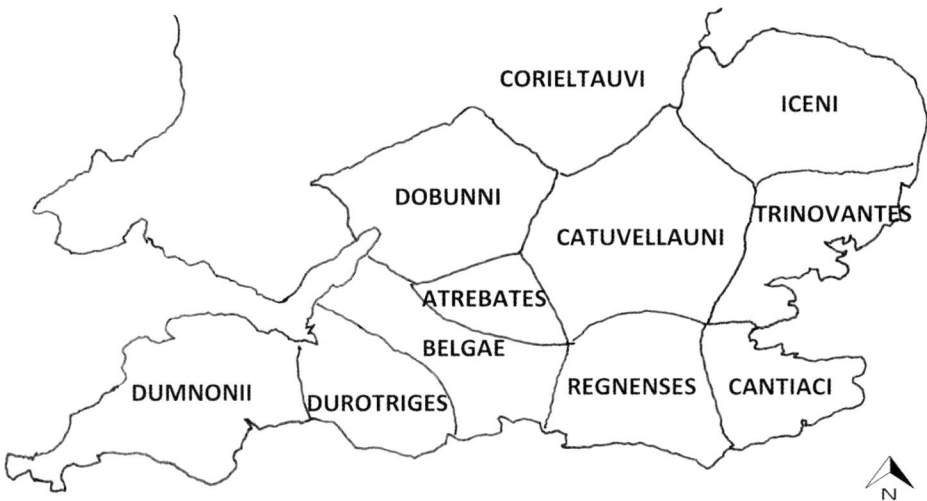

General indication of the late Iron Age tribal lands of the Trinovantes and their near neighbours

LANDFORM ***'The Land of the Fanns is about land and water and the often shifting relationship between them.' (TellTale working with the public 2018)***

Gradually as the Late Bronze Age developed into the Iron Age some farmsteads became fortified often being surrounded by single, double or triple ditches and banks and with wooden fortifications they developed as **hillforts** (see Bronze Age Chapter). These could more properly be called 'defended settlements' that could provide shelter for local people at times of threat. On the ridge of highland at Chadwell Heath there is evidence of a Late Bronze Age/Early Iron Age enclosure at Marks Warren Farm (Tier 1 Archaeological Priority Area, APA) that may have been an early hillfort 'on a naturally defensible position on a small hill, overlooking both the Rom and the Thames River valleys.' (Inner London National Character Area 112) also a Late Iron Age/Early Roman enclosure (also Tier 1 APA) which is similar to one at Orsett and may have been a religious centre (ILNCA 112).

On Thameside in East Thurrock, **Mucking** is a hillfort site and was a pre-existing settlement from Neolithic times and is very favourably located on a prominent bend in the river Thames giving it clear views straight downriver to the estuary. During the Iron Age the people constructed a series of enclosures here with round houses and other structures, some built outside enclosures, also cemeteries with burials and cremations. It is a rich location beside the river and marshland for fishing, fowling, salt drying and river travel, and with an elevated hinterland for farming, also pottery and metalworking. Grain and salt production at Mucking drove its long-term economy from the Middle Bronze Age onwards (*Current Archaeology*) with the success of the settlement continuing through the coming Roman and Saxon periods.

Towards the west of the Trinovantes lands is the very large and well organised **Uphall Camp** or hillfort, constructed on the east bank of the river Roding between Barking and Ilford, it was a major centre from around 200 BC that would have been of importance to this area. The Iron Age settlement was laid out in a regular form apparently with streets and various areas for different uses including granaries, barn, sheds and working areas. The people lived in round-houses made of local materials constructed of interwoven timbers or wattles and daubed with mud or clay (wattle-and-daub) and with thatched roofs, typical of Southern Britain.

Artist impression of a large Iron Age roundhouse of wattle and daub with a thatched roof
– here it is imaginatively decorated in the Celtic art style –
based on Little Woodbury roundhouse in Wiltshire reconstructed at Butser Ancient Farm

As a hillfort, Uphall Camp had massive earth defences and it is strategically positioned particularly facing outwards to the west and south and with good views of the Thames. It may also have had a small port for trade on the river Roding controlling the river and giving easy access to the Thames (Greenwood, Dr Pamela, 1989, *London Archaeologist*, Vol 6, *Uphall Camp, Ilford, Essex*; also, Historic England: PastScape, Millward, Jonathan *2016, Uphall Camp* and *London Borough of Redbridge: Archaeological Priority Areas Appraisal* Oxford Archaeology). However, crucially it was abandoned during the last 100 hundred years BC (Isca Howell, Dan Swift and Bruce Watson with Jon Cotton and Pamela Greenwood, 2011, *Archaeological Landscapes of east London* pub. MOL) when the tribes were warring and the Roman politician and general Julius Caesar was campaigning in Britain.

• • • • • • • • • • •

The fertile soils were suitable for the development of arable farming and, like the Bronze Age people before them, the Trinovantes were it seems essentially peaceful farmers (Edwards, A.C. *A History of Essex*) and traders. At this time the climate had worsened becoming colder and wetter while the economy now relied more on farming and landownership rather than trade in metals as previously. The people generally lived and worked on small farms supplying their own needs and, unlike the earlier bronze or wooden ploughs they used a more efficient and simple, light, iron-tipped wooden *ard* plough that was guided by the farmer and pulled by oxen, and could till heavier clay soils so bringing more land into farming use.

Also from 400-300 BC the use of the rotatory hand quern arrived in Britain, probably from ideas brought by travelers (Shaffrey, Ruth, 2019, *The Movement of Ideas in Late Iron Age and Early Roman Britain: An imported Rotary Quern Design in South-Western England* pub. Cambridge University Press November). This was used for grinding grain between two flat stones to make flour, and was an extremely important and time-saving device and many fragments of rotary and the earlier saddle querns were found at the Mucking site for example.

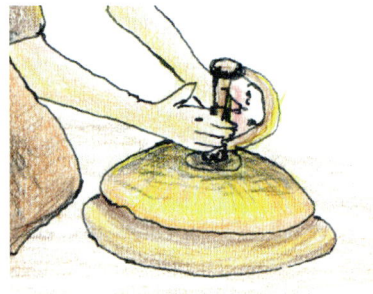

A rotary quern worked by grain being poured into the hole in the top stone, that stone was then turned by the handle crushing the grain against the stationary lower stone

Farmers kept cows and sheep, pigs, goats and geese, they grew hardy cereals of wheat, barley and spelt, and oats, rye and beans, storing grain in granaries or underground. They gathered oysters and cockles, and salted or smoked fish and meat to preserve it. They had domesticated dogs for hunting, they wove on looms, used pole lathes with an iron knife to shape wood into bowls and plates, they played board games and had glass pieces for example, and by the end of the Age were producing wheel-made pottery.

Now a rare breed sheep, Manx Loaghtan are similar to those in the Iron Age, a small primitive sheep with usually four or sometimes six horns, dark brown faces and legs, these sheep are not wooly but were kept for their meat

• • • • • • • • • • • • •

From the Middle Iron Age (c.400-100 BC) around the time of the arrival of the Trinovantes people, there are far more signs of settlements locally, again often along the river valleys and often on pre-existing sites. Locations include:

- an occupation site at Ockendon School, South Ockendon (*Archaeology in Essex* 2008);
- enclosures at Belhus Park and Stifford Clays (Wilkinson 1988);
- Middle Bronze Age and Middle Iron Age pottery fill at East Brook End Park (K. MacGowan, Passmore Edwards Museum – now Newham Museum Service) in the river Beam Valley;
- in the Ingrebourne Valley there are several Iron Age settlements being part of continuous occupation of earlier sites and additionally Middle Iron Age round house features and a possible droveway at Maybank Ave, Hornchurch (Greenwood and Maloney 1992) as well as evidence for a Late Iron Age settlement there;
- Middle/Late Iron Age features and a roundhouse at Berwick Ponds Farm, Rainham (*Archaeological Landscapes of east London…*) ;
- at Passingford Bridge north of Havering-atte-Bower there is evidence for an unenclosed settlement during the Middle/Late Iron Age period 'of perhaps two or three households' of farmers raising cattle and sheep or goats and growing wheat, barley and spelt and also metalworking and making pottery;
- features of this date at Fairlop Quarry near Chadwell Heath also extend into the Roman period;
- at Newbury Park a Late Bronze Age/Late Iron Age occupation site was revealed in what was a mixed woodland landscape with meadow and scrub clearings (K. Hulka *et al. London Archaeologist Vol 11.4* 2006);
- a farmstead site of probably the Middle/Late Iron Age at Sandy Lane, Aveley;
- a farmstead site at High House in Purfleet of possibly Late Iron Age date;
- in Upminster an Early/Middle Iron Age farmstead at Great Sunnings Farm is recorded (MOL Archaeology 2013) with five wells and a Late Iron Age/Early Roman defensive site (*Transactions of the Essex Society for Archaeology & History*);
- a Late Iron Age enclosure and evidence for Early Roman potters at Codham Hall, Brentwood;
- a Late Iron Age/early Roman pottery and building material at the Rainham Federation Cemetery with Roman remains nearby in Launders Lane (P. Greenwood 1982);
- pottery making at Hobbs Hole, Brentwood (Evans and Lucy 2008);
- at Orsett there is a Middle/Late Iron Age enclosure at Baker Street and at 'Bishop Bonner's Palace' north of Orsett village (both SAM's). In places like Orsett local iron deposits in the gravels and bog iron in the marshes are likely to have been exploited making the need for imported copper and tin for making bronze no longer necessary.

Iron Age wooden trackways were used to move cattle out into the Thames marshes and have been found west of here in Newham and at Rainham Marshes where an Iron Age farmstead has also been identified between Rainham village and Brookway. People were continuing to take advantage of the dry gravel bank that runs across the marsh edge here that would have been an excellent resource interface ideal for cattle grazing, agriculture, fishing and fowling, with sites at:

- 105-109 New Road, Rainham, which is an Early Bronze Age and Middle Iron Age (MIA) site where 'The MIA features supplement the growing picture of an increasingly settled landscape along the terrace edge, as at the former Rainham Football (Club) Ground' (Costello 1997);
- at the nearby Early/Middle Iron Age and later Iron Age/Early Roman settlement at the former Rainham Squash & Snooker Club site, Ferry Lane/Wennington Road 'The archaeological remains correspond well to those revealed at the adjacent site of Rainham Football Club (Ground) and the pattern of settlement previously attested in the region.' (*Transactions of the Essex Society for Archaeology and History* 2009).

Several of the Iron Age sites demonstrate continued occupation into the Roman period and 'The emerging picture of activity of mid to later Iron Age/early Roman Rainham is of a continuing spread of settlement ... with more marginal sites (such as the Rainham Squash & Snooker Club site) being used on a more intensive scale possibly due to the need to exploit the lowland areas as the uplands became unfit for settlement due to climatic variations.'. Further along the gravel bank there are also surviving Late Iron Age features at South Hall Farm, Rainham (GLSMR 062231 and *Archaeological Landscapes of east London...*).

Altogether the changes in development led to an increase in population, and 'after 150 BC agricultural growth demanded new fields and settlements' (*From Ice Age to Essex* Pamela Greenwood *et al.* 2006, pub. MOL) and 'this new land management' of the larger field system appears evident at Orsett as well as 'Managed ancient woodland near Aveley and Mucking' (Tripp, C.J., 2018, *Thurrock's Deeper Past*,). In general the life of the Trinovantes seems settled but obscure for nearly 400 years (Edwards, *A History of Essex*) following their arrival while it appears they peacefully occupied the land.

ECONOMY *'This area is justly famous for trade, commerce and industry: these have been important here for many centuries.'* **(TellTale working with the public 2018)**

The Iron Age Celts had brought a cultural revolution rich in traditions such as their craftsmanship, storytelling, poetry and music and they introduced new things to Britain such as coracle boats for river fishing and two-horse chariots. They were skilled metalworkers, making iron cooking pots, tools and nails, horse harnesses, plough tips and weapons and also copper, tin, bronze and gold jewelry such as broaches, bracelets, necklaces and neck rings called torcs, and they had a distinctive swirling, intricate and stylized art form depicting animals and plants.

Celts also had a monetary system with gold, silver and bronze coins, and by 100 BC tin-bronze (potin) coins or tokens were first minted in Britain and some have been found in this area, so their economic power and strength enabled them to spread across Europe. During this latter period of the Trinovantes rule they had a significant Celtic mint from 100 BC- 43 AD, at what appears to have been their capital at Braughing, west of Bishop's Stortford. The settlement may also have been a trading post as it is on the navigable limit of the river Rib which is accessible to the river Lea and out to the Thames.

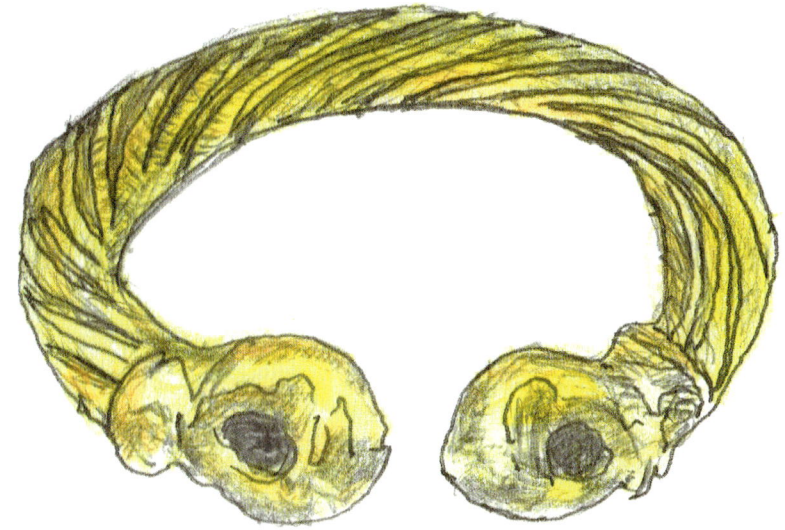

Torc – high status neck ring jewellery

Regional links between communities for trading metals for example, developed along trackways such as the Ridgeway which forms part of the Icknield Way (*Thurrock's Deeper Past* 2018) that is said to be of New Stone Age (Neolithic) origin, it runs between Avebury in Wiltshire above the Dorset coast, to Norfolk running along the chalk escarpment that crosses England. It is thought that an Iron Age track also ran east/west across this local landscape perhaps roughly along the route of the District railway line. However the ancient St. Marys Lane may also be a likely contender for the route, once the longest lane in England it runs, by extension, from Ilford nearby Uphall Camp in the west to Norsey Woods at Billericay in the east. Another route along Ripple Road towards Barking is thought to predate the Roman period and here:

- an Iron Age farmstead is located at Beam Parklands on the Rainham/Dagenham boarder;
- there is a 'late Iron Age pyre site at Beam Washlands, Dagenham located on the floodplain of the Wantz Stream' (Biddulph *et al.* 2010);
- and a small farmstead at the corner of London East Leisure Park, Dagenham (Barking and Dagenham Post 2019, AOC Archaeology);
- and two millennia of activity probably with a settlement close by surviving until the Early Iron Age at Goresbrook Village, Dagenham (Catherine Douglas *London Archaeologist* Vol 14.12).

• • • • • • • • • • • •

The Late Iron Age period (c.100-50 BC) The Trinovantes northern neighbours were the Belgic **Iceni tribe.** Arriving in c.200 BC they had settled what would become Norfolk, and the two tribes shared a similar lifestyle. The Iceni name may mean 'tribe or nation', they were a wealthy, civilised people who seemed true to their name.

A 1st century BC amphora was discovered at Hunts Hill Farm that would have contained Mediterranean wine indicating a 'trade in luxury goods with the Roman world some 50 years before the final successful Claudian invasion.' (*Archaeological Landscapes of east London...*). It seems that native British people

Chapter 6 Iron Age

living here were trading goods with the Continent and in effect advertising trade by the images on coinage of king Cunobelin in the early part of the first century AD depicting the high-sided, flat-bottomed ships for carrying coastal and seaborne goods.

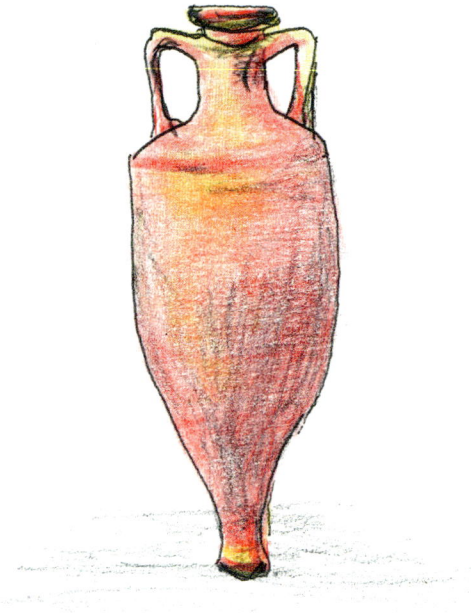

Terracotta Roman amphora – wheel-thrown, then the neck and handles were added in clay coils to the partially dry body; the pointed base of this style was very strong and would be embedded in soft ground for storage. It also aided both in stacking layers of the storage vessels while being transported by boat and again for unloading onto a sandy beach

However, this Late Iron Age period spans the arrival of the aggressive **Catuvellauni tribe** as well as the Roman Caesar's incursions into Britain, and Celts could be fierce fighters. They fought guerilla-style for personal glory using slings, javelins and larger spears, knives and swords. They grew their hair long and men wore moustaches but shaved their bodies and dyed their skin blue with woad, (a plant of the cabbage family) that would create a frightening warrior appearance. Their life expectancy was around 25 years, and generally their practice in South East Britain was to cremate their dead.

Artist impression of a reconstructed Iron Age war chariot also suitable for hunting and racing with one person sitting and one standing, with inbuilt suspension and drawn by two horses

The more warlike Belgic tribes began to arrive in Britain in about 75 BC. These latest newcomers, the Catuvellauni, occupied the land to the west in Hertfordshire and beyond. Their name may mean 'good in battle' and they indeed became a very powerful people, and in time relations began to break down between the Catuvellauni and their neighbouring tribes including with the Trinovantes people.

The Catuvellauni were skilled metal workers and enamellers and their pottery was wheel-thrown. Their heavy ploughs were better able to cultivate the clay soils than those of earlier people and they 'soon spread from Kent to Hertfordshire, passing up the Lea Valley and constantly harrying the peaceful Trinovantes, who were forced to take refuge in their hill-forts on the Epping ridge.' (Edwards, *A History of Essex*) where there is a north/south line of hillforts beyond Uphall (APA), at Loughton Camp (SAM), Ambresbury Banks (SAM) and Wallbury Camp (SAM) near Bishops Stortford in the north. A boundary line of hillforts between occupied territories such as these may have been used as look-outs and for protection for people and stock enclosures for their animals and generally remained in use for 150 – 200 years (Historic England).

At only some 32 km (20 miles) apart, the Trinovantes capital at Braughing, was now uncomfortably close to that of the fearsome Catuvellauni at Wheathampstead near St. Albans (Verlamion). Historical records show how the various peoples occupying this landscape have over the millennia consistently valued it – including these Celts who fought for the land. In military defence, this landscape would have played its part in defending this area from the Catuvellauni tribe from the St. Albans area to the west and in aiding in the defence of the country from Roman invasion – but not before the Trinovantes had in fact first welcomed Caesar as an ally.

Locally other fortified sites have also been identified:

- some 2 km (1.25 miles) northwest of Mucking, the Orsett Cock (SAM) is a well defended enclosure site that remained in use for some 3,000 years from the New Stone Age until well into the Saxon period;

- occupation of Hunts Hill Farm, Upminster extends through from the Late Bronze Age/Early Iron Age to the Roman period when the farmstead was fortified (MOL 2011) shortly before AD 40, then initially disused from c. AD 40-AD 60/70 but then remained in use until c. AD 120, well into the Roman occupation when there was no longer any need to fortify the settlement (*Archaeological Landscapes of east London...*);

- similarly, two Middle Iron Age enclosures at Moor Hall, Aveley continued in occupation by native people through to the Roman period, when the farmstead was 'fortified around the time of the Roman invasion'(*'Archaeological Landscapes of east London'...*);

- at Ardale School site in North Stifford the enclosed settlement is from the Middle and Late Iron Age with occupation surviving the traumas through to the Roman and Saxon periods;

- a Late Iron Age hill fort at South Weald west of Calcott Hall Farm is now traversed by Sandpit Lane, it includes a defensive bank and external ditch and dates between 100 BC-100 AD, which is the time spanning the periods between the first arrival of Julius Caesar, to the invasion proper by the Emperor Claudius i.e. either side of the Roman invasion/s and when this land of the Trinovantes was at the same time at war with the Celtic Catuvellauni tribe.

The names of the Trinovantes rulers during the later Iron Age period were recorded by the Romans who first mention their **king Imanuentius** in Caesar's *'Gallic War'* records. At this time **Julius Caesar** was Governor of Gaul, he would have been aware of trade which was carried out between Gaul and these islands which were to him 'beyond the known world' and he planned to also cross the dangerous currents of the English Channel and reach Britannia in pursuit of riches in land, grain, slaves and metals.

His first was a futile foray in 55 BC; at that time Caesar regarded the Trinovantes to be the most powerful of the British tribes and their capital to be the capital of the whole land. However, some time before Caesar's second expedition in 54 BC the Trinovantes king was overthrown and killed by **Cassivellaunus**, who is thought to have been leader of the Catuvellauni tribe and who forced the king's son **Mandubracius** into exile. Mandubracius fled to Caesar in Gaul for protection and the Trinovantes provided grain and hostages to Caesar in return for Roman support against Cassivellaunus. The Catuvellauni then abandoned hostile relations with neighbouring British tribes and instead Cassivellaunus led the British resistance against the Romans. But Caesar defeated him, this was probably near his capital at Wheathampstead and the Catuvellauni were suppressed, and so with Roman support peace prevailed for the Trinovantes for the following thirty-odd years.

• • • • • • • • • • •

During that time, in around 20-15 BC, **Addedomaros** the next king of the Trinovantes began his rule that lasted for about 10 years. By now it was clear that there was a great market for produce to supply Rome and Britain was soon exporting grain. So it is perhaps not surprising that Addedomaros was a person of great power and wealth and his was the first inscribed coinage of the Trinovantes. He is recalled as one of the founders of Britain in medieval manuscripts known as the **Welsh Triads**.

However, inter-tribal warfare at this time caused Addedomaros to almost immediately make a strategic move and resite his capital as far away as possible from the St. Albans neighbourhood of their enemies to a new site on the east coast of the Trinovantes lands, which he named **Camulodunon** (modern Colchester) meaning the 'fort of the war-god Camulus'. The move was not unjustified as the Trinovantes king either warred with **Tasciovanus** who was now king of the Catuvellauni, or Tasciovanus claimed he was the rightful heir to Mandubracius, or Addedomaros became client king to him because Tasciovanus seems to have taken control of Camulodunon in c.15-10 BC and issued his own coinage from there, but he was later forced to withdraw and Addedomaros was restored.

• • • • • • • • • • •

Addedomaros died during this unsettled period, but he left the Trinovantes in control of their capital at Camulodunon. He was briefly succeeded by his son **Dubnovellaunus** who formed the two warring tribes into one kingdom. Dubnovellaunus also produced his own coinage and developed Camulodunon, which allowed flourishing trade routes to develop with the Continent exporting grain, metal, dogs and slaves and with the import of luxury foreign goods such as wine, oil and pottery.

By the end of the Age there were about 1 – 1.5 million people living in Britain. Locally the Trinovantes had a thriving Iron Age rural economy here with many farms and settlements on these Thames gravel terraces and as a high status site Mucking must have been particularly important to this. In 2016, *'Current Archaeology - Writing Mucking: lives in land'* reviewed the outcomes of the major archaeological excavations at Mucking and concluded that during the Late Iron Age Mucking had about ten households and an overseer's residence with a major granary supplying about 150 families. It seems to have been a major grain and salt exporter at the time probably supplying to the Continent. It also produced pottery 'some of its products being destined for the military on **Hadrian's Wall'**. The settlement had set aside a large possibly ceremonial area that would indicate its position as a high status place of social power. This seems to have determined its later development as a Romano-British estate with an attached settlement.

By this time elsewhere a few settlements were developing into **oppida** which were large, fortified Iron Age settlements with the best known of these being in this area – at Camulodunon and Verlamion (St. Albans), one each on the borders to the west and east of this local landscape, and not surprisingly these oppida reflected the local tribal powers here. While at the Orsett Cock site numerous changes took place at the critical late Iron Age date when the tribes were warring and Caesar was making his first forays into Britain. In *'Thurrock's Deeper Past'* 2018, Christopher John Tripp explains that a large crossbow was found at the Orsett Cock site and a 'hoard of spearheads was found in one of the ditches, and they were probably used in its defence, as the excavators interpreted part of the site had been destroyed, either from internal tribal warfare or during the AD 43 invasion.' before the site become 'less defensive during the middle of the 1st century AD.'

From this point the story of the Trinovantes and their neighbours is recorded by the Roman invaders and so begins the historic period with a clearer picture available indirectly through Roman written records telling the strategic importance of this landscape and its people.

Places to visit near and far:

- Butser Ancient Farm, Hampshire, an experimental archaeology site in the South Downs National Park
- Cranbourne Chase Ancient Technology and Outdoor Education Centre, Dorset
- Maiden Castle, Dorchester, Dorset is in the care of English Heritage, 'one of the largest and most complex Iron Age hillforts in Europe'
- Danebury Iron Age hillfort in Hampshire 'was excavated by Professor Barry Cunliffe between 1969 and 1988 and is one of the best-studied sites of the British Iron Age.' It is also a Local Nature Reserve and a Scheduled Ancient Monument; the site story and its artefacts are held at the Iron Age Museum, Andover

Ideas for further projects:

- Iron Age trade routes with the Continent and the local response to Roman invasion may bare study
- Across this landscape it is said that an Iron Age track runs east/west and is thought to have been roughly along the route of the District Railway line. However the ancient St. Marys Lane may be a likely contender for the route, once the longest lane in England it runs, by extension, from Ilford, nearby Uphall Camp, across Becontree and Chadwell Heath to the 'broad or roomy ford' at Romford. From here across the promontory at St. Andrews Church and the Dell, Hornchurch and on to Upminster alongside the north bank of the old Bell River past Puddle Dock at the edge of the Mardyke marshes and on to Dunton Wayletts. Here the land dips down between the Brentwood Heights and Langdon Hills leading to the multi-period site at Norsey Woods, Billericay with its important Iron Age cemetery dating from c.50 BC to the Roman period and its relationship with the small Romano British town at modern Billericay c.1 km to the south-west and from there on via Stock to Chelmsford and Colchester.

References for further research:

- See Section B: Prehistory & Archaeology Introduction, p. 59

Further Reading:

- Hagger, Nicholas (pub 2012) *A View of Epping Forest*
- Howell, Isca J.; Swift, Dan; Watson, Bruce with Cotton, Jon & Greenwood, Pamela (2011) *Archaeological landscapes of east London: six sites excavated in advance of gravel quarrying in the London Borough of Havering'* pub. MOLA 2011 ISBN 978-1-907586
- Tripp, Christopher John (2018) *Thurrock's Deepest Past: A Confluence of Time* pub. Archaeopress ISBN 978-1-78969-111-5; ISBN 978-1-78969-112-2 (e-Pdf)

Section C
History Introduction

Generally, historic periods are dated forwards from the time of the first written records, which here are denoted as from AD 1 ('Anno Domini'); earlier records generally relate to pre-history periods and date backwards from then commonly beginning with 1 BC ('Before Christ') as being used here.

Despite eons of migration to, from and through this landscape in all directions, local people seem always to associate themselves positively with the area and have shown a certain independence and affection for the landscape and its particular sense of place – whether the Celts who fought for the land when it was the Iron Age Land of the Trinovantes; the Romans who valued its productivity; the Saxons who resisted invasion of the place they called Lundein; to the Danish invaders this land was under the Danelaw and part of Guthrum's kingdom, until eventually it became East Seaxe. Each of the defence forces played their strategic role in protecting Britain right through to modern times.

Local people were also accepting of new types and forms of religion; and migration into, out of and through the area with the expansion of settlements and employment; even the effect of national service routes, outlaws and gangsters, plague or day-trippers, this area has experienced them all. All these factors have shaped the resilient nature of local people and an appreciation of the place and its character so that here, surrounded by townscape as it may be, at the heart of the landscape is found the peace and quiet of the countryside and beautiful views as well as places to visit and the outdoor recreational and learning opportunities that are found along its river valleys and marshes and across its hillsides with their quaint villages and broad lowland plain still with its remote settlements at Bulphan, Orsett, the Horndon's and Childerditch and all over dotted with clusters of historic Essex buildings.

As a consequence of the position of this landscape between two major arteries (the A12 and the river Thames) from the coast into London, so much of the events of national historical interest have actually occurred across this area, creating an enviable legacy historical record and giving importance of this area to the national story. This may be recalled and collated as a compendium of great British historical events, each with a local aspect adding colour and clarity to the heritage and making both local history and national events easier to understand and identify with, both for local people and as an invaluable educational tool.

This Section C – History, is designed to record how this landscape has helped shape local, regional and national historical events and how in turn those events have affected this area and its people. It also provides information on the heritage of the landscape, as well as its history, its valued historic buildings and structures, historic areas and parklands. Here are also ancient routes, local craftsmanship, cultural traditions, and the natural heritage, its flora and fauna, rivers, hills, marshes and panoramic views.

Here are the secret histories of this key locality now extensively hidden in the mists of time, historic events of the defence of London and the realm, the development of agricultural, industry and quarrying, national commerce and trade routes, the introduction and development of Christianity to England, as well as people, animal and plant migration over the millennia from prehistory to the future. There are many historic figures associated with the area relating to royalty, to the development of language, science and mathematics; examples of both local vernacular buildings and villages and great historic houses by the most famous architects of their day such as James Paine; examples of the whole range and development of historic landscape design from Bridgeman to Repton and including Lancelot 'Capability' Brown; as well as stories, legends and folk law of witches, highway robbery, press gangs, smuggling and the like.

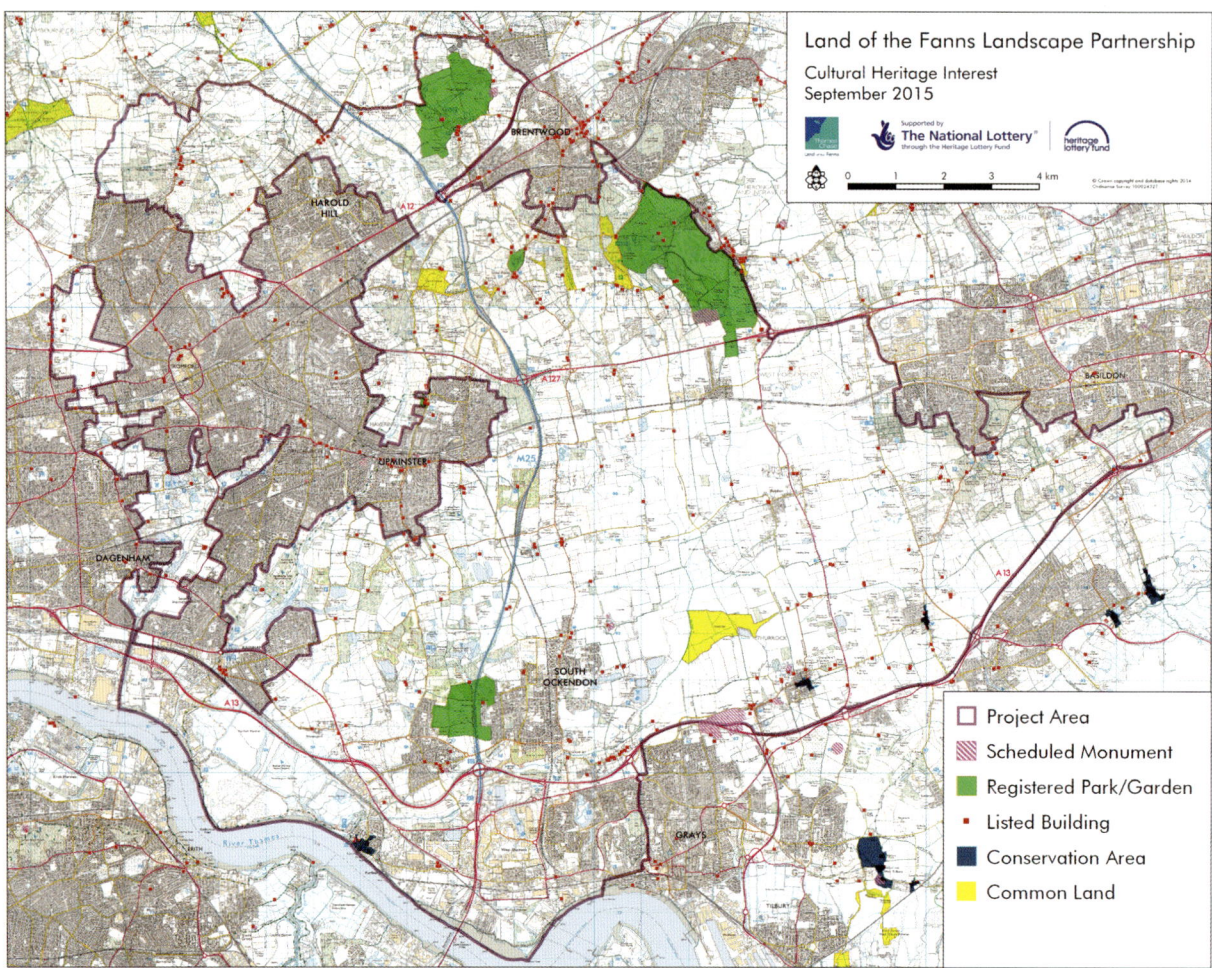

Sites and areas of protected Built Heritage interest within the LotF landscape (the LotF together with its adjacent urban areas of Dagenham, Havering and Brentwood town, has 24 conservation areas and some 500 statutory listed buildings with many additional local heritage buildings and areas of archaeological interest), (Courtesy LotF and Alison Farmer Associates 'Land of the Fanns Assessment Report')
© Crown copyright 2021 OS LICENCE no. 100064852

Places to visit nearby:

- Havering-atte-Bower Conservation Area is a linear village that grew up between the two Palaces of Havering and Pyrgo and today the village has numerous attractive listed and historic buildings
- Great Warley Village Conservation Area and adjoining Warley Place Essex Wildlife Trust Nature Reserve
- South Weald Conservation Area historic, rural, hilltop hamlet with a sense of history

- Cranham Conservation Area is a hilltop hamlet on a medieval route with historic Georgian and Victorian buildings and surrounded by farmland that retains its historic feeling of rural isolation
- Horndon-on-the-Hill Conservation Area is a beautiful hilltop village with numerous listed buildings of the 18th and 19th century often with older buildings hidden behind
- Orsett Conservation Area is another attractive rural hilltop village with many listed and other historic buildings. Immediately on the west side of the village is the historic hamlet of Baker Street with its smock mill (grade II), now in residential use.
- North Ockendon Conservation Area is a rural area with two historic hamlets linked by a footpath crossing the fields to the medieval church
- Purfleet Conservation Area is based on the 18th century planned village by the Whitbread family and houses the Purfleet Heritage & Military Centre in the Government Powder Magazine No.5, a grade I listed building and Scheduled Ancient Monument

Ideas for further projects:

- Compile a register of all national, regional and local built heritage (including landscapes, routes and views) in order to map the built heritage of this landscape
- Scope for a children's book of the history of the landscape
- Scope for a coffee-table pictorial book
- Draw out curriculum links for each time period that could be explored further in local classrooms
- Given significant interest of people in genealogy and human interest stories there may be scope for a more detailed account of the lives of notable local personalities
- There may be scope for a further chapter on the impact of the 21st century of this landscape followed up in an organised way by close consideration given to major Planning Applications across the landscape including major strategic government infrastructure proposals. This may be informed by a study on the impact of 20th development on this landscape.
- Seek to set up Neighbourhood Planning Forums for Rainham historic parish area (Beam Park, South Hornchurch, Rainham and Wennington) and for Aveley with Purfleet-on-Thames

References for further research:

- The National Curriculum Key Stages 1, 2, 3, 4 & 5
- The National Heritage List for England (NHLE) is the register of all nationally protected historic buildings and sites in England and includes listed buildings, scheduled monuments, protected wrecks, registered parks and gardens and battlefields https://historicengland.org.uk/listing/the-list/
- The Heritage Gateway is a single online access to many of England's local and national historic environment records
- Greater London Historic Environment Record (GLHER)
- Essex Historic Environment Record (EHER) is a database of all known archaeological sites and monuments, historic buildings, parks and gardens in Essex
- Unlocking Essex Past (UEP) provides online access to the Essex Historic Environment Record
- English Heritage (EH) cares for over 400 historic monuments, buildings and places to visit

- The National Trust welcomes visitors to the places of historic interest or natural beauty in its care
- Historic England (HE) is the public body that helps people care for, enjoy and celebrate England's historic environment
- Museum of London (MOL)
- London Metropolitan Archives (LMA) holds a huge and diverse collection of many aspects of London's history
- The National Archives, the website includes a *London for Researchers* guide to additional London archives
- British Library includes manuscripts, journals, newspapers, magazines, sound and music records, patents, maps and drawings and the records of the India Office
- Imperial War Museum
- Archives for London (AfL) 'an independent voice for archives, archive users and archives enthusiasts in London'
- Black Cultural Archives is the national heritage centre for collecting, preserving and celebrating the histories of African and Caribbean people in Britain
- *Dictionary of National Biography*
- Local Studies libraries and archives:
    - Havering Local Studies Library, Romford
    - Havering Museum, High Street, Romford
    - Thurrock Local Studies, Grays Library, and Thurrock Museum, Thameside Complex, Grays
    - Barking & Dagenham Archives and Local Studies Service and Valence House Museum, Becontree Avenue, Dagenham
    - Brentwood Museum, Lorne Road, Brentwood
    - Essex Records Office (ERO), Wharf Road, Chelmsford

Further Reading:

- Bowman, Karen (2010) *Essex Girls* pub. Amberley Publishing ISBN 978-1-84868-895-7
- Bowman, Karen (2013) *Essex Boys* pub. Amberley Publishing 2013 ISBN 9781445608532
- Cherry, Bridget; O'Brian, Charles & Pevsner, Nikolaus (2005) *The Buildings of England – London 5: East* pub. Yale University Press ISBN 0 300 10701 3
- Kemble, James (2007) *Essex Place-Names* pub. Historical Publications
- Mills, A.D. (1998) *Oxford Dictionary of English Place Names* pub Oxford University Press ISBN 0 19 280074 4
- Morant, Philip (1768 re.pub. 1978) *The History and Antiquities of the County of Essex, Vol. 1*
- Ogborne, Elizabeth (pub. 1817) *History of Essex*
- Pevsner, N. & Bettley, J. (2007) *The Buildings of England: Essex,* pub. Yale University Press
- Powell, W. R. ed. *Victoria History of the Counties of England: A History of the County of Essex*, Vol. II pub 1907, Vol. III Pub 1963; Vol. VII pub. 1973; Vol. VII, pub.1978; Vol. VIII pub.1983
- Warren, J.B. (2001) *Origins of Havering's Road Names* (see Havering Local Studies Library)
- Warren, J.B. (2001) *A Companion to Havering's Local History* pub. by the author (see Havering Local Studies Library)
- *The Royal Commission on Historical Monuments (RCHM) Essex* Vol. II & Vol. IV

Chapter 7
Romans
AD 43 – AD 400

NATIONAL CURRICULUM Hints

The Romans and their Empire made a great and lasting impact on world history but this local area has its own stories to tell about the Romans and the attempted invasion of Britain by their emperor Julius Caesar in 55-54 BC; also the invasion proper in AD 42; the subsequent British revolt led by the Iceni Tribe and the final Romanisation of Britain with its impact on this lowland farming area and its people, their culture and religious beliefs.

SURPRISE *'The Land of the Fanns is an intricate landscape, full of surprises and 'hidden gems' and rewards exploring.'* **(TellTale working with the public 2018)**

At first there is little obvious that is Roman on the surface of local history here, but this landscape was in fact a significant witness to Caesar's incursion and to the later Roman invasion and to the subsequent Boudican rebellion.

This period begins with the written record of events by the Romans, which reveal much about their view of what happened. While in Britain the Celtic tribes remained in control, on the continent the Roman Empire was dominant and by the early 1st century AD it was flourishing all across from Spain in the west to Syria in the east. In 27 BC **Augustus** had become the first Roman Emperor and he was watchful of Britain and its promise of bounty with resources in iron, tin, lead, silver and gold, slaves, cattle and hides, hunting dogs and most especially wheat, but these islands were at that time still 'beyond the known world' of the Romans.

The peace that Julius Caesar had earlier (in 54 BC) brought about between Dubnovellaunus the Celtic king of the Trinovantes tribe that ruled this area, and the king of the neighbouring Catuvellauni tribe to the west, eventually became fragile. Dubnovellaunus evidently had also forged links with the Atrebates tribe who were also troubled by the Catuvellauni and by AD 7 those leaders travelled together to Rome and paid tribute to the Emperor Augustus – as recorded in the *Res Gestae*[1] that was produced following the death of the Emperor in c AD 14.

Meanwhile Tasciovanus had been king of the Catuvellauni since c 20 BC, he had established a new capital at Verulamium (modern St. Albans) and one of his sons expanded the Catuvellauni south from there into the land of the Atrebates tribe. By the time that Tasciovanus died in AD 9 it seems that the Trinovantes had been finally overcome either by Tasciovanus himself or by his son **Cunobelinus** (the Cymbeline of Shakespeare's play of that name), who succeeded him. According to the 12th century

---

[1] Literally 'things done', originally this was a written record by Augustus about his own life and achievements.

historian Geoffrey of Monmouth, Cunobelinus had been brought up in the court of Augustus – it seems that amongst the Celtic tribes both sides were courting the powerful Romans.

But at this time Rome was preoccupied not by the warring Britons but by having lost three legions of their army in the forests of Germany. Cunobelinus was now able to thrive, ruling primarily from his own rebuilt and well-fortified capital at Camulodunon (modern Colchester) in the land of the Trinovantes and becoming the most successful of the Catuvellauni kings. Among the various British exports the depiction of an ear of wheat or barley on some of his coinage advertised British grain exports; while imports of luxury goods included olive oil, wine from Italy, fish sauces from Hispania, Gallo-Belgic tableware, drinking vessels, glassware and jewellery.

Dubnovellaunus died in the late 30s AD followed by Cunobelinus in AD 41 who was succeeded by his son **Caractacus**. Whilst also in AD 41 in Rome, **Claudius** had become Emperor and to survive politically he needed a Roman military *Triumph* for which he looked to Britain despite the inherent Roman fear of these islands that were beyond their civilised world. The continued local friction here in Britain gave Claudius the excuse to carry out an Invasion proper in AD 43, supposedly in support of the defeated Trinovantes and Atrebates but also to give him his Triumph and lead to greater prosperity for Rome.

<u>MIGRATION</u> *'This is a cross roads landscape: because of its location on the Thames ... people have always travelled into, through and away from this area.'*
(TellTale working with the public 2018)

Because Claudius believed the Trinovantes to be the main British tribe and their capital to be the capital of Britain, so Camulodunon became the target for his invasion in AD 43. However the Roman army is thought to have landed at Richborough in Kent and so early clashes took place in that county.

Claudius sent four Legions to Britain from Gaul under the leadership of the distinguished Roman senator, General Aulus **Plautius**, this was an army of about 25,000 soldiers supported by about the same number of auxiliaries. Heading west they were harried by the British guerrilla tactics before meeting the army of Britons at the river Medway where Caractacus and his brother **Togodumnus** led the initial defence of the country in a battle lasting two days. However, the British were defeated and pushed back across the Thames, most likely in the Tilbury area, bringing Essex into the fray as they were pursued by at least one division of auxiliary Germanic mercenaries and with some Roman losses in the Essex marshes.

Soon after Togodumnus died and Plautius sent for Claudius to join him for the final push. Claudius brought his personal **Praetorian guards** and a number of **war elephants** that would have intimidated the British. Now the Romans swept further westwards with the main army as the heavy war elephants could only cross the Thames further upstream famously at Brentford in West London. Then turning eastwards the large Roman army marched into Essex crossing the river Lea at Old Ford and heading east probably camping at Moulsham in Chelmsford before the final advance on Camulodunon where Claudius received the submission of eleven local chiefs achieving his Triumph at Britain's Iron Age capital.

> Having defeated the Celts, not surprisingly the Romans took control of Camulodunon as their capital then renamed as **'Camulodunum'**. Claudius then returned to Rome after only sixteen days, leaving his troops quartered in the Colchester area. From this base at Camulodunum over the first four years of the invasion Plautius was able to fan out the conquest to other areas of Britain.

By AD 50 the south-east of England had been conquered to become client kingdoms of the Romans who went on to over-run the other Celtic kingdoms by military occupation – northwest to the lands of the Catuvellauni and to the Corieltauvi tribe beyond, the Celts were driven west over-running the lands of the Dobunni tribe towards Wales, and south-west to the Atrebates land and that of the Durotriges beyond, towards Cornwall. This was followed during AD 47-52 under the direction of Ostorius **Scapula** pushing into Norfolk and the lands of the Iceni and driving the Celts before them further into Wales.

In AD 60 Tacitus the Roman historian recorded the Roman attack that devastated the **druids** on the island of Anglesey, those ancient mysterious religious peoples whose extreme practices the Romans could not tolerate. Subsequently other Roman leaders pursued their invasion north to Scotland and the lands of the Caledonians and returned across north Wales again to the druids refuge of Anglesey to crush the spiritual driving force of the Celts.

LANDFORM *'The Land of the Fanns is about land and water and the often shifting relationship between them'* **(TellTale working with the public 2018)**

Meanwhile In this area, following their conquest and the eventual cooperation of the Trinovantes, the Romans restored the tribe with local self-government subject to Rome. They were awarded the status of **civitas**, which was an administrative area of the new Roman Province of Britannia with Camulodunum as its capital - although as a 'colonia' (a Roman settlement in conquered territory) Camulodunum could only be inhabited by Romans or Roman citizens. The town became a centre for Roman soldiers to retire as a farming community with considerable areas of land (perhaps 400 sq. km (640 sq. miles) granted across the surrounding landscape for their farmsteads.

• • • • • • • • • • •

The road from Camulodunum to **Londinium** (London) was one of the main Roman roads constructed under the direction of Plautius following the Celtic revolt in c. AD 60, and tying the new **Province Britannia** with the existing continental road network. *The Great Road* lies roughly along the line of the A12 following the higher ground well above the marshes and via the fording places of the rivers at Chelmsford, Romford, Ilford, Stratford and Old Ford and via Aldgate leads to the Thames crossing point where the Romans erected the first bridge across the river (where London Bridge stands linking the City to Southwark), which enabled Roman Londinium, founded in AD 47-50, to develop as a trading post.

Along the route of The Great Road a Roman Staging Post was built at **Durolitum,** near Romford that, in his paper on the subject archaeologist Nicholas Fuentes convincingly places on the Marshalls

Park estate on the side of the Rom valley overlooking the river (Essex Journal 21(1).18-21). The Great Road became one of the major routes in and out of Londinium and provided a strategic axis for the Romans to dominate the area. A link road, the *Via Trinobantina* through London along Old Street and Oxford Street connected this area from Colchester in the east (and Norfolk beyond) to Silchester in Hampshire in the west.

Roman roads were typically at least 2 metres (7ft.) wide or more and flanked by drainage ditches, however in this area that lacks natural stone the road had a thin gravel surface and in time identification of the actual road became lost, although a supposed section at Gidea Park is designated a Scheduled Ancient Monument (SAM).

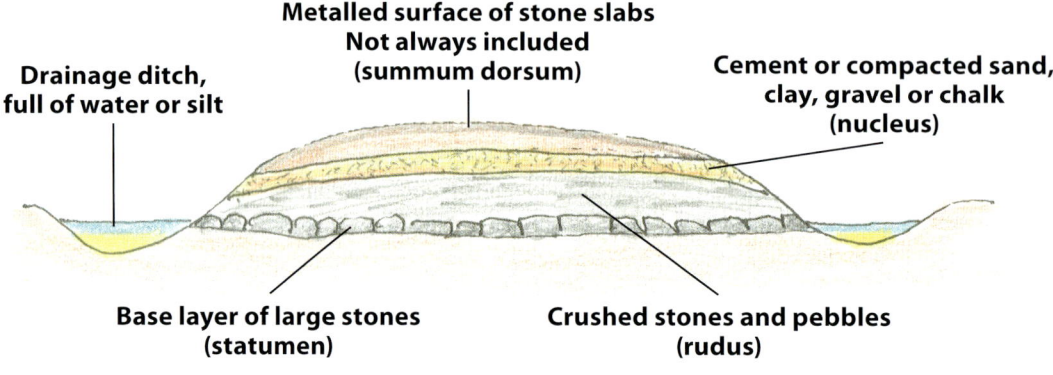

Cross section showing the makeup of a typical Roman Road – in this area there was no local stone to provide a metalled surface

Another road clips the northwest corner of Havering Borough, running from London to Colchester via Chigwell and to the north of Abridge it seems to have continued in use through to the Saxon period (*London Archaeologist* Vol 1.6). Following the Roman custom this road has cremation burials along it, and a Romano-British villa (SAM) at Abridge overlooked the river Roding and dates from AD 100-350 and was possibly one of the richest in this part of Essex. A second villa also a SAM, is situated a little further to the west, and there is another villa site in Havering Park.

Within little more than a decade of the Conquest there was a trackway and a relatively unusual and fairly richly-furnished mixed rite cemetery on an earlier site at High House, Purfleet that has possibly the earliest recorded case of leprosy in Britain. The development of a local road network linking local farms to Camulodunum and London on the strategic network would have enabled an organised commercial agricultural production area to be developed. Over time these tiers of more local Romano-British roads were laid out linking local Romano-British property onto the main route as farmsteads or villas were built across the district for the invaluable production of wheat. Such a track survives on the east side of Marks Warren Farm running south to join The Great Road and serving a Roman building and site of at least one cremation.

There are also possible Roman Roads in the Langdon Hills area at Dry Street and at Dunton Wayletts and Horndon-on-the-Hill. Also possibly Ripple Road in Dagenham, (that may be of prehistoric origin), with cremation burials dating from the first two centuries AD found in various places along its route and a stone coffin of the 3rd century AD. There is also evidence for a Roman marching camp (an overnight or longer defensive stop) at Orsett and possible Roman-British settlements at South Ockendon and at Bulphan.

From the beginning Essex remained firmly under Roman rule, except at the time of **Queen Boudicca's revolt** in AD 60 or 61 that followed her outrageous ill-treatment by the Romans following the death of her husband the king of the Iceni. The Trinovantes were keen to join with Boudicca's fight, perhaps because the Romans had taken over their capital at Camulodunum as their first Legionary Fortress in Britain and developed it by taking much of the surrounding land for Roman citizens.

Boudicca's bold uprising swept south and united with the Trinovantes setting fire to the unprepared Camulodunum and raising it to the ground and destroying its fine Roman buildings. The united Celtic armies swept across the area killing all Romano-British they could find, they then took, the by now abandoned Londinium before sacking Verulamium. Soon after the main Roman army finally returned from subduing Celts on the Welsh borders and now prepared and ready they met and defeated Boudicca, driving the remaining local Celts back to their homelands and killing all Celts they could find on the way. It is said that 70 – 80 thousand died in the Celtic rampage and the Roman revenge.

ECONOMY *'This area is justly famous for trade, commerce and industry: these have been important here for many centuries.'* (TellTale working with the public 2018)

Although by the time of the unsuccessful uprising the Celts had generally been pushed westwards to Wales and beyond, others had settled to become the **Romano-British people** as peace was finally restored and Roman civilisation took over in Britain. The Trinovantes appear to have returned to a cooperative existence despite being ousted from their capital.

Some farmers became wealthy as they were obliged through taxation in kind to increase production to meet the demands of a secure Roman market at home, in the new towns, supplying the Roman army here and abroad and using the improved trade routes and a strengthening currency. Perhaps this is why from circa AD 60-65 the Moulsham area of Chelmsford was developed as **Caesaromagus** meaning 'Caesar's market place'. This was a civitas or small town that was permitted to be occupied by non-Romans as well as Romans, and had an eastwards route out of the town to a port at Heybridge. Caesaromagus became the Trinovantes capital with the Trinovantes ruling themselves as one of the client kingdoms of the Romans.

Until that time Londinium had been only a planned trading centre on the Thames river crossing but now it became developed almost from scratch to become the most significant town in Britannia economically and politically and it was only some 15 km (9 miles) west of our area from Barking and Dagenham. By AD 197 Londinium had become the capital of the province of southern Britain – *Britannia Superior*. With Londinium's transformation the lower Thames Valley took on a new importance that had previously been concentrated on Verulamium and Camulodunum. The Thames flowing across here to London would have been significant to this as flourishing trade routes developed with the Continent including the import of luxury goods, and possibly using the Ingrebourne Valley as a trade route for wheat to Gaul perhaps using Coldharbour (some speculate the name refers to a Roman staging post) on the Thames on Rainham Marshes to access the river where a ferry is said to date from the Roman period.

As well as exploiting Britain's natural resources and taking slaves, the Romans learned about coracle boats from the Celtic people and their use of chariots in warfare, while Roman Latin influenced and entered into the language, Romans gave us the solar calendar, the basis of our legal system and censuses and they imposed their sense of order on the landscape.

• • • • • • • • • • • •

The people eventually settled into 400 years of peace by which time farming communities were common on the lowlands (*Kingdom, Civitas and County: the evolution of Territorial Identity in the English Landscape* by Stephen Rippon 2018). Climatically this was an unusually warm period across Europe that lasted from around 250 BC to 400 AD and this landscape was essentially used by the Romano-British people for wheat production to feed the Roman armies. In the previous age the British had produced only enough food for their immediate use, but now the Romans needed to improve production, storage and transportation for export and introduced the necessary tools and techniques.

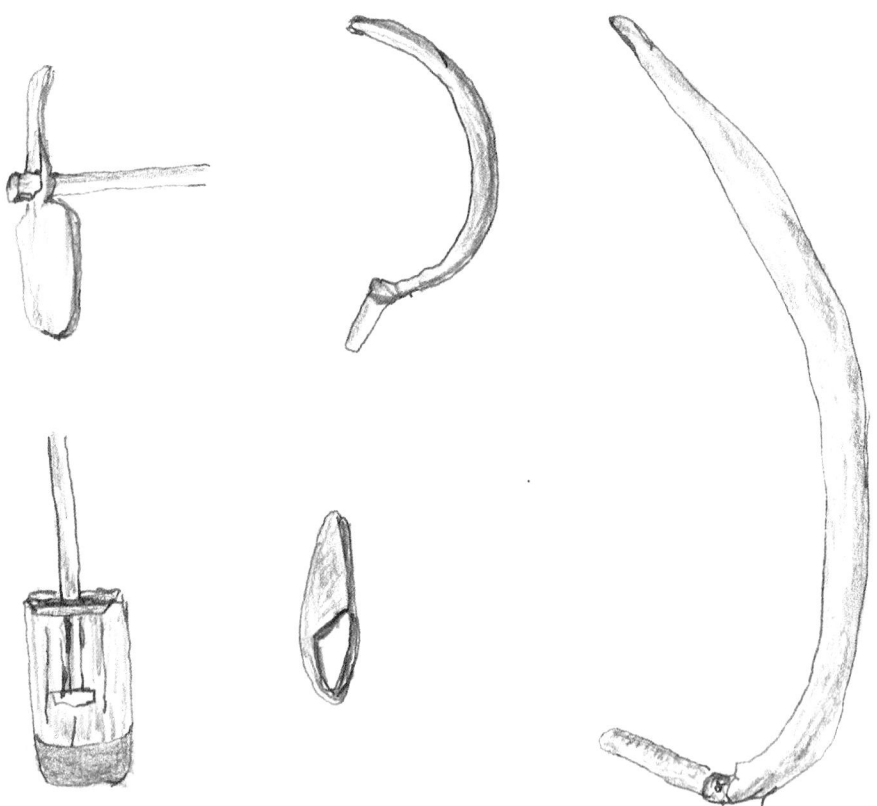

Roman farm implements: the mattock, sickle, iron clad spade and shears;
the large two-handed scythe made it faster and easier to cut cereal crops

The Romans agricultural system used light, wheel-less ploughs with flat iron shares suited to light soils and, unlike the Celtic four-field rotation system, practised a two-field system with one field planted while the other had any weeds ploughed in and left fallow.

Roman plough pulled by a pair of oxen

The Romans constructed fen ditches in the Mardyke Valley to control local flooding and improve the productivity of the land here with a mixture of arable and pasture (Wilkinson 1988) and people had to learn new techniques to dry and store grain ready for export.

By the 4th century AD most lowland areas, even clay lands were supporting farming communities and generally Roman Britain was densely settled and there were many farms and settlements on these Thames gravel terraces. Oaks, willows, alder trees and heather were growing locally and used for firing pottery; dung beetles and honey bees have also been found here from the Roman period. Roman fields were a standard size based on the amount of land that one person could plough in a day and there is surviving archaeological evidence for Roman field systems:

- around Cranham and Manor Farm in North Ockendon;
- at Great Sunnings Farm and a farmstead site in Harwood Hall Lane, both in Corbets Tey;
- also at Whitehall Woods, Rainham;
- a farmstead site in Aveley;
- cropmarks at Linford;
- farming at Passingford Bridge;
- crop marks at Baker Street and occupation at Orsett;
- cropmarks, an industrial site, occupation and likely a villa at Mucking;
- occupation at North Stifford;
- evidence of occupation in Rainham at the old LESSA (London Electricity Sports & Social Association) Sports Ground; also at Warwick Field; South Hall Farm; and possibly in Bridge Road and at Brookway, Rainham;
- archaeological work at Beam Valley Country Park revealed a site west of the Beam river dating from the late Iron Age with a cremation cemetery of 16 graves through to the 1st century AD and important evidence of a Roman farmstead with cattle and horses and growing wheat and with pottery kilns manufacturing a large range of goods in around AD 125, and with a Roman lead coffin revealed on the east side of the river that is now held at the British Museum.

Some sites indicate defensive enclosures and/or temporary abandonment around the time of the Invasion such as at Passingford Bridge and at **Hobbs Hole** near Brentwood. Later on Roman villa estates of medium to high status are indicated at both sites with evidence for hunting red deer and digging clay pits at Hobbs Hole, and woodland coppicing, ale brewing and medicinal plants used at Passingford Bridge. It was also important to improve livestock and in the 3rd and 4th centuries AD animals were being raised at both sites for breeding, milk production and as draught animals with meat being processed at Hobbs Hole. At **Goresbrook Fields** in Dagenham work by Newham Museum Service revealed a possibly late Iron Age to early Roman site and a possibly palisaded rectangular ditched site from the 1st century AD together with four cremation burials (*Essex Archaeology & History* Vol 27).

In Havering at **Hunts Hill Farm** in the period AD 40-70 and at **Moor Hall** during AD 40-60 the Iron Age farmsteads already had defensive enclosures constructed during the time of so much local warring between the British tribes followed by the Roman invasion. But the trappings of Iron Age life were thrown out at Moor Hall in c AD 60-70 as Romano-British life settled down and now these farms were surrounded by organised ditched fields with wells and stock waterholes in mixed farming use, and there were Roman burials. During AD 120-260 these farms concentrated on livestock farming and, following the general pattern of increased productions, agriculture intensified here from AD 260 until the later 4th century when new field systems were laid out. Generally by the 3rd century Roman objects became commonplace even among the poor and Roman finds at Hunts Hill and Moor Hall include coins, glass jewellery and bottles as well as pottery.

There are other Roman features revealed at Eastbrookend in Dagenham, Manser Road and Launders Lane and the old Rainham Football Ground in Rainham and a multi-period site at Berwick Ponds in Rainham extended through to late Roman; also a Roman burial mound (SAM) originally accompanied by two others, on a site once taking advantage of views over the Mardyke river valley; a Roman building at Shenfield and at Noak Hill with further sites and finds beyond the immediate LotF area at places including Barking, Billericay, Norsey Wood, Stock, Stanford-le-Hope, Fobbing, East and West Tilbury, Little Thurrock and Chadwell-St. Mary and, as a vital commodity there were Roman salt workings at Tilbury. Local finds include clues to materials and features of better quality buildings such as Roman roof tiles, bricks, Roman cement, mosaics and hypocaust underfloor heating.

• • • • • • • • • • • •

However as time passed Rome was less able to focus on Britannia. During the 2nd century AD Rome increasingly had to turn its attention to other areas of the Empire and in AD 122 **Hadrian** visited Britain and ordered the building of Hadrian's Wall in response to the need to hold the north of Britain while soldiers were pulled out to deal with problems on the continent. Rome continued to face serious social, political and economic problems and the Roman army in Britannia was reduced from about 50,000 in AD 150 to perhaps 15,000 or less by the 4th century AD. There was a brief 50 year interlude of agricultural prosperity from c. AD 312 after the conversion of the **Emperor Constantine the Great** who granted religious toleration to all faiths and reorganised Britannia under the military control of the **Count of the Saxon Shore** to protect the economically important southeast of the country. But, after some four centuries of control the Roman Empire itself finally began to collapse, institutions began to break down and plantation owners were unable to prevent their slaves escaping and yields fell to subsistence levels.

As Roman Britain descended into a state of political and economic collapse the Romans began to withdraw from about AD 388 finally abandoning their Province Britannia in AD 410 as the Anglo-Saxon peoples from north Europe continued their incursions. The Roman army left the Romano-British people to defend themselves from the **Saxon Shore forts** built along the southern and eastern coastline towards the end of the 3rd century as Saxon raids on the Province increasingly became a problem. Like the others the local fort at **Othona** (Bradwell-on-Sea) soon fell to the Saxon incomers and their devastating seax swords. As the Romans withdrew from Britain so the local Romano-British people here showed familiar fortitude against the incoming Saxons and resisted the invasion with some success, the local people only gradually over time pulling back towards the north-west and their old heartland near St. Albans, being one of the last areas to yield to the Saxons.

Places to visit near and far:

- The Roman coffin from the Dagenham/Mardyke border is held at the British Museum
- Colchester Castle Museum
- Lullingstone Roman Villa, Kent
- Bignor Roman Villa, Bignor, West Sussex, including educational visits for schools
- Ostia Antica, Italy an ancient Roman port at the mouth of the River Tiber that is now an archaeological site with significant building remains

Ideas for further projects:

- Further study of the local Roman landscape and *find* spots including places like the Launders and Gerpins areas
- Investigate Roman routes including trading routes
- Investigate the relationship and development of this area with London
- Use the local story of the Roman invasion and subsequent life here as inspiration for all ages to use as a basis and/or as ideas for schools and other theatre productions

References for further research:

More information on the Romans may be found through:

- See Section C: History Introduction, p. 99
- Council for British Archaeology (CBA), CBA London branch (CBA-L) and CBA East
- Ancient Monuments Society (AMS) now Historic Buildings and Places
- English Heritage Roman sites
- Historic England Greater London Archaeological Advisory Service (GLAAS)
- Museum of London Archaeology (MOLA)
- Museum of London Archaeological Archive & Research Centre (LAARC), Hackney

- Recent archaeological report records for Havering Borough are held at Havering Local Studies Library, Romford
- West Essex Archaeological Group (WEAG)
- Essex Society for Archaeology and History (ESAH)
- The Roman Military Research Society (RMRS)

Further Reading:

- Graves, Robert (1934) *Claudius the God* ISBN 10: 0140004211 an historical novel where the author places a battle between the Celts and the Romans at Brentwood Hill

Chapter 8
Saxons & Danes
c.410 AD – c.1066
(The Early Medieval Period)

NATIONAL CIRRUCULUM Hints

With the fall of the western Roman empire, Rome eventually withdrew from Britain in c. AD 410 as the Anglo-Saxon advance was stepped up. This time marked the end of Classical Antiquity and the beginning of the Medieval period (the Middle Ages) that lasted from the 5th to the late 15th century. With the departure of the Romans new people came to settle and Britain was again divided into smaller kingdoms with village settlements leaving a legacy in new local place names.

Saxons brought their own laws and justice, religion, art forms and culture. Eventually Christian conversion of the country again took place before the Danish Viking raids and invasion brought back paganism once more to be met by the resistance of King Alfred the Great. Further Viking incursions introduced the Danegeld pay-off and brought Danish kings of England before King Edward the Confessor restored Saxon rule and administration. His death in 1066 and succession by his brother-in-law King Harold II (Godwinson) led to the invasion of William the Conqueror and a move into the High Medieval period (the High Middle Ages).

SURPRISE *'The Land of the Fanns is an intricate landscape, full of surprises and 'hidden gems' and rewards exploring.' (TellTale working with the public 2018)*

The Early Medieval Period (or Early Middle Ages) is often called the Dark Ages because until recently little historical detail was known about this time, but now increasing archaeological study is improving understanding of this period of Saxon history. This area is important to the national story of invasion by the Saxons and by the Vikings through its resistance and defence, the presence of the river Thames, migration and settlement, and importance to the economy in agriculture, quarrying and industry. This was an Age dominated by its political and religious leaders, and religion became a highly political matter.

Before the Romans departed from Britain it is possible that Saxon settlers were already arriving here and farming land in return for providing military service. With the departure of the Roman military there followed some 40 years or so of conflict, famine, disease and chaos and then more disastrously the climate began an extended cooling period, affecting farming. Evidently one **Vortigern**, or High King, eventually emerged as leader of the federated states of the Britons.

The late 9th century *Anglo-Saxon Chronicle*[1] records (after Bede)[2] that in the year AD 449 Vortigern invited in Germanic mercenaries to fight the threat of the Picts in the north and the Scotti from Ireland. Led by legendary Jutish brothers **Hengist** and **Horsa** they later turned against Vortigern and chose to remain in Britain. Amongst other areas, Essex is said to have been ceded by the Britons to Hengist and the Saxons in return for sparing the life of Vortigern after the 'Treachery of the Long Knives'. This is when the Anglo-Saxon mercenaries are said to have massacred native British chieftains at a peace conference on Salisbury Plain in c AD 460.

In the 8th century, in his *Ecclesiastical History of the English People* the brothers are recorded by the Venerable Bede as the first chieftains among the Angles, Saxons and Jutes in Britain (see below). Hengist may also be the Hengist of the Old English epic poem *Beowulf*. Other legends that thrived during the Middle Ages emerged about King Arthur, Camelot and the Knights of the Round Table of West country fame. What we do know is that it is during this turbulent period that this local area became part of the minor kingdom of Lundein with its capital at Caer Colun (Fort Colonia) – previously Camulodunum and now modern Colchester.

MIGRATION *'This is a cross roads landscape: because of its location on the Thames ... people have always travelled into, through and away from this area.'*
(TellTale working with the public 2018)

Saxons AD 440 - c.830 In their time the Romans had imposed their sense of order on the landscape but after they abandoned Britain Saxons from Germany spread to Essex (East Saxons), Wessex (West Saxons), Middlesex (Middle Saxons) and Sussex (South Saxons); Jutes arrived from Jutland and mainly settled in Kent; Angles came from South Denmark settling mainly in East Anglia, and legend has it they had been invited into the country by Hengist and Horsa. However it happened, between them these latest newcomers battled and divided most of Britain into Seven Kingdoms during the early 6th century – Northumbria, Mercia, Anglia, Wessex, Sussex, Kent and Essex.

Despite the Romano-British farmed land, much of the country was still covered in thick oak forests and in having to contend with local resistance it's not surprising that the Saxons appear to have established their early settlements here along the Thames where access was easier. These sites seem to be named after local leaders including Mucking (Mucca's settlement or creek), where the Romano-British villa had been left abandoned during the 4th century until Saxon settlement had begun by the early 5th century. Mucking held an important strategic position on a bend in the Thames, with a population of at least 100 people it flourished and gradually moved northwards over the following centuries surviving until at least the 8th century, until eventually the field system was taken over again in due course by the Saxo-Normans. Other early local settlements were Barking (Bereca's settlement – or possibly settlement by the birch trees), Wennington (Wynne or Wenn's settlement) and Rainham (Regna's settlement).

---

[1] A collection of historical records created during the reign of Alfred the Great of Wessex.
[2] Bede was an Anglo-Saxon monk writing in the monastery at Jarrow.

Later settlers penetrated further inland along the local rivers. From Rainham the Saxons would have been able to use the river Ingrebourne and the Ingrebourne Valley to access the hinterland and establish settlements in that wide valley as people had done before them through the Bronze Age and the Iron Age and Roman period, for example at the old LESSA Sports Ground, Rainham that was occupied from the late iron Age to the 5th or early 6th centuries. By a short overland extension from the head of the Ingrebourne valley the wooded hills of Brentwood and Havering could be reached, and the settlement at Havering also indicates an early settlement name ('Haefer's settlement' or otherwise 'goat pasture'), its Romano-British fields continued to be ploughed until the 7th century. In similar fashion Havering Ridge would also have been accessible from the Thames via the rivers Beam and Rom along the Dagenham Corridor where the multi-period Marks Warren Farm site (Tier 1 APA and surrounded by Tier 2 and 3 APA's) revealed a 5th century Saxon site with a building and cremation burials.

Place names Settlements here grew up and acquired Saxon place names like Langtons (long settlement), Ingrave (a settlement place) and Kenningtons (Cylia's settlement).

It is also thought that the Saxon use of *-ing* or *-ingas* at the end of place names might provide more clues about a place than the simple fact that it was someone's settlement, and scholars have put forward various theories as to the extra meaning (e.g. John McNeal Dodgson; Dr Margaret Gelling OBE; Susan Laflin *Do -ingas Place-Names Occur in Pairs?*, and others). For example the plural '-ingas' form of Havering (or Haueringas) may possibly indicate an administrative centre on the highland that together with the alternative name for Rainham (Roegingaham, meaning 'settlement of the ruling people') on the lowland, may give some clue to Saxon control of these villages and people movement and travel routes both along the Ingrebourne Valley and between area boundaries during the earliest period, and over time as trackways grew up as a network of paths between settlements. Others suggest that maybe *ingas* has a royal reference, or perhaps other meanings will come to light as these theories are studied further.

Despite being warriors with their fierce **Seax swords**, after which both their name and that of their national god Seaxneat are derived, the Saxons were mainly farming people. Although the newcomers and their pack animals could still use old Roman roads and tracks they also worked with the geography of the landscape in establishing settlements and creating new trackways. They left vital clues in local place names that describe the landscape – and hence its workability and accessibility through:

- the Saxon 'fanns' or fens of Bulphan (fortified marsh) that stretch down from the Brentwood Heights towards the Thames marshes;
- its hills like Horndon the 'horn-shaped' hill and Wocheduna or 'Wocca's hill' that is now Ockendon;
- river fords at Stifford and Stanford-le-Hope;
- the 'good lands' of Shenfield;
- 'herepaths' are military tracks such as Hare Street in Gidea Park;
- also Crau's or Crows ridge which is Cranham;
- Aveley means 'Aelfgyth's wood clearing or meadow' and Kenningtons is 'Cylia's settlement';
- Purfleet is 'Purta's stream or tidal inlet';

Chapter 8 Saxons & Danes

- 'Turroc' refers to the bottom of a boat and that describes the winding shape of the Thames at Thurrock;
- Warley may mean 'weir meadow' and here agricultural or industrial finds were made at Codham Hall dating to the 5th or early 6th century;
- 'ton' refers to a settlement or farmstead and gives us Suttons Farm (southern farm) and Langtons (long settlement);
- Ingrave (a settlement place)

Rulers and Religion Irrespective of legends that abound from the early days of Saxon England, in the early 6th century the Saxon **Escwine** is credited with unifying the kingdom of Essex from a number of sub-kingdoms or Saxon tribal groups from places along Thameside like Barking, Havering, and probably from Mucking to Vange as well as others further north. The kingdom also included much of Hertfordshire and Middlesex and for a time it extended into Kent and possibly Surrey, and incorporated both London and Colchester. So that by c. AD 575-600 Lundein had finally became the kingdom of the East Seaxe or *Essex* and ruled it seems by the overlord king of Kent and by Escwine, who claimed descent from the Saxon gods Seaxneat and Woden. Later Essex kings were of this dynasty but at times family members were co-regents.

In the late 6th century Escwine's son **Sledda** had married Ricula, daughter of the king of Kent and sister of Ethelbert the next king of Kent and overlord of Essex. Sledda's son **Saebert** followed his father as the next king of the East Saxons around the time in AD 604 that Bishop (later Saint) **Mellitus** arrived in the international trading centre of **Ludenwic**, which was then the capital of Essex (Bede: *Ecclesiastic History of the English People*). He was sent by **Augustine**, Archbishop of Britain to convert the Anglo-Saxons by integrating pagan and Christian rituals and customs. His patron King Ethelbert as overlord helped in the conversion of his nephew, King Saebert to Christianity and then built the first church dedicated to St. Paul in London. Saebert may have a more local connection to this area as by tradition he lived at Great Burstead and was buried there – although a medieval legend also has it that he and his queen were buried on the site of Westminster Abbey.

The early Christian princely burial at Prittlewell is most likely to have been that of **Seaxa** the brother of Saebert and the impressive artefacts from that burial can be seen at Southend Central Museum and indicate an extensive trade network abroad at that time. However, after Saebert's death in AD 616 whether for political or religious reasons, Mellitus was driven out and Essex and Kent reverted to paganism. Succeeding Ethelbert as bretwalda (overlord) the High King of nearby East Anglia was **Raedwald** (ruled c.617-625) and it's thought to be his burial that was discovered at **Sutton Hoo**. The fabulous burial artefacts are now in the British Museum and some can be seen at the National Trust Sutton Hoo visitor centre near Woodbridge in Suffolk.

At times during the 7th century the Jutes of Kent expanded across the Thames and at Gerpins Farm, Rainham many rich artefacts of the 6th and 7th centuries were excavated from a pagan Jutish cemetery of national importance at Gerpins Gravel Pit. The finds included swords, brooches, rings, spear heads and a magnificent pair of glass drinking horns – now in the British Museum with an exact copy on display in Havering museum and more of the objects are held at Valence House Museum.

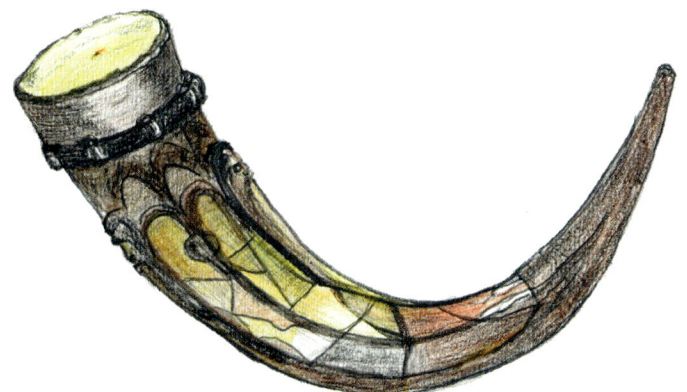

7th century, rare Saxon glass drinking horn found near Gerpins Farm, Rainham and now held by the British Museum

Although King Saebert's successor kings returned the East Saxons to the old religions his grandson **King Sigeberht the Good** invited **St. Cedd** to convert Essex back from paganism and in AD 653 Cedd landed at Othona Quay on the Essex coast. Here he founded a Celtic-style community at the monastery converted from the old Roman Saxon Shore fort of Othona, at modern Bradwell-on-Sea, and he built an Anglo-Celtic Cathedral at the fort gatehouse, the **Chapel of St. Peter-on-the-Wall** which can still be visited.

Travelling westwards along the Thames, Cedd landed at Tilbury (*Tilaburg* – 'Tilla's fortified place') where there was a crossing point to the Kent side. Here he founded a monastery at Tilaburg and passing through this area his name is commemorated in Chadwell St. Mary, Chafford Hundred itself, Chafford Heath and Chadwell Heath and he may have brought about the naming of Upminster ('an important church on high ground'). St. Cedd's Well (Thames Chase Walk no. 1)[3] survives at the un-Scheduled moated site beside North Ockendon church (grade I) in North Ockendon conservation area east of the M25 motorway that lies on the path heading towards the Chafford Hundred Gathering Ground.

St Cedd's Well (Photograph courtesy of Paul Sainsbury)

---

[3] Thames Chase Trust have produced a number of Walks leaflets, available on their website, crossing the LotF landscape linking people with local places and wildlife and with details of local heritage interest.

Chapter 8 Saxons & Danes

In AD 664 a great plague arrived killing King Swithelm of Essex and the following year the king of Mercia was able to establish himself as overlord of Essex. In AD 666, following St Cedd's work **Barking Abbey** was founded by St. Erkenwald, Bishop of London for his sister St. Ethelberga the first Abbess. This was a 'double house' for monks and nuns, and a missionary centre. It was a timber construction infilled with wattle and daub (thin wooden strips woven between upright wooden stakes and covered with a sticky mix of clay, straw and dung, dried and lime washed) and archaeological finds have revealed how affluent the occupants were (Valence House Museum). The Barking Abbey ruins are a SAM and a proposed Tier 1 APA near Barking town centre (proposed Tier 2 APA) and open to visitors.

A settlement was soon built around the Abbey and would have benefitted from the Abbey's spiritual, social and economic support. The Abbey would also have had an influence over local industry and commerce and importantly international relations. In c.687AD, about 20 years after the Abbey was established, **Sebba**, king of the East Saxon's gave Old Dagenham village (proposed Tier 2 APA) to Barking Abbey. As Daeccanham or Daecca's home, on the Wantz Stream a tributary of the river Beam, this is thought to be one of the earliest Saxon settlements in Essex and nearby at Dagenham Heathway a long abandoned ancient site seems to have been reoccupied for a time in the 6th century as one or more farmsteads.

In AD 693 Erkenwald died while on a visit to Barking Abbey. He was soon after declared a saint and his shrine at St. Paul's Cathedral became a place of pilgrimage. At the time the Catholic Church in Rome maintained a widespread cultural influence across western Europe through providing some education in Latin and in the art of writing and through the organisation of its network of Bishops.

Meanwhile, Ludenwic had quickly grown as an East Saxon metropolis of market and ship building just outside the abandoned Roman Londinium and achieved its peak during the late 7th and early 8th centuries. While locally, the Saxon king established a royal hunting lodge in the wooded hillside of Havering overlooking both Lundenwic and the passage of the river Thames – advantageous both for commerce and for any possible invasion threat. In time this hunting lodge grew into a **Royal Palace** for centuries serving many subsequent kings and queens of all England. With the palace came the establishment of the 10.36 ha. (40 sq. mile) Saxon royal manor of Havering enriching the economy of the local area as goods and services were supplied to the palace.

In c. AD 730 the western parts of Essex beyond the river Lea were lost to Mercia and London passed to Wessex in AD 825. By the mid 9th century Essex came under the control of Mercia, then of Wessex while being ruled from Kent.

Daily life Archaeological work between 1963 and 1997 in advance of gravel quarrying in Havering revealed ancient multi-period sites of occupation (*Archaeological landscapes of east London*, Museum of London, 2013) including a probable farmstead from the early to the middle Saxon periods, c AD 410-850, at Whitehall Woods and another at Hunts Hill Farm together with a cemetery that was probably early Saxon in date.

At Rainham an impressive number of **Grubenhaus** hut sites were revealed by Birkbeck College on high land overlooking the Ingrebourne valley and the Kent hills. More of these pit-houses have been located locally at North Stifford and another from the early Saxon period at Barringtons Farm, Orsett Cock (Milton, B., 1987 *Excavations at Barrington's Farm Essex Archaeology and History* 18).

Left: A reconstructed 'Grubenhaus' Saxon pit-house or store
Right: Cross section showing sunken floor

At the substantial Mucking settlement over 200 of these Anglo-Saxon sunken-floored pit-houses were located with 20 larger rectangular hall buildings some up to 15m long (50 ft), and two cemeteries including families and warriors buried with their weapons. Original finds from Mucking are held at the British Museum, while some replica pieces are at Thurrock Museum. The Mucking archeological finds are most important for the significant information they provide about everyday life and people.

A 6th century Saxon Grubenhaus pit hut was revealed at Chadwell St. Mary Primary School on Chadwell Hill overlooking the tidal marshes and the Thames crossing point at Tilbury to Higham in Kent. Pieces from a range of pots made from local clay were found and remnants from a loom, likely indicating sheep or goats were kept for their wool and meat, and their bones used to make combs and knives. Remains of seed included barley, wheat, oats, rye and pulses and apple and bramble.

Another pit-house was revealed at West Tilbury from c AD 600. A Scheduled Anglo-Saxon round barrow cemetery (SAM) lies south of the Orsett Cock in the vicinity of the A.13/A128 junction on a natural platform of the Thames terraces. Here a small Saxon settlement grew up surrounded by open countryside with at least 5 round barrow burials, now ring ditches, that form one of only a handful of confirmed Saxon round barrow groups in East Anglia (Essex County Council). Two graves were examined containing wooden coffins, one likely to have been that of a lady with a bag of seemingly magical or amuletic objects with a late 7th or even 8th century burial date suggested (Hedges, J.D. et al. 1985, *Journal of Medieval Archaeology* Vol 29, issue 1).

LANDFORM *'The Land of the Fanns is about land and water and the often shifting relationship between them'* **(TellTale working with the public 2018)**

Danish Vikings c. AD 830/878-1042 In due course the local Saxon people showed typically great resilience in defence against the Danish raiders and invaders and would no doubt have played their part within the local Essex militia as this landscape stood witness to the Danish attack forces along the Thames in the AD 800s and 900s. The Viking attacks on England had begun at the end of the 8th century. By c. AD 830 Danish Vikings were plundering England along the coast and rivers and the undefended Saxon settlements and farmsteads of Essex fell to the invaders – 'the Great Heathen Army' as they were described in the *Anglo Saxon Chronicle*.

Chapter 8 Saxons & Danes

The Vikings sacked Barking Abbey in AD 870, the buildings were destroyed and it is thought that the nuns fled to their London estates – later the parish of All Hallows Barking by the Tower. **Alfred the Great**, of 'burning cakes' fame, King of Wessex from AD 871-899, led the Saxon resistance. During his struggles Alfred hit back at the Danes on the Essex borders in AD 878 and achieved a negotiated peace restricting the invaders to eastern Britain between the rivers Thames and the Tees – the area of the **Danelaw** and so this area became part of the Kingdom of Guthrum.

Even after Alfred's peace with the Danish King Guthrum (baptismal name 'Athelstan') and with this area now subsumed into his kingdom, there is little memory of the Danes here in this southern area of the Danelaw by way of place names for example. Although, Wennington as the place of Wynne's people, 'whynne' means 'white' in Anglo-Saxon (Old English) and could perhaps be a reference to the fair haired and fair skinned Viking people. Mainly this north Thameside seems to have largely stood witness to the passing of the aggressive Danish vessels[4] along the river and the Essex coast.

In AD 886 Alfred successfully re-established English control of London, which then became **Lundenburg** (London Fort), and renewed its fortifications. By the late 8th and 9th centuries although Lundenburg remained an important settlement it had now begun to decline: 'London's position on the edge of both Danish and Anglo-Saxon kingdoms, which would have been a trade advantage during times of peace, instead accentuated problems ... thought to have been intrinsically linked to its failing transport links, whether due to the docks silting up or to Viking raids.' (*London Archaeologist* Winter 2019 Vol. 15).

> To the east the battle at the Danish fortified camp at **Benfleet** took place in AD 893 or 894, when the Danes were driven off by the Saxon's while Alfred was fighting with his main force near Exeter. For an element of surprise the smaller Saxon force with more local reinforcements from London and led by Alfred's son and son-in-law, are said to have approached on the landward side despite the thick forests and marshes. Haesten, the leader of the Danes was with his men plundering for supplies as the fort was stormed. The surviving Danes fled eastwards to Shoebury and built another fort there and King Alfred returned Heasten's captured wife and children to him.
>
> Never-the-less hostilities continued and in AD 895 the **Battle of the River Lea** took place west of here. The previous year the Danes had rowed up the Thames and built a fortress 20 miles up the Lea. This was attacked by a local force in AD 895 and in that autumn the king blockaded the river to prevent the Danish ships escaping and to stop the Danes from raiding local areas for the harvest. The Danes then abandoned the area and lost their boats to King Alfred who later used them against the Danes on the south coast.
>
> The Danish force was driven from Essex between AD 911 and 916 under **King Edward the Elder**, son of King Alfred, with the English gradually regaining control of the Danelaw.

---

[4] Try drawing a fleet of Viking longships in the Thames.

During this period Barking Abbey was rebuilt as a Benedictine nunnery under the patronage of the **Edgar the Peaceable** who was king from AD 955-979, and it became the second richest in the county with vast estates and revenues. The king appointed all abbesses, who were also Lords of the Manor, and chosen from highly educated women of noble rank and high status birth.

However, savage and unremitting Danish raids continued and in AD 991 after attacking Folkstone, Sandwich and Ipswich, the **Battle of Maldon** was fought by an Essex militia of East Saxons led by Ealdorman Byrhtnoth but he was killed and the battle lost to the Danes. The battle is celebrated in an Old English battle poem *The Battle of Maldon*. This area was one of the last in England to yield to the Danes, retreating eventually westwards – as the Celts had done long before them. **King Ethelred** was now on the throne and for the first time the Danes were bought off by payment of a tribute called Danegeld that became a land tax that would continue until the 12th century.

Despite that payment, three years later the **Norwegian King Olaf Tryggvason** led a force of 94 ships along the Thames, only to be repulsed at London Bridge. Peace came with the conversion of King Olaf and the **Danish King Harald Bluetooth** from paganism, but Harald's murderous successor son **Sweyn I Forkbeard** continued to wage war for 20 years. Finally, in 1013 for his last 5 weeks of life Sweyn became England's first Danish King. Sweyn's son **Canute the Great** eventually gained control of the Danelaw, and succeeded to all England in 1016 following the **Battle of Assandun** in Essex against **King Edmund Ironside**.

Now the English landscape developed with farms, villages and towns together with a feudal social system with its hierarchy of reciprocal obligations. According to legend it is King Canute who tried to turn back the tide at the Wash (in Norfolk) in an effort to show his flattering courtiers that he was not all-powerful. Canute died in 1035 and now began the High Medieval period or High Middle Ages of around 1001-1300 AD a time of warm climate with good harvests and prosperity when the peasant population grew.

Today in the county of Essex the **1st Battalion the Royal Anglian Regiment** is nicknamed *The Vikings* after the influence of the Nordic warriors on the eastern part of the Regimental area and in November 2012 hundreds of people lined the streets of Romford to welcome home The Vikings after a six-month tour of duty.

ECONOMY *'This area is justly famous for trade, commerce and industry: these have been important here for many centuries.'* (TellTale working with the public 2018)

The Saxons were great administrators and once they had settled here they gradually brought order back to the land and the people. By the 7th- 9th centuries Essex is recorded (in the *Tribal Hidage*) as containing 7,000 **hides**. Hides are thought to represent the amount of land needed to support a family however both the amount of land per hide and numbers of hides may be variable or inaccurate but generally it places Essex in a mid-range size of kingdoms.

By the 9th century Saxons had begun to introduce land division into **shires** administered by an Alderman (ealdorman) and a sheriff or shire-reeve in the shire court (Essex was one of 15 Danelaw shires). By the 10th century shires were subdivided into administrative areas called **Hundreds**. The origin of the term 'Hundreds' is obscure but may originally have referred to 100 hides or perhaps to an area that could provide 100 fighting men and they were named after their meeting-place or **moot**. The west of this area was allotted **Becontree** (*Beohha's tree*) Hundred that included the Royal manor of Havering, **Barstable** Hundred is to the east with **Chafford** in the centre ground.

The Ingrebourne Valley ('Inga's boundary') was first established as an administrative divide by the Saxons to form the boundary between Becontree Hundred and the Hundred of Chafford – and reflected in its name 'bourne' being the Saxon word for 'boundary'. Similarly the word 'Mardyke' means 'boundary ditch' – here between Chafford and Barstable Hundreds, previously under the Romano-British it may have been the Celta, (it has also been the Flete or 'small estuary' and the Brook). The Mardyke tributaries collect across the great landscape bowl anciently carved out by the Thames at that past time when it flowed westward here. Now only the Mardyke flows westwards before it finally joins the Thames as a tributary at Purfleet. The Saxon fanns or marshes of the Mardyke were first tamed by the Romans into fens and were worked by the fann men for generations. This great enigmatic bowl of low-lying landscape would one day become the heart of the 'Land of the Fanns' and the home of the Thames Chase Community Forest.

• • • • • • • • • • •

The Saxons had established moots in around the 7th – 9th centuries, these were gathering grounds for the democratic resolution of local disputes and so on and had local routes leading to them. The Chafford Hundred moot was at Chafford Heath (now Bush Farm) on the Rainham/Upminster borders and even today there are vestiges of numerous public footpaths all around that may give clues to ancient routes. An example may be The Chase that runs past Cranham Hall, which is an ancient route linking the northern-most tip of the Hundred at Great Warley to the gathering ground at Chafford Heath, and south it continues as a footpath or bridleway (f. p. 228) to join Ockendon Road and beyond as it once continued through Stubbers (now an Adventure Centre).

A little to the east of Chafford Heath, Havering footpaths 249, 251 and 231 via the churchyard of St. Mary Magdalene, North Ockendon continue to head directly east across the fields (fp272) where a route can be traced via Fen Lane, Doesgate Lane, Old Church Hill and Dry Street (or possibly Staneway) to the Langdon Hills and towards the meeting ground of Barstable Hundred (possibly meaning a battle axe and post or pillar marking the place) that is now in central Basildon (Beorhtels Hill) (N.B. on the Chapman Andree map of Essex 1777, Barstable Hall stood approximately where the Eastgate Shopping centre stands today). First named literally as the 'long hill' or 'Langdon' by the Saxons, the tall, hilly countryside range of Langdon Hills would have been a clear geographical vantage point for these people. From the Langdon hilltop the Saxon gathering ground at Chafford Heath could have been visible to the west and similarly no doubt the moot at Barstable to the east, likely giving a clear view of the central areas of both Chafford Hundred and Barstable Hundred.

Saxon routes from the outlying areas of Chafford Hundred to their gathering ground at Chafford Heath are now becoming clearer with these long distance linkages evident here both east to Barstable moot and beyond and also west to the Becontree gathering ground at Becontree Heath and on to join the old Roman road at Ilford (meaning 'ford over the trickling stream' – the river Hyle, now the Roding) and onward to the early 8th century trading town of Ludenwic. These possible Saxon routes incorporating Chafford Hundred gathering ground are an intangible heritage asset in this area and something that may benefit from further study to better understand the Saxon landscape here.

Following development after the Norman Conquest the shire moots went on eventually to form the basis for the representation of local people in Parliament's **House of Commons**. While the Saxon **Witan** ('meeting of wise men') was a council called by the king at his discretion and eventually went on to form the basis for the **House of Lords**. The earliest reference to a Witan here was called by Ethelberht, king of Kent in c.600 AD and overlord of Essex. From that time with the introduction of Christianity to the country, the church and state became intertwined in the Witan membership and its decisions and is reflected today in the **Lords Spiritual and Temporal** in the Upper House of Parliament (UK Birth of Parliament.uk).

The last of the Saxon Kings 1042-1066 Like the rest of Essex the people had remained ethnically and culturally Saxon in character under the rule of the Danish kings, and would no doubt have welcomed the return of a Saxon king, Canute's stepson the saintly **Edward II** the Confessor[5] who finally succeeded to the throne in 1042 following Canute's other sons. He is said to have spent much of his time seeking quiet at his palace at Havering that was conveniently built in a glade (or bower) on a high position in the forest and with direct overland access from the capital and with easy river access fairly close by.

Edward was particularly fond of his Saxon palace and there are many well related legends of his banishing nightingales from there for their incessant noise interrupting his prayers; also the story of the naming of the village through the return to the King of his generous gift of his ring to a poor man, by St. John the Evangelist with the words 'have-a-ring' and foretelling Edward's death. He is said to have died reportedly, although disputed, at his palace at Havering in 1066, and Havering palace is alleged to be depicted in the Bayeux Tapestry. Historically the districts all around provided goods and services to the royal palace at Havering and remnants of medieval tracks can still be discerned across the landscape (see Chapter 9).

The Havering Ring is on display at the British Museum. This is a 4th century, Romano-British gold finger-ring with an onyx paste engraving of the mythological figures of Bellerophon riding the winged horse Pegasus and slaying the fire-breathing, havoc-making monster Chimaera.

💡 *Perhaps a metaphor for how the Romans viewed their conquest of Britain?*

Photo © The Trustees of the British Museum

---

[5] *Confessor* reflects King Edward's reputation as being saintly but one who did not suffer martyrdom

Elsewhere, at Horndon-on-the-Hill the village and conservation area is atop the hill half way between Orsett and Langdon Hills. The village is of Saxon origin possibly with an 11th century Saxon mint and defended enclosure sited off the main north/south route from Brentwood to Tilbury dock and ferry. Nearby at Hangman's Wood (between Orsett Heath and Grays) some 70 medieval chalk and flint mineshafts were excavated, and it is said to be the most extensive and best preserved surviving Denehole site in the United Kingdom (Essex Field Club) and a biological SSSI for its bat colony.

Following the death of King Edward the successor controversially chosen was Harold Godwinson Earl of Essex whose name is recorded from the 13th century in the king's Manor as Harold Wood. He became King Harold II and last of the Saxon Kings of England. Only eight months later Harold marched north from London to successfully repulse an invasion by his rival Norwegian Viking claimant, then immediately back south again passing through London to finally lose his throne to William and the Norman Conquest at Hastings only two weeks later.

Places to visit near and far:
- St. Cedds Well
- Southend Museum for the Prittlewell Prince
- Chapel of St. Peter-on-the-Wall, Bradwell-on-Sea, Essex – originally constructed as an Anglo-Celtic church for the East Saxons by St. Cedd in AD 654 from the ruins of the abandoned Roman fort of Othona on the 'Saxon shore'
- St. Andrews church, Greensted, nr Chipping Ongar
- Barking Abbey ruins, originally built c. AD 666 and one of the most important nunneries in the country, and from which William the Conqueror very briefly (6 days) administered the country following his invasion. Barking Abbey lands extended well into this landscape.
- Sutton Hoo, near Woodbridge, Suffolk (National Trust property)
- An Anglo-Saxon village, reconstructed on its original site at West Stow Country Park near Bury St. Edmunds is open for visitors to explore
- The Viking city of Jorvik has been rebuilt on its original site for visitors as the Jorvik Viking Centre in York
- The British Museum holds a Viking collection and St. Edward the Confessor's ring and the Saxon glass drinking horns are held there (not necessarily on display)
- Local museums:
  - Valence House Museum, Becontree Avenue, Dagenham
  - Havering Museum, High Street, Romford
  - Thurrock Museum, Thameside Complex, Grays

Ideas for future projects:

- A study of Saxon organisation and administration of this area
- A study of Saxon routes across this landscape in particular looking at the influence of the Saxon moot/meeting or gathering grounds of the Hundreds at Becontree Heath, at Chafford Heath, Upminster and Barstable in Basildon, as well as the influence of the royal Palace and royal Manor of Havering
- A study of King Edward the Confessor's life and legends in relation to this area and the Saxon Royal Palace of Havering see also for example *Life of St. Edward the Confessor* by St. Aelred of Rievaulx trans. by Fr Jerome Bertram, pub. The Saint Austin Press 1997
- A study of the role of the Jutes in this landscape and any relationship with the 'lost' north Kent Jutes
- Looking for Havering Palace – working with the Havering-atte-Bower Conservation Society (HABCOS) and also note that a student report prepared for English Heritage (now Historic England) may offer some help and may be obtainable from Havering Local Studies Library. The site is an Archaeological Priority Area (APA) – the APA and APZ map of Havering Borough can been viewed on Havering's Heritage Supplementary Planning Document (SPD) 2011, or through Historic England, both on-line. This work became overdue for review in 2021 and may be prepared in connection with Havering's latest revised Local Plan

References for further research:

More information on this historical period may be found through:

- See Section C: History Introduction, p. 99
- The Council for British Archaeology, CBA-London branch (CBA-L) and CBA East
- Ancient Monuments Society (AMS) now Historic Buildings and Places
- Historic England GLAAS
- Museum Crush is part of a charity aiming to bring arts and heritage organisations closer to audiences, and includes on their website an introduction to Viking museums and collections

Further Reading:

- Bertram, Fr Jerome (1997) *Life of St. Edward the Confessor by St. Aelfred of Rievaulx* trans. pub. The Saint Austin Press
- Evison, Vera I. (1955) F.S.A., *Anglo Saxon finds near Rainham, Essex, with a Study of Glass Drinking-horns* article pub. Soc. of Antiquaries
- Historic England (reissued 2018) *Pre-industrial Roads, Trackways and Canals*

Chapter 9
Norman & Plantagenet
1066 – 1485

Monarchs: 'Willie, Willie, Henry, Steve...'

NATIONAL CURRICULUM **Key Stage 3 hints for the Middle and Late Medieval Periods**

This was the time of the Norman and the Plantagenet ruling dynasties in medieval Britain from 1066-1485. From the time of the Norman Conquest this marks the struggle between church and state with the importance of religion and the development of Christendom and the ensuing Crusades, the signing of the Magna Carta in 1215 and the emergence of Parliament with its promise of democracy. To local people matters of concern involved society and religion in daily life in the parishes, and abbeys; also, feudalism and the economy in farming, trade and towns especially the wool trade; and culture in matters of art, architecture and literature, were all important. The country as a whole and local people alike had to wrestle with the Black Death plague in 1348 and again in 1361 and its social and economic impact that led to the Peasants Revolt in 1381, and later the Hundred Years War from 1337-1453 and finally the Wars of the Roses from 1455-1485.

Introduction The Saxon **Early Medieval period** (Early Middle Ages) now moved into the **High Medieval period** (High Middle Ages) that was beginning to develop between around AD 1000-1300. This was a time of warm climate with good harvests and prosperity when the peasant population grew, however their increased numbers and strength would become challenging to the new Norman authority that kept the people ruthlessly under control. The following **Late Medieval period** (Late Middle Ages) saw the development of cultural influences in education, legislation, religion and social institutions that would still be of influence today. However, at the time, the period also saw the population decimated through famine, plague, wars and economic stagnation and ended with the Wars of the Roses and the establishment of the Tudor royal dynasty in 1485 that heralded the **Early Modern period**.

Surprise *'The Land of the Fanns is an intricate landscape, full of surprises and 'hidden gems' and rewards exploring.'* (TellTale working with the public 2018)

Normans 1066-1154 Remarkable as it may seem, once **William of Normandy**, the Conqueror, and his army had battled their way into Britain defeating **King Harold II** (Godwinson) on the south coast famously near Hastings, he did not make straight for the capital at London to set up the royal court but instead came to this area and Barking Abbey. Here the Abbess was Elfgiva sister to King Harold, and who may also be depicted on the **Bayeux Tapestry**.

The Abbess received the Conqueror who remained at the Abbey for the first six days of his rule. William issued a royal charter confirming Elfgiva's control of the abbey and she emerged as one of the few Saxon women who managed to retain her lands after the Conquest. In fact, William ruled England from Barking Abbey during those first few days and following his coronation at Westminster Abbey on Christmas Day he returned to the abbey for the latter part of 1066 and the New Year. Here he received the surrender of the two Saxon Earls brothers-in-law to the defeated Harold, and other lords (Valance House Collections).

All of these things would no doubt have impacted on the people of this area who may have played a peripheral role during William's time there and likely have benefitted from a continuation of regal influence from a Saxon Abbess who was also Lord of the Manor. The Abbess was responsible for the spiritual care of local people and the practical care of the monastery estates. Elfgiva was a prudent manager who had new shrines to her predecessors built at the Abbey, that would put them on the road to sainthood and thereby increase prestige and attract pilgrims and bring in revenues to the Abbey. Indeed, over the next 20 years Barking went on to become a large and wealthy settlement (Domesday record) extending to Collier Row and in time the Abbey lands expanded into Chafford Hundred at Rainham and to the Abbey infirmary at Warley.

Migration *'This is a crossroads landscape: because of its location on the Thames ... people have always travelled into, through and away from this area.'*
(TellTale working with the public 2018)

Although William had good claim to inherit the English throne, he owed his battle success to the Norman barons who were his equals in France. Under the Norman **feudal system**, the King owned everything, renting out manor estates to the Barons in return for the security of their fealty (support); the Barons granted (leased) the land to the knights who provided military service and who in turn leased to the local peasant workforce (serfs) who produced the food and provided services when required. England was soon divided out between William and those to whom he owed allegiance including the Roman Catholic Church that was now the religion of Europe.

Castles In 1078 William began building the **Tower of London**, just some 27 km (17 or 18 miles) from here, the first stone 'keep' in England, one that would display Norman domination and permanence. For the same reasons other keeps, or castles, protected by knights and soldiers, were later built elsewhere by the new landholders and their successors.

Artist's impression of a motte and bailey castle

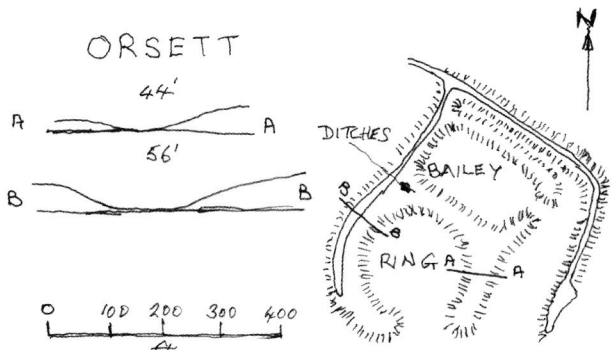

Plan of Orsett castle – the Ring is c.60m (200ft) across (Original source Wilson, Imperial Gazetteer, 1870-72)

Chapter 9 Norman & Plantagenet

The Normans brought the fortified motte-and-bailey castle design to England. The **motte** was a large hill built up of earth with a keep (a lookout) constructed on top and surrounded by a large protective palisade fence. The earliest keeps were built of timber for speed and only later constructed in stone – which is a scarce material in this area. The **bailey** was a large open area in front of the hill where people lived and kept animals and beyond this a large ditch or moat would be dug all around, with a drawbridge for access to the bailey and a wooden bridge from the bailey for access to the motte.

In the Hundred of Chafford only the earth works survive to the Norman motte and bailey castle at Orsett that was owned by the Bishops of London and known as 'Bishop Bonner's Palace' (SAM) after the infamous 16th century Edmund Bonner, Bishop of London (see Chapter 10) during the rule of Queen Mary I, who was the last of the Bishops of London to hold the land. The earthworks similarly survive at Ongar Castle (mid 12th century, SAM) that was built by Sir Richard de Lucy, High Sherriff of Essex and here the village grew up, as was common, on the approach to the castle for both protection and opportunity for trade.[1]

Domesday Record In 1086, William ordered an account of all the land, its value and who was responsible or held it both prior to the Conquest and after so that he could impose accurate taxation. The old Danegeld was still used as a land tax until the reign of Henry II and was last recorded in 1161-2. Essex was surveyed during the early stages and is recorded in great detail in the **'Little Domesday Book'** that includes careful and informative entries of both the old Saxon Hundreds and the Norman manors that make up this landscape. The previous Saxon landholdings were largely confirmed as Norman manors and the Saxon ecclesiastical parishes also often follow the long, narrow form of precedent set by the Saxon Hundreds. The population in England by then was estimated at 1.2-1.5 million and there were only 18 towns with a population of over 2,000, the only one near to here being London one of the two largest.

The Domesday record did not include London but locally the record is excellent and confirms that William kept the royal manor of Havering for himself and other land at North and South Ockendon and Little Thurrock and also in Childerditch that had formerly belonged to the Saxon Queen Edith, wife of King Edward the Confessor. The Saxon royal hunting lodge stood on the forested Havering Ridge only 32 km (20 miles) from London and by the early 12th century a park was in existence with the house (VCH).

At 110 households Grays and West Thurrock was very large and had five entries, the largest having 17 villagers, 45 smallholders and 8 slaves and 16 ha (40 acres) of meadow, pasture for 500 sheep, woodland sufficient for 200 pigs and two fisheries, it was held by Robert, Count of Eu – the place in France where William the Conqueror had been married at the castle chapel.

As a sample of other landholdings and landholders:
- the king's half-brother Bishop Odo held land at Chadwell, Rainham, Upminster, Cranham (Bishops Ockendon), Aveley, Thornden (Horndon), Ingrave, Stifford, Thurrock, Dunton and Barstable. It was Odo who instigated the making of the Bayeux Tapestry which some say includes a picture of the palace of Havering;

---

 [1] Working in a group, plan a medieval pageant and consider what life was like in a castle during the period 1066-1485.

- Barking Abbey continued to hold 'one of the most populous manors in Essex' (Oxley 1966; Williams & Martin 2002) Barking manor, which included Dagenham, and also held Bulphan and land at Great and Little Warley;
- Westminster Abbey continued to hold Wennington;
- the Canons of Waltham Abbey continued to hold land at South Weald;
- the Bishop of London held Laindon and continued to hold Orsett along with Count Eustace II of Boulogne – who also held Shenfield and who may have been the patron of the Bayeux Tapestry;
- amongst several other high-ranking landholders, Swein of Essex was related to both King Edward and to King William and he held Basildon and Langdon and land at other places including Horndon-on-the-Hill and Tilbury and the Early Norman Rayleigh Castle (SAM) and he was a Tenant-in-Chief at Kenningtons.

Manors The Normans looked down on the seemingly inferior Saxons who managed to retain their own culture, but Norman French became the language of the elite. The manors were generally self-sufficient agricultural estates that also had to produce a cash crop for the market. They would have a manor house for the Lord of the Manor who set local taxes, minted money and administered justice from the manorial court; the land would include arable land, meadows, woods, orchards and ponds. It was also likely to contain glebe land to support the local church and the priest, who would likely be uneducated and would be responsible both for preaching and for looking after the village sick; there would also probably be a mill, a bakery and a blacksmith, for example.

However, **peasants** (also known as serfs or villains) were without rights, they were tenant farmers who typically lived in single-roomed buildings with a yard and vegetable garden and had to work for the lord of the manor and for the knights as well as providing for themselves, they had to attend church on Sundays and were not allowed to leave their manor.

Examples of peasants clothing and the more refined noble men and women during the Early Medieval period

Chapter 9 Norman & Plantagenet

Restoration work on Pages Farmhouse (grade II) in Harold Wood revealed that the original 13th century frame survives within the present house; Kenningtons in Aveley is a late 13th century house (grade II*) and at Wrightsbridge restoration work found that Angel Cottages (grade II) were originally a 14th century hall house (a single-roomed, one and a half story, timber-framed dwelling); Bretts on Romford Road, Aveley is a late 14th or early 15th century (grade II* RCHM 5) with a Tudor barn (grade II).

Many local settlements grew from the old Saxon/Norman manors and the names of Norman landholders at times became place names of local estates including the 12th century Bretons in South Hornchurch; Gaynes of Upminster from the de Engaine family originally coming from Engen near Boulogne; Gerpins from the 13th century Jarpenville family of Gerpenville on the Seine; and the place name of Grays which is of Norman French origin came from Henry de Grai (Henry de Grey) who was granted the manor of Grays Thurrock in 1195 by King Richard I.

Landform *'The Land of the Fanns is about land and water and the often shifting relationship between them'* **(TellTale working with the public 2018)**

The Saxon administrative divide of the Ingrebourne River Valley was reinforced by the Normans who confirmed the large royal manor in Becontree Hundred forming the western side with several smaller manors along the eastern side. Eventually the idea of an east/west divide in this area became embedded and naturally reinforced perceptions when establishing the modern boundary between the outer spread of London from Essex County.

Historically in the Hundred of Chafford, much of the eastern part of the Ingrebourne Valley as far north as South Weald is associated with the **Abbotts of Waltham** and, like the Barons the church leaders were wealthy and powerful people. The manor of Upminster Hall had been granted to Waltham Abbey by Earl Harold in 1062 but after the defeat of Harold at Hastings it became **'Mannes Land'** or land for the use of all, and in 1191 Waltham Abbey was fined by King Richard the Lionheart for enclosing 104 acres of this 'waste land' that later shrunk over time and became Tylers Common – from 'Tigelhurst' – woodland where tiles were made. Here the monks built Upminster Hall (15th – 16th century and grade II*) originally as a hunting lodge for themselves, now a Golf Club house. Adjoining Upminster Hall is a grange barn, now the Upminster 'Tithe' Barn Museum of Nostalgia, erected c.1450 (SAM) where Cecil A. Hewett first identified the unusual *reversed assembly* timber building form he also identified in the 13th century tower of St. Lawrence church, Upminster (grade I) (Hewett, Cecil A., 1969 *The Development of Carpentry 1200-1700: an Essex Study*).

As well as building the hunting lodge and great barn in Upminster the Abbotts are also associated with Great Tomkyns house (grade II*) on a moated site a little to the north where they built a small aisled barn (grade II) in the 13th century by the same unusual 'reversed assembly' method. Here they would have been neighbours of the king at Havering Palace just across the Valley - and rivalling the Abbess of Barking whose land adjoined the king's land to the west in Collier Row.

The river Ingrebourne remained navigable along the valley until at least the 13th century when Hornchurch village still had its own hythe (landing place). Close by in 1159 the foreign **Hornchurch Priory** ('Hospice of St. Nicholas and St. Bernard of Montjoux in Savoy') had been founded by Henry II for religious and political reasons - probably to gain an alliance against France but effectively creating a manor within the manor. St. Andrews church was given to the Priory and it's here in 1938 that workman uncovered a treasure trove of some 448 silver coins from the reign of Henry III. Prof Ged Martin intriguingly attributes this to a possible theft from within the Priory during the winter of 1260-1 (*Romford Recorder* 2017). Other land was endowed for Priory support including Newbury in Havering and Suttons Farm and farmland - that are now part of Hornchurch Country Park.

At Suttons the meandering Gaynes and Hacton Parkways lie mid-way along the Ingrebourne Valley stretching south to Rainham (see Thames Chase Walk no.5) where Dovers moat survives on the king's manor side. From Dovers, further along the edge of the Thames marshes the low gravel ridge running west to east from Dagenham and Rainham continues past the 17th century South Hall Farm (grade II) and bridge that are reminders of the Norman manor of South Hall, and on to the tiny Wennington village with its medieval church (grade II*). The modern A13 road is partially diverted across the Rainham, Aveley and West Thurrock Marshes, an open, flat expansive area of reclaimed medieval grazing marsh divided by ditches and characterising the area that from prehistoric times were managed for fishing and fowling, then as reed beds and for sheep and cattle grazing. Here Section 24 of the London Loop continues along Thameside and on the way, walkers are able to look down on either side of the path both over the marshes of the RSPB Reserve and at the Thames, its medieval sea wall and its foreshore that from those times attempts have been made to defend London from inundations from the tidal river.

Churches In this area east of the Ingrebourne, numerous **Norman parish churches** survive built by individual Lords of the Manors so that Hornchurch Church was at first the only one, other than the private palace chapels, within the huge royal manor of Havering, but smaller manors would have their own like the Minster church at Upminster in Chafford Hundred. As with the later castle keeps Medieval churches were also built of stone and commonly in this area being of flint with Kentish ragstone rubble and Reigate stone for more detailed work, such as the 12th-14th century church of St. Mary the Virgin, North Stifford (grade I) that lies on an ancient east/west route with the manor house once standing nearby in the vicinity of the early 19th century Stifford Clays Farmhouse (grade II).

The round-towered church of St. Nicholas, South Ockendon (grade I)

South Ockendon village has an unusual **round towered church** (grade I) dating from the 12th century, the round tower is 13th century with the main body of the church 15th century. The reason for round towers is unclear but it is said to be a Saxon not Norman building technique that hung on into the Norman period in outlying areas and it has been suggested that the round shape is easier to construct when building in flint (Hart, Stephen, 2003 *The Round Tower Churches of England*).

North Ockendon is a two-centred historic settlement still linked across the fields by a public footpath (fp272), now the North Ockendon Conservation Area it has Saxon origins but is centred on the 12th century medieval Grade I listed church and a fine moat (RCHM2) and a cluster of later listed and other historic buildings and can be reached from the Thames Chase Visitor Centre Walk No.1.

Dating from the 12th century, St. Mary Magdalene Church, North Ockendon (grade I) contains beautiful monuments, including a large alabaster tomb-chest unusual as the tester is unsupported by columns. The path on the left (beside St. Cedd's well), through the churchyard led directly west to the Saxon meeting ground nearby at Chafford Heath; eastwards it can be traced to the Langdon Hills and towards the Barstable Hundred meeting ground

At West Thurrock the medieval church of St Clements (Grade I) is strikingly flint-faced in bands, and close by on a promontory of the marshes was the original 11th century West Thurrock manor house where it could control the Thames ferry to Greenhithe. Here the 14th century Stonehouse (SAM) was located in 2002 during archaeological excavations for the CTRL (High Speed 1) and, unusually for a rural, domestic building in this area also constructed as its name suggests, in stone.

In Barstable Hundred, Bulphan village also has a medieval origin, with late medieval listed buildings surviving at the Church of St. Mary (grade I) and the Old Plough House (grade II*) that was formerly Appletons Farm.

Moated sites In time wealthier people felt the need for a means to defend their homes in something of the way of castles and there are a significant number of medieval moated sites across the Land of the Fanns area. In Becontree Hundred there were 13 manors across Barking and Dagenham most of which had a moated site including at Frizlands Lane and Sedgemoor Drive, Dagenham; the moat at Valence House is thought to date from the 1200s. From the early 14th century there were hamlets grown up at Becontree and Chadwell Heaths – where the surviving but unscheduled moated site of

Marks Manor dates from the 14th century. In Havering Manor, the Cockerels moated site in Dagnam Park, Harold Hill is a SAM (LBH) of 13th century date. In Chafford Hundred, South Ockendon moat is a SAM but North Ockendon moat is unscheduled (RCHM2) and the mid 12th century - c. early 14th century moated enclosure off Launders Lane near Wennington, is thought to be of Launders Manor (MOL Archaeology 2013, *Archaeological Landscapes of East London*).

Dispersed moated sites continue across the central plane of the Land of the Fanns area in Barstable Hundred. Records indicate that virtually all parts of this landscape that was not fanns or marsh supported a moated site, many of which remain unscheduled but often referenced in the Victoria Country Histories (VCH) or the Royal Commission on Historic Monuments of England (RCHME) volumes.

Crusades & Civil War In the wider area, from 1095 for several hundred years of the medieval period the Crusades were a series of religious wars taking place in the Middle East, but they were also about politics and culture. Through them new knowledge in science and medicine was brought to Europe, there were developments in castle design, trade was stimulated, and the Arabic numbering system was spread, but thousands of lives were savagely lost.

These invasions occurred first sanctioned by the Church and led by European knights and nobles and with the founding of various religious military orders including the Knights Hospitallers from 1113 to aid sick or injured pilgrims and the Knights Templar established c.1119 to protect holy sites and pilgrims. Locally the Knights Templar owned a water mill where the river Mardyke enters the River Thames at Purfleet through the Mardyke Canal lock. They also held land at places like Rainham and Berwick manors, later taken back by the king when the Templers were disbanded in 1312 with the land handed over to the Knights Hospitallers.

Knights Templar & Knight Hospitallers both had medieval origins

There was a hiatus across the country between 1135-1153 during the civil war, (which the Victorians later referred to as **the 'Anarchy'**), between the cousins Stephen of Blois and the legitimate heir the Empress Matilda, never queen but instead titled *Lady of the English*. This brought a widespread breakdown of law and order in the land. This area in the south east was for King Stephen, while the Empress had control of south-west England and the Thames Valley and with events taking place mainly in the West Country. Peace came finally with the naming of Matilda's son Henry as Stephen's heir. At one time King Stephen with his Queen and whole court visited Barking Abbey for a period of several days and granted Becontree and Barstable Hundreds to the Abbey. Like his predecessor Henry I, King Stephen also appointed his wife Abbess of Barking, and later on illegitimate daughters of both Henry II and King John were made Abbess there.

Both Stephen and King Henry II in turn sent fighters to the Crusades but with limited impact. It was Henry's second son, **King Richard the Lionheart** who himself fought in the Crusades and brought fame and fable to England during the Third Crusade with tales of chivalrous Knights, 'a veray parfit, gentil knight' as Geoffrey Chaucer puts it in his *The Knights Tale,* and stories of the fabled Robin Hood of Nottingham, both dating from the late 14th century. By the end of the Third Crusade in 1192 the rights had been won for pilgrimages to again be made to the city of Jerusalem.

Economy *'This area is justly famous for trade, commerce and industry: these have been important here for many centuries.'* **(TellTale working with the public 2018)**

'...Henry II, Dick, John, Henry III. One, two, three Neds, Richard two...'

Plantagenets 1154 – 1485 Although still medieval kings and descendants of the Conqueror, England's kings from Henry II to Richard III adopted the dynastic name of Plantagenet, which distinguished them from the French branch of the (Angevine) dynasty. Under the Plantagenet kings England transformed back into an independent Kingdom and King John set in train the founding of English democracy in 1215 by signing the **Magna Carta** to appease the old rights descending with the Norman Baronial families and limiting the power of the monarch.

Pilgrimages King Henry II it seems was fond of this area visiting his palace at Havering on some twenty or so occasions and having improvements and repairs carried out. However, it is the murder of **St. Thomas Beckett**, Archbishop of Canterbury late in December 1170 during his reign, which had a profound social and economic impact on this area both through the lucrative 13th century pilgrimage routes that grew up across this landscape and also through the social support provided to people here by the monks of Lesnes Abbey in Kent:

> Two of the knights involved in the murder owned land here, one became the manor of Bretts in Kenningtons, the other, Sir Reginald Fitzurse was Lord of the Manor of North Ockendon, the knight who smote the first blow. King Henry II is said to have undertaken great penance for the unintended murder of his Archbishop and friend, he famously walked in sack cloth and ashes to the shrine at Canterbury Cathedral. He also installed Mary Beckett sister to Thomas, as the Abbess of Barking as an apology for the murder and he had intended to take part in the 3rd Crusade in penance, but he died the year the Crusade began so that was left to the new King Richard.

The murder had led to Becket's sainthood and pilgrimages to the shrine of St. Thomas Becket began soon after his death. Beautiful stained-glass windows depicting the pilgrims were already installed into the Cathedral within 20 years (Canterbury Cathedral 2018) and his tomb at Canterbury became the most popular shrine for pilgrims in England. **Chaucer** evocatively describes such pilgrimages across north Kent in his **'Canterbury Tales'** some 200 years later (between 1387 and 1400) and gives an idea of those taking place across this landscape at the time that did not come to an end until King Henry VIII banned pilgrimages in 1538.

As his Chief Justiciar (chief advisor) Sir Richard de Lucy also felt some responsibility for the murder. De Lucy's penance was to found **Lesnes Abbey** at Erith together with satellite churches including Rainham parish church (grade I). This building is remarkable for being a surviving Norman church erected complete and of a piece and with quality stone carved decoration. The monks from Lesnes set up a ferry across the Thames to a hamlet of Rainham Ferry on Rainham marshes to conduct church services and minister to the people at Rainham. Today Rainham is on the London Loop and linked to Thames Chase Walk no.5 which also takes in Berwick Glades to Abbey Wood in Rainham, named for its association with Barking Abbey and later its ownership by Lesnes Abbey.

• • • • • • • • • • •

During the latter 14th century, the king's master mason was **Henry Yevele**, who owned land at Wennington. During 1377-1400 Yevele rebuilt the nave where Becket had been murdered in Canterbury Cathedral in the new Perpendicular gothic style. His name is thought to be linked with Aveley where there is a moated manor house site (SAM), and the tithes from the medieval church of St. Michael went to endow Lesnes Abbey. The church is itself a grade I listed building, with its earliest fabric dating from c.1120 its origins were celebrated at its's 900th anniversary in 2020.

• • • • • • • • • • •

The pilgrim routes that grew up between Canterbury and York passed through this area resulting in a significant pilgrimage impact here from around 1220 during the reign of Henry III at a time when the Plantagenet kings were beginning to consider themselves more English than French. Here as the pilgrims moved southwards down through this landscape our communities today tell us that: from the 'Top of Folkes Lane, the view of the intervening area towards London would have looked similar in medieval times'.

Clues to pilgrim routes are recorded in local place names across the Brentwood Heights as at Pilgrims Hatch ('gate') and St. Thomas a 'Becket Chapel (SAM) that was founded in c.1221 in the hamlet of Brentwood as a chapel of ease to South Weald church. Below South Weald, Brook Street was originally Sideburgbroc where the leper hospital was founded in 1201, from here Dark Lane (Protected Lane) takes the traveller to Great Warley where five ancient roads meet and open out onto the heart of the village. This is a conservation area around The Green surrounded by historic and listed buildings of Group Value, in a rural setting. Wallets (grade II) on The Green by the War Memorial is stationed at the entrance to the pilgrim route as it descends along Hole Farm Lane down to the marshes and where tradition says the pilgrims left their wallets for safe keeping while crossing the dangerous marshes. This route descends via the manor of Warley Franks (grade II listed) and moated site (Thames Chase Walk no.3) to Puddle Dock on the marsh edge near the old Bell river (now all but lost except for the ditch line and brick bridgeworks surviving beneath the ground surface at the listed Clockhouse in Upminster – Clockhouse photograph in Chapter 13).

Pilgrims needed local, hardy fann men to guide them across the marshes, work which supplemented their income from agriculture, fishing and fowling. Pilgrims crossed the Mardyke river at Stifford Bridge where above the north bank of the Mardyke, Low Well Wood, Millard's Garden and Brannett's Wood cushion the riverside edge and are individually separated by medieval wood banks which are tree-topped earth mounds. Pilgrims travelled on to Grays town to the Thames ferries from places like Grays, West Thurrock, Purfleet, Rainham and Tilbury (that had earlier been a fording place) across to Kent as they travelled southeast to Becket's shrine at Canterbury.

Another route appears from Brentwood to Tilbury via Ingrave and Herongate with its 13th century moated site at Heron Hall (SAM), past Horndon-on-the-Hill to Grays where the 1170 church of St. Mary (grade II*) in Dock Rd, Little Thurrock is one of the pilgrim churches (Thurrock Local History Society). At Canterbury pilgrims were given a metal badge token stamped with the symbol of the shrine and one has been recovered, along with various other artefacts from close by Stifford Bridge. These copious travelers would have stimulated the local economy and established better links with the wider world including the spread of news and gossip. Other pilgrims travelled northwards through here heading for York and the old Pilgrim routes remain an intangible heritage asset in the area.

Forest Law William the Conqueror had introduced restrictive Forest Law with harsh punishments for lawbreakers to protect game animals and their habitat, and he determined that wild animals such as deer and boar belonged to him. Although at the time of the Domesday Survey only about a fifth of Essex was wooded by 1100 William had designated all the land, other than Thameside and the coastline, to be under Forest Law whether wooded or not and including settlements and fields, so that the land was more like a modern game reserve with the king having the hunting rights. Later King Stephen relaxed those laws, but his successor, Henry II, reinstated stricter controls.

By the 13th century the **Royal Forest of Essex** was disestablished and reduced to only the more wooded areas including Waltham Forest that is made up of Epping Forest and Hainault Forest that we know today. By this time King Henry III was on the throne (reigned from 1216-1272) and making use of Havering Palace in the forest, in fact he adopted Edward the Confessor as his patron saint. In around 1215 records show that he provided for the upkeep of the Park and frequently arranged for building repairs including the construction of a bath for the king. The extensive building works undertaken at the Palace during that century enabled many future monarchs to stay there.

In 1262 Henry granted the palace to his queen and it became a favoured residence which from that time until the Tudor period usually belonged to the queen consort or the dowager (queen mother). By 1267 the Palace and park, village, forest with woodland, pastures and marshes of some 6,500 ha (16,000 acres) were all part of the **queen's dower property** and by 1272 Havering had acquired its 'atte Bower' appellation from *ladies chamber* or an *arbour*.

Food & Products Elsewhere across the area, Barking Abbey also remained an important economic driver with its wealthy market town and fishing industry supplying the London trade. The Abbey appears to have had its own water mill, and the Abbess had control of the grinding of wheat for flour across its area. Mills were important to the economy and as Marks Manor was outside of the control of Barking Abbey it was permitted to have its own windmill during the medieval period and with a 'Newemylle' recorded in 1396 (within an APA). The large number of medieval mills in that area indicates how important **flour production** was to the economy and is evidence of the wealth of a manor.

Otherwise beyond Barking and Dagenham village and the gravel pit at Church Lane (NMR no. 1255101), the thirteen manors across Barking and Dagenham were mainly in **pastoral agricultural use** and sparsely populated. Similarly, from the 12th – 14th centuries land around the farmstead at Hunts Hill, near Aveley from Rainham to North Ockendon was also mainly open fields of mixed farming probably producing grain for the London market, in fact Rainham was supplying grain, beans and hay to St. Bartholomew's hospital in London in c.1200. Creeks like those at Rainham and Wennington were outlets for local produce and by this time many types of vessels were occupied on the Thames (Historic England *Ships and Boats: Prehistory to 1840*).

West Thurrock manor house on the Purfleet to Grays road along the junction of the marshes and uplands, had a route for the manor stock out into the marshes. These were used for grazing mainly sheep and later cattle and increasingly produced hay as the marshes were reclaimed. Pig husbandry took place on the inland wooded areas although they were also being cleared. In North Ockendon for example by the early 14th century only 10 acres of woodland remained. Close to All Saints church, Langdon Hills where the original 14th century church stood with its village, long deserted, the oddly shaped fields on the escarpment above the river Thames, are thought to be from piecemeal assarting (grubbing out) woodland to create fields.

In the royal manor, Hornchurch was a centre for the **leather industry** and presumably exporting by river from Hornchurch hythe. In the 13th century the main street was called Pallestrate (Pell Street) after the pelt-mongers or skinners there (Muilman: *History of Essex*), behind were the lime kilns. Romford was a hamlet of Hornchurch and closer to Oldchurch at first where there was a chapel of ease (the 'old church') to St. Andrews, Hornchurch. Romford had a cloth working industry in the 13th century when it became more developed with the king granting a weekly market in 1247 and an annual fair in 1250 and by 1259 it had a goal.

To the north of the manor a number of apparently medieval roads are still discernible around the village of Noak Hill at Manor Farm and crossing Lower Noak Close. Via 'Mozzies Lane' that once curved across Dagnam Park (locally 'The Manor') these trackways could have brought people to Havering Palace crossing the old Roman Road (A12) and Putwell Bridge from Chafford Hundred at Brook Street and linking to more distant routes such as Wingletye Lane, and via crossing points of local rivers to neighbouring manors such as Hacton Bridge an important entrance into Havering Royal

Chapter 9 Norman & Plantagenet

Manor from Chafford Hundred. At Hacton the evocative deep road cutting on the bridge approach is a clue to its antiquity.

Locally goods and services would have been supplied to the Palace, for example close by at Harold Wood the manor of Redden Court, meaning 'reedy valley' and presumably referring to the river Ingrebourne (Prof. Ged Martin), originated as a tenement that in 1212 was required to supply the king's chamber at Havering Palace with fresh rushes. Similarly at the time, the tenants of Earls, Romford and Gooshays manors had to provide serjeanty (services exclusively to the king) being keepers of the royal woods. Also, in 1270 King Henry III granted a market license for Rainham across the Ingrebourne in Chafford Hundred that would have boosted its trading economy whilst being in competition with Havering's Hythe (Ogborne, Elizabeth, 1817, *The History of Essex*,) in the king's own manor. While at Paternoster Row in Noak Hill, there was a large pottery manufacturing kiln until 1365 or 1405, revealed by the finds of the West Essex Archaeology Group (WEAG) (*Archaeology In Essex* 2001).

Wool trade By 1086 sheep wool had become the principal product of the Essex marshes and Horndon-on-the-Hill became an important collection point. By the mid 13th century, the wool trade had become the staple and driving force of England's economy and by now the Norman church at Horndon had been replaced, and there was a market and fair. Horndon became an important administrative centre leading to the village achieving town status and with a magnificent surviving 14th century Woolmarket (grade II). But later Horndon failed to develop leaving us today with the medieval street pattern surviving with a number of medieval and post-medieval buildings and burgage plots[2] forming an impressive core of listed buildings including the grade I, 13th century church.

Wool had become England's 'main export and source of wealth' and Rainham was shipping wool to Calais in the late 15th century for example, and a graffito of a ketch of the time is hidden in the old rood stair at Rainham parish church. During the 15th century the moated Bretts at Aveley was home to the Cely family who were prominent wool merchants (VCH) and leading members of 'the Staple' – the kings' designated market for the wool trade and export tax. Their family and business papers are a rare and important survival describing their life and business activities as London wool merchants at a time at the end of the Wars of the Roses. Cely Woods are close by Belhus Woods Country Park on land they purchased in 1492 to escape the bubonic plague and is now part of Thames Chase Community Forest.

Famine, war, plague, punishments, flood, the Peasants Revolt and Civil War The population growth of the High Medieval period meant that during the 14th century when the weather patterns changed to prolonged rain spoiling the crops it became hard to feed everyone and famine soon followed especially for the poorest. The **Great Famine** of 1315 became so bad that on one occasion when King Edward II passed through St. Albans his entourage had great difficulty in finding bread to buy even for the king.

Historic strains between England and France had rumbled on with a gradual rise in tension between their respective kings ever since the Norman-French William had become king of England. The French kings saw the English monarchs as owing them feudal allegiance. In 1327 Edward III became king of England and ten years later he declared himself heir to the French throne too and in that year of 1337

---

[2] Deep, narrow-fronted town rental property, often with voting rights, owned by the king or lord.

began what became a virtually continuous war between England and France that lasted for over 100 years until 1453.

Sir Walter de Manny, had arrived as an esquire of Queen Philippa of Hainault, he owned the manor of Romford and Mawneys is named after him. He was a great soldier and a commander in the campaigns of Edward III during the **Hundred Years War** and was quickly appointed Admiral north of the Thames in that same year, 1337. He fought at the Battle of Crecy in 1346 where cannons were used for the first time and became a turning point in the development of warfare away from the rules of chivalry and feudalism. He founded the monastery of Charterhouse in London on land he bought where many of the victims of the Black Death had been buried.

On top of the continual war, the **Black Death** – bubonic plague – had arrived in England in 1348, it was in London by the autumn of that year and arrived here in 1349. It killed perhaps 45 percent of the population (Prof. Carenza Lewis 2016), and it continued to return to the country periodically. On Thames Chase Walk No.5, Berwick Glades leads to Abbey Wood Open Space in Rainham. It is said that bodies were brought out by barge at night from Barking Abbey along the waterways to be buried on these Ingrebourne marshes.

The devastation of the Black Death led to major economic crisis and a time of civil unrest. Crime was already severely punished during the medieval period but after the plague stocks became common in England by the mid 14th century as part of the means to control the surviving population and restore the economy.

Facsimile stocks and whipping post on The Green at Havering-atte-Bower protected as a grade II listed building

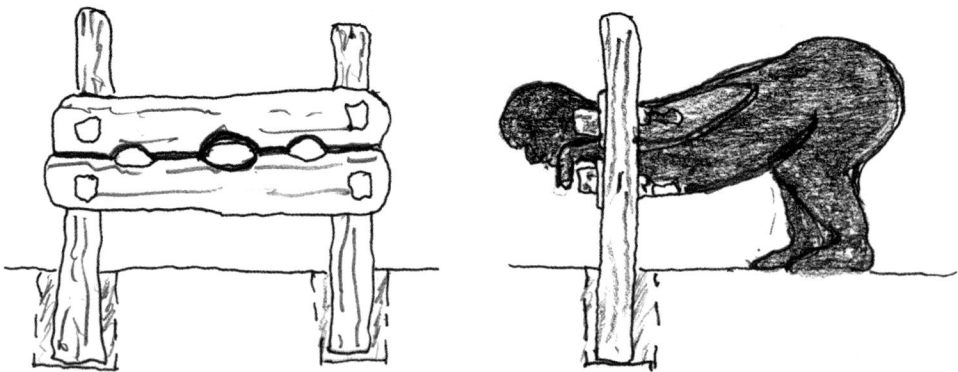

Reused timbers from Saxon pillories, the earliest known in Europe, were discovered by archaeologists at Barking Abbey (Research Report Series No. 36-2013 Barking Abbey). In the late 13th century both the Lord of Suttons and the lord of West Thurrock claimed the right of gallows; locally there were gallows sites in Dagenham and outside Brentwood and Romford. In Romford itself the stocks, the ducking stool and cage were all in the Market Place. Over time villages like Hornchurch and Rainham also had a cage or lock-up for miscreants and the late 17th or early 18th century Orsett lock-up survives as a grade II listed building next to the village pound that would hold stray livestock.

Amidst all the turmoil, King Edward III made the most of Havering Palace making more than thirty visits and often staying for weeks at a time, in 1343 he and Queen Philippa spent Easter there. For a period of five months in 1358 Edward held a **Marshalsea Court** at the Palace for local people to air their grievances, a privilege normally reserved for royal domestic servants.

In 1377 at the age of 10, Edward's grandson became King Richard II with regency councils for advisors and in that year a **poll tax** was first introduced. This was a personal taxation to prevent migration of working people seeking higher wages. It brought about the need for people to have surnames by this time and here local family names survive like Bumpstead and Aylett or Yeldham from north Essex. This was also the year that great problems befell Barking Abbey when the **Thames flooded** with around 280 ha (700 acres) lost mostly from Dagenham marsh and never recovered despite every effort being made including enforced labour, repair of dikes and enormous expenditure.

Under the rule of the new young king the economic stagnation that followed the Black Death and the war with France going badly for the English, led to protests by local people, artisans, village officials and the poor alike that broke out as the **Peasants Revolt** in June 1381 against a third and fiercest Poll Tax levy. Resistance against the tax began locally in Fobbing in Thurrock, then, with local people from Corringham and Stanford was followed by an attack in Brentwood where men were killed, from which there was no turning back and news was quickly spread across Essex and throughout the Thames estuary.

Kentish men burst into Lesnes Abbey, which at this time was being misgoverned, and the Abbot was made to swear allegiance to the cause and taken hostage. Then they crossed the Thames by boat to Barking and held a conference with some of the leaders including **Wat Tyler** and the enigmatic **Jack Straw**. Then from the Thameside villages around they drew more than 100 recruits armed with whatever tools were to hand as weapons, and gathered at Rainham. Wennington Hall, home to a leading official Sir John Gildesborough, is thought to have been plundered in one of the first Essex attacks and curiously Rainham church's Priest's door has been proven to have been remade at about this time (and with oak shipped from the faraway Baltics).

Having gathered the riled folk then crossed back into Kent spreading chaos and rioting against the land-owning class and misgovernment. Both the Essex and Kent armies marched on London, led by Wat Tyler and others to meet the king at Mile End. The peasants were betrayed as Richard went back on his promises and the last stand was again near here in Billericay where battle took place in Norsey Wood in June 1381 where some 500 were killed in the **Battle of Billericay**. That same year King Richard held a court at Havering Palace for some of those peasants seeking mercy but many were tried and executed.

The struggle of the Peasants Revolt was similar to the Chartists movement of the 19th C and the Suffragettes (qv) of the 20th C (BBC Bitesize KS3 History).

'...Henry IV, V, VI – then who? Edwards IV, V, Dick the bad...'

The royal Houses of York and Lancaster Medieval monarchs ruled through strength as well as through at times complicated matters of inheritance and now the son of a younger son, Henry IV (Bolingbroke) of Lancaster seized power from King Richard II and began the dispute amongst the descendants of Edward III and between the royal Houses of Lancaster and York that would in time lead to the **Wars of the Roses**. Henry's wife, Queen Joan of Navarre, outlived both her husband and her stepson Henry V, against whom she was accused but never tried, of witchcraft, after finally being reconciled with him she passed away at her home of Havering Palace in 1437.

Despite the ongoing 100 Years War and national economic stagnation continuing until 1485, locally life went on. At Thorndon for example, the former St. Nicholas church and churchyard (SAM) were constructed in West Horndon parish and nearby the small, medieval moated manor of 'Old' Thorndon Hall (SAM) was built soon after in the early 15th century and the deer park created c.1412 is now protected as a SSSI. In 1414 the house was improved by Lewis John of West Horndon, Dunton, Ingrave and Bishops Ockendon (Cranham), knight of the shire for Essex and Hertfordshire and Steward of Havering-atte-Bower and elsewhere, by a licence of King Henry V. This was the popular king who led his army to victory in the battle of **Agincourt** in 1415. One of the king's commanders was Sir Richard de Vere the hereditary Steward of the Forest of Essex and brother-in-law to Lewis John; Sir Richard Arundel of Bretons also accompanied the king to war. Close by Thorndon, in Ingrave, Salmonds Farmhouse (grade II) was also constructed in the early 15th century, and the granary at Heron Hall (grade II*) is of early 15th century date as well as the grade II property at 13 Cricketers Lane.

England finally lost its claim to France in 1453 when King Henry VI suffered a mental illness and the king's cousin Richard of York was made protector. In 1455 **civil war** broke out between the king's Lancastrian branch of the royal family and the supporters of Richard of York – with the red rose badge

Chapter 9 Norman & Plantagenet

of the House of Lancaster and the white rose of the House of York that eventually named the period the Wars of the Roses. A time of turmoil followed. Locally, in 1436 Henry VI had granted the manors of Dagenhams and Cockerels in Havering to his Lancastrian supporter Henry Percy, but Percy was killed at the Battle of St. Albans in 1455 and his son at the battle of Towton in Yorkshire in 1461, after which the Yorkists victors confiscated the manor. Towton was a decisive battle, Henry was deposed and Richard's son took the throne as King Edward IV.

In 1465 **Liberty status** was granted to Havering manor. It is thought that Sir Thomas Urswick, a prominent Yorkist, may have had a hand in obtaining the royal charter as he acquired additional land within the Liberty, with all its advantages, rights and privileges for his manor of Marks. However the greatest impact on this area began in 1485 when finally, the Welsh Henry Tudor of the Lancastrian line defeated the **Yorkist King Richard III** at the **Battle of Bosworth Field**, and the Early Modern Period began with the reign of the Tudor dynasty – that would in turn have a dramatic effect on the economy of this local area.

 Usefully, this is the same Richard of York and Battle of Bosworth Field that is recalled in the well-known Rainbow mnemonic: '<u>R</u>ichard <u>O</u>f <u>Y</u>ork <u>G</u>ave <u>B</u>attle <u>I</u>n <u>V</u>ain'.

Red, Orange, Yellow, Green, Blue, Indigo, Violet
(Image by Clker-Free-Vector-Images from Pixabay)

<u>Places to visit near and far:</u>
- Curfew Tower and St. Margaret's Church at the ruins of Barking Abbey
- Mountfitchet Castle which is a Norman, timber Motte and Bailey Castle and Village, re-constructed on its original historic site and depicting life in Domesday England.
- Hedingham Castle is a Norman stone keep, built c.1140 and with four floors to visit
- Lesnes Abbey, Kent
- Canterbury Cathedral

- the 12th century Hospital Chapel of St. Mary the Virgin and St. Thomas of Canterbury, Ilford
- Wat Tyler Country Park & Fobbing Peasants Revolt monument (metal sculpture by Ben Coode-Adams, erected 1981)
- Fobbing Memorial
- All Saints Church, Vange, SS16 4PX, grade II* listed church (RCHM 1) cared for by the Churches Conservation Trust with some WW2 war graves in the churchyard

Ideas for future projects:

- A study of the Domesday records across this area comparing and contrasting the changes between the Saxon and the Norman political and administrative practices as a foundation for the following millennia (see also for example *Domesday Book - Essex* ed. Alexander Rumble pub. Phillimore 1983)
- Further research on the lost and nearly lost medieval roads across the area would be an invaluable aid to the Pilgrim Story of the landscape
- Research historic ferry crossing points of the river Thames in connection with informing the story of 13th century Pilgrim routes through this area to Canterbury and to York
- A study of the influence of historic Abbeys and religious houses on the history of this area
- Study and record the history and the surviving fragments of the Domesday East Horndon village, which was broken up and lost through major roadworks (the A127 'Halfway House' intersection), and the closed and listed All Saints Tudor brick church and churchyard at East Horndon; a study and history of the lost villages of Hacton and Langdon Hills
- Further research into the history of the fenland area and its villages

References for further research:

More information on the medieval period can be found through:
- See Section C: History Introduction, p. 99
- Council for British Archaeology – London branch (CBA-L) and CBA East
- Ancient Monuments Society (AMS) now Historic Buildings and Places

Further Reading:

- Bowden, Muriel (1966) *A Commentary on the General Prologue to The Canterbury Tales* pub. The Macmillan Company
- Bowman, Karen (2012) *Essex Girls* pub. Amberley Publishing ISBN 13: 9781445606927
- Hewett, Cecil Alec (1969) *Development of Carpentry, 1200-1700: An Essex Study*
- Hitchins, H.L. (1948) *Canterbury Tales* – Chaucer pub. by John Murry, to get a feel for the life and times of the 13th century pilgrims travelling to Canterbury
- Maldon, Henry Elliot (1980s edit) *The Cely Papers: selections from the Correspondence and Memoranda of the Cely Family* Royal Historical Society (Great Britain) pub. Camden.
- Rumble, Alexander ed. (1983) *Domesday Book - Essex* pub. Phillimore
- In similar vein to the Cely Papers are the *Stonor Letters*, the *Paston Letters* and the *Plumpton Letters*, all relating to gentry families of the time with connections to the English wool trade

Chapter 10
15th – 17th centuries: Tudor & Stuart
1485 – 1714

NATIONAL CURRICULUM Key Stage 3 hints – the development of Church, state and society

The new King Henry VII brought a close to the Wars of the Roses, increased Government wealth and set up his Tudor dynasty with a secure throne for his son to inherit. Thus began the Early Modern Period from c.1500 – the 'Age of Discovery' with great changes coming in the arts, science, politics and fashion.

In turn, King Henry VIII was a handsome man of stature who encouraged the Renaissance – a revival of classical culture influencing Britain, and he hung on to the ideals of chivalry and encouraged the rise of the gentry (middling) class. But he still acted like a medieval monarch, all-powerful and brutal. He worked towards uniting more of the British Isles, and under him England became a sovereign state, responsible only to its own government. Henry built war ships and returned to warring with France. He was determined to leave a male heir on the throne, which led finally to the break from the power of the Pope and the Roman Catholic church.

The power struggle between State and Church that had begun emerging generations before continued now throughout the reigns of the Tudor and Stuart monarchs. It provided the opportunity for the extreme Puritan Interregnum followed by the restoration of a dissolute monarchy and led to the necessity to invite in the succeeding protestant Hanoverian monarchs that continues to this day.

SURPRISE *'The Land of the Fanns is an intricate landscape, full of surprises and 'hidden gems' and rewards exploring.' (TellTale working with the public 2018)*

'...Harrys twain (VII, VIII), Ned VI the lad, Mary, Bessie...'

16th century: Tudors 1485-1603 Through its long riparian border with the great river Thames this area continued to bear witness to, and play its part in some of the nation's great historic events. After the turbulent final years of the medieval kings with wars, plague and economic stagnation, the establishment of the new Tudor dynasty heralded the modern age nationally and with a new golden economic period locally especially in and around the royal manor of Havering in the western half of this landscape.

Henry VII had seized Havering Palace which was again a favoured spot and many members of the Tudor royal family and some Stuart monarchs stayed at the palace. Henry VIII considered the hunting excellent in the area. He held court and entertained French hostages at Havering Palace[1]

---

 [1] Draw King Henry's feast at Havering Palace – what did they eat? What would you have at a feast if you could have anything you wanted?

144　　　　　　　　　　　　　　　　　　　　　　　　　　The Land of the Fanns and its history

and granted the palace to the first three of his wives, Queens Catherine, Anne and Jane. As a child the future King Edward VI was nursed at Havering Palace and it is said that the game of Real Tennis[2] began close behind Havering Palace at the rear of the 19th century Fairlight (locally listed).[3] At the north end of the village stood the newly built Pyrgo Palace (or 'Portgore' - perhaps named for being sited at the Park Gate to Havering Palace) built by Sir Brian Tuke, the king's steward of the manor of Havering. After the death of his queen Jane Seymour, Henry purchased Pyrgo in 1541 where he was reconciled to both of his daughters Mary and Elizabeth.

MIGRATION *'This is a crossroads landscape: because of its location on the Thames ... people have always travelled into, through and away from this area.'* **(TellTale working with the public 2018)**

Some twenty years earlier in 1465, the 10,360 ha. (40 sq. miles) royal Manor of Havering had been granted Liberty status and now stood apart from Becontree Hundred. The new Royal Liberty of Havering possessed its own freedoms and special rights and privileges including countrywide freedom from paying tolls and the right to charge its own tolls and taxes that boosted the local economy influencing a wide area. With the new political stability of the early Tudor period, the Liberty went on to become a wealthy place of trade and employment encouraging a huge migration of young workers into the area, many of whom also died there perpetuating the inflow of migrant workers (ref. Marjorie McKenzie).

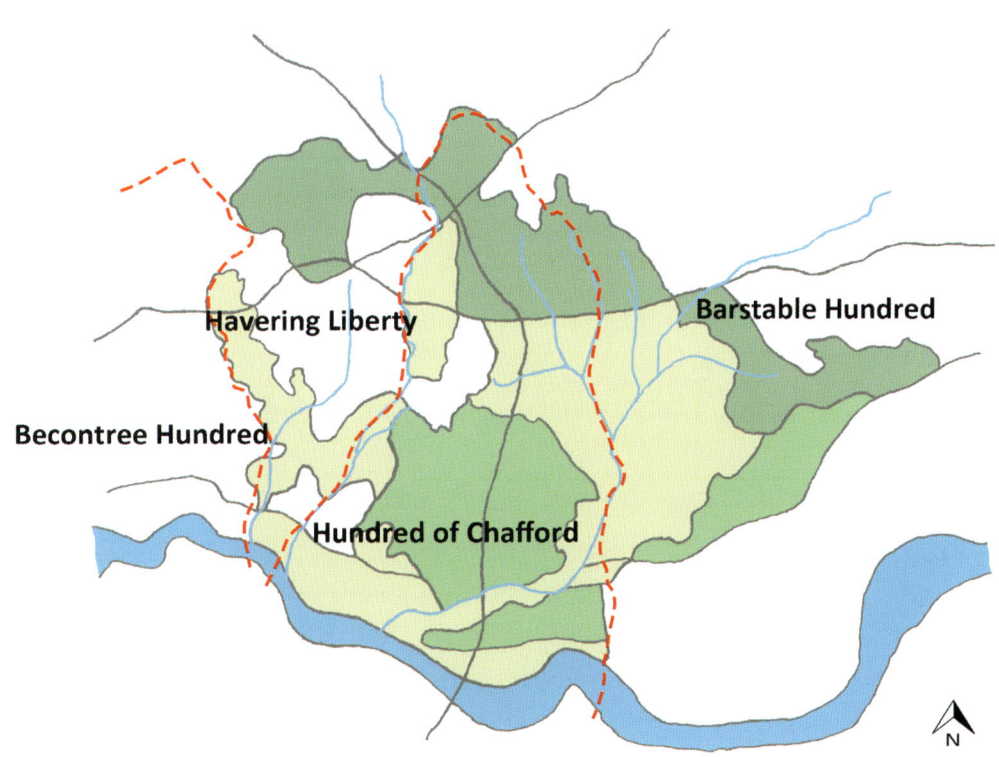

Map of the LotF area with the Hundreds and Royal Liberty

 [2] Research the game of real tennis and write a paragraph about the game and how it was played and is different from tennis today.

[3] Locally Listed buildings are those included on a list of historic buildings or structures compiled by Local Authorities, but which are not of sufficient national importance for formal Listing by the Secretary of State.

Chapter 10   15th – 17th centuries: Tudor and Stuart

Across this landscape many buildings remain that originated from this period and are now listed buildings.[4] Within **the Liberty**, Church House survives in Romford Market Place, originally part of a much larger Tudor building. In Emerson Park the Tudor house of Nelmes was demolished in 1967 but the staircase survives (RCHM), rebuilt into Capel Nelmes house that also retains a Tudor wing reputed to have been a chapel; the Well Tower nearby is of the Stuart period.

At Hornchurch the alien Priory (one under foreign control) had long before been suppressed and sold off by Richard II and a new hall (Chaplaincy) erected there in c.1400, was altered or extended in the 16th century and concealed within later fabric with all trace of the location of the original Priory being lost. The Chaplaincy building was later discovered by a young Mr Caldwell in 1969 in connection with Hornchurch & District Historical Society, enabling an impressive timber-framed wall of the solar (private chamber or room) to be eventually recovered and recorded by Passmore Edwards Museum, Newham (now Newham Museum Service), providing a rare link to the ancient Priory. Another clue is in the adjoining parish church of St. Andrew (grade I) that was originally called the 'monasterium cornutum' (horned monastery) after its bulls-head decoration.

Thomas Scargill of Bretons (now an Outdoor Recreation Centre) in South Hornchurch left money in his will for the 'making of a steple att Hornchurche' and that landmark spire to the church was completed in 1491/2 and later clad in copper. Later the Ayloffe family acquired Bretons where, surviving from this period are two Tudor barns and orchard garden walls originally with ten niches or bee boles for straw skeps (bee hives). Other great houses within the Liberty at the time are shown on a map of c.1618 illustrated in the Victoria County History of Essex Vol.7.

Illustration of a woven bee skep in a bee bole built into a garden wall

---

[4] Commonly historic buildings (or other structures) from this period that survive in anything like their original condition are included on the List of Buildings of Special Architectural or Historic Interest as 'listed buildings'. Grade II (two) listing is the usual grading for these buildings of special interest; particularly important buildings (less than 6 percent nationwide) are starred (grade II*) and the most exceptional buildings (some 2.5 percent) are grade I (grades I and II* are indicated here in the text). (Some historic buildings of lessor importance are recorded as Locally Listed – see earlier).

In the **Hundred of Chafford** the picturesque village of South Weald is a conservation area[5] with many listed and historic buildings including the Tudor 'Queen Mary Chapel' and 'Rochetts' farmhouse, and stands at the high point with Weald Country Park (grade II on the 'Register of Parks & Gardens of Special Historic Interest in England') covering the slopes down the hill to the north and west. The Park, originally to the Tudor Weald Hall, built in c.1540-1545 (demolished in 1950), was laid out from the late 17th - early 18th century and now has a Visitor Centre and special 'Stickman Play Trail' for children complementing the 'Gruffalo Trail' nearby at Thorndon Country Park.

Below the hill at Brook Street, a master of the lepers' hospital here had once lived at the Golden Fleece (II*) (Sylvia Kemp, local historian) that was erected in around 1400 with further work in the 15th century and later. By the 16th century Brook Street was a scattered settlement where numbers 17, 19 and 21 are of early 16th century date and were originally a 2-bay open hall with two storeyed end bays (a 'Hall House')[6]. The Moat House (II*) is also of early 16th century origin, known as *The Place* in 1514, it is said to have been frequently visited by Henry VIII when it was is the ownership of Henry Roper who held office in the household of the Tudor Queen Catherine of Aragon. This became the manor of Ropers with Great Ropers house and Ropers Lane, and was otherwise called Mary Green manor. Nearby, the Bull Inn dates from around 1600.

The name *Brentwood* indicates that the town originated as a forest clearing, this is seems was extended by the abbey of St. Osyth who held the manor of Cocstede (Costead) in the late 12th century. The wide main street developed on the pilgrim route around St. Thomas' chapel where there survives a degree of Tudor building fabric in adjacent buildings. By this time Brentwood had grown as a market town popular with travellers at its coaching inns and with London merchants who acquired property (Stephen Alsford). Around the area the surviving 16th century domestic Tudor buildings are invariably timber-framed hall houses; the 17th century Stuart buildings may be either timber-framed and rendered or encased in the new incoming brick and all are generally grade II listed.

---

[5] Conservation Areas are areas designated by local authorities that are 'of special architectural or historic interest the character or appearance of which it is desirable to preserve or enhance' (Planning (Listed Buildings and Conservation Areas) Act 1990). For specific information see the *Conservation Area Appraisals & Management Plans* for individual conservation areas.

[6] The single-roomed, one and a half storied 'hall-house' design with a central open hearth was favoured by yeomen farmers from the 13th century (e.g. Pages in Harold Wood) and 14th century (e.g. Angel Cottages, South Weald). Hall-houses were constructed in timber with panels infilled with wattles (timber strips) and daub (daubed with clay and horsehair mixture and painted with lime when dry). In time smoke stacks (an early form of chimney) were installed high up to guide the passage of smoke (e.g. Warley Franks), and houses often had a two-storey wing added on one side with a solar (for private use of the family) and on the other side a buttery (for storage of wet goods) and a pantry (for dry goods) (e.g. Upminster Hall). By the 16th century lower ceilings had often been inserted into the large hall to make these entirely two storey houses. There are numerous examples of Hall Houses in this area, such as Courts Farmhouse in Aveley and Hole Farmhouse, Warley and also 4 & 5 Boyles Court Cottages (RCHME) erected in 1533-1566 and later 'ceiled' over and later still divided into two cottages, always responding to the economic (often farming) conditions of the times. These traditional, largish timber hall houses were originally designed for communal use – the family and their servants and workers - but were beginning to be out of place as domestic building needs changed to suit more individual households with smaller two-storey units requiring less stout timbers at a time when suitable woodland was becoming scarcer.

Chapter 10 15th – 17th centuries: Tudor and Stuart

The church at Little Warley dates from the 15th century (grade I, RCHM) and there are Tudor farmhouses at 'Old England' and 'Little Bassetts', and 'Roses Farmhouse' is late 17th century, the Greyhound public house is a surviving timber and plastered hall house of the period. The early 16th century Little Warley Hall (II* and RCHM) was originally part of a larger building on a moated site and during the 1930s was the home of the actress Mary Clare.

In Childerditch Street, 'Rosebrook' is a hall house of c.1500 origin (II*); 'The Fruit Farm' is a late medieval and 17th century house and 'Woodlands' dates from the mid 16th century – here the National Heritage List for England (NHLE) description includes an historical note of the changes taking place at the time to the ubiquitous hall house: 'the house demonstrates the persistence of the open hall house for ordinary folk well after the open hall had been abandoned in favour of individually heated chambers of the fully storeyed house by the more fashionable.'.

Old Thorndon Hall was extended into a large and rambling medieval house before being remodelled into a fine example of a grand Elizabethan red brick mansion by Sir John Petre of Ingatestone (later first Lord Petre) in 1573-93, when it became the main family seat (Queen Elizabeth I had previously stayed at Ingatestone Hall in 1561 the guest of Sir John's father William Petre, her Catholic Secretary of State - and previously to Queen Mary, Edward IV and Henry VIII). The gardens were transformed, laid out in squares and quarters and planted with Elizabethan knot designs typical of the period (illustrated on John Walker's map of 1598) (SAM). A central feature is the Pigeon mound (RCHME and SAM) for Sir John, probably originally a dovecote and viewing mound.

At North Ockendon the 16th century garden walls of Hall Farm survive with its early 16th century moated enclosure (RCHM2). The Hall was lost to a WW2 bomb, but from 1768 during its ownership by Richard Benyon, it was home to his tenant Richard Woods, the Georgian landscape architect (Cowell, Fiona, 1986, *Journal Article Vol. 14, No. 2* pub. The Gardens Trust).

At South Ockendon next to the church the Royal Oak Inn and Quince Tree Farmhouse on South Road are both Tudor timber-framed hall houses. Belhus was a Tudor house, said to be 'newly builded' in 1526. By the mid 17th century Belhus was one of the largest estates in Essex. Although the mansion was demolished after WW2 some of the fabric and fittings are held at Valence House Museum (LBB&D) and at Thurrock Museum (TBC) and elsewhere (VCH) and the estate is included within Thames Chase (see *Belhus Country Park Walk*). East of Belhus the timber-framed 'Little Belhus' (II*) is mid 16th century and its brick garden walls are also grade II* with entrance gateway containing the Stuart Royal Arms. Other 16th and 17th century buildings are 'Street Farmhouse', the former gateway at 'Groves' and a red brick barn and a timber-framed granary at 'Great Mollands'.

At Aveley the manor house (SAM site) stood beside the church (grade I) but had gone by 1593; close by in Aveley High Street are a listed Tudor hall house (RCHM 7) and the 15th century Crown & Anchor Hotel. This cluster of surviving historic buildings stand at the village end of Ship Lane leading to the Mardyke which was tidal for some 8 km (5 miles) until the latter 18th century enabling the trading of goods from the heart of the LotF out to the tidal Thames.

• • • • • • • • • • •

In **Barstable Hundred** there are also outlying timber-framed Tudor and Stuart listed farmhouses across the fens in Bulphan at 'Garlesters', 'Old England' and 'Little Tillingham Hall' and in Orsett include 'Whitfields' house and barn, 'Poplars Farmhouse' and the 'Bothy'. Near Baker Street are 'Slades Hold Cottages' and 'Larkins', and 1& 2 'Malting Cottages' are 17th century and in red brick. 'Doesgate Farmhouse" in Dunton is 17th century and timber-framed; at East Horndon 'Dunton Hills' house and cottage is in black brick; Horndon-on-the-Hill has 'Great Malgraves', 'Wrens Park' and outbuilding and dovecote at 'Arden Hall'. At Langdon Hills the Church of St. Mary & All Saints (II*) is in early 16th century red brick and stone.

ECONOMY *'This area is justly famous for trade, commerce and industry: these have been important here for many centuries.'* (TellTale working with the public 2018)

A new, middle social class of yeoman, some with voting rights and increased wealth had begun to develop in England. Better off yeoman farmers were able to afford improved living accommodation developing the timber-framed and rendered hall house style that survives across this landscape. Fashionable dress also became important about now and, for example, there are two pairs of brasses in Rainham church where 'one from c.1489 is of a civilian and his wife, she has an unusual form of butterfly headdress and high-waisted gown with a very low neck, tight sleeves and fur-trimmed collar and cuffs; the other pair are of a merchant and his wife from about 1500, he has a fur lined gown and she has a pedimented headdress, and both of them have a Shield of Arms.[7]

The districts all around the Royal Liberty likely provided goods and services to the palaces and it is the crossing points of local rivers into the Liberty that would have been key locations to boost local economy in and outside Havering manor. In the north the river Rom crossing from Becontree Hundred into Romford was near Stickleback Bridge in Brooklands Lane. In the south the Beam Bridge (previously 'Fleetsmouth' or 'Dagenham Creek') crossing from Becontree Hundred was into South End (South Hornchurch), also from South End on the east side via Red Bridge across the river Ingrebourne into Rainham at Dovers. Other crossings of the Ingrebourne are at Putwell Bridge on the Roman Road into Brentwood, Cockabourne Bridge at Harold Wood leading to Great Warley; Upminster Bridge crosses from Hornchurch into Upminster and Hacton Bridge crosses near the old Hacton Village where Hacton Lane may have been a key route to the palace via the ancient Wingletye Lane and Harold Wood.

The Thameside villages would especially have benefitted from the additional trade imports from their wharves such as at Rainham Creek, and in Barking Henry VIII ordered boats to be built at Barking quay. In the Hundred of Chafford the effect of local wealth and widespread changes in land-ownership can be seen in an increase in building during the 16th century at places like Great Warley and South Weald that continued to expand, with the market towns of Brentwood and Aveley being the largest centres at the time and new settlements developed at places like Wealdside and Coxtie Green where the Black Horse pub, originally a house, survives. In Becontree Hundred settlements began to grow from the early 1600s with many manors and farms on the excellent agricultural land

---

 [7] The gown and butterfly headdress were a smart style from Burgundy in France, wire 'feelers' at the back of the headdress supported a veil in a 'V' shape; a pedimented headdress is pointed like the gable roof of a house. Take a 30 minute challenge to create your own headdress inspired by the brasses in Rainham church OR make a LotF Tudor bonnet OR design your own Shield of Arms for your family, town or organisation.

including Hooks Hall Farmhouse in The Chase built around 1690 and Bentry Heath House in the late 17th or early 18th century.

Throughout all periods this whole landscape continued to be mainly an agricultural area growing produce such as corn, wheat, barley, hay, peas and potatoes (newly discovered from c.1586), fruit and nut trees, and by the Mayesbrook in Dagenham hops were grown for beer-making. Poor weather brought bad harvests in 1562 and from 1594-97 with good years in 1592 and 1593. **Windmills** for grinding corn into flour were at Mill field, Hornchurch and near Eastbury House before 1746, Baker Street Windmill is said to date from 1674 while its Mill House is 15th or early 16th century. Other mills are indicated on a map of the Liberty of Havering 1618 (VCH) on the east bank of the Beam river south of Beam Bridge, one outside Stewards Park at Romford, and another outside Gidea Hall Park and one at Marks Manor. Also watermills at Aldborough Hatch, one at Barking and, until 1614 at Dovers.

Pigs were raised in woodlands, cows grazed and pigeons were kept in dovecotes for mainly winter meat at places like Eastbury Manor and Padnall Farm, Chadwell Heath. Commoners had rights on the 536 acres (217 ha) of flood prone Dagenham marshes that continued to be used for seasonal sheep grazing until the late 19th century and reeds were grown for thatching, hurdles and basket-making at Horseshoe Corner on the Thames and along the Beam river.

• • • • • • • • • • • •

In 1539 the **Dagenham Breach** at the estuary of the Beam River formed the present Dagenham Pond or Lake; in Barking, the marshes were also breached in the time of Queen Mary (1553-1558), and £300 was sent to the Surveyor to help with its repair. In another breach in 1621 the Dagenham pond became 'the Gulf', which the Dutch drainage engineer Sir Cornelius Vermuyden repaired and that lasted until a further devastating breach in 1707 then remained unrepaired. Eventually some 1,000 acres were spoiled and the affected area spread as far as Dagenham village and from across the Dagenham Levels eastwards beyond the Beam River and across the Havering Levels almost to Rainham Creek. Each tide swept more acreage into a mud bank that formed in the Thames and became a danger to shipping, threatening national trade. After attempts by others eventually the breach was stopped by the hydraulic engineer Captain John Perry RN, over a five year period of work, finally completed in 1719 and involving a workforce of 300.

The location of the river Thames along the southern border of this area has always been instrumental to its economy and to the defence forces that played their strategic role in protecting Britain from the Medieval period to modern times and the 16th and 17th centuries were no exception when the river Thames was 'the most important route into England'. At a time of international tension, east of this area **Tilbury Fort** was first erected in 1539-40 by Henry VIII as West Tilbury Blockhouse at the important Thames ferry crossing. The fort was equipped with heavy guns and its job was to sink enemy ships on their way to attack London and its naval dockyards. Together with four other gun forts at the head of the Thames estuary, these defences was part of the king's national programme of fortification that transformed the old medieval army into a formidable armed force with these gun forts and others along the east and south coasts and a powerful Navy of warships, all to protect the country from invasion by powerful European Catholic forces.

• • • • • • • • • • • •

In this rural location traditional and rustic materials and detailing often clung on much later than in the larger towns, with timber structures often clad in weatherboarding and with simpler architectural detailing. In this manner in Hornchurch the little 17th century house at 195 High Street has an ancient shopfront and in Corbets Tey at Bearblock Cottages, the 16th century no's 1-3 Harwood Hall Lane were built as a single timber-framed house with a shop front at no. 1 and a chimney for smoking hams and likely served the village probably as a **butcher shop**. Although no's 4, 5 and 6 are thought to have been infilled in the 18th century, no's 7 and 8 are 17th century, and no. 8 at the end of the row has a bread oven and likely supplied the **village bread**.

1-3 Harwood Hall Lane, 16th century grade II listed building in Corbets Tey Conservation Area and bearing a L.B. Havering Environmental Award Plaque for restoration of the row of listed cottages

In Dagenham the village developed along Crown Street and retains the early 17th century vicarage, and the early 15th century timber-framed hall-house and former **tannery** is now the Cross Keys public house. Before clearance in 1976 buildings at 2-8 Church Street included a Tudor fireplace and what was probably a **butchers shop** and a slightly earlier **wheelwright's** workshop. Dagenham also had a **pin maker** and **archery bow maker** in 1519 and two **tailors** in 1573. Other occupations included **spinners and dyers**, **blacksmiths**, **carpenters**, and **fishing and oyster catching**. Collier Row was a hamlet at the edge of Hainault Forest that had acquired its name from the ancient method of **charcoal burning** during the 15th and 16th centuries.

The wealthy were able to import stone for architectural detailing from the West Country via London and brick was newly available locally from the many brick earths in the area such as Cranham Brick Works and with local **brickmaking** in the Dagenham manors of Valence and Parsloes – where a Tudor brick kiln was located at Parsloes Park (GLSMR no. 060496). The fine Tudor brick church of All Saints, East Horndon (II*) mainly dating from the last quarter of the 15th century is a rare example of a complete church in Tudor brickwork and stands sentinel on the hilltop, almost all that remains of East Horndon village after extensive A127 road layout changes in the 20th century, and is an example of patronage by the Tyrell family of Herongate who developed the brick industry in this area.

East Horndon Tudor brick church is now vested in the Churches Conservation Trust and open at times by the Friends of East Horndon; the modern wind turbine stands in stark juxtaposition in the wider view (Photograph courtesy of Debbie Brady, Heritage Engagement Officer LotF, 2017)

By 1500, other industry was beginning to develop in the area and chalk extraction in the West Thurrock area had a significant impact on the economy and the landscape. The medieval **chalk mines** or deneholes (of geological interest, a SAM & SSSI for bat hibernation) just outside the area at Hangman's Wood between Grays and Orsett Heath are said to be 'the most extensive and best preserved' survivals (Essex Field Club).

The Dissolution of the Monasteries (1536-1541) was brought about over establishing the heir to the throne and a power struggle – yet King Henry VIII in fact remained a Catholic throughout his life. Religious foundations were clustered around the king's royal manor - to the north in Ongar Hundred the land was held by the Abbey of Bury St. Edmunds; to the east in the Hundred of Chafford were the Abbotts of Waltham and to the south-east were the Knights Hospitallers at Rainham and Berwick; and west in Becontree Hundred was the Abbess of Barking. Here, until 1539 when the king finally closed Barking Abbey, the maintenance of roads and bridges and land transfers were all dealt with by the manor court held at the Abbey, and as Lord of the manor the Abbess also enforced correct weights and measures at the market and maintained social hierarchies. However, with the dissolution of the monasteries came the break up and sale of some large land holdings and that provided opportunity for economic growth by new entrepreneurial owners.

Barking Abbey lands were sold to wealthy families such as the Fanshawe's and country houses were built amongst the farmlands of Dagenham leaving Barking itself to survive as a market town. Similarly, Eastbury Manor House (grade I), now in the care of the National Trust, is a brick built *H-shaped* Elizabethan gentry house erected by a wealthy merchant Clement Sisley, in 1572-73 on what had been Barking Abbey land. It stands on rising ground that would have had views of the Thames across the marshes to the south. Tradition says (as repeated by Daniel Defoe in 1727 in his book *A Tour Throughout the Whole Island of Great Britain*) that in 1605 the Catholic Gun Powder plot conspirators schemed there; while others say that Lord Monteagle was in residence there when he received the letter that led to the Plot's discovery; it's also said that the necessary boats were hired from 'a rogue of a sailor of Barking', a man called Johnson (alias Guy Fawkes).[8]

In the Hundred of Chafford, at Warley, the extensive land holding of the manor of Warley Abbess and its settlement were sold to private owners in 1540 and subsequently broken up through inheritance and resale to descend separately as Warley Magna (Great Warley) and Warley Place. The settlement of Great Warley developed over time in a pattern of scattered dwellings and farms down through this elongated manor. Numerous timber-framed buildings were erected during the Tudor period and several 16th century hall houses remain as listed buildings in the heart of the village conservation area and the Tudor and Stuart Franks Farmhouse survives at Warley Franks. While at Rainham the lands were also taken back from the Knights Hospitallers (the Order of St. John of Jerusalem) following their confiscation in 1540 and sold on in 1545 including those of Sir William Weston of Berwick manor, the last English Prior of the Hospitallers and associate of the Cely family wool exporters; locally wool was being exported from Rainham to Calais from the time of King Henry VII.

In Barstable Hundred, at Horndon-on-the-Hill wool production continued to be important and Sir John Shaa, former mayor of London and owner of the Horndon estates, was licensed to trade in wool and woollen cloth, and held the market and fair that were still operating in 1504 at the time of his death. But from 1525 to 1685 the Essex wool trade fell into decline and the Woolmarket at Horndon was being used for other commercial purposes and for manorial court sessions. There were also nearby competing markets at Orsett and Bowers Gifford, and Thameside markets at West Tilbury, Fobbing, West Thurrock and South Ockendon (Stephen Alsford).

Queen Mary (ruled 1553-1558) After the short reigns of the Protestant monarchs Edward VI from 1547-1553 and Lady Jane Grey in July 1553 – who was never even crowned - there was turmoil when England again became a Catholic country under the rule of Queen Mary who revived the old heresy laws. The Tudor Marian persecutions and terrible burnings of local religious martyrs that took place here were through the tragic efforts of Edward Bonner, Bishop of London. Bonner is recalled locally in the so-called Bishop Bonner's palace at Orsett (q.v.).

Four men from Rayleigh were arrested by the Bishop in connection with the Tudor Marian Inquisition and eventually publicly burned at the stake in their local market town as well as the young Brentwood lad William Hunter, martyred in Brentwood in 1555. Hugh Laverock, an elderly invalid of Barking and John Apprice, a blind man were martyred together at Stratford where others met the same fate including Henry Wye, a brewer of Stanford-le-Hope. Bonner also arrested two local men of some standing from Horndon-on-the-Hill. He had them taken to Colchester Castle where he personally interrogated them. Eventually they were also both condemned for heresy according to the turbulent religious politics of the time. Both were burned at the stake on 26 March 1555, Thomas Causton in Rayleigh and Thomas Higbed back at his home village of Horndon-on-the-Hill where a blue plaque on the Bell Inn records the gruesome event that took place in the courtyard of the coaching inn.

• • • • • • • • • • • • •

---

[8] Plan a *moving story* for pupils to hear the story of the Gunpowder Plot in different parts of the room before a final role play in the 'cellar' of the Houses of Parliament.

Essex was also known as the *witch county* and witchcraft was a serious offence, particularly after the Civil War. However in 1558 a case of witchcraft arose in North Ockendon village when a local man and his cattle all died after supposedly being bewitched by a local spinster. In 1589 three so-called witches of Dagenham were indicted and hanged outside the court at Chelmsford for bewitching several people to death. By the following century people no longer believed in witchcraft, which was seen as confidence trickery, and in 1736 it was decriminalised; eventually the spectacle of public executions was stopped in 1868.

Queen Elizabeth I In 1559, just three months into her reign, the new Protestant queen granted Pyrgo Palace to the uncle of the ill-fated **Lady Jane Grey**. The reign of Queen Elizabeth was, like her father's, another 'Golden Age' of achievement and prosperity; and during the summer months she and her court *progressed* or visited the southern counties, staying and being entertained at her courtiers' lavish expense at their great houses.

During her **progress** to Essex in 1578 the queen is said to have visited Belhus mansion and thought to have breakfasted there. But for Elizabeth, Havering Palace was her gateway to Essex, she often began her progresses into Essex from there despite that in her view, the ancient Palace's clogged garderobes (lavatories) had made it 'a noxious place'. Elizabeth had Lord Burghley arrange for a survey and plan of the palace in 1578 that survives to today, and the palace was extended. Local man Derek Rowland, produced an excellent depiction of how the Palace is likely to have looked at this time and it is portrayed on a plaque on Havering Green, and from that he and two other members of Romford Historical Society produced a model of the palace (held at Havering Museum). The Queen's chapel is said to have stood when the parish church of St. John the Evangelist stands today and so gives a clue to the precise location and orientation of the palace at Havering Green. As queen, Elizabeth made numerous visits to Havering Palace with her Privy Councillors. On one visit a story is told of a fabled blue boar slayed by an archer who was called to account to the queen, who was amused by his cheeky response to her questioning; the Tudor 'Blue Boar Inn' survives, now as part of Blue Boar Hall facing the Green.

In military defence, when facing the **Spanish Armada** in 1588 Warley Garrison played a strategic role, being used as a meeting place for contingents from eight eastern and midland counties including 900 horsemen assembled, before travelling on to Tilbury. Havering Palace was prepared as a command post and it is said that the Queen stayed there on her way to rally her troops camped on high ground at West Tilbury just north of the refortified Tilbury blockhouse, before facing the great Armada of ships.

Elizabeth's **privateers** with their armed ships, and other travellers are well known to have brought back strange tales as that of shipwrecked sailor David Ingham of Barking who claimed he walked the length of America, as well as exotic new plants brought to England like the potato. Such new plants like rhubarb were amongst 342 species that William Coys, the greatest English botanist of the time, listed and cultivated in his walled gardens at Stubbers on the Cranham/North Ockendon borders in the period from 1580-1627. Here he introduced the ivy-leaved toad flax that is still found locally growing wild in old garden walls and in 1604 he was the first to coax the white yucca to bloom in England. Coys focussed on economically productive plants including turnips, lentils, panic-grass, barley and peas and the forage crop red clover. In 1605 it was through Coys that hops were first introduced into ale and transformed beer. At the time Coys made Stubbers as important and famous as the Royal Botanic Gardens at Kew are today. In 1689 Stubbers was purchased by Sir William Russell (an acquaintance of

Charles II, William Pitt and Samuel Pepys). In 1796 Russell's grandson employed Humphry Repton to redesign the grounds with some garden features surviving today (see Georgian Chapter).

On a comic note, in the year 1600 **Will Kemp**, the beloved Elizabethan clown and then recent ex-member of William Shakespeare's acting troupe, danced the Morris Dance through here on his way from London to Norwich as a publicity stunt to promote his solo career – by his account Kemp's 'Nine daies wonder', apparently drinking and carousing as he went. The stunt has since been repeated on occasions in modern times for publicity and charitable reasons including Morris dancers from across the UK dancing the 120 miles course in 2000 and a lone Morris Dancer in 2008, celebrating the original epic journey.[9] Locally the event is recalled in the name of the Morris Dancer public house in Harold Hill - originally the listed New Hall farmhouse, which once had a priest's hole concealed as an offshoot on the staircase.

LANDFORM *'The Land of the Fanns is about land and water and the often shifting relationship between them.'* **(TellTale working with the public 2018)**

'...James ye ken,
Then Charlie, Charlie, Lords Protector (two) and James again,
Will & Mary, Anne Gloria...'

17th century: Stuarts 1603 – 1714 This is a landscape busy with industry and trade on the Thames and with a quiet and desirable hinterland accessible to the coast and London. The history of the fann lands and the fann men who worked the interior during the 17th and 18th centuries is an intangible heritage asset of this area. Their management of this marshy landscape and their lifestyle is well recorded in local parish records from Rainham in the west, to Canvey Island in the east and is recalled in Leslie Thompson's local history book *The Land that Fanns* (pub.1957).

An artist impression of the 17th century elm barn at Thames Chase's Broadfields Farm

• • • • • • • • • • • •

[9] Take 5 minutes to re-enact Will Kemp's Morris dance.

Chapter 10 15th – 17th centuries: Tudor and Stuart

In terms of purpose designed buildings for their appearance rather than their use and convenience, architecture is credited as being introduced to Britain at this time by Inigo Jones with his 'Queens House' (built between 1616 and 1636) at Greenwich as the first purposely classical building in England. This influenced building development through the Stewart period – so that by the end of Queen Anne's reign the old traditional smaller timber-framed, 'lobby-entry'[10] style of house that became common in this area even into the 19th century, were being 'dressed up' with new frontages, like the Old Vicarage, Rainham (re-fronted c.1711), or were giving way to the new 'polite' design of house coming from Italy as architecture really began to flourish in Britain during the following 18th century Georgian era.

In the royal Liberty, the mansion of **Gidea Hall** (dem. 1930) originated in the 13th century and became the home of leading local families for many years. It was rebuilt and crenellated (battlemented) by 1568 when Queen Elizabeth stayed there. In 1638, following a formal, grand procession led by twelve trumpeters preceding two long trains of coaches and horsemen, Marie de Medici, Queen of France stayed overnight at Gidea Hall after landing at Harwich en route to London. She was accompanied by her son-in-law King Charles I who had joined her at Chelmsford although he himself stayed at the palace, as his father James I had regularly done before him, but by this time it was too old-fashioned for her majesty, and this being the last occasion that a monarch stayed at Havering Palace.

In the Hundred of Chafford, **Warley Place** (dem.1939) was 'an ancient house' by c.1725 (VCH) but with a surviving avenue of ancient sweet chestnut trees, planted in 1629 (Historic England Registered Garden). Thames Chase Walks No. 2,5, & 6a take a southern loop to **Corbets Tey** village, a conservation area with a fine cluster of listed buildings in addition to those already mentioned and centring on High House (II*) c.1700 and earlier and the 18th century Old Anchor that was once the Anchor Inn, and the 17th century Old Cottage that was once the George Inn. While the complex of listed buildings at High House in **Purfleet**, close by the London Loop and Purfleet rail station, are a significant feature in the area. This High House was originally a high-status timber farmhouse constructed in the 1550s and some of the mid 16th century Elizabethan timbers survive in the building; it was rebuilt in brick during the Stuart period in 1684. At about the same time the octagonal brick dove cote was built (SAM and listed) (access is close by Section 24 of the London Loop).

In Barstable Hundred, **Herongate** forms the backdrop to Thorndon Park, another village conservation area with several 17th century vernacular, listed buildings in Cricketers Lane and in Billericay Road including the late C17 Heron Hall and stables.

In Becontree Hundred, **Valance House** Museum in Dagenham (II*) is mostly of the 17th century with some parts older and on a 13th century moated site. It is timber-framed and contains a late Stuart marble fireplace and two panelled rooms and is the only manor house to survive in Dagenham. It is now a local history museum, and part of the grounds and moat are now Valance Park which is also a Nature Conservation Area of local importance.

---

[10] A 17th century and later design of small timber-framed house with a large central chimney stack heating a room on either side, the front door and tiny lobby formed on one side of the chimney stack, and a winding staircase built into the other side. It may be of one or two stories and may have a basement, sometimes an additional unheated room was added at one end and a later brick skin with a more polite (formal) window arrangement may be added, local examples include Mill Cottage, Hornchurch, and Kilbro (the Old Bakehouse), North Ockendon.

In 1641 a perambulation of Hainault Forest by Commissioners appointed by the Crown took place defining the boundary of the Forest of Waltham and the Liberty where the physical boundary was perhaps less clear by setting up marker stones, now all listed buildings. Marking the extent of the Liberty of Havering are the Collier Row Stone in Hog Hill Road, the two Marks Stones in Whalebone Lane North inscribed with their name and date, and a single Warren Stone all set up in 1642. This was most important for securing the rights and privileges pertaining to the Liberty. Also in Whalebone Lane North the Forest Bounds Stones (RCHM) were to define the limit of the Forest of Waltham, again inscribed and set up at the junction where the ditch line meets the road (photographed in 1910 by George E. Tasker *Country Rambles by Field Path and Road in and around Ilford*).

Civil War 1642 Two Civil Wars between King Charles I and Parliament broke out, firstly in 1642, for political, religious and financial reasons. The king, with his Protestant and Catholic **Royalists** held the north and west of England from his base at Oxford; mainly Protestant and Puritan **Parliamentarians** with some Catholics held London, the south and the east, making this area along the Thames estuary once again essential to the defence of London.

Politically, the king espoused the doctrine of the **'divine right of kings'** and ruled as an absolute monarch and had dismissed parliament in 1629. In the matter of religion, despite Elizabethan efforts through new laws to unify the Church after the religious turmoil of the Tudor period, there were Dissenters even from the established Church of England and locally included the rectors of Little Warley who were said to be Puritans during the reign of Charles I (VCH). While the Puritan Lawrence Wright of Dagnams, was one of **Oliver Cromwell's** physicians before 1651 and it was said 'he was reputed to be in particular favour' (Furdell, Elizabeth Lane, 2001, *The Royal Doctors, 1485-1714*).

Similarly, the aristocratic Sir William Ayloffe Bt. of Bretons and Thomas Legatt of Hornchurch Hall (dem. 1941) were both prominent Puritans although they were also long-time adversaries. Whilst Sir William's son and successor Sir Benjamin Ayloffe, High Sherriff of Essex, was by comparison a Royalist, for which his property was sequestered (confiscated) and he narrowly escaped banishment to the plantations in the West Indies (his fortunes later revived when he was elected MP for Essex in the Cavalier parliament in 1661 under Charles II). Financially, the monarchy was nearly bankrupt, while sequestration of Catholic land and property, goods and animals was important to the Parliamentarian cause and common enough in this area. Other local noble families that also supported the king included those from South Weald, Little Warley and East Horndon. This also led to conflicts and later sequestration of manors including that of Sir Edward Sydenham at Gidea Hall, and Sir John Fanshawe at Parsloes in Dagenham, while Sir Thomas Fanshawe was fined and others of the family fought for the king or fled the country.

Between 1640 and 1642 intense fear and suspicion had arisen in large cities like London and smaller towns like Colchester, that local Catholics were plotting against their Protestant neighbours. The Parliamentarians were fiercely anti-Catholic, whether they were Royalists or neutral in the war and some of the worst attacks on them, often by way of ransacking, pillage and arson, were in the Essex and Suffolk Parliamentary heartlands. But local communities seemed to stick together and, for example, in 1647 local people went to help defend the Catholic Lady Petre at Ingatestone

Hall[11] against the trained marauding bands of Parliamentarian troops. During the Reformation (of the Catholic church and development of Protestantism led by the German monk **Martin Luther**, in 1517) the Petre family were recusants remaining loyal to the Roman Catholic Church and yet were able to profitably survive the extreme religious changes during the Tudor monarchies. The Petre's had even entertained Queen Elizabeth I at Ingatestone Hall for several nights during her royal Progress into Essex despite having two priest holes hidden within the walls of the building for the secret shelter of Catholic priests during those troubled times.[12]

The militias of these rich agricultural regions of Essex, Hertfordshire, Norfolk, Suffolk and Cambridgeshire quickly became the successful Parliamentarian *Eastern Association*, which included a unit of troop of horse (cavalry) raised by Oliver Cromwell as its captain. The Eastern Association established Parliamentarian control over East Anglia and in 1644 it went on to form part of the establishment of the **New Model Army** where Cromwell was one of the principal commanders under General Sir Thomas Fairfax.

> Civil War reignited against Parliament in 1648, and this area saw troop movements with clashes along the Great Essex Road including a skirmish at Chadwell Heath against retreating Cavaliers.
>
> The revolt had begun in Kent and troops from both sides passed through here as Royalists pursued by Parliamentarians rushed north across these fens after crossing the Thames at Tilbury, where a Parliamentarian garrison held Tilbury Fort, to join the revolt in Essex where some had declared themselves to support the king. Meanwhile the Royalist troops from the west held siege at Marks manor house in Chadwell Heath, and the Parliamentarian owner, Carew Harvey Mildmay had to swim the moat to flee into the forest to escape the Royalist troops who then passed through Romford all the while with Lord-General Thomas Fairfax chasing in hot pursuit. His Parliamentarians made an overnight stop at Romford before marching through Brentwood.
>
> Meanwhile some 500 of Kent's Royalist soldiers united with the Essex regiment so that the total force numbered around 4,000 and moved on to the county magazine at Braintree but the magazine had already been secured by loyal Parliamentarians and the force carried on to Colchester intending then to gather more Royalists across Suffolk and Norfolk. After passing through Brentwood Fairfax with over 5,000 experienced troops and 1,000 cavalry also carried on to Colchester and he immediately attacked and the kings men were forced to retreat behind the towns walls – where they were unwelcome among the Parliamentarian townspeople. A siege ensued and tragically lasted for eleven weeks and was perhaps the most significant event of the war.

---

 [11] Pre-book a school visit to Ingatestone Hall and grounds, particularly for history studies for 'pupils in the last year of primary school but older and younger students are welcome too' and for 'study and project work in Art & Design, Geography, Science and Mathematics'.

 [12] Draw a map for an escape route for a Catholic priest hidden in a wall.

In the year 1649 **King Charles I** was caught, tried and executed. Following his death Havering Palace was abandoned, the Park tenant Montagu Bertie 2nd Earl of Lindsey having already been sequestered in 1643. The palace was now purchased by Col. (later Admiral) Richard Deane, regicide (one of those who had signed the king's death warrant). He began dismantling the buildings, so that by 1650 the palace was described as 'a confused heap of ruinous decayed buildings'. Many trees were being cut down now for the building of Navy ships and Deane cut down the mature Palace parkland trees for the same purpose and turned the land into permanent farms retaining one and tenanting the other to Lt. Gen. Thomas Hammond - also a party to the king's death and who later had his lands confiscated.

The monarchy was now replaced by a **Republic** until 1653 when Oliver Cromwell became **Lord Protector** backed by his New Model Army. Catholics were ruthlessly persecuted and Puritanism, an extreme form of Protestantism, now dominated. This insisted on a simple form of religious worship and the people led a plain existence often devoid of fun according to Cromwell's new *moral laws* designed to *improve* behaviour. These included forbidding alcohol and banned the celebration of Christmas. But Cromwell increased the navy and defeated the Dutch who were Britain's great rival trading nation, giving England supremacy at sea, he reorganised public finances and enabled the growth of mercantilism (commercialism) bringing wealth to the country.

In 1649 **John Evelyn**, famous diarist of the period, had purchased the manor of Great Warley, but quickly sold it again in 1655 complaining that 'the taxes are so intolerable that they eate up the rents etc., surcharged as that county has been during our unnatural war.' In 1655-57 there were royalist uprisings and as a result direct military government took over. In this area, one Hezekiah Haynes of Colchester was in charge as deputy major-general for Charles Fleetwood overseeing Essex on behalf of the Lord Protector. Haynes raised a county horse militia, and he was responsible for having suspects disarmed and imprisoning a number of Royalists.

Restoration When Cromwell died in 1658, he was succeeded by his son Richard, but he lacked the skills to govern (VCH), there was a time of chaos and the Protectorate collapsed. Charles II was restored as king shortly afterwards bringing a freer but more hedonistic way of life, the restoration of the Church of England and gradual acceptance of Catholics. New Protestant groups also started up around this time with some Quakers (the Society of Friends) apparently from Dagenham in 1658, Presbyterians at Aldborough Hatch during the 1660s and Baptist meetings taking place from around 1700. At Havering the palace was extensively repaired, now called 'Havering House' it was occupied by Robert, son of Montague Bertie. As for Carew Harvey Mildmay – remarkably it seems he worked his way back into the new kings employ.

• • • • • • • • • • •

Economic stability in the country grew through the continued practice of mercantilism and led to the development of capitalism. England continued to develop as a great trading nation, much of this relying on the river Thames and its docks and wharfs. Locally this included places like Grays and Rainham and the wharf on Barking Creek where the fishing and boat building industries were growing (VCH) and in the 1660s they were fishing as far away as Iceland. As wealth poured into London so these Essex marshes, their creeks and 'drains' continued as a haven for **smugglers** along Thameside and there is a story that a number of tunnels large enough for the passage of horse and cart run from Bretons to the river, perhaps for the purpose of smuggling. More tales of tunnels occur from Salmonds Farm in Ingrave in connection with Catholic priests and from Burton's Corner in Hornchurch to Hornchurch Priory.

Samuel Pepys (1633 – 1703) and his famous diaries (1660-c.1670) make numerous mention of his efforts in relation to the Thames along this stretch of the river from his position as Head of the Admiralty, particularly in relation to Wars with the Dutch. In 1665 plague hit London and on Thameside checks were carried out on incoming vessels at Canvey Island and at Tilbury. But plague had previously severely affected Barking in 1574, 1582, 1603 and 1665 and that year there were 90 deaths recorded in Romford. Victims of plague and of the Great Fire of London are said to have been buried at Frog Island in the Dagenham marshes. In his diary for 1665 Pepys mentions that he visited Grays in the late summer on what was 'a very calm and curious morning' and that he purchased 'a great deal of fine fish'. He also made much of his labours as a matchmaker at Dagnams, Noak Hill where he was a frequent visitor, between Mr. Carteret and Lady 'Jem' (Jemima daughter of Lord Sandwich had an arranged marriage with Philip Carteret in 1665). Although the mansion has gone Dagnam Park survives with its Humphrey Repton landscape still discernible close by the London Loop section 21.

The year after, 1666, saw the **Great Fire of London** where no doubt the conflagration would have been visible from here.[13] Following the Fire a Coal Duty on coal imports to London was imposed at the ports and later on loaded carts and rail wagons too, to help the costs of rebuilding London including St. Pauls Cathedral. In the mid 19th century cast iron Boundary Posts inscribed with the coat of arms of the City of London were set up on roadsides to mark the tax point – here listed posts are in Collier Row, in Romford and two in Rush Green, and similarly, the tall stone obelisk on the railway embankment near Whalebone Lane South marks the limit of the Metropolitan Police district. Of the many that were set up around London there are other unlisted surviving examples locally, including a cast iron post on display at Valence House Museum, while other posts and obelisks, mainly along the Beam river at Dagenham have been lost (Martin Nail).

Compounding local fears in the following year during the **Second Anglo-Dutch War** in 1667, the Dutch fleet sailed into the Thames, where the British were ill-prepared for defence with few guns at Tilbury for example. The king ordered a blockade by sinking ships at Barking Creek and elsewhere, and the mobilisation of all militia around London - which repelled a Dutch landing party on Canvey Island. But the Dutch continued engagements and attacked the British fleet in the 'Raid on the Meadway' with the terror of its cannon fire audible as far as London; it was one of the worst British naval defeats. With London so vulnerable, in 1668 work was planned for a new much larger fort at West Tilbury that was substantially completed by 1685.

> In 1670, the bold Anglo-Irish scoundrel Colonel Blood had returned to England after having first fought for the king, then for Parliament and fleeing back to Ireland when Charles II came to the throne, he then became involved with a failed plot to storm Dublin Castle and so had a price on his head as he hid out in Romford Market posing as an apothecary named Ayloffe.

 [13] Draw or paint a picture of the Great fire of London in daylight or darkness as seen from the Land of the Fanns in colour with silhouettes, smoke and fire fanned by a strong east wind.

> In 1671 he hatched an audacious plan to steal the British Crown Jewels from the Tower of London.¹⁴ 💡 His plot failed but he won over the king who both pardoned him and gifted him lands in Ireland. Blood then became a familiar figure at Court where he was employed as an advocate. Several of his descendants later had distinguished careers in Britain and Ireland.

The Catholic James II succeeded his brother as king and, in 1686 was the last monarch to hunt stag locally around Brentwood and Romford (Prof. Ged Martin, Historian). He was followed on the throne by his Protestant daughter Mary and her Dutch, Protestant husband and cousin William of Orange as joint monarchs and then by Mary's sister Queen Anne. Despite having had 17 children before Anne had even succeeded to the throne, none survived her. She reigned from 1702-1714 and the Act of Settlement of 1701 ensured that the crown would pass to a Protestant heir, bypassing her Catholic relatives and bringing a close to the House of Stuart.

Places to visit near and far:

- Eastbury Manor House, a brick built manor house erected during the reign of Queen Elizabeth I, now Grade I listed National Trust property and Discover Me(tropolitan Essex)
- Tudor Church of All Saints, East Horndon managed by the Churches Conservation Trust
- Tilbury Fort, English Heritage property, originally built by Henry VIII as part of his coastal defences of London and its dockyards
- Queen Elizabeth's Hunting lodge, Epping Forest, Grade II* listed building
- Valence House Museum and grounds, Chadwell Heath, listed Grade II* it is a timber-framed and plastered house built in the 17th century on a much older moated site
- Essex Houses & Gardens are a group of historic buildings and gardens independently opening to the public and include the Tudor Ingatestone Hall and gardens and Layer Marney Tower which is a Tudor palace and the early 17th century Audley End House
- Thames Chase Forest Visitor Centre, Cranham, with a 17th / 18th century timber barn
- William Hunter Memorial (grade II), Brentwood (erected 1861) and Stratford Martyrs Memorial (grade II), Parish Church of St. John, Stratford (erected 1879)
- National Maritime Museum, Greenwich
- Oliver Cromwell's House in Ely and Cromwell Museum in Huntingdon – with school visits, virtual education sessions and family friendly events
- Mary Rose, Portsmouth, ship in Henry VIII's navy, which sank in the Solent in 1545 during action against the French

---

 ¹⁴ The 'Outrage' board game is based on the escapade of Colonel Blood and challenges players to try themselves to 'steal' the Crown Jewels and escape.

Chapter 10 15th–17th centuries: Tudor and Stuart

- Portland Castle, Dorset, one of Henry VIII's coastal artillery forts, an English Heritage property, similarly Deal Castle and Walmer Castle in Kent
- Weald & Downland Living Museum, at Singleton near Chichester with its famous collection of historic buildings through the ages
- Visit the Tower of London and see the Crown Jewels for yourself

Ideas for future projects:

- A study of the importance of All Saints church East Horndon together with the history and fragmentation of East Horndon village, its impact and potential for interpretation and recording
- A study of Aveley village in its heyday including writing its local history
- A study of 15th and 16th century buildings across this landscape including the royal Tudor Palace of Pyrgo at Havering-atte-Bower
- Consider the likely effects of the Tudor economy of the royal manor and Palaces on the surrounding area across this landscape (see also McIntosh, Marjorie Keniston, 1986 *'Autonomy and Community: the Royal Manor of Havering, 1200–1500'* pub. Cambridge University Press, and also by her in 1991 *'A Community Transformed: The Manor and Liberty of Havering, 1500-1620'* pub. Cambridge University Press)
- A study of Samuel Pepys, his visits to and influence on this landscape, on smuggling and defence of the realm (see reference books for example Meeres, N.V. ed. 1933 *The Diary of Samuel Pepys Selections* pub. Macmillan & Co.)
- A study of the inter-twined political, economic and family relationships of the local nobility and upper classes

References for further research:

More information on this historical period can be found through:

- See Section C: History Introduction, p. 99
- Ancient Monuments Society (AMS) now Historic Buildings & Places
- The Society for the Protection of Ancient Buildings (SPAB)
- Victorian & Albert Museum British Galleries for style, taste and innovation of the times
- Historic Environment Records (HERS) by county are available through 'Heritage Gateway' online; details of conservation areas are held by the relevant Local Authorities and available online
- The London Gardens Trust
- Essex Gardens Trust
- John Walker, 1598, *Old Thorndon Hall* map

Further Reading:

- Bowman, Karen (2013) *Essex Boys* pub. Amberley Publishing 2013 ISBN 9781445608532
- Browne, Montagu (1889) *Yearly Records of Pyrgo Park*
- Hewett, Cecil Alec (1969) *Development of Carpentry, 1200-1700: An Essex Study*

- Kemp, E.G.W. (1884) *Kempes Nine Daies Wonder, Performed In A Journey From London To Norwich: Wherein euery dayes iourney is pleasantly set down, to satisfie his friends the truth against all lying ballad-makers; what hee did, how he was welcome, and by whome entertained* pub. 2009, ISBN 9781120307651
- Maldon, Henry Elliot, Royal Historical Society (Great Britain) (1980s edit.) *The Cely Papers: selections from the Correspondence and Memoranda of the Cely Family* pub. Camden
- Mildmay, Lieut.-Colonel Herbert A. St. John, (compiled 1913) *A Brief Memoir of the Mildmay Family* Privately printed by John Lane the Bodley Head MCMXIII
- Moore, Lucy, *Lady Fanshawe's Receipt Book: An Englishwoman's Life During the Civil War.* About *The Life and Times of a Civil War Heroine* her book includes the first recipe for 'icy cream'
- Sutherland, Lucy Stuart (1962) *A London Merchant 1695-1774* ISBN 9789333393676)
- Thompson, Leslie (1957) *The Land that Fanns* pub. the Tindal Press

Chapter 11
18th century: Georgian
1714 – 1837

'...Georges four (I,II,III,IV), Will and...'

NATIONAL CURRICULUM Key Stage 3 hints

After Queen Anne the next 56 royal family members in line for the throne were all Catholics and under the law, the Act of Settlement 1701, they were bypassed for their next Protestant relative. This was an Hanoverian, George I of Great Britain, who reigned from 1714-1727. Catholic opponents to him rallied as Jacobites supporting James (III), the *Old Pretender* as the Stuart heir. During this period the South Sea Bubble major financial crisis erupted in 1720, when the South Sea Company, that had been founded on slavery, collapsed. In Parliament the political position of Robert Walpole strengthened through his handling of the crisis and power in Britain began to move away from the monarch and towards a more democratic system with a cabinet government led by a prime minister. In effect Sir Robert Walpole became the first British Prime Minister (from 1721-1742), and led the Whig party against the Tories.

George II was the son of George I and reigned in Britain from 1727-1760. He was the last British monarch to lead the army into battle (in Bavaria in 1743). In 1745 Charles the *Young Pretender,* wanted a return to the 'divine right of kings', and tried to depose George II in the last Jacobite rebellion known as the *Forty-five*. But this was unsuccessful and Charles fled to France and as *Bonnie Prince Charlie* he has become a romantic icon with the story being told of his flight aided by Flora MacDonald in the traditional Scottish lullaby *The Skye Boat Song*.

SURPRISE *'The Land of the Fanns is an intricate landscape, full of surprises and 'hidden gems' and rewards exploring.'* **(TellTale working with the public 2018)**

Despite this being a period of continual foreign warfare this area remained in agricultural use during the Georgian era (as it is known from the first four Kings who all took the name of George as monarch). The stable and prosperous economic end to the Stuart period continued during this time and the resultant accumulated wealth enabled a flourishing of the Arts and this became a reasoning *Age of Enlightenment*. Now people found they had time to be thinkers and to debate, they wanted to improve on nature and had ideals of freedom and equality and this landscape and its people continued to play their part. Here the landscape, its location and connections quite naturally present opportunity for being inventive and for developing social awareness, and it has done so over time and the independent minds of social thinkers, improvers and reformers is of significance here particularly from the 17th century onwards.

MIGRATION *'This is a crossroads landscape: because of its location on the Thames ... people have always travelled into, through and away from this area.'*
(TellTale working with the public 2018)

By the Georgian period, as pressure for the outward expansion of London developed, aided by improvements to transport systems for people and goods, north-east London relentlessly migrated into historic south-west Essex, bringing new cultural and business ideas. These included the new professions of architecture and landscape architecture, as well as developments in religion, and ideas of academics and social improvers in literature, philosophy, music and politics as well as in agriculture and industries like quarrying.

Political and societal status still revolved around land rather than commerce but now was an opportunity for merchants to step up to have more importance and influence. However their business dealings are now considered at times to have been dubious at least (ref. the Norman & Plantagenet Chapter for the Cely and similar papers and see *A London Merchant 1695-1774* below), and even immoral or abhorrent in the case of slavery for example. Some of that new-found wealth, directly or indirectly, would have funded the grand houses and parklands of the time including some in this area.

Highway Improvements The Havering Palaces that had been highly influential on the economic development of the area, had been demolished and this landscape that is close to London and close to the Thames now became a significant area for development. In his *Tour Through the Eastern Counties* by **Daniel Defoe** in 1724, Defoe includes a description of Brentwood town at the time as 'full of good inns and chiefly maintained by the excessive multitude of carriers and passengers who are constantly passing this way to London with droves of cattle, provisions and manufactures.' From the time of Queen Elizabeth I a postal service had begun along the Great Essex Road between London and Harwich. In time stage posts were set up providing fresh horses and by the early eighteenth century Essex was organised into the Eastern District and mail was checked by Surveyors along the road.

However, highway robbery had continued from the Middle Ages and became a capital offence. From the early 17th century it was being recorded in isolated places like Romford Common and Chadwell Heath (which tradition says at one time was frequented by the notorious highwayman **Dick Turpin**). Stealing from travellers had become commonplace by the 18th century as improved roads and increasing trade led to more horse and stagecoach traffic between often isolated settlements and with travellers frequently carrying large sums of money as there were few banks.

> Between 1781 and 1787 Edward Carder, prominent Romford brewer, was held up on three occasions by highwaymen and footpads when returning home. On the last occasion he was better prepared and called for help. The three criminals were caught and later hanged at Chelmsford.
>
> In 1800 a local, Jimmy Wood, was shot near Gallows Corner while attempting to rob a mail coach; he managed to return to his mother at Hornchurch where she hid him and he at first recovered but still met an early death.

Even in 1807 in his *General View of the Agriculture of the County of Essex Vol. 2* the writer Arthur Young comments that the forest of Epping and Hainault are the hunts of robbers and deer thieves.

The introduction of toll charges enabled **Turnpike Trusts** to finance road improvements. The Middlesex and Essex Trust operated from 1722 improving what would become the A12 road running directly through Romford Market to Brentwood, Billericay and on to Chelmsford, Witham, Colchester and beyond to the coast. In 1793 the Thundersley to Horndon Trust linked to Brentwood and Tilbury and in 1808 the Barking and Tilbury Fort Road Trusts also opened.

The new toll roads made travel quicker and easier, and with increasing control of highway robbery in the 19th century, together provided good access for business and commerce. This enabled the area to attract development as it became possible for the wealthy to acquire country estates that were accessible to their London places of business. As the area opened up the new professions of building architecture and landscape architecture were becoming available and desirable to the wealthy.

The early 18th century, old Toll House, Shenfield with later extensions, as it may have appeared when this was the first road in Essex to be turnpiked

Architecture & Planned Landscapes The hills and high wooded ridges here with their clean air and distant landscape views were most attractive for development and much of the most desirable landscape was at first taken up by the wealthy employing the best professional people to put fine houses into purpose designed parklands across this landscape. Great houses in the grand manner were erected in brick or stone or rendered to look like stone, especially in towns and when in the ownership of richer and fashion-conscious people.

Famous architects like James Paine (b.1717 d.1789) and James Wyatt (b.1746 d.1813) were employed here and produced some fine examples of houses and landscaped Parks some of which are now open to the public. Well-known landscape gardeners were also employed across the area including Charles Bridgeman (b.1690-d.1738), and local men Richard Woods (b.1715-d.1793) tenant of North Ockendon Hall, and Humphry Repton (b.1752-d.1818) of Hare Street, as the planned Parkland also became fashionable.

Bower House & Stables 1729 (both grade I listed): In the royal Liberty at the end of his well-established career, the early landscape architect Charles Bridgeman took a landscape commission from John Baynes, Sergeant-at-Law, on the slopes south-east of the site of Havering Palace and gave the young Henry Flitcroft his first building commission – to put a house into Bridgeman's landscape.

Bridgeman physically divided the house from its farmland by his early very simple form of a ha-ha (a sunken walled, boundary ditch), and provided early landscape tricks to create views and a ride and viewing area in the adjacent woodland. Flitcroft had recently been working under the guidance of William Kent at Holkham Hall in Norfolk and may have brought some of the ideas he had learned in Norfolk to his design for Bower House, originally called 'Monthavering'. The allegorical wall murals by Sir James Thornhill seemingly reference the neighbouring palace site. Some of the family portraits in natural style were in the manner of William Hogarth. He was the son-in-law of James Thornhill and famously a pictorial satirist and social critic at these times of both extreme luxury and of great poverty, he was even suspected by the French of being a secret agent in 1748 (Hogarth House room guide and McQuade MA, Brian Thom, *Seven Painters who changed the course of Art History*).

Illustration of a traditional ha-ha – a vertical barrier to grazing animals that retains an uninterrupted view from the house to the landscape beyond (compare with the 20th century ha-ha at Hylands House, Writtle)

Between 1797 and 1816, during the time of the Napoleonic Wars, wings were added to each side of Bower House, and there was a royal visit by the young Princess Charlotte in 1801 and in 1804 a fete and military display and grand dinner were held for 'About 200 of the neighbouring nobility and gentry and others from the town...' (*About Bower House* by S.D. Pomeroy, pub. Ford Marketing Institute 1970). In 1832 a grand dinner for the local poor was held to celebrate the Great Reform Act that brought about electoral reform – although the labouring class still did not get the vote. It seems the final grand event was another royal visit between the two World Wars, this time by Queen Mary in 1934. After WW2 the property was purchased by Ilford Ltd and then by Ford Motor Company, it is now owned and occupied by the Amana Trust.

Rainham Hall 1729: The neighbouring Hundred of Chafford also became a desirable area for fine houses and landscaped Parks, some of which survive in whole or part and some properties in private ownership are open to the public occasionally, others are regularly open to the public like Rainham Hall in National Trust ownership (on the London Loop junction of section 23 and 24, just south of the Ingrebourne Valley and Thames Chase Walk 5). At Rainham the village was regenerated from c.1728 prompted through investment in its wharf by an entrepreneurial newcomer to the area, Captain John Harle who built Rainham Hall in 1729.

In time the Captain's son, also John, and his wife occupied Rainham Hall where they hosted the new Methodist meetings. In 1767 John Valton, a contemporary of John Wesley, brought Methodism to Rainham at their invitation and the Hall became the scene of a near riot by an angry mob led amazingly by Harle's father-in-law William Dearsley who had the visiting Methodist Minister horsewhipped out of the house. Valton escaped via the back door, across the pond and off to Purfleet village where Methodists were better tolerated at the time, Valton recorded the detailed story in his diary.

Rainham village centre boasts a variety of both red brick and timber constructed Georgian properties, many originally with a commercial use in this riverside village. The listed buildings from this period include Rainham Hall and its outbuildings (all II*), Redberry and the Old Vicarage in Broadway, and in Upminster Road South no's 2-6 were originally a barn and at one time an inn called the 'Horseshoe & Cann' (a wide drinking vessel) with a tiny shop and covered passageway at no. 8. A late 18th century property survives at 12 Broadway, while terraced shops at no's 9-27 Upminster Road South were originally Georgian cottages when this was Back Street and converted to shops some years later (photograph held at Havering Local Studies Library), all Locally Listed.

Bretons 1740/2: In the Dagenham Corridor Bretons (II*) is a gentry house (of high social class) erected in c.1740 although there had been some four earlier houses on the site with areas of medieval masonry surviving. Like others from this period, Bretons is within its own farmland setting but this house is smartly separated from its working landscape by the Georgian introduction of a fine bowed clairvoyee (II*) of low walls and railings with beautiful wrought iron gates and overthrow that encloses the forecourt to the house via a short carriage approach and with a mature Cedar of Lebanon tree before the house.

Sketch of Bretons house and farm as it would have appeared in c.1820 with the house separated from the farm and its early 16th century Tudor barn & walled garden

Several of the 16th century farm buildings survive as listed buildings in the remains of the walled garden beside the manor house. There is anecdotal evidence of large tunnels running from the house to the river – possibly for smuggling during the Tudor period. The old farmland is now in use as parkland and sports pitches and a 4.5ha (11-acre) fishing lake created as part of the river Beam flood plain that separates Bretons from The Chase LNR in Dagenham.

Gaynes 1748: Sir James Esdaile (c.1714-1793) was one of the first to be attracted to develop in this area. He was a banker and co-owner of Rose Hall, a Jamaican Georgian plantation house, now run as an historic house museum. He moved to Upminster in 1748 where he had Gaynes Mansion built for himself by James Paine a leading architect of the day. Esdaile also developed some ten significant properties around the village, restoring prosperity to the local area. His surviving buildings include the listed Tadlows gardener's cottage and Gaynes Cross Lodge in Corbets Tey Road; Clockhouse on a moated site was originally the stable block to Esdaile's mansion of New Place erected in 1775 to replace an earlier 18th century house (modern development works revealed below ground arched brickwork bridging over what is thought to be the now dried up Upminster Bell River); also Harwood Hall, which was built c.1782 but altered in gothic style in c.1840, and is now in use as a Montessori school.

Esdaile's own mansion was demolished after only 50 years although part of the grounds survive in this area as Parklands Open Space (see Thames Chase Walks no. 5 & 6a). The grounds are thought to have been laid out by Esdaile's gardener Mr Tadlow to the design of James Paine. They once extended to 40.5 ha. (100 acres), the stream running from Cranham marsh was dammed here to form the large ornamental lake with a listed bridge and a small island (extant); today it leads on to Bonnetts Wood in Thames Chase and accesses the Ingrebourne Valley. An extensive greensward survives as Parklands Park where at the west end the original waterfall and rapids have long-since been replaced by a concrete weir however north from the weir the Walk traces through an area of Ancient Woodland along the path of a holly-lined woodland walk to another listed bridge, apparently once giving access from Gaynes House, which it faced in picturesque fashion, to the neighbouring Hacton House, the two owners at times being on friendly terms.

Hacton House 1762/5: During the reign of George III (1760-1820) William Braund built Hacton House for himself. He was associated with the Branfill family of Upminster in the East India Shipping business. The house is now converted into private flats and bungalows. Braund is famed for his papers that convey a rare account of aspects of 18th century commercial life (see *A London Merchant 1695-1774* below). His estate is shown on the Chapman Andre map of Essex 1777 where it extended to include Park Corner Farm with its red brick listed barn (Braund's papers indicate that he was producing his own bricks in 1773). In his *A History of Upminster & Cranham* John Drury records that until the early post-War period a tunnel existed from the grounds into Hacton House and led to a small room hidden behind a dresser in the hall.

Belhus Park bet. 1753-1763: Belhus Park is a grade II registered Historic Park on the At Risk Register. Here was an Elizabethan Tudor mansion, built 1523-1525 that is said to have been visited by Elizabeth I during her *Progress* to Essex in 1578. Recent exciting archaeological evidence of the Tudor and Jacobean (early Stuart reign of King James I) gardens has been found to still lay beneath the ground surface (LotF 2021). Christopher Laine, Historic England Landscape Architect commented that 'We already knew that Belhus Park was a special place, and a designed landscape of great historic interest. This research ... will help to inform strategies for improving management and conserving this important heritage for current and future generations.'

By the mid 17th century Belhus was one of the largest estates in Essex. The house was given a gothic appearance by Thomas Barrett-Lennard, the 17th Lord Dacre, between 1744-1777. His friend, the architect Sanderson Miller (1716-80), was a pioneer of Gothic revival architecture and a landscape designer who advised on the building. The mansion was demolished in 1957 after wartime damage, some of the 16th century panelling is held at Valence House Museum and a bird's-eye view of the property in the late 17th /early 18th century is held at Thurrock Museum together with an oak fireplace, panelling and other fittings.

Belhus Park landscape survives in Essex County Council ownership with leisure facilities. This Park was designed by Lancelot 'Capability' Brown[1] between 1753 and 1763 with additions by Richard Woods of North Ockendon in 1770. Humphry Repton (who coined the term 'landscape gardener') may also have later given some landscaping advice and Belhus appeared in the pocket companion or almanac *Peacock's Polite Repository* for 1807.

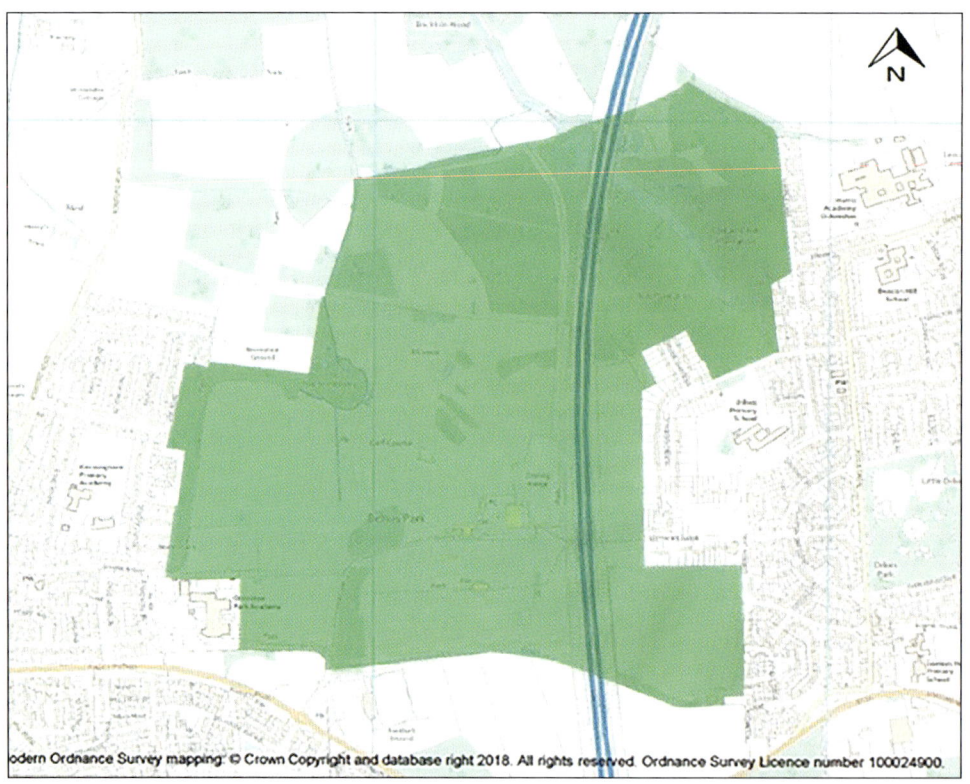

Belhus grade II Registered Park © Crown copyright 2021 OS licence no.100064852 © Historic England 2021
The National Heritage List Text Entries contained in this material were obtained on 26 October 2021.
The most publicly available up-to-date National Heritage List Text Entries can be obtained from
http://www.historicengland.org.uk/listing/the-list/

 [1] Lancelot Brown was called 'Capability' because he often said Parks had 'capability for improvement'. He swept away formal gardens with a large scale, polished, naturalistic approach with great, smooth lawns, trees in clumps, belts and specimens and long views. Plan your own landscape Park like Brown adding a curving lake, bridges, an island, earth mounds, sweeping drive, garden buildings, sheep and a ha-ha (Curriculum link to Geography – maps and Art).

Today the landscape and the Long Pond are bisected by the M25 motorway but the high-level road provides an over-looking view for travellers and with the open parkland linked by pedestrian footbridges to the woodland areas including Belhus Chase and Gurnett's Fields. The walls of the 18th century walled garden and an 18th century Tudor 'chimney' stench pipe² are listed buildings, and other original references survive from the planned gardens including woodlands, shrubbery, two mounds and mature specimen trees. On the east side of the motorway Thurrock Borough Council maintain the adjoining woodlands linked historically with Belhus Mansion - Oakwood, Rookery Wood and Ash Plantation, located on either side of Long Pond.

To the north Belhus Park adjoins Belhus Woods Country Park, also within the Thames Chase Community Forest and south of the Visitor Centre. The Country Park is a mixed landscape with grassland, lakes and ancient woodland. In 2001/2 the Forestry Commission extended the woodlands by purchasing and planting Cely Woods (named after the local 15th century family of wool merchants).

Thorndon Hall 1764: On Brentwood Heights, James Paine built the new Thorndon Hall (grade I) for the 9th Baron Petre. The mansion is now converted into private flats and is situated at the north end of the Park, which is a grade II* registered Historic Park.

Thorndon Hall, Ingrave by James Paine neo-classicist and the leading architect of his day, begun in 1764, grade I listed (Photograph courtesy LotF)

There are various listed buildings in and around the Park including the listed Lion Lodges North and South, and Lion Gates with Railings, The Avenue, probably by James Paine, 1764, and the early 19th century Hunters Lodge (Octagon Lodge) in The Avenue. Nearby the listed Hatch Farmhouse and farm buildings in Thorndon Park built in 1776 were designed by Samuel Wyatt as an animal feeding place grouped with an earlier repurposed, listed timber-framed granary.

---

² See story no.10 of 'Fens Forests and Fields' pub. Thames Chase Trust (LotF) 2021 ISBN 978-1-5272-8981-9.

Chapter 11 18th century: Georgian

The parkland is now Thorndon Country Park, it is within the Community Forest and at some distance north-east of Thames Chase Visitor Centre and provides its own visitor facilities. The Park was designed by Lancelot Brown but retaining some fragments of the earlier Park by the 8th Baron Petre, his plans drawn up in 1733 by the surveyor Sieur Pierre Bourguignon who also seemingly worked on Weald Park in Brentwood in 1738 (he was a colleague of Hogarth and possibly a French spy),[3] and with some later work by Richard Woods.

South and west of Thorndon Park are the dispersed settlements of Little Warley and Childerditch with numerous listed buildings of the period amongst the older timber-framed survivals including the Greyhound Inn on Warley Common of 1769 which has early 16th century origins and an early 19th century outbuilding. The A128 Brentwood to Tilbury road runs alongside Thorndon Park through the linier villages of Ingrave and Herongate (a conservation area) where there are numerous 18th century listed buildings amongst those dating from the previous century.

Hare Hall 1769-70: A country house (II*) built in Gidea Park for the merchant J.A. Wallinger by James Paine; Richard Woods later laid out the grounds and Humphry Repton, who lived in Gidea Park, included a drawing of the Hall in *The Polite Repository*. The site was occupied by a regiment of the British Army Reserve, 2nd Battalion of the Artists Rifles as Hare Hall Camp during WWI earning battle honours during the Boar War and WWI (see Early 20th century Chapter). Since 1921 Hare Hall has been the Royal Liberty School.

Bedfords 1771: In the royal Liberty on Havering Ridge, the lawyer John Heaton[4] bought Bedfords in 1771 rebuilding the house soon after together with a walled garden with an unusual horizontal chimney arrangement heating the hot houses. He acquired a great deal of the newly enclosed common land and rebuilt the adjacent listed Upper Bedfords farmhouse and established Heaton Grange model farm beyond. The estate was described at the time as having 'much the appearance of a park and all the uses of a farm'. Later a Victorian owner of the mansion introduced all sorts of new garden devices between his purchase in 1853 and 1862, including a scheme for water management, a fernery and a pineapple house inside the walled garden.

Bedfords was sold to the District Council in 1933 for a park and the house used as a local museum. The house was demolished in 1958 and a café with an unusual cantilevered roof erected in 1964. That was itself replaced in 2003 by an Essex Wildlife Trust Visitor Centre that echoes the earlier café design and together with the parkland and Heaton's walled garden survive as Bedford's Country Park.[5]

Dagnam Park 1772: Here on Havering Ridge was an important Tudor house, rebuilt in c.1660 and on several occasions visited by Samuel Pepys. That house was also demolished and rebuilt in c.1772 by Sir Richard Neave, at one time a Governor of the Bank of England, he owned property and enslaved people in the Caribbean and was one of those merchants intent on elevating themselves. Humphry Repton designed the landscaped Park and some of his landscape ideas and features survive such as the treed mound and cattle pond near the house. These are illustrated in Repton's *Fragments on the*

---

[3] David Jacques (2017) *Gardens of Court and Country: English Design, 1630-1730*; Brogden, William Alvis (2016) *Iconographia Rustica: Stephen Switzer and the designed landscape* pub. Taylor & Francis.
[4] *Georgiana Duchess of Devonshire* by Amanda Foreman features John Heaton, legal adviser to the Duke.
[5] Supported by Friends of Bedfords Park (FOBP) volunteers.

Theory and Practice of Landscape Gardening published in 1816. That house too was demolished after army occupation during WW2. Today the parkland is locally referred to as 'the Manor' where there is an older water filled moated site at Cockerels (SAM) and deer herds roam freely, and the woodlands that Repton considered to be 'sufficient' survive as Cockerels Wood, Hatters Wood and Duck Wood amongst the post-War Harold Hill housing estate.[6]

Boyles Court, South Weald/Great Warley 1776: The mansion was rebuilt or possibly partly remodeled in 1776/1788 by the architect Thomas Leverton and acquired by Joseph Lescher as a country seat. It is designed as a central block with pavilions in red brick and listed in 1958. The Lescher family went on to acquire Boyles Court Farm in about 1807 where the barn was built in 1774, the barn and late 19th century farm stables are also listed buildings. The property was used for war work during WW2. Following use as Leverton Hall Secure Unit, in 2021 the mansion is set to be converted to residential apartments with houses constructed in the grounds.

Cranham Hall c.1790: Cranham Conservation Area is a hilltop hamlet on a medieval route with historic Georgian and Victorian buildings and surrounded by farmland that retains its historic feeling of rural isolation. Here, Cranham Hall (Thames Chase Walk no 2, 5, 6a) is privately occupied, a listed Georgian house built in c.1790 on the site of an earlier mansion that was once the home of General James Oglethorpe (1696-1785) and from which the earlier walls of the walled garden survive as a listed building.

General Oglethorpe was a British General (c.1745) and MP (from 1722), a visionary and philanthropist interested in social justice. He founded the State of Georgia in America in 1730-33 and established many forts along the Georgia coast and colonial towns including Frederica and Savannah, which he designed. Today Savannah has heritage protection in America as an outstanding example of 18th century town planning. At the site, the Fort Frederica National Monument quotes Oglethorpe – 'We are resolved not to suffer defeat. We will rather die like Leonidas and his Spartans if we can but protect Georgia and Carolina and the rest of Americans from Desolation'. In 1742 his military leadership of English and native American Indian forces against the Spanish in the **War of Jenkins Ear** and his tactics and daring action in the **Battle of Bloody Marsh**, were vital to retaining Georgia as an English possession and protection for British North America. But the peace also left Georgia susceptible to the incoming migrant slavers from South Carolina as Oglethorpe returned to England.

Many of the friends Oglethorpe entertained at his Cranham home were great academics and thinkers of their day, including **Dr Samuel Johnson** (d.1784) and **James Boswell**, all close friends for many years. Boswell was interested in intellectual, philosophical, and academic thinking and in time met a great variety of powerful people with those interests. He admired and looked up to Oglethorpe, and he became known for writing Johnson's biography, which has been described as 'the most famous single work of biographical art in the whole of literature'. Johnson is most famed for writing the pre-eminent English dictionary and has been described as 'arguably the most distinguished man of letters in English history'. He also made satirical allusions to public concerns of the times including corruption and crime, finance and immigration.

---

 [6] Discuss the pros and cons of the earlier formal gardens of the Elizabethan Age against Brown's reforming (or vandalising) parklands and Humphry Repton's later ideas of Picturesque landscapes with terraces, balustrades and steps, pleasure grounds and flower beds (Curriculum link to English – presenting a point of view).

Oglethorpe died at Cranham and is buried in the listed Victorian All Saints' parish church that immediately adjoins Cranham Hall and his association makes this a place of occasional modern-day pilgrimage for American visitors.

Hawkesbury Manor, Barstable Hundred: To the east of the area on Langdon Hills, Hawkesbury Manor was one of the two original manors of Fobbing. This private house is a timber framed, listed building of mid - late 18th century origin and, together with St. Michael's church, it is said to have once served as a line of sight for Thames shipping in the Tilbury Hope. Historically, Fobbing marsh was famed for smuggling activity.

The site adjoins a 3.6 ha (9 acre) site of grass, scrub and woods rich in flora and fauna leading onto Basildon Meadows SSSI and the Dry Street Hill Fields Wildlife Site in Thurrock to form an important hillside wildlife site.

Woodlands, formerly Scrimpshires, at Becontree Heath is a late 18th century listed house in brown brick with some fine features. In more recent times it was used as a hostel for older people and then as a children's home, is now in use as the Barking and Dagenham Registry Office. Nearby in Dagenham places like Chadwell Heath were known at this time for reputable apothecary shops and also for 'quack' doctors – that Dr. Samuel Johnson described in his Dictionary as '...An artful tricking practitioner in Physic'.

The Round House 1792: In Havering-atte-Bower village this grade II* listed villa was built in 1792 for William Sheldon and attributed to the architect John Plaw. It has an unusual oval plan form and said to 'provide all conveniences of a country seat in miniature' (London Parks & Gardens Trust). Sheldon was a barrister, highly appreciated for his diplomatic skills in negotiations between the two sides in the Italian Opera controversy (Neil Burton, Architectural Historian) that dominated polite society on mainland Europe and had spread to England. The Italian cause was to promote modern development in opera with the introduction of fun into classical music. The Round House has often taken part in Open House London.

Stubbers Park 1796: Stubbers House was demolished in the 1960s and extensive gravel extraction undertaken during the 20th century destroying much of the landscaped Park. The landscape gardener for the Russell family (for earlier history see Tudor Chapter) was Humphry Repton, a local man residing for many years in Gidea Park, and the last great English landscape designer of the 18th century. He was seen as a successor to Lancelot Brown producing managed Parklands for Gentlefolk at the expense of working farmland. However his commissions were on a smaller scale and as a consultant only rather than a contractor. He also moved towards the controversial *picturesque* approach to landscape design and considered the importance of placing the house within the landscape. He advised on many local properties as illustrated in Peacock's *Polite Repository* in 1793, including Belhus and Langtons in Hornchurch and Stubbers in 1804.

Although the famous **'Red Book'** of Repton's designs for *improving* Stubbers Park in 1796 is damaged, it does survive and is held at the University of Essex (ref. Essex Gardens Trust). South of The Chase in Cranham a footpath or bridleway (fp228) joins Ockendon Road at Stubbers (Thames Chase Walk no 2) and as part of his scheme Repton re-sited the Stubbers section of road further west as Stubbers Lane. Some of Repton's ornamental tree planting and his treed grounds and lawned area survive to the front of the site along Ockendon Road and Stubbers drive. Also an 18th century walled garden and 'crinkle-crankle' or serpentine wall and entrance gate survive as a listed building and are a feature within the present use of Stubbers as an Outdoor Adventure Centre that makes popular use of the water-filled reclaimed gravel pits. Nearby in North Ockendon village, the listed Russell Cottage was constructed just a few years after Stubbers House and is associated with the Russell family.

LANDFORM *'The Land of the Fanns is about land and water and the often shifting relationship between them'* **(TellTale working with the public 2018)**

From 1820-1830 George IV was king, followed from 1830-1837 by his brother King William IV who became the last monarch of the Georgian period, a naval man he was nick-named the 'Sailor King'. Much of this landscape is about the relationship between the land and the water and related matters such as social change, science, slavery, naval reform, the army, royalty, politics and religion, were all issues current at that time.

The Land By this period people were travelling with greater ease and safety and writing about their observations and their studies of landscape. In this way *Picturesque Beauties of Great Britain – Essex* was written by Thomas Wright in 1834 and comprised engravings of pictures of all the very best of Britain's noble properties and views and includes Thorndon Hall, Weald Hall, Little Warley Hall and Bell House (or Belhus) in Aveley, together with views of Langdon Hills and Purfleet. Earlier, *The New & Complete British Traveller* pub. 1784 included Thorndon Hall and a print of the newly rebuilt Dagnams that also feature in a travel guide *Excursions in the County of Essex* 1818, which includes illustrations of other residences of the nobility and gentry such as Heron Hall, Weald Hall, Hare Hall in Gidea Park, Gidea Hall and Belhus.

At over 117 m. (385 ft.) the Langdon Hills Country Park (One Tree Hill and Westley heights) adjoins the Langdon Nature Reserve and Visitor Centre (Dunton Plotlands, Lincewood, Marks Hill and Willow Park). As a day-out destination these hills have enjoyed visitors as day-trippers, walkers and picnickers since Georgian times, being famous for their *prospect* or sudden very fine views, south and west over the landscape plain of this area as well as eastwards towards the Thames estuary. Indeed several Georgian writers and others have been inspired by the beauty of this landscape when viewed from the hills around. The historian **Philip Morant** was struck by the amazing views here towards London, recording that from the Langdon Hills this was the 'finest prospect in all England' *(The History and Antiquities of the County of Essex* pub. 1768).

In 1777 **Chapman and Andre** produced their excellent and reliable map of Essex that must have been a great aid to travellers and continues as an established work for historians today. By 1848 this 'finest prospect' was being advertised in William White's History, Gazetteer & Directory of the County of Essex with 'Pleasure parties from the metropolis and other places often assemble around a large tree on the highest point, to enjoy the extensive and delightful view, in which is seen the broad bosom of the Thames for a distance of nearly 40 miles, thickly studded with steam and sailing vessels; and a wide range of country in this county and Kent.' In a similar way, in the vicinity of Fairlop Waters, a local landowner founded Fairlop Fair at Aldborough Hatch in 1725. Beginning with picnics under the large and shady Fairlop Oak it continued until 1900 for a time attracting vast crowds, entertainment and a marching band.

In matters of science, **Dr. Derham** FRS (1657-1735), was once the village physician and Rector of Upminster (1689-1735). He became chaplain to the Prince of Wales in 1714 and a Canon of Windsor Castle in 1716, and he was a scholar with books published between 1696 and 1731. Amongst his extensive research interests he was curious about the significant medieval deneholes near Grays (see Tudor Chapter). Notably he was the first to accurately measure the speed of sound which he did in 1709 from the tower of the parish church of St Laurence in Upminster town centre and from other local landmarks, including North Ockendon church (both grade I listed buildings).

Sea Defence From the early 1600s **Barbary Pirates** were infamous for taking captives at sea to be sold into slavery or ransomed and at Rainham for example, vestry minutes describe assistance given to freed captive seamen traveling home in the early 18th century (*A History of Rainham with Wennington & South Hornchurch* by Frank Lewis 1966). A double gibbet fate for river pirates and other criminals stood at the mouth of the Beam river around 1777 (*Map of the County of Essex 1777* Chapman & Andre) and for three years from 1701 the Scottish privateer turned pirate Captain William Kidd, hung from the gibbet near Tilbury as a warning to others against piracy.

Around this time Samuel Bonham had at first been a navel Captain but then become a slave trader until 1740 when he retired to Orsett (*Basildon, Canvey, Southend Echo* 2007; BBC Essex, October 2014). Orsett House is a grade II* listed gentry house of the early to mid 18th century, divided into apartments and with listed garden walls and gates, one bearing the Essex Coat of Arms.

In Aveley, John Newton (1725-1807), was also at first a sailor until 1757 and later a Calvinist clergyman in c.1764. He lived in Marshfoot House, Aveley for a time in his youth and joined his first merchant ship at Long Reach, Purfleet.

Fear of invasion by the French under Napoleon led the Government to expand the Royal Navy and it was common for the **Press Gangs** to capture disembarking trained merchant seamen down river at Tilbury and press them into Navy service. The British Newspaper Archive records that a Press Gang of 150 men attacked East India Company Ships at Purfleet in January 1771 'armed with carbines, cutlasses and every necessary implement of war'. Like many experienced sailors of the age Newton was seen as valuable to the Royal Navy and he was also captured and pressed into Navy service, and in time flogged for trying to desert because of the terrible conditions.

Newton himself became a slave to a princess in West Africa and was abused and mistreated before being rescued, but later as a ship's Captain he became himself a slave trader. Later he became a Curate, then Rector, and eventually an abolitionist of slavery - which became law in 1807. Poignantly he wrote the hymn 'Amazing Grace ... that saved a wretch like me'. His extensive journals and letters provide much of what is known about the 18th century slave trade. Thurrock Borough Council propose a plaque in memory on the Green at Purfleet and there have been other commemorations and numerous films, novels, TV and stage productions on aspects of his life.

In Naval reform towards the end of the 18th century, during his time ashore Admiral of the Fleet, John Jervis 1st Earl St. Vincent GCB, PC, lived and eventually died at Rochetts, where the listed farmhouse, barn and Lodge cottage are associated with South Weald Park (Registered Park) lying outside St. Vincent's Hamlet that is said to have been part of the Rochetts estate. His title was awarded for his outstanding victory at the battle of Cape St. Vincent, with **Nelson** who was a Commodore and his protégé at the time. One of his awards for the victory was the Freedom of the City of London presented in a 100 guinea gold box with a ceremonial sword from the grateful City, both now held in the National Maritime Museum, Greenwich along with a gold topped baton later presented to him by King George IV. He was a disciplinarian, keeping firm control during that time of mutinies and he was skilled in administration and logistics and he brought cleanliness, hygiene and good health to the crews of the Navy ships. He became First Lord of the Admiralty in 1801 and made tireless efforts for naval reform, all matters of great relevance to people of this riparian area.

Land Defence At Tylers Common it is said that in taking precautions against the Napoleonic threat, the trees were cut down for Nelson's navy. The army were also preparing themselves against likely invasion by Napoleon and included the development of Warley Camp (Garrison) in 1742 with back-up stabling facilities for six troops of cavalry built at Romford in 1795 and the Havering Company of Volunteer Cavalry raised in around 1802. Warley Camp become the permanent Warley Barracks in 1805 and the remains of Warley Barracks military camp with its typical early 19th century military buildings, are at Warley Common to the north-east of Great Warley village. The Barracks turned Brentwood into a garrison town from George III to the mid-20th century, and is now the headquarters of 124 Petroleum Squadron, part of the Royal Logistics Corps of the Reserve Forces London.

At the height of military threat Warley Camp was one of the largest with some 10,000 soldiers when it was visited in 1778 by Dr Samuel Johnson. In the same year a grand **Review of Warley Garrison** and visit to the resplendent Warley Camp by King George III and Queen Charlotte took place and following the Review the king and queen were entertained by Lord Petre at Thorndon Hall. The event was recorded by Thomas Sandby, and by Philipp Jakob de Loutherbourg, and the canvases were originally acquired by King George III and are in the Royal Collection Trust.

Thomas Sandby (1721-98) 'The Encampment at Warley Common (Essex) in 1778'
By kind permission of the Royal Collection Trust/© Her Majesty Queen Elizabeth II 2021

The location of the picture by Sandby is from Shenfield Common with one of the two windmills in the foreground (evidenced on the Chapman Andre *Map of the County of Essex 1777*), looking south over Warley Common towards the Encampment with the main north face of Thorndon Hall on the far left in the middle ground and an area supplying the soldiers 'necessaries' is on the right. (The temporary huts were vulnerable it seems as the Royal Collection Trust notes from the *Chelmsford Chronicle* that a fire fanned by an east wind destroyed more than 50 of the huts and booths together with 'a butcher's shop, a brewhouse and three public houses').

Philipp Jakob de Loutherbourg (1740-1812) Warley Camp: 'The Mock Attack' painted in 1779
By kind permission of the Royal Collection Trust/© Her Majesty Queen Elizabeth II 2021

The pictures by Loutherbourg record the view of the encampment looking to the southwest over Childerditch Common and Little Warley Common, from Thorndon Hall Park on Brentwood Heights.

Philipp Jakob de Loutherbourg (1740-1812) 'Warley Camp: The Review' dated 1780
By kind permission of the Royal Collection Trust/© Her Majesty Queen Elizabeth II 2021

In depressing contrast, in 1821 the two-day, rain-soaked funeral cortege of Queen Caroline of Brunswick, wife of George IV (king from 1820-1830), who was scandalous but popular with the masses, passed through here en route from London to Harwich. Here the retinue passed unmolested after the riotous protests the company had experienced in travelling across London.

ECONOMY – *'This area is justly famous for trade, commerce and industry: these have been important here for many centuries.'* **(TellTale working with the public 2018)**

Agriculture From the earliest times, in common with the London basin this has been a prime agricultural area. From about 1750 **market-gardening** began to develop serving London and producing crops such as wheat, barley, hay, beans, and turnips, and fruit including apples, cherries, pears and peaches and hazelnuts and walnuts. Using the local wharfs in Rainham, Wennington, and Purfleet, City dung was brought out by Thames barge to manure the land and goods returned by barge or farm carts using the new toll roads to deliver produce into London.

Although In the west of our area much of the landscape has been subsumed in suburban development but even here surviving agricultural buildings of the period include an 18th century brick farm barn at Warren Farm in Marks Manor near Chadwell Heath, and a late 18th century red brick granary at the late 16th century Crown Farmhouse nearby. East of the Liberty in Upminster and Cranham, Apse Tree Cottages are a tiny pair of late 18th century farmworkers cottages (now one house), with a larger pair (again now one house) at 265-267 St. Mary's Lane with the more substantial early 19th century Bury Farmhouse close to West Horndon and the rather smarter Mascalls House in South Weald, the home of the high sheriff of Essex at the end of the century, all listed buildings and originally associated with the business of farming.

Across the central low-lying fanns of the river Mardyke from Thames Chase in the west across to Dunton, Langdon Hills and Vange (with its grade II* church of Norman origin), are many dispersed 18th century listed farmhouses like Fanns Farmhouse in the Mardyke valley. Also a number of local agricultural settlements including Bulphan and East and West Horndon surviving with core 18th and early 19th century buildings. Some of these buildings are in red brick, but most hark back to the earlier vernacular building form of timber-frame and weatherboarding, re-fronted in brick and 'improved' to suit Georgian taste, others are cottages with thatched roofs. From Thames Chase Forest Centre, Walk no.1 takes in North Ockendon where the late 18th century brick built Old Rectory stands next to the medieval church, while there are more listed Georgian properties in Ockendon Road.

The little village of North Stifford overlooks the Mardyke Valley, with many attractive 17th, 18th and 19th century listed and historic buildings; the Dog & Partridge Inn (rebuilt in 1934) was an alehouse in 1757. The listed Copped Hall was rebuilt in 1753 and later altered to the designs of **James Wyatt** (VCH), nearby are the 18th century timber-framed former granary and Stifford Lodge (Europa Lodge Hotel) that is of mid 18th- early 19th century date. Here the Mardyke river was tidal to Orsett Hall until the *Poorfleet* sluice gate was constructed at Purfleet in 1760 as part of the Royal Gunpowder Magazine development. However, the Mardyke river and ditches continued to be used by barges to transport agricultural produce and London manure to and from the Bulphan fens farms with the barges passing under Stifford Bridge into the 20th century. Today the village maintains a sense of peace and calm with an atmospheric combination of ancient woodlands, the Roman and Dutch fens and the marshes cutting through this landscape of the fanns. The old Stifford Clays Farmhouse was replaced in about

1840 by the present listed building a little to the south that was then part of the extensive Orsett Hall estate and the largest farm in Stifford.

At Orsett the village is surrounded by open countryside and survived as a small, historic settlement until the 20th century when Orsett Hospital was built on the site of the Victorian Workhouse together with residential developments, that are well integrated behind the main village streets the core of which is also a conservation area around the medieval church. Orsett Hall originally dated from the 17th century but was enlarged and reconstructed in brick from c.1750 with 4.9 ha (12 acres) of parkland at the centre of the Orsett Hall agricultural estate. However the house was destroyed by fire in 2007 and is now rebuilt in similar style to the original and is in commercial use; the 18th century boundary wall and fine wrought iron gate survive and are listed buildings.

Perhaps the greatest of all English writers on agriculture, **Arthur Young** (1741-1820) carried out an information gathering agricultural tour of the southern counties of England and Wales including this area in 1767 and remarked on the comparative benefits of the exceedingly large size of farms in the Mucking and Horndon area with rich soil and considerable flocks of sheep. He also commented magnificently on the beauty of this farmland landscape from the Langdon Hills as reported in *England's Gazetteer Vol. 2* by Philip Luckombe in 1790. While here Young stayed at the old Kings Head pub at West Tilbury and Thurrock Borough Council has included him in their Commemorative Plaques scheme in memory. Horndon-on-the-Hill is still a beautiful hilltop village with a Conservation Area and numerous listed buildings of the period focussing on the listed Wool Market and the importance of the wool trade to the area until the end of the 16th century.

King George III was an enthusiastic **agricultural improver**, known affectionately as 'Farmer George'. So too the Georgian landowners like John Heaton at Bedfords, were interested in the relationship of the best economic farming practices with the development of parkland landscapes by integrating good practice in farming and horticulture with good design. Local landowners were also interested in modern developments in agricultural machinery such as the two successful but rival Wedlake family agricultural Iron Foundries in Hornchurch.

Prompted by the years of War with France and with opportunity presented through the technological innovations of the time, the Government sought to increase agricultural production to feed the expanding population and canvassed opinions from experienced local farmers. In facing the Napoleonic threat, the Neave's of Dagnams at Noak Hill were amongst others advising on agriculture in Essex. As part of this drive, **Upminster Windmill** was newly built and in use by 1805 by local farmer James Nokes. By 1812, as a step towards industrialisation in the district the sails were being supplemented by steam engine alongside the mill. A grade II* listed building, its quality, completeness and significance with original wooden machinery makes it one of the very best surviving English smock mills (Thames Chase Walks no. 6a & 6b). There were other mills around the time in West Thurrock, Horndon-on-the-Hill and Orsett for example.

Ancient attempts to **enclose common land** continued, removing people's common rights over the land, harvesting the timber and turning the land to private farming. After 1811 the Common land along the edge of the Royal Forest was being sold off and farms created. Now on the Havering and Dagenham boarders around Marks Gate, farms such as the early 19th century Furze House Farm (listed) and new, improved roads were created with some land retained as commons such as the small patch of common land in Havering village where Havering Palace once stood. By 1814, the year before the famous battle of Waterloo, over 1,000 acres of commons land at Collier Row, Noak Hill, Straight Road and Squirrels Heath were taken into additional food production and mangel-wurzels (like sugar beet) were introduced as a crop in the area. Local farmers were also known for rearing exceptional Friesian cattle.

Distinctive black & white Friesian cattle stock as at Berwick Farm in Rainham, also exceptional Marino sheep from the flocks of George III were raised by the Sturgeon family in Thurrock

By 1815 with the end of the Napoleonic Wars there followed a period of economic depression and unemployment, with social discontent and unrest and political uncertainty that led to support for electoral reform,[7] and an evangelical revival. The two-party system of rival political parties – the **Tories and the Whigs** – developed during this period. Generally Tories represented the Anglican gentry (like Dr Johnson) while the Whigs supported constitutional monarchism, Protestant dissenters and industrialists.

It is claimed that the Congregational Church originated c.1797 through great dissatisfaction of local agricultural workers in the farming district around Upminster over the payment of **farm tithes** to the demanding Vicar giving rise to a major dispute between two Upminster rectors and their congregation. This led to the growth of Congregationalism in Upminster and the listed Old Chapel in Upminster (Thames Chase Walks 6a & 6b) was built in 1800 and re-fronted 1847, as an alternative place of worship for Protestant dissenters. It was used for non-conformist worship until 1989, now it is in private ownership and has a Friends Group and is opened to the public on occasion. (This Walk also gives easy access to the Upminster town centre retail area famed for its own Independent Department Store and a mainline railway station bringing people direct from London, Essex and the coast)

Quarrying The rich resources of sand, gravels, brickearth and chalk across this landscape are also an economic factor important to this locality. Quarrying for clay and gravel took place in South Ockendon during the 18th century with later extraction for **sand and gravels** mainly from the southern area where quarrying for minerals continues in the Ingrebourne Valley, and also in recent times from the shallow deposits on the ridge top of the Dagenham Corridor.

---

[7] Led to the 1832 Reform Act extending voting rights to the middle class.

Quarrying at the Mill Field by St. Andrews church in Hornchurch resulted in a bowl-shaped depression known as The Dell. It became popular as an arena for sporting events including bare knuckle fighting – most notably for the infamous prize fight between champion pugilist Daniel Mendoza and 'Gentleman' John Jackson for 'Champion of All England' (see Victorian Chapter).

Believed to be a depiction of the famous Jackson vs. Mendoza fight in 1795
By the kind permission of the National Trust for Scotland, Brodick Castle

Brickearth had been quarried anciently at Tylers Common recorded from the mid 11th century, and there was brickmaking during the 16th–18th centuries at Stony Hills Farm between Tylers Common and Great Warley including supplying Ingatestone Hall. In Cranham the Upminster Brickfields was operating from 1708 with its first brick kiln built in 1774 and operated under the Branfill family of Upminster Hall producing bricks and other clay goods, and amongst others for a time leased by T. L. Wilson (local historian). The bricks were known for their quality and supplied Upminster Court for example, but brickmaking finally ceased here in 1933. The Grays Brickearth was quarried from a 5.5 km (4 mile) stretch between West Thurrock and Little Thurrock and Grays town developed around the brickmaking industry that in 1804 employed some 500 men. In Brentwood in 1750 Thomas Munn known as 'the gentleman brickmaker' or 'Tom the Smuggler', was hanged at Chelmsford for robbing the Yarmouth mail, after a life of self-confessed exploits, and his body exhibited in chains at Gallows Corner, Rumford (Romford) (VCH). Brentwood Brickworks in London Road were in operation from at least 1878 until the early 20th century and an important geological site at the time.

Quarrying the **chalk outcrop** at Grays and West Thurrock was an ancient industry still taking place at this period. In 1768 Arthur Young complained of the heavy use by wagons hauling chalk from Tilbury to manure the fields in Billericay that created impossibly poor road conditions. The Thameside wharfs and proximity to London had already brought trade to the area and industries grew here in brick, chalk, lime, cement and straw boards and paper. These works continued to expand through the 18th century and together these uses absorbed the old village of West Thurrock and spread west to South Stifford village where there had also been a hythe and wharf since the 16th century and the listed Ship Inn originally a house, was first mentioned in 1761 (VCH). Now the village was absorbed as it expanded to provided additional homes for the local workforce.

In 1777 the brewer **Samuel Whitbread** (d.1796) bought West Thurrock manor and became the owner of Purfleet chalk quarry. He was another of the upwardly mobile merchants or lessor gentry moving into the area at this time. He built a planned village for his quarry workers in the Dipping or Church Hollow with the listed Hollow Cottages and the Schoolhouse and Schoolmaster's House built in 1790. In 1791 he built Purfleet House (demolished) with its own detached Chapel of Ease that was possibly the inspiration for Bram Stoker's Carfax House in *Dracula* (Thurrock Borough Council Museum). The Whitbread family supported the Methodist Movement that played a lead in many social issues of the day including prison reform and the abolition of slavery and they required their quarry workers to attend church meetings. It was back to the Methodists he knew at Purfleet that the preacher Valton ran from the horse-whipping incident while speaking at Rainham Hall in 1767 (see above). Botany Gardens with its paths and grottoes was set up by the Whitbread's in an old chalk quarry that later attracted Victorian day-trippers by boat and rail (see Victorian Chapter). Besides the outfall of the Mardyke, Purfleet village is now a conservation area including the Dipping and a substantial riverside green.

<u>Gunpowder Magazine</u> Earlier, during the reign of George III and following an explosion at the Woolwich Garrison, five large gunpowder magazines were built (mostly between 1763 and 1765) at Purfleet within approximately 10 ha (25 acres) of ground occupied by the government, which was moated round and walled. At this time all gunpowder supplied to the Government was tested, graded and transported out. In this connection the government also improved the road from Wennington to Purfleet but, met with local hostility they had to guard the road with a locked gate called the Purfleet turnpike south of Noke House (dem.) near by the listed Tudor/late Georgian Lennard Arms Inn (previously the Crown and Cushion). A great deal of shipping called at Purfleet to take on a gunpowder load including **Captain Cook's** expedition ship HMS Resolution in 1772 and **HMS Bounty** in 1787 when Captain Bligh is recorded as having gone ashore for stores (Thurrock's Past: Echoes from a Place by Alan Leyin). There was a Thames short ferry from Erith until well into the 20th century when it could still be hailed from the bank. In 1784 the antiquarian Thomas Pennant in *A Journey from London to Dover* described crossing here and the precautions taken against danger from explosions at Purfleet Magazine.

As well as an American Founding Father, **Benjamin Franklin** was a prodigious inventor and dubbed the 'Father of Electricity', he invented the lightening rod in the 1752. While living in London he visited Purfleet in view of concern about the how to protect the 5,000 tonnes of gunpowder stored there at the magazines. Franklin recommended that the magazines be equipped with a lightning rod and a plaque recording the event is affixed to the last remaining magazine No.5 at Purfleet. Purfleet Garrison protected the magazines with the West Essex Militia guarding from 1797. Three buildings from the Purfleet magazine are SAM's and of these, the Purfleet Heritage & Military Centre for all three Services is also linked with RAF Hornchurch in the Ingrebourne Valley and is housed in magazine No. 5 (grade I, built 1763-5), The Proof House (II*) and the Royal Magazine Clock Tower and walls are also listed.

'The Temeraire, painted by Turner, last trip past Purfleet' as it was reported in the London Courier and Evening Gazette in September 1838. It appears to have been painted from north Thameside looking towards Rotherhithe © The National Gallery, London

J.M.W. Turner painted and drew sketches of Purfleet riverside, mainly the Powder Magazines, in 1805-8 now in Tate Britain, while his *Purfleet and the Essex Shore* 1808 in oil on canvas, is in a private collection. *The Fighting Temeraire* the naval warship that fought so valiantly for Lord Nelson at the Battle of Trafalgar in 1805 was tugged upriver along the Thames on 6th September 1838 on its final journey. Turner's painting is an allegorical depiction of the Industrial Revolution supplanting traditional technologies and values and was voted the nation's favourite painting in 2005; it hangs in the National Gallery, London.

Smuggling continued along Thameside with its heyday coming as taxation increased from 1700 into the 1830s although prime minister William Pitt lowered import duties in the 1780s so reducing the demand for smuggled goods. It was seen as a victimless crime by those who benefitted from cheap luxury goods, tea, tobacco, spirits, silks and lace. Different areas of the Thames specialised in different approaches to smuggling, whether off mud banks, or along the drainage ditches and creeks across the Thameside marshes such as at Rainham (*A History of Rainham* by Frank Lewis). Whilst like Dickens' *Fagin*, a woman at Barking paid boys to obtain smuggled tobacco to supply London merchants (Smith, Graham, 2005, *Smuggling in Essex*).

Places to visit near and far:

- Grade II*Rainham Hall and Gardens, Broadway, Rainham, National Trust property and its Rainham Conservation area setting
- Grade II Old Chapel, Upminster
- Grade II Fairkytes Arts Centre, Hornchurch
- Grade II Langtons House and Gardens, Hornchurch, the gardens may be attributed originally to Humphrey Repton
- Stubbers Adventure Centre, Upminster with Grade II garden walls
- Grade II* Upminster Windmill, Upminster, smock mill built in 1803
- Grade II listed Stock Tower Mill built in 1804, near Ingatestone, Essex
- Grade II* Mountnessing Post Mill built 1807
- Purfleet Heritage & Military Centre in the Grade I listed Government Powder Magazine No. 5 (built 1763-5) and see the nearby Grade II* listed Proof House (erected mid 1760s) Centurion Way, Purfleet
- Grade II* Valentines Mansion & Registered Gardens, Emerson Road, Ilford, built in 1696 the walled garden, dovecote and grottoes were created in the 1720s and the house given its Georgian façade in the 1760s
- Hylands House, Writtle nr Chelmsford grade II* listed and with a notable 20th century ha-ha before the house
- Open House, an architectural festival giving free public access to many buildings, walks, talks and tours over one weekend in September each year
- Open House London is a free festival of London's architecture, engineering and urban landscape from the medieval to the thoroughly modern, held annually in the 3rd weekend in September
- Walk the Two Forts Way path which links Coalhouse Fort at East Tilbury and its Napoleonic and Victorian history with that of the older Tilbury Fort – where 300 rebels from the Battle of Culloden were held on the king's orders in 1746
- Oakwood & Ash Plantation are two adjoining woodlands linked by Long Pond and are an integral part of the Thames Chase Community Forest. They were part of the original landscape garden of Belhus House and were designed in the 18th century by locally-based and respected landscape architect Richard Woods and the renowned Lancelot 'Capability' Brown
- Belhus Woods Country Park is a diverse landscape of ancient woodland, grassland and lakes once part of the Belhus Estate
- Essex Houses & Gardens are a group of historic buildings and gardens independently opening to the public and include Hylands House built in 1730 and its early 18th century gardens and the Georgian Spencers Garden at Great Yeldham
- General Oglethorpe is buried in the chancel of the church of All Saints, Cranham and the parish retains links with organisation/s in Georgia, USA, which are dedicated to his memory, note also the *National Society of The Colonial Dames of America*, that promotes appreciation for the people, places and events that led to the formation and development of America

Ideas for future projects:

- A study of the development of architecture and planned landscapes and the contribution made across this landscape from the 17th century with local examples
- A study of the moral business stance of merchants of the day including attitude to slavery and its abolition and see for example *The Cely Papers: selections from the Correspondence and Memoranda of the Cely Family* by Henry Elliot Maldon Royal Historical Society (Great Britain) pub. Camden 1980s edit, and Lucy Stuart Sutherland *'A London Merchant 1695-1774'* pub. Routledge ISBN 978-1-138-86603-4
- To improve the interpretation of the historic land use patterns and increase awareness of designed parklands by notable figures such as Capability Brown and maximising the opportunities of any anniversary celebrations
- Research into unused or underused jetties and their potential investigated for reuse as community facilities
- A study of the Charles Bridgeman parkland landscape at Bower House including the early ha-ha, pine tree-lined ride through Bower Wood with its Victorian ice house, larch plantation and once managed woodland; the historic timber and brick barns at the rear of the Orange Tree public house in Havering-atte-Bower in regard to any relationship with Bower House and also hints to the original farm complex in this location before the erection of Bower House
- A possible study at the Grangewaters Outdoor Education Centre for its quarry origins and earlier fen landscape and comparing the implication of, and informing, the Lower Thames Crossing proposals
- Unpicking the Repton landscape and the successive houses at Dagnams (LBH owned)

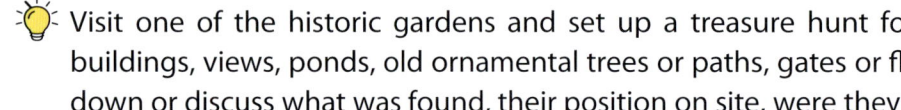

Visit one of the historic gardens and set up a treasure hunt for historic features like buildings, views, ponds, old ornamental trees or paths, gates or flowerbeds. Draw, write down or discuss what was found, their position on site, were they for artistic effect or for practical reasons? (Historic Landscape Features Spotter, Key Stage 1-3)

References for further research:

More information on this historical period can be found through:
- See Section C: History Introduction, p. 99
- Georgian Group
- The Society for the Protection of Ancient Buildings (SPAB)
- English Heritage
- Historic England
- Museum of London (MOL)
- University College London: Legacies of British Slave-ownership
- Victorian & Albert Museum British Galleries for style, taste and innovation of the times
- Historic England *Register of Parks & Gardens of Special Historic Interest in England*
- Thompson, Leslie (1957) *The Land that Fanns* pub. the Tindal Press;

- Muilman, Peter (1769) *A new and complete history of Essex ... By a Gentleman*
- Peacock, William (1793) *The Polite Repository*
- Repton, Humphry (1816) *Fragments on the Theory and Practice of Landscape Gardening* pub. London
- Stroud, Dorothy (1962) *Humphry Repton* pub. Country Life
- Young, Arthur (1772) *A Six Weeks' Tour Through the Southern Counties of England & Wales* ISBN: 9781166542696 and Volume 1 (1769)
- Young, Arthur (1807) *General view of the Agriculture of Essex vol. II* comments on the work of local farmers such as the Earl of St. Vincent at Rochetts, Lord Petre at Thorndon, Sir Richard Neave at Dagnam Park, Mr Newman at Hornchurch and Sir Thomas Barrett-Leonard at Aveley
- Walker, John (1598) *Old Thorndon Hall* map,
- Chapman, John and Andre, Peter (1777) *A Map of the County of Essex*
- Mudge, William (1801) *An Entirely New & Accurate Survey of the County Of Kent, With Part of The County Of Essex*
- Saunders, Ann (ed. 1991) *Facsimile of the Ordnance Surveyors' drawings of the London Area 1799-1808*
- See works of art by artists of the time such as Thomas Gainsborough, Sir Joshua Reynolds and the young J.M.W. Turner, illustrating the changing world of the Georgian period

Further Reading:
- Body, Val (1989) *Stubbers – A Short History* pub. Havering Libraries ISBN 0 9500008 4 1
- Cowell, Fiona (2019) *Richard Woods (1715-1793): Master of the Pleasure Garden* pub. Boydell UK ISBN 10: 1783274328/ISBN 13: 9781783274321
- Martin, Frank (1983) *Rogues River: Crime on the River Thames in the 18th Century* pub. Ian Henry Publications Ltd. 1983 ISBN 10: 0860258742
- Smith, Graham (2005) *Smuggling in Essex* pub. Countryside Books ISBN 1 85306 917 5
- To get a feel for Georgian life and times also read novels by writers of the time including Jane Austin, Mary Shelly, Bram Stoker and Henry Fielding or the romantic poets like William Wordsworth, Samuel Taylor Coleridge, Percy Bysshe Shelley, William Blake, John Keats and Robert Burns, also:
  - *Robinson Crusoe* by Daniel Defoe, first pub. in 1719 (TDC identified that in c.1694-1703 Defoe operated a tile and brickworks at his 'Brick House' farmstead on Chadwell Marsh and the marsh features in his 1722 novel *Moll Flanders*
  - *Gulliver's Travels* by Jonathan Swift, first pub. in 1726
  - *Auld Lang Syne* written by Robert Burns in 1788
  - *A Red, Red Rose* written by Robert Burns in 1794
  - *Waverley* by Sir Walter Scott, first pub. in 1814
  - *Rob Roy* by Sir Walter Scott, first published in 1817
  - *The Skye Boat Song* lyrics written by Sir Harold Boulton to an air collected by Anne Campbell MacLeod, first published in 1884

Chapter 12
19th century: Victorian
1837 – 1901

'...Victoria...'

NATIONAL CURRICULUM Key Stages 2 & 3 hints

By the time the young Queen Victoria inherited the throne in the early 19th century, the great flamboyance of the Regency period was ended by an acute economic depression and the Industrial Revolution and growth of the British Empire had begun. Any increase in foreign competition was being delayed by continued war and revolution on the Continent and enabled British commerce and industry to begin to expand and prosper again.

The Victorians, like the Georgians before them, glamourized history giving us a romantic and even jolly interpretation of the times through their Arts and literature, and so were effective in clouding our view of history. The glamour of the Arthurian tales of the Knights of the Round Table were elaborated and the idea of 'Merrie Olde England' persisted, while the darker side of history - including how wealth was often acquired at the brutal expense of others - became hidden or brushed aside.

At the same time many charismatic people were also coming forward with new ideas, and they brought forth a renewed energy, looking to the future with increasing sensitive and philanthropic ideals. These influences brought about great change in the social, physical and economic landscape.

For some people, and for the nation as a whole, this became a Golden Age. However, for many - especially the poorest - it was a dark time of change that brought harsh conditions and poverty that the stories of Charles Dickens brought to the notice of the masses. Decade on decade this was a century of rapid change that laid the foundations of modern Britain.

SURPRISE *'The Land of the Fanns is an intricate landscape, full of surprises and 'hidden gems' and rewards exploring.' (TellTale working with the public 2018)*

Throughout history, the effect of the presence of the river Thames in this area has meant that the great constants here have been trade routes, defence, agricultural trends and migration, and across the ages this landscape and the independence of local people has produced significant social thinkers, improvers and reformers and the Victorian period was no exception.

LANDFORM *'The Land of the Fanns is about land and water and the often shifting relationship between them' (TellTale working with the public 2018)*

Restructuring As London expanded so the old system of **local government** based on the Saxon Hundreds and the parishes and vestries[1] set up by the Normans that had remained in use down through the centuries, finally came to an end with the passing of new laws. These effectively reorganized local government and public services introducing new sanitary authorities. So that over the 19th and 20th centuries the Hundreds and parish administrative areas were variously broken up and merged with others.

In 1834 the Poor Law Amendment Act removed responsibility for the poor from the old parishes, setting up Boards of Guardians to administer groups of parishes or Poor Law Unions (PLU). This 'Land of the Fanns' area was divided into three **Poor Law Unions** - Romford, Billericay and Orsett each with its own Workhouse for the poor. The Public Health Act 1875 consolidated previous efforts to improve sanitary conditions in Britain and introduced Urban (USD) and Rural Sanitary Districts (RSD). The Local Government Act of 1894 established District Councils and civil (rather than religious) parishes.

So, in 1834 the Hundred of Chafford was split into three and the western parishes of Great Warley, Cranham, Upminster, Rainham, and Wennington, together with the Liberty parishes of Havering-atte-Bower, Romford and Hornchurch, and Dagenham and Chadwell Heath from Becontree Hundred along with some other parishes, became the Romford Poor Law Union, and then the Romford RSD. During these changes some of the old Workhouses for the poor became redundant, for example the little mid-18th century Upminster Workhouse was converted and still survives as a row of listed cottages (Ingrebourne Cottages) with its Crown Fire Insurance Mark still visible. The Liberty had been sold by the Crown in 1828 and finally lost its privileged status in 1892 (VCH) and in 1894 **Romford became an Urban District** (UDC) and the surrounding parishes including Noak Hill became the vast **Romford Rural District** (RDC).

Meanwhile, the north-east parishes of Brentwood, South Weald, Little Warley, and Childerditch together with West Horndon with Ingrave (or West Thorndon), East Horndon, Dunton Waylett and Basildon from Barstable Hundred, and others, formed the Billericay Poor Law Union, later Billericay RSD and then the **Billericay Rural District**. In 1899 Brentwood parish became the **Brentwood Urban District**.

The south-east parishes of Aveley, North and South Ockendon, Stifford and West Thurrock, and in Barstable Hundred Bulphan, Horndon-on-the-Hill, Langdon Hills and Orsett, with others formed the Orsett Poor Law Union, which later became the Orsett RSD, and from 1894 was the **Orsett Rural District**. All with further changes taking place during the following century.

As these administrative changes took place, so smart municipal buildings were put up, but the minutes, accounts and statistics of the old Hundreds were at times broken up, lost or repackaged. The stories of the past were in the same way fragmented to be retold within the new areas and linkages were forgotten. The history of the area as a whole became difficult to grasp as generations passed and its value and wider context were increasingly lost, leaving more of just a *feeling* that this landscape, the Land of the Fanns is special for its past, and that holds good in its promise for the future.

---

[1] Vestries were the governing body of the parish, in effect local government for each Church of England parish area. Eventually civil parishes were formed and purely local government evolved.

Land Defence Although extensively an agricultural area the significant military Camp on Warley Common and its fortunes inevitably had a great impact and turned Brentwood into a garrison town so that at the beginning of the 19th century the soldiers at **Warley Garrison** outnumbered local people by up to 11 to 1. But then at the beginning of Queen Victoria's reign the Camp was closed for more than a decade before being taken over in 1843 by the enormously powerful and vastly wealthy, global trading **British East India Company** that exploited India and in the previous century had relied on the labour of enslaved people.

At Warley in 1853 a young Irish doctor, William O'Shaughnessy set up a training camp that would enable the Company soldiers to establish a suitable telegraph network on the Indian sub-continent (work for which he was later knighted). The design had to include for wiring high enough for **pack elephants** to pass underneath and strong enough for **storks and vultures** to perch on and **monkeys** to climb (Romford Recorder, Dec. 2017).

Soldiers doubled the numbers of people in the local area, training significant numbers more, and this may explain why at the time there were said to be more public houses along the road to Brentwood than dwellings. It also led the Company to make extensive modifications at the Barracks and in 1857 to erect the (Anglian and) Essex Regimental Chapel by Matthew Wyatt, with its furnishings designed by Sir Charles Nicholson. The chapel is now a listed building open monthly for services and on regimental heritage days. Amongst other memorabilia the old regimental *colours* or flags hang from the ceiling and make this an extremely evocative space. 1857 was also the year of the brutal 'India mutiny' which led to the return of the barracks to Government control soon after, leading to further expansion, modernisation and reorganisation of military services here for at least the following century.

The listed Blenheim House, Depot officers mess for the Bedfordshire, Hertfordshire and Essex Regiment, built in 1878 on Clive Road, Warley is now the 124 (Essex) Transport Squadron Royal Logistic Corp, **Army Reserve Centre**. In 1881 the Church of Holy Cross and All Saints, was built as a Roman Catholic mission church for the soldiers of Warley barracks. Donated by Countess Tasker, it was built by her cousin the architect Frances W. Tasker and is grade II listed.[2]

> By this period the national census and other records can shed light on local events including the effect of the Camp on local people. Through these records we know part of the story of one local lad, Harry, who was born into a family of agricultural workers. Harry enlisted at Warley Camp in 1892 aged 17 and presumably looking for opportunity, employment and no doubt adventure. Here he received his Army training and two years later was sent abroad

---

[2] In 1850, after almost three centuries Catholic dioceses were re-established in England putting this area into the Westminster diocese. In 1917 the diocese was split creating the Diocese of Brentwood covering historic Essex, and having the same boundary as the Anglican Diocese of Chelmsford. This gave cathedral status to Brentwood Catholic parish church of St. Mary and St. Helen, built in 1861 under the patronage of Lord Petre. After various modifications the building was considerably enlarged in 1989-91 in an Italianate Classical style by the architect Quinlan Terry and dedicated by Cardinal Basil Hume. The cathedral is within the Brentwood conservation area and stands within a complex of other associated 19th century church buildings including a convent for the Sisters of Mercy also built by F.W. Tasker.

for a tour of duty in India. Embarking soldiers were marched to Brentwood railway station, opened in 1840, then by train to Tilbury Docks and from there by sea (in earlier years they had been marched to Tilbury Docks).

Four years later Harry was serving in Burma near the Chinese border. In 1901 he was embroiled in the Boar War in South Africa and not finally home until 1903.

A further three years later while still stationed at the Warley Home Base he married a local girl whose family for generations had been farm workers here. The young couple were promptly shipped with the Garrison to Ireland where a few years later, their baby died from an infection, apparently common among soldiers' families and local people alike in the terrible living conditions of those times.

Sea Defence The Thames continued to play its part in coastal defences, but at the resumption of hostilities between Britain and France in 1803, **Tilbury Fort** was still the only fortification protecting the Essex coast and north Thameside. Soon there were more installations, including the barracks at Romford until 1825, and at Warley. As part of the recommendations of the Royal Commission on the Defence of the United Kingdom, **Coalhouse Fort** (SAM) at East Tilbury was rebuilt between the 1860s and 1874 and continued in its role defending London during the next century throughout both World Wars and its setting is now the Coalhouse Fort Park open space. In 1889/90 Coalhouse Fort was reinforced by constructing the 'invisible' East Tilbury (or Coalhouse) Battery (SAM) with 'disappearing guns' nearby.

Steam ships From the 17th century three major routes had been established on the river Thames for hoys (sailing boats carrying freight) and tilt-boats (rowing boats carrying up to 40 passengers). By 1802 there were also the much larger passenger packet boats (regular chartered boats for passengers, mail and cargo) running from London to Margate during the summer months. The fast **paddle steamers**[3] were beginning to ply their trade on the Thames in c.1815 followed in 1857 by the Thames Conservancy Act to try to ameliorate problems thrown up on the busy Thames between the modern steamboat companies and owners of the Thames barges, ferries and other small sailing craft. The steam ships became a most popular means of travel on the Long Ferry route between London and Gravesend before the arrival of the steam railways, it being considered the quicker, cheaper and safer means of travel. Cross river ferries were set up (and modern versions still operate) at Woolwich and Tilbury.

There was nothing to stop the vessels from racing one another and Rev. Palin, for fifty years the forthright and uncompromising rector of Stifford, fell into the Thames from a racing paddle-steamer when transferring from ship to a small wherry (light rowing boat) intended to land dry shod at Grays (Prof. Ged Martin). When Grays pier was built in 1841 it ended the necessity of passengers transferring vessels mid-stream.

---

 [3] Draw a picture of a paddle-steamer or a Thames barge.

Chapter 12 19th century: Victorian

In 1878 on a 'Moonlight Trip' the paddle steamer **SS Princess Alice** sank at Galleons reach near Woolwich Pier after a collision, with the loss of the 600-700 passengers in the foul, sewage laden water from London's sewage pumping stations and nearby gasworks and chemical factories. Unsurprisingly the sinking blighted the pleasure trips in the tidal Thames. After the disaster care began to be taken to purify raw sewage flowing into the Thames and the Marine Police force were supplied with steam launches to replace their slow moving rowing boats. A memorial was erected at the time and a plaque at Barking Creek marks the 130th anniversary of the sinking.

Illustration of a Thames paddle-steamer

Sewage Farming Lieutenant Colonel **William Hope VC** was an expert in sewage and guns. He won the Victoria Cross at Sevastopol in 1855 and the famous painting by Louis William Desanges of Hope winning his Victoria Cross hangs in the Royal Fusiliers Museum, in the Tower of London. He went on to carry out further extraordinary heroics in Sardinia winning the Sardinian Medal, for Military Valour and being awarded the Crimea Medal and the Turkish Crimea Medal for fighting in the Crimea War.

William Hope was an engineer and inventor and became an expert in sewage farming while working with his relative, the celebrated diplomat Lord Napier and proposed an extension to the London sewerage system across Essex. For a decade from 1867 he settled in Parsloes in Dagenham (LBB&D have installed a Plaque in his memory in Parsloes Park) and from 1869 he also leased Bretons (see Georgian Chapter) as a Sewage Farm in the Dagenham Corridor from the Romford Local Board of Health. He employed sewage farming methods utilising local muck that was the beginning of a century of sewage treatment at Bretons serving the local area. However, as a farm soil improver muck failed as sewage became polluted with industrial chemicals and watered down with the introduction of Water Closets (lavatories). Here, as ever greater demands were made on the system from local developments so rows broke out between the Romford UDC and Romford RDC until a point in the 1960s that there was a moratorium on new housing for a time until the capacity of the sewage treatment could be increased.

After the closure of the 20th century Treatment Works at Bretons, the park and historic buildings have increasingly been restored for public use and access including a footbridge link across the river Beam to the Beam Valley Country Park in 2014.

MIGRATION *'This is a crossroads landscape: because of its location on the Thames ... people have always travelled into, through and away from this area.'*
(TellTale working with the public 2018)

Over the course of the 19th century the pattern of development in the area generally followed the outward expansion of the north and east London boroughs particularly after the arrival of the railway lines into this area. East London villages like East Ham expanded and Little Ilford became the suburban settlement of Manor Park and all were absorbed into the metropolis.

Often local people can see this for themselves in their own family trees through ancestry research as generations gradually moved out from the East End, and during the 20th century the population gradually moved through this area onwards towards the Essex coast or north into East Anglia.

Railways The arrival of the railways and the expansion of the London, East End and Tilbury docks attracted new industries and workers along Thameside. Romford station opened in 1839 close to the old Calvary Barracks and was at first called *Barrack Lane* Station, and opened up opportunity for housebuilding in the town (see below). The railway reached Brentwood in 1840 (Graces Guide) and at Shenfield Common the listed Seven Arches road bridge over the London to Norwich railway line was constructed that year for Eastern Counties Railway Company, its design gives the name to the road running across it. In 1854 the London, Tilbury & Southend railway line opened including stations at Barking, Dagenham Dock, Rainham, Purfleet and Grays and with a station opened at Dagenham (East) in 1885. That same year the Great Eastern Railway had arrived at Upminster with a travel time of only one hour to the City and this encouraged commuting with new 'dormitory' suburbs built on London's outskirts.

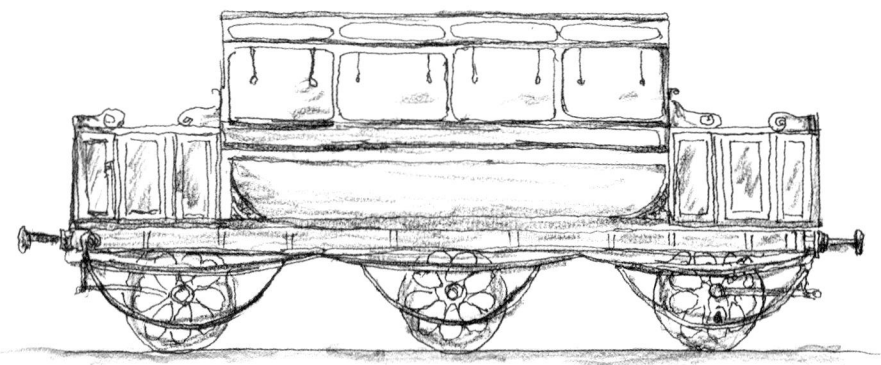

Eastern Counties Railway 'Smoking' Carriage, 1846

Over the turn of the century as more new railway lines began to cut through the area they brought commuters from as far as Kent via the Tilbury ferry and train to the City (*Thurrock Past* by Alan Leyin) and returned with visitors from the City and the East End of London coming out on day trips by steam train. The single-track branch line connecting Romford, Upminster and Grays opened in 1892-3. Along that line at North Stifford the Davy Down Riverside Park in the Mardyke Valley is now open to visitors giving access to explore the Mardyke Valley as well as be impressed by the Victorian, 10m (33 ft.) high, **Stifford Railway Viaduct**, known locally as 'Fourteen Arches'. The viaduct still carries trains, now the C2C Upminster to Grays railway line, affording passengers panoramic views of the valley between South Ockendon and Chafford Hundred (and Lakeside Shopping Centre) railway stations.

Town Planning As the population grew, and the railways enabled more people to live further from London's unhealthy housing conditions, large scale housing development began in the towns around London. In Romford, the first new housing of the Victorian era was built in the 1840s on the site of the Napoleonic Barracks. These houses were described in a public health report in 1851 as 'The houses are nearly new and two stories high, and in every case the privy is built close to the back kitchen of the house' (Havering Libraries – Local Studies), they provided housing for the families of laborers and other workers often connected with the Romford Brewery and the railway.

A grander scheme of 'new town' villas, by John Laurie at the eastern end of Romford market came in the 1840s but was never extended beyond the initial villas, large middle class houses, and two public halls. Much of **Laurie Town** was demolished for the ring-road and largely became Ludwigshafen Place in the mid 20th century (VCH). The 1850s saw the start of large scale redevelopment on places like Stewards manor, and the example of Romford where many of these houses and new streets still exist, tells us much about the types of housing typically built in the era.

As the areas fanning out from London grew, more thought was given to the wider impact of housing development and new, progressive ideas about towns, gardens, industry and transport emerged. During the latter 19th century town planning came into vogue following the ideals of Ebenezer Howard and his foundation of the **Garden City Movement** whereby self-contained communities are built surrounded by *greenbelts*. This introduced architect-designed homes for the middle classes in places like Gidea Park based north and south of Hare Street (Main Road). Subsequent entry designs for a House and Cottage Competition and Exhibition in 1910/11 were in the Arts & Crafts tradition[4] by influential architects including Parker & Unwin, M.H. Baillie Scott and Clough Williams-Ellis. This is now a conservation area and a number of the buildings are listed.

Philanthropy Amongst academics and social improvers, philanthropy is evident here through the efforts of early movers in such matters including public wellbeing and planned housing developments, and Victorian landowners who provided estate cottages for their workers as at Boyles Court in Great Warley. At Noak Hill, a hamlet of numerous listed and local heritage buildings including cottages originally for farm workers employed at the adjacent Dagnams Estate, the lady of the manor had the (listed) Church of St. Thomas built in 1841-2 for the local workers to save the long walk to South Weald.

At Cranham, several successive members of the **Benyon** family, all named Richard, owned and carried out philanthropic works often employing the architect Richard Armstrong on the family estates that also included North and South Ockendon. Benyon's planned model farm at Cranham had a fine quadrangle of buildings designed for the efficient transit and processing of livestock and farm produce and is now converted to private residences. The farm together with the listed Cranham Hall and Benyon's listed Church of All Saints form a landmark and focus for views across the farmland. The Benyon's also donated land, built schools and teachers houses and restored the churches and chapels from at least 1775 until 1902, until their estates were finally broken up and sold in 1937.

At South Weald, Sir Anthony Browne (d. 1567) had provided in his Will for charity almshouses in connection with his foundation of Brentwood School. Having passed through several owners, in 1851

---

[4] The Arts & Crafts movement promoted traditional craftsmanship and materials, and taking design ideas from medieval, romantic and folk styles.

Christopher Tower obtained an Act of Parliament to build ten almshouses. These, Brown's charity Almshouses and Chapel, were designed by the English Gothic Revival architect Samuel Teulon and erected c.1858. They were upgraded, listed and extended in the 20th century.

Education Until the 19th century education in England was mostly linked to religious institutions, such as St. Mary's Church of England (C of E) School In North Ockendon conservation area, built in the 1840s and now in residential use and St. Thomas's, C of E School, Noak Hill.

Following campaigning The Elementary Education Act 1870 created in addition **School Boards** providing non-denominational education for children aged 5-10 years. Dagenham's first school board for example, was formed in 1874 when there were 5 elementary schools covering Dagenham, Chadwell Heath and Collier Row. Numerous old school buildings survive, some are locally listed such as Romford's Albert Road (Manor) School built in 1884 now in community use, and Crowlands School built in 1908 and still in school use.

Under the Poor Law, School Districts were also set up for poor children from the metropolitan area to receive a basic education and training for employment in the rural districts. In this way under the Brentwood School District, children from Hackney and Shoreditch were sent to Harold Court in Harold Park and to the school building at Brentwood erected in 1852-4 on Brentwood Hill opposite Brentwood Brickworks (Later St. Faiths Hospital for epileptic patients). Today the grounds form the 16 ha (40 ac) St. Faith's Country Park that is managed especially to benefit wildlife and biodiversity.

> Some boys from Hackney, Poplar and Whitechapel went to the Training Ship *Goliath* moored off Grays from 1870 until, with nearly 500 on board, it tragically caught fire in a winter gale in 1875 with the sad loss of life of 22 of the trainees and a schoolmaster (Lloyd's Weekly Newspaper December 26, 1875). Despite this disaster more Training Ships followed through into the next century.

The pioneering **St. Leonard Cottage Homes** were built in Hornchurch between 1887 and 1889 by the Shoreditch Board of Guardians seeking a healthier, rural lifestyle for children in their care, it remained in operation until 1984. Cottage Home Villages were built to house orphans and destitute children and prepare them for future employment – the boys mainly in the Armed Forces and the girls mainly in domestic service. St. Leonard's is now a conservation area and the Hall is listed. The artificial stone statue of a woman (possibly *Abeona* Roman goddess of children) with a boy and girl of the period, taken from Shoreditch to be placed in a niche at the Hall, was later removed to the Bethnal Green Museum of Childhood. In Chapter 5 of his 'culturally important' novel *A Son of the State*, William Pett Ridge describes the arrival and reception of children to the Home.

Health During the Victorian period, the high, open-aired Brentwood heights were found to be an ideal location for specialist hospitals catering for new ways to improve health, hygiene and well-being such as for mental health, with buildings mainly on the fringes of the town. At Warley the hospital foundation stone was laid in 1851 and opened in 1853. Certainly in the latter part of the 20th century there seemed to exist a general compassion and support amongst the local community for those recovering and recuperating.

Although several old Victorian hospitals are now closed and brought into reuse (such as Warley Hospital, Highwood Hospital, and the Maternity Hospital in Ingrave Road - all now used for housing), the area remains favoured by a number of specialist nursing and treatment centres, such as the Marillac Hospital, now accommodated in the old Officers' Mess at Warley and caring for patients with neurological and complex physical disabilities.

Romford's original Victoria Cottage Hospital, is locally listed, built in 1888 it remains in health care use. The centenary of a visit to lay a memorial stone by Princess Louise, fourth daughter of Queen Victoria, when all local worthies were present, was celebrated in 2012 by local people and organised by Laurie Ford of *Havering Heritage* and with guest representatives of Havering Council and NHS North East London and the City (NELC) (Romford Recorder).

Police With the increasing population also came an increase in crime and the need for better organised crime prevention. Romford already had a single metropolitan horse patrol but in 1840 was included in the new Brentwood Division of the Essex Constabulary until transferring to the Metropolitan Police in 1965 (Havering Libraries – Local Studies). The police station in Brentwood was built in 1844 and survives in Coptfold Road although the police have long since moved on to other premises. After the first official Metropolitan police force was opened in 1829 Dagenham became part of their K Division in 1840 with a purpose built Police Station opened by 1851 housing a sergeant and six police constables (Valence House Archives & Local Studies Centre). This survives as a listed building on the outskirts of Dagenham village by the railway station.

> Police struggled to gain public support during the early years. In Dagenham the murder has never been solved of the young PC George Clark at Rush Green in 1846 and in 1885 Romford police Inspector Thomas Simmons was shot and killed in Upper Rainham Road in the Dagenham Corridor close to Bretons House where a memorial stone has been placed nearby.
>
> In 1921, one local man was presented with a fine silver-topped cane for saving a police officer who was attempting to break up an alcohol-fueled street brawl in Queen Street in Warley Garrison town (pers rec. of Jack Smith). But in 1927 PC George Gutteridge, who served in Essex including at Romford, Grays and Stapleford Abbots, was murdered in the performance of his duties by known criminals from the East End and Liverpool. A memorial stone stands close to where he died in Gutteridge Lane, Stapleford Abbotts (Essex Police History Notebook Number 19 *The Silent Detective* by Martyn Lockwood).

One of the police constables at Dagenham for a time around 1881 was George Bales, his married daughter Maud lived nearby at another surviving listed building Stoneford Cottage, erected in c.1858 on Beam Lands on the west side of the river by the **Beam Bridge**. The one-time Librarian for Dagenham, local historian John Gerald O'Leary suggests the cottage likely got its name when there was a stone bridge or even an earlier stone ford across the river here on what is now Rainham Road South. In 2018 the cottage was bequeathed to the National Trust by Maud's daughter Mary Maud White MBE. She, together with her sister, is recalled in years past as smartly stepping out daily for Dagenham Station and her work at the Home Office.[5]

An earlier occupier of Stoneford Cottage was Henry Gentry the Dagenham Village thatcher, cutting his reeds at Horseshoe Corner (Barking & Dagenham Local History Society) by Dagenham Breach where the landscape was flat with reedy drainage ditches and few trees. Nearby the Beam Valley Path now follows the line of the ill-fated **Romford Canal** of 1875-7 from the A1306 road where a lock survives in the Beam Valley Country Park, northwards to the Beam Bridge as far as Eastbrookend Country Park. The canal was intended to transport mainly potatoes to London from Collier Row, but was never completed through lack of investment (*London's Lost Canals* online).

Religion Finally freedom of religious expression began to be accepted by this era. Catholic Emancipation came in 1829 with the Roman Catholic Relief Act and the subsequent building of new churches such as the listed Roman Catholic (RC) chapel of 1837 that adjoins Brentwood Cathedral. Also the listed RC chapel of St. Edward the Confessor, in 'Laurie New Town', Romford designed by Daniel Cubitt Nicholls in 1856 in the recommended Gothic revival style pioneered by A.W.N. Pugin.

On the theme of public service, the Victorians were busily restoring - or more commonly over-restoring - many old parish churches such as St. Andrews Hornchurch and St. Laurence Upminster by William Gibbs Bartleet of Brentwood and London in 1862-3, both grade I listed medieval buildings. A more sympathetic restoration of the 12th century Rainham parish church was carried out by the architect Rev. Ernest Geldart (by comparison he decorated his own church at Little Braxted, sumptuously in gold and bright colours).

Elsewhere new Anglican churches, now listed buildings, were erected with some incorporating older material, including:

- the Church of St. Peter and St. Paul in Grays, built in 1846 but retaining the 13th century tower and South Chapel;
- the Church of St. Edward the Confessor (II*) erected in 1849 and the Church of St. Andrew, 1862 both in Romford and both by John Johnson;
- the former Church of St. Mary, Church Road, Dunton in 1873 in red brick also by Bartleet;
- St. Mary's Church, High Road, Langdon Hills, built in 1876 and nearby old Parsonage 1875 both by William White, who is noted for his Gothic Revival architecture and church restorations;
- and the Church of St. John the Evangelist, Havering-atte-Bower, 1875-8 by Basil Champneys.

Thankfully, in around 1869 Rev. William Palin (qv) usefully researched and published the church records of Stifford and surrounding villages after some records of Little Thurrock had been deliberately destroyed by church officials.

---

 [5] Mary was said to have also been a hospital volunteer and to have been friends with Winston Churchill, perhaps there is truth in a local tale that Churchill's cat is buried in the garden here. Can you write a short story about this tale? (See Chapter 14 Future Projects list)

The trend for non-conformist religious thinking also continued and, before 1849 and only some 12 years after their missionary work had begun in Britain, the Mormon Church of Jesus Christ and the Latter Day Saints founded a branch at Orsett.

Science Evolution was contrary to mainstream thinking at this time when **Alfred Russell Wallace**, sometimes called the 'father of biogeography' was working. Independently of Darwin he conceived 'the theory of evolution through natural selection' and their papers on the subject were jointly published in 1858 and led to **Darwin** publishing his larger work *On the origin of Species*. Wallace's house at The Dell (an old chalk pit of 1.6 ha or 4 acres) in Grays is now converted into three flats, built for him in 1872 by Thomas Wonnacotlutyns (who was experienced in this early use of concrete) in shuttered concrete making use of the nearby cement works and on-site gravel, with asbestos slate roofs (grade II listed). Wallace was also interested in social reform including anti-slavery and women's rights, and spiritualism as a 'new branch of anthropology'. Thurrock Council with the A.R. Wallace Memorial fund have placed a heritage plaque on the house.

Horticulture At Great Warley, the late 17th century Warley Place was purchased in 1875 for the Willmott family moving from London. Soon after, their daughter **Ellen Willmott** (1858-1934) began to develop the c.13.4 ha (33 acres) of land as gardens in a natural style. She became influential as an horticulturalist and as a member of the Royal Horticultural Society she received the society Victoria Medal of Honour in 1897. She was admired even by the great **Gertrude Jekyll** who described Ellen as 'the greatest living woman gardener'.

In 1894 Ellen employed (Sir) **Edward Lutyens** to remodel Warley Lea house opposite her own, for her sister Rose. Lutyens worked in the Arts & Crafts style and was known for his imaginative new designs and clever modernisation of older properties, and he collaborated with Gertrude Jekyll and the 'natural style' of garden design. Three of Lutyens sketches for Warley Lea survived as part of the house sales brochure in 2010 (The Lutyens Trust).

In time Miss Willmott was said to have employed 104 gardeners on her estates here and abroad, but as she became elderly and with her finances spent the house was left to deteriorate and eventually Warley Place was demolished in 1939. However the Lodges both survive, and the remaining gardens of Warley Place are now a grade II Registered Garden and also a Nature Reserve run by Essex Wildlife Trust.[6] South Lodge was originally thatched, built in the 'cottage orne' style, a picturesque form popular between c.1790-1820 and is grade II listed; North Lodge was probably built later but before 1875 and likely before 1866 (ref. Brentwood Borough Council), it is now in private ownership.

Miss Willmott's godmother Countess Tasker, is said to have encouraged the young Ellen in her work when she may even have carried out some planting at Hill Place, Upminster for the Countess. That house is listed and contains some fine stained-glass windows from the workshops of William Morris to the designs of Edward Burne-Jones in Pre-Raphaelite art form.

• • • • • • • • • • •

---

 [6] Warley Place is open for visits periodically through the year.

At The Round House in Havering village, the Rev. Joseph Pemberton originated the new **Hybrid Musk rose** with its almost continuous blooms on large bushes. By 1896 he was producing some 4,000 varieties of roses at The Round House and The Hall. Of special interest he also produced the *Queen Alexandra Rose* in 1915 and the vigorous *Havering Rambler* in 1920. During WW2 the house was occupied by the army and for storage, it stood empty but cared for in private ownership after the war until being restored in 1982. In memory many of the Pemberton roses are now grown around the village with the largest collection in the grounds of the adjoining The Hall, now St. Francis Hospice.

Leisure There was more time for Leisure pursuits for some. At Hornchurch the old gravel pit (see Geology and Georgian Chapters) called *The Dell* by the old mill field had long since become a beauty spot, it formed a simple amphitheatre and was anciently occupied on Christmas Day by a wrestling match for a boars head prize until 1868 (C.T. Perfect); both cockfighting and bare-knuckle fights took place with its most famed fight between Mendoza and Jackson (see image in Georgian Chapter) referenced in the novel *Rodney Stone* by Arthur Conan Doyle, first published in 1896.

• • • • • • • • • • •

During this period Purfleet was popular with tourists and then as now known as 'Purfleet-on-Thames' it attracted day-trippers, geologists and naturalists.[7] The philanthropist Samuel Whitbread MP, had been improving conditions for his workers at Purfleet since the latter part of the previous century (see Georgian Chapter for earlier history). By this time the Whitbread family's botanical **'Botany Pleasure Gardens'** were developed out of the old chalk pits cut into the well-worked chalk cliffs, and became a great tourist attraction by steamboat and for 'city men and their families' arriving by railway with a bridge leading from the station direct into the Gardens. In 1848 White's directory of Essex described the harbour at Purfleet as being 'often full of shipping business' as well as the 'barracks for a company of artillery'.

The Purfleet Conservation Area in urban West Thurrock actually extends to the Thames here to include the listed Royal Hotel, once the Ship Inn, and later the Bricklayers Arms amongst others, it was rebuilt in the early 19th century and one room is said to be haunted. In 1862 the publican's White Bait Dinners were of note and it is also said that during the 1870s, Edward the then **Prince of Wales** visited the hotel from which it earned its name of the 'Royal'. Local lore says that when he was king he had secret assignations at the hotel with the actress Lily Langtree – who did indeed take a river trip to visit Purfleet for lunch one Sunday in September 1899, according to *The Penny Illustrated Paper*, which described Purfleet at the time as 'the pretty and interesting little town'.

In literature, Purfleet claims the inspiration for Abraham 'Bram' Stoker's 'Carfax House' in his novel **Dracula** (1897), being Purfleet House, built by Samuel Whitbread snr. for his own occupation in 1791. Indeed, while he was working in London it is quite likely that Bram Stoker would have visited this Victorian tourist attraction with its village, beach, walks and panoramic views. Thurrock Council has placed a plaque on St. Stephens church in the grounds of Purfleet House recording the association.

The High House site in Purfleet also commands great views towards the Thames that were promoted by Walter White in 1865 in *Eastern England from the Thames to the Humber*. High House, Purfleet, is now an international centre of excellence for creative industries in association with the **Royal Opera House**.

---

 [7] Where would you go on a day trip today, how would you travel and what would you see there?

The old pits and the Royal Hotel were also used as a film location until the First World War, finally closing in 1917. Nearby in Aveley the pianist, author and music teacher **Alice Mangold Diehl** was born in 1844 and Thurrock Council have placed a plaque in her memory nearby at Aveley Christian Centre (Thurrock History Society).

• • • • • • • • • • • •

Hornchurch Cricket Club was an early pioneer of Essex cricket with its home ground from 1785-1889 at Langtons Park, which is now Fielders Field behind Langtons House (listed buildings, Havering Registry Office and public park). Established by 1783 the Club attained 'important match status' and played against the **MCC** (Marylebone Cricket Club) on five occasions between 1790 and 1793 - when cricket was halted by the Napoleonic Wars. Hornchurch returned with an unbeaten record from 1822-29, when the Bearblock brothers of Hornchurch Hall (dem.) were long time players. It then moved next door to Grey Towers Park (house dem.) on the Langtons estate. Cricket is still being played on Fielders Field two centuries later.

By 1803 the Aveley Cricket Club had also been established at Belhus Park and in 1815, just four days after the battle of Waterloo, a match took place there between Aveley and 'Eleven Gentlemen of the Liberty Club'. As 'Belhus Cricket Club' their first match is recorded in 1888 against an Orsett team, where Belhus won.

ECONOMY *'This area is justly famous for trade, commerce and industry: these have been important here for many centuries.'* **(TellTale working with the public 2018)**

Agriculture Initially this was still an agricultural area. Deforestation continued as did the enclosure of common land through successive Acts of Parliament during the 19th century, concentrating land ownership amongst fewer people.

In the north, the **Forest of Waltham** had at one time stretched from London's Bow Bridge to Colchester. It included Hainault and Epping Forests (that contained the Iron Age hill forts of Loughton Camp and Ambresbury Banks – see Iron Age Chapter) and had been used by successive kings for hunting with rights for local people to graze their livestock and to gather foodstuffs and firewood since the 12th century. In the medieval period they had been divided into bailiwicks (administrative areas), and that of Hainault (known as the King's Woods) was mainly in Barking and Dagenham. However so much of the Royal Forest had been cut back for ship building in the 17th century that by c.1641 the actual woodland only extended as far south as Aldborough Hatch. By 1851 there remained little demand for timber for war ships, but instead the deforestation continued with over 16,000 hectares (4,000 acres) of trees speedily cut down so that the ground could be turned over to agriculture.[8]

Now all that remains of Hainault Forest is Hainault Forest Country Park and after public pressure, areas of Epping Forest also survive west of Loughton, and Havering Country Park.

Here in 1890 the Macintosh family planted an avenue of Wellingtonia trees (Sequoiadendron giganteum or giant redwoods, see Geography Chapter) to their mansion called Havering Park (dem.),

---

 [8] Consider by comparison where this is happening abroad today.

now forming an exceptional treed avenue into the Park. The Crown Estates purchased additional land including Marks Manor and Gobions (present farmhouse built by the Crown in 1899), Pigtails (Crown Farm, listed) and Warren Farm (listed red brick barn).

• • • • • • • • • • • •

Of other areas with **common rights**, Humphry Repton was permitted to enclose some 18 metres (20 yards) of common land outside his cottage in Hare Street, Gidea Park so as to 'improve' the view, but today the land is a carpark with just a plaque to mark its history. There were exceptions however, such as at Tylers Common, Upminster that survived enclosure in 1846 through the action of the Victorian Lords of the Manor the tough **Branfill** family. The Branfills had owned Upminster Hall for longer than two hundred years and during the 17th and 18th centuries had been involved in the East India Company and the slave trade. In the 19th century Mrs Anne Branfill became the family matriarch from her widowhood in 1844 until her death in 1873. Her second son Benjamin Aylett Branfill inherited the Upminster Hall estate at that time and it was presumably he who in 1875 warned strangers off the common land with their sheep and cattle, their lighting fires or camping.[9]

Chafford Heath, once the Saxon meeting place was common land at the heart of a long established local farming community including Broadfields Farm, which is now the Thames Chase Forest Visitor Centre in an historic farm complex. Many of the nearby farmhouses survive as listed buildings, most were already present in the previous century and are shown on the Chapman Andre *Map of the County of Essex 1777*, many are medieval with some moated sites like Baldwins and (Warley) Franks, and some farmland such as at Hunts Hill, Manor, Great Sunnings and Moor Hall have been farmed since Roman times or even earlier, for example South Hall Farm in Rainham that has late Iron Age origins (See also Tony Benton's *Upminster History site: south Upminster: gravel pits and ancient bits* and William Mudge *Map of Kent 1801* extract for this area).

• • • • • • • • • • •

By around the decade 1852-1862 the period of acutely distressed Essex farming had begun to recover as demand for food increased from the expanding population of London together with the improvement in farming methods brought on by the Agricultural Revolution and local farmers continued to supply the London markets. While, almost in living memory the convoys of horses and carts along the old Roman road (A12) are said to have still been making a weary return journey, the drivers nodding asleep while the lead horse turned the attendant train into the local tap room and stables at Woodman's Cottages (dem.) by Gallows Corner outside Romford before tackling the hill at Brentwood.

In the Orsett Poor Law Union area, by 1861 extensive drainage operations carried out in South Ockendon encouraged **market gardening** and brought an increase in population to the local area (Wilson, John Marius, 1870-2, *Imperial Gazetteer of England and Wales*). Similarly nearby in Stifford, Davy Down had been a farming area and then used for market gardening until road working divided the landholding and made its agricultural use uneconomic. However, the Mardyke river and ditches

---

[9] Benjamin Branfill emigrated in 1881 to New Zealand where as an engraver (see his illustrations for Wilsons Upminster History 1881) some of his work is held in the collection of the National Library and his extensive papers are held at the University of Toronto, Canada (see Tony Benton's Upminster History website).

continued to be used by the 'dumpy barges' to transport agricultural produce, corn and hay for the horses and return with London muck to manure local farms, to and from the Bulphan fens farms with the barges passing under Stifford Bridge into the 20th century.

The next agricultural depression from around 1874 was exacerbated in 1868 and 1880 by foreign competition, enabled by the opening of major Thames docks in London's East End bringing the first imports of frozen meat from Australia, New Zealand and Argentina and wheat from America. Numerous farms fell out of production across the county and many people generally drifted towards the towns and the metropolis looking for work. The population of Corbets Tey, for example, shrank between 1891 and 1911, and led to the closure of the Anchor Inn in 1896 and The George Inn (both listed buildings) in 1901. In the Romford Poor Law Union, rather than join the migration out of the area at least one local fellow, John Cook, is known to have walked 20 miles from his family home in Great Warley village to find work.

The cheap farm rents that resulted from all the changes together with a chance of expansion did attract numerous long-experienced cattle farmers from as far afield as **Ayrshire** in Scotland who settled successfully here in places like Bulphan Fen and Orsett farms at this time (Janet McCheyne, 2020, LotF 100 Stories Project, and the Frank Lewis papers held at Havering Libraries – Local Studies).

Also bucking the trend, on the Rainham/Wennington borders Henry Swann became a successful farm manager for the trustees of South Hall Farm in 1876 (plan illustrated opposite). He proudly 'farmed 413 acres (167 ha), employing 72 men, 42 boys and 13 women' and in 1879 won first prize for the farm in the Market Garden Class (*The Journal of the Royal Agricultural Society of England, 2nd Series vol.15 Report upon the Market-garden and Market-Garden Farm Competition 1879*). The judges heaped praise on Swann's efforts and highlighted the importance of liberal application of London muck to the fields producing 'extraordinary results'. Nearby, Ayletts Farm in Warwick Lane was another of the important market garden farms in the Rainham area. In 1875 it was advertised with 'luxuriant growing crops of market garden and farming produce' (Havering Libraries-Local Studies).

While as a young man, Francis Whitmore became responsible from 1896 for restoring the run-down Orsett Hall and the agricultural estate. He did so with both fine agricultural and commercial acumen to achieve a thriving farming enterprise. The estate documents from the 19th and 20th centuries are now held at the Museum of English Rural Life at Reading. The revolution in Agriculture increased output and as the proportion of the workforce in agriculture fell this helped drive the Industrial Revolution. Together with an expanding empire this set the scene for change in the Victorian period and into the modern age.[10]

• • • • • • • • • • • •

The **fishing industry** centering on Barking had boomed at first and in the latter part of the century local farmers were supplying ice from Dagenham marshes to the Barking fishing industry. However, when the railways arrived linking east coast ports direct and speedily to London so the local fishing industry began to collapse too.

---

[10] Typical traditional farming equipment and farming life for this time can be explored at the Upminster Hall 'Tithe' Barn Museum of Nostalgia (Thames Chase Walk 6b).

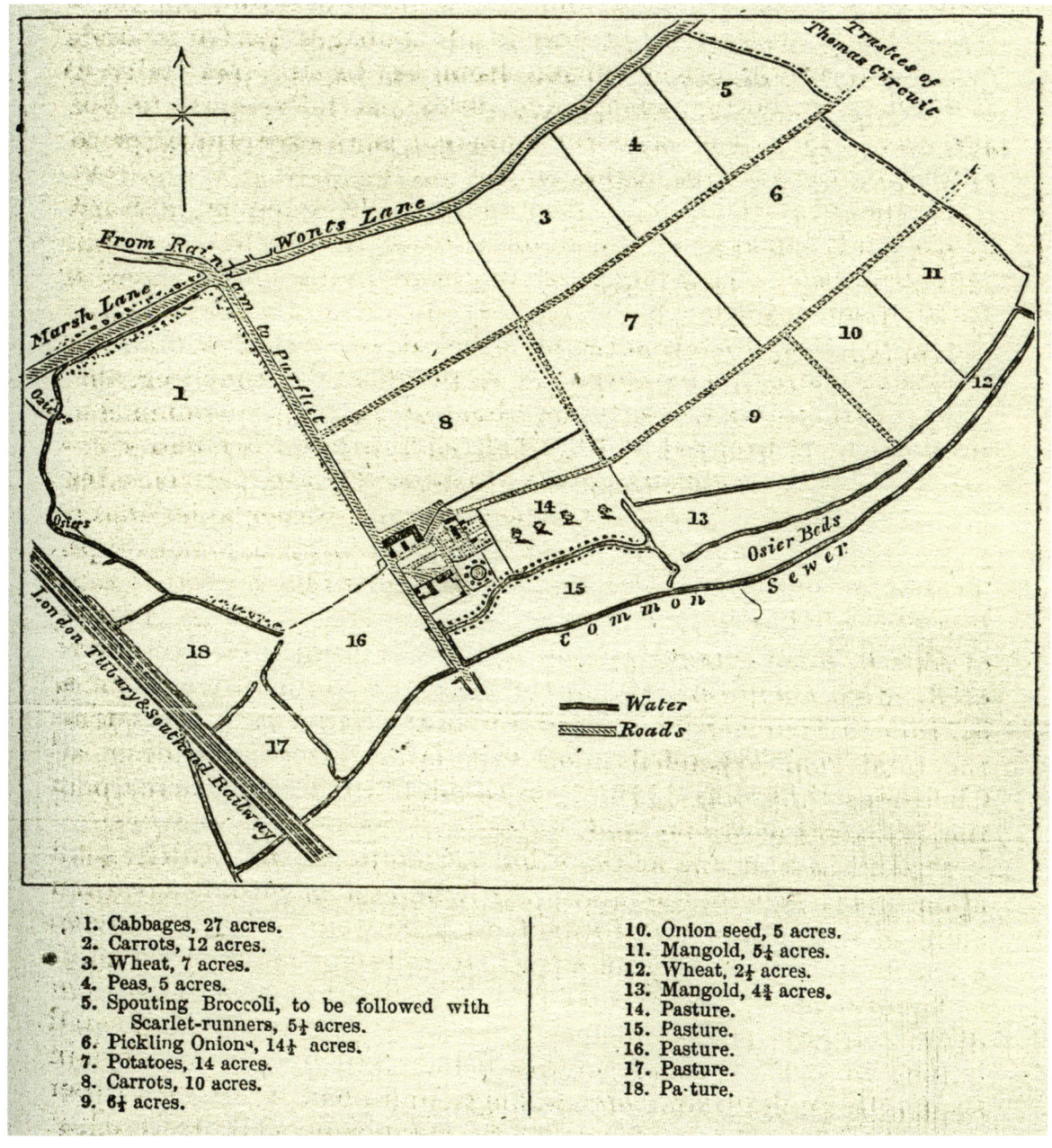

The planting plan for South Hall Market Garden Farm, Rainham, 1879 illustrates the importance of market gardening to the area (Courtesy of Havering Libraries-Local Studies)

Industry It is with the arrival of the railways from the mid 19th century, that industry began to develop along Thameside with factories and malthouses, and had accelerated by the turn of the century with the development of new industrial processes and new building materials like cement manufacturing taking place.

By the late 19th century Dagenham Dock industrial estate had been established at Dagenham Breach with wharves on the marshes importing coal and exporting manufactured goods. At Rainham the Ferry House inn was the cornerstone of the little community at Rainham Ferry and had long served the passengers of the long (along the river) and short ferries (crossing the river). By 1869 industry began to arrive here on the marshes, a manure works was built in 1873 and with far more industry developing over the next century.

Chapter 12 19th century: Victorian

The chalk along Thameside from Purfleet to Grays provided the basis for the growth of industry in that area and as a side product in the 1860s brought the beginnings of mass provision of tap water (see Geology and Edwardian Chapters) to Brentwood, Romford, Ilford, Barking and elsewhere. Here was easy access to the Thames with its wharfs and jetties and proximity to the London market. Chalk and lime were exported and later coal and oil brought in. In 1848 there were around 400 people working some 34 ha (85 acres) of chalk pits at Purfleet.

The Lion **Cement works** opened in South Stifford in 1874. The village was absorbed as it expanded to provided additional homes for the local workforce so that by 1894 South Stifford village had become a township that continued to grow over the next 30 years (VCH). The wharfs at West Thurrock also brought trade including in brick and chalk until closed by Portland Cement in the early 1920s, and in cement from 1897 until closed in 1976, and straw boards and paper from the 1890s until 1902. As heavy industry grew up between here and Grays so that this village too was absorbed.

• • • • • • • • • • •

Thames Chase Walk No. 3 from the Forest Centre is a circular walk to the historic Cranham **Brickfields** at Pot Kiln Wood. This brick and tile kiln from 1708-1933 with its first brick kiln in 1774, is now a Nature Reserve and a grade I site of Borough Importance for Nature Conservation. It is also an informal recreation area, and once clay excavation for brick making ran out in around 1920 there was a boating lake here, a football pitch and during WW2 it was cultivated for food as part of the 'Dig for Victory' campaign.

• • • • • • • • • • •

Now private **gas works** began to be established in Romford, Brentwood, Ingatestone and Fryerning and Grays - that after 1913 also supplied the rural areas beyond. Of these, Romford Gas Works was established in 1825 (White's Directory) leading at first to some street lighting and gas supplied to a limited number of Romford houses. By 1892 those gas works had moved from South Street to Crow Lane in the Oldchurch area of Romford with a gasometer for gas storage erected in c.1925. The gas industry was nationalised in 1949 following WW2 and within the decade, and ahead of the national move, Romford was receiving gas from the oil refineries of Shell Haven and Coryton as refinery gas was converted to town gas. Following the eventual industry move to natural gas the familiar Crow Lane gasometers were demolished in 2018 (Oxford Archaeology, 2018, *Former Gasworks at Crow Lane, Romford – Historic Building Investigation and Recording*). The makers plaques from the gasholders were donated to Havering Museum (Romford Recorder).

• • • • • • • • • • •

In the early days most families **brewed beer** for their own consumption and properties like Rainham Hall in 1729 and Hare Hall in 1768 had their own brewhouses. At that time local places such as Rainham had maltings beside the wharf where malt was prepared from grain, usually to a brewer's specification and Rainham was supplying the noted Westminster breweries and distilleries from the maltings at Rainham Creek (Frank Lewis *Rainham Parish Church*).

A licence was required for a publican to sell alcohol, others were wholesale brewers. The Hornchurch Brewery Co. was a wholesale brewery established early on by John Woodfine opposite the Kings Head public house in Hornchurch. It was a local rival to the more famous Romford brewery, and was revived in 1889 as the Old Hornchurch Brewery Co. In all it operated from 1789-1925 when it was sold to Mann, Crossman & Paulin Ltd with its 40 public houses. Quickly the public houses were sold off and the brewery demolished, today the site forms a shopping parade.

The long recorded history of the origins of the brewery in Romford seems now to be clouded in doubt (Matthew Abel *The Journal of the Brewery History Society* 167, 2-12, 2016). However, Edward Ind did purchase a brewery in Romford in around 1799 that went on to become Ind, Coope & Co. in 1845 with major investment and linking the brewery to Romford station by its own sidings. It later became Allied Breweries that went on in 1993 to become part of Carlsberg-Tetley. In 1864 'Ind Coope's Own Regiment' company of soldiers were attached to the Essex Rifle Volunteers (q.v.) with its own Company Battalion Brass Band, and in 1883 became part of the 1st Volunteer Battalion of the Essex Regiment, which from 1888 was to gather at Warley in case of invasion (The *Stanhope Memorandum*). The Company also maintained its own Fire Department up until the Company's closure in 1993 when the remaining brewery buildings in High Street, Romford became home to Havering Museum.

• • • • • • • • • • •

Over the following years this area became very popular with Londoners and the scene was set for future country retreats, Plot-lands developments and 'Homes for Heroes' during the next, the 20th, century; as well as the industry, commercial and warehousing uses that remain important here along north Thameside today.

Places to visit near and far:

- The railway viaduct at Davy Down Urban Riverside Park
- Although now converted to private housing some of the original Warley Hospital buildings survive as listed buildings including the Lodge, the Main Block and the Tower House
- Essex Regiment Chapel, Warley was the only individual regiment to have its own freestanding chapel. The imposing interior has a rich display of the Regimental Colours, as well as the pew ends and memorials of the regimental history. The Essex Regiment Museum is included within Chelmsford Museum, Chelmsford
- Havering Museum in Romford Conservation Area is housed in the Edwardian office building and part of a Victorian Warehouse, later offices, of the old Romford Brewery and is locally listed. It houses exhibits, tells the stories and celebrates the achievements of local people
- Upminster 'Tithe' Barn Museum of Nostalgia houses memorabilia of the area's Victorian agricultural and folk past in a thatched roofed medieval grange barn, which was originally constructed for the Abbots of Waltham and is now a Scheduled Ancient Monument

- Brentwood Museum, Cemetery Lodge, Lorne Road, Warley is the original Sexton's cottage now housing social and domestic objects from around 1840-1950. Outside is the closed cemetery, once the sexton's responsibility, some graves are maintained by the War Graves Commission and are testament to the First World War military camp in Warley, the grounds are now a Nature Reserve
- The Victorian kitchen at Valentines Mansion & Gardens, Ilford
- The Victorian kitchen at Audley End House, managed by English Heritage
- Essex Police Museum, Chelmsford, CM2 6DN, including the *History Notebook* free publications about the stories of people like PC Gutteridge
- V&A Museum of Childhood, Cambridge Heath Road, Bethnal Green
- Open House, is an architectural festival giving free public access to many buildings, walks, talks and tours over one weekend in September each year https://openhouselondon.org.uk
- London Open House is a free festival of London's architecture, engineering and urban landscape from the medieval to the thoroughly modern, held annually in the 3rd weekend in September
- Essex Houses & Gardens are a group of historic buildings and gardens independently opening to the public
- Several Walks from Thames Chase Visitor Centre start from Broadfields Farm with its older grade II listed barn and a Victorian stable block with a king post roof structure rarely found at this date and also a 19th century cart shed and farmhouse, now offices, originally built to look like a medieval hall-house
- Cranham Conservation Area is a hilltop hamlet on a medieval route with the historic Georgian Hall and the railed tomb to Thomas Woodruff (d.1746) in the churchyard and Victorian buildings all surrounded by farmland that retains its historic feeling of rural isolation. At the heart of the conservation area Walks no.2, 5 and 6a pass the Victorian farm complex built by the great local benefacting Benyon family
- Thames Chase Walk no. 3 takes in Cranham Brickfields, a Local Nature Reserve and Site of Borough Importance for Nature Conservation with links to the introduction of brickmaking into this area by the Tyrell family of Herongate at the time
- For a feel for the royal forest of Essex and further information and forest walks, see the Epping Forest Gateway (The View) with the Tudor Queen Elizabeth's hunting lodge, (II*) the c. early 19th century Butlers Retreat interpretation centre and café (II) at Rangers Road, Chingford (a former Victorian coach house and stables)
- The Victorian Coalhouse Fort built between 1861 and 1874 to protect England from invasion by the French. It was used again during WWI and WW2 before being closed in 1956 following the abolition of Coastal Defence and now its setting is the Coalhouse Fort Park open space
- Tilbury Fort, owned by English Heritage is the best example of a low-profiled artillery fort in England with a circuit of moats and bastioned outworks. It has protected London's seaward approach from the 16th century through to WW2. It has Victorian magazine houses where vast quantities of gunpowder were stored, and underground bastion magazine passages to explore

- The Two Forts Way along the Thames riverbank links Coalhouse Fort at East Tilbury and its Napoleonic and Victorian history with that of the older Tilbury Fort. The path is about 5 km (just over 3 miles) and is described as 'a challenging route suitable for able bodied walkers and experienced cyclists'
- Blists Hill Victorian Town at Ironbridge Gorge Museums, Telford, Shropshire, including school visits
- Victorian & Albert Museum British Galleries for style, taste and innovation of the times

Ideas for future projects:

- Given the significant interest by people in genealogy and human interest stories there may be scope for a more detailed account of the lives of significant local personalities and their impact both locally and in the wider world, for example the famous gardener Miss Ellen Wilmott who developed her interest and career locally from her home base at Great Warley
- A study of the history, development, decline and impact of Warley Garrison on Brentwood town and Warley district and across the wider landscape area, and its role in the national story
- Develop an increased interest in the grand houses of this period through reading (e.g. Bryson, Bill, *At Home – A Short History of Private Life* ISBN: 9781784161873); and period dramas (e.g. Downton Abbey television series) to explore historic social interactions and relationships/a study of class rules etc. between the nobility, local wealthy, the merchants and skilled and unskilled local people and their lifestyles

References for further research:

More information on this historical period can be found through:

- See Section C: History Introduction, p. 99
- The Victorian Society champions Victorian and Edwardian buildings in England and Wales and advises on their adaptation to modern living whilst retaining their special interest
- The Society for the Protection of Ancient Buildings (SPAB)
- The Nation Archives, Kew for Metropolitan Police records
- The Metropolitan Police Historical Collection via the Friends of the Metropolitan Police Historical Collection
- *The Hundred Best Houses* Gidea Park Exhibition Brochure 1911, reprint 2016
- Gotto, Edward, 1853 map of Romford, held at Havering Local Studies Library
- Victorian Ordnance Survey maps online or at larger scale at the Local Studies Libraries or at Essex Records Office

Further reading:

- Beeton, Isabella (ed. 1861) *Mrs Beeton's Book of Household Management*
- Le Lievre, Audrey (2008) *Miss Willmott of Warley Place: her Life and Her Gardens* pub. Faber & Faber
- Leyin, Alan in partnership with Thurrock Council (1997) *Thurrock's Past – Echoes from a Place* pub. Lejins Publishing ISBN 0 9528789 0 9
- Perfect, Charles Thomas (first pub. 1917) *Ye Olde Village of Hornchurch*
- Pett Ridge, William (1900) *A Son of the State* pub. Horse's Mouth 2020 ISBN 9781839671869
- Phillips, John (2015) *Victorian Cranham – and the Boyd School*
- Poe, Edgar Allan (1843) *The Gold Bug* inspired by the story of the 18th century privateer and pirate Captain William Kidd
- Rhodes, Linda; Sheldon, Lee & Abnett, Kathryn (2005) *The Dagenham Murder* pub. London Borough of Barking & Dagenham, ISBN 9780900325373 Won the Crime Writers' Golden Dagger in 2006
- Rhodes, Linda & Abnett, Kathryn (2007) *Foul Deed and Suspicious Deaths in Barking, Dagenham and Chadwell Heath* pub by Wharncliffe Books ISBN 978 1 84563 034 8
- Rhodes, Linda & Abnett, Kathryn (2012) *The Romford Outrage* pub. by Pen and Sword Books
- Scott, Sir Walter (first pub. 1819) *Ivanhoe*
- Stevenson, Robert Louis (1883) *Treasure Island*
- Tasker, George (first pub. 1911) *Country Rambles by Field Path and Road in and around Romford, Hornchurch and Upminster*
- Thompson, Flora (1945) *Lark Rise to Candleford* ISBN 978-1-5290-2405-0

Chapter 13
Early 20th century: Edwardian era 1901 – 1939

'...Edward VII, George and Ted...'

NATIONAL CURRICULUM Key Stage 3 hints *are about changes in national life and challenges for Britain, Europe and the wider world*

The 20th century began a new time of great change, innovations and significant events. This was a time of fast-paced highs and lows, dominated initially by the Great War (WWI) followed by the strange inter-War mix of gaiety, Modernism and the Great Depression, with emancipation, socialism and workers' rights. But the said 'war to end all wars' did not achieve that high ideal and just one generation of fighting men later erupted in 1939 into the brutal Second World War (WW2).

SURPRISE *'The Land of the Fanns is an intricate landscape, full of surprises and 'hidden gems' and rewards exploring.'* **(TellTale working with the public 2018)**

In this age of speedy innovation, discovery and change, here alongside the river Thames, London continued to have a dominating effect on developments and this had a great part to play in defence measures, industrial developments and migration, all of which put this agricultural landscape under considerable pressure. Fortunately, from 1990 some 9,800 ha (38 square miles) of urban fringe[1] countryside has been managed as the Thames Chase Community Forest central to this area, to renew and regenerate the natural landscape whether damaged by mineral extraction, landfill or visual intrusion, for the future for all.

MIGRATION *'This is a crossroads landscape: because of its location on the Thames ... people have always travelled into, through and away from this area.'* **(TellTale working with the public 2018)**

This has historically been an area of people movement across it, mainly in response to economic conditions. This trend continued during the 20th century and even today is no different as there remains a constant flow of generations eastwards out from London towards the coast for cheaper housing and long-distance commuting and for gentle seaside retirement.

Local Government Reorganisation As the suburban expansion of the metropolis continued so a new civic emphasis developed bringing more public buildings, schools and parks, hospitals and civic centres. Alongside this further changes across the local administrative areas took place (and adjustments continue to take place to today).

---

[1] The *urban fringe* is the edge of towns and cities where town meets country with competing pressures for agricultural, urban development and natural landscapes.

During the interwar period Dagenham became an Urban District (UDC) in 1926 and was elevated to a Municipal Borough from 1938 until 1965 when it became part of the London Borough of Barking but reasserted itself in the **London Borough of Barking & Dagenham** in 1980; the Ilford part of the Becontree Estate transferred from the London Borough of Redbridge in 1994. In his Architectural Guide Sir Nikolas Pevsner remarks that 'Dagenham remained an Essex village into the early 20th century' but it was 'the LCC's Becontree Estate after 1919 that forced its absorption into suburban London.' and 'Contemporary with the shift from rural to suburban, agricultural Dagenham became industrial, beginning with the establishment of the deep-water Dagenham Dock and confirmed by one of the largest industrial enterprises of the 20th century, the Ford Motor Works ... new civic buildings were symbolically placed at its geographical centre on Becontree Heath...' Here the Civic Centre was erected in 1936 and the main building and Council Chamber are now a listed building.

Romford Rural District (RD) was abolished in 1934 and Noak Hill and Havering-atte-Bower became part of Romford UD, which become Romford Municipal borough in 1937 with a Town Hall built in 1935 by HR Collins & AEO Geens. This is a listed building, in International Modern style[2] but keeping the traditional use of brick walls as cladding onto a metal frame. In 1926 Hornchurch had become one of the largest Urban Districts in England when it gained Rainham, Wennington and most of Great Warley, Upminster and Cranham (the remainder went to Brentwood), and part of North Ockendon parish was added in 1936. When London Government was reorganised to form 32 Boroughs in 1965, Romford and Hornchurch were combined to form the new **London Borough of Havering**, named after the historic Liberty. Pevsner says of Havering '...the character of its buildings is shared equally between the suburbia of its western neighbours and the rural vernacular of the Essex countryside. This mix is unique in East London, comprising still remote medieval parish churches along the Thames marshlands, tiny rural villages, farmhouses set in open fields, a scattering of mansions, leafy Edwardian suburbia, and at its heart the brash commercialism of Romford.' Much of this diversity across the LotF landscape is now encapsulated in Local Authority designated conservation areas.

Brentwood UD gained South Weald, Little Warley, Childerditch and the remaining portions of Great Warley, Upminster and Cranham in 1934. In 1974 it joined with part of Epping & Ongar RD and part of Chelmsford RD to form Brentwood UD, becoming **Brentwood Borough Council** (BC) in 1993. A considerable development from its origins as a hamlet that grew up in a burned forest clearing first mentioned in relation to a 12th century outlaw Reginald de Bosco Arso ('of the burnt wood').

Also in 1934, Billericay RD became Billericay UD until 1955 when part of Orsett RD was added to make Basildon UD. In 1974 the smaller, developed part of Langdon Hills was also transferred in to make up **Basildon BC**. Built in 1949, Pevsner describes Basildon as the largest of the eight New Towns developed after WW2 in a ring around London. Sited just beyond the Metropolitan Green Belt (MGB) these towns were designed to be self-contained and to accommodate London's overflow population and industry in pleasant surroundings. The New Town spread some 6 miles eastwards from the plotlands of Dunton and Langdon Hills - where between 1831 and 1931 the population of Langdon Hills had already risen from 224 to 2,103 people.

---

[2] International Modern style makes use of new building materials such as glass and steel and reinforced concrete and achieving a visually weightless quality. It is characterised by an emphasis on volume, rectilinear forms, asymmetrical compositions with open interior spaces and minimal ornamentation.

In 1936 Thurrock UD was formed from Grays Thurrock UD, Purfleet UD, Tilbury Town Council and Orsett RD (including Langdon Hills Civil Parish) and the remainder of North Ockendon parish. It became Thurrock Borough Council with a mayor in 1974 and **Thurrock Unitary Authority** in 1997 when it took on various additional powers from Essex County Council. Although the Thurrock Thames Gateway Development Corporation exercised the Planning function from 2003 it was taken back under the Council in 2012. Thurrock aptly describes both itself and its ambition by its motto: 'By Thames to all people of the world.'

Communications Transportation improved throughout the century with the better **road and rail networks,** and the Thames short **ferry** from Erith remained until well into the 20th century when it could still be hailed from the bank. The introduction of **bicycles** made reasonably distant journeys possible for many people and opened up evening outings to local dances and cinema trips and jaunts to Thameside and to the seaside. The **radio** (called a *wireless*) kept people in touch with what was now available for them to buy and to enjoy. Public telephone boxes like the listed **Type K6** box made it easier to keep in touch with friends and family and make arrangements to meet.

The iconic K6 Red Telephone Boxes were designed by Sir Giles Gilbert Scott in 1935 to commemorate the Silver Jubilee of the coronation of King George V. Here the listed K6 box stands outside the listed Clockhouse (q.v.), in the vicinity of the lost Bell River at Upminster; other local examples are at Rainham village, Great Warley village and at Horndon-on-the-Hill (Photograph courtesy of Debbie Brady, Heritage Engagement Officer LotF, 2017)

In the early years of the century there was also much interest in developing **powered flight** – by plane or other airship (and continued throughout the century and to today). According to *Aviation in Essex* (ed. K.A. Cole, 1976), Essex was considered one of the *cradles* of British aviation history - but the story here goes back rather further is seems. In *Essex: A Hidden Aviation History* Paul Bingley and Richard E. Flagg tell of a hot air balloon flight across London by Jean-Pierre Blanchard in 1785. Taking off at Chelsea the balloon landed on Langdon Hills where a witness said he 'pac'd it up in a post-chaise and went to London.' But *balloon alley* was then born of the prevailing wind on this route and by 1853 the frequent flights had become a nuisance to local farmers. By 1860 George Faux was experimenting with *flapping wings* in Chigwell Row commenting 'I'm a real good flyer, but I cannot alight very well.' (Basildon, Canvey, Southend Echo, 2007).

Chapter 13 Early 20th century: Edwardian era

Early on, and in conjunction with the War Office Dr F.A. Barton, flight pioneer, was secretly producing an airship at Alexander Palace. A number of incidents occurred, the most serious involving an explosion whilst generating the highly flammable hydrogen gas needed to fill the balloon. However in 1905 the, by now independent Barton-Rawson airship finally made its maiden and only flight. The ship was 55m (180 ft.) long with a bamboo platform below for the operators, the balloon made of varnished Japanese Silk and filled with about 200,000 cubic feet of hydrogen (Bill Welker, USA, 2020). The ship performed well but was inadvertently blown across East London to Heaton Grange at Havering where it landed in a potato field close by a garden party in progress. Two farm labourers grabbed hold of the tail rope but were thrown tumbling off as the airship rebounded in the air. The anchor caught into the field hedge and gracefully landed until the crew shifted weight by moving to the bow, making the ship rapidly rise again. One operative, still in the stern grasped the ships 'ripping gear' that tore open the balloon and released its gas with a terrific noise and the ship was wrecked. The 14-mile flight had been a great success with a near perfect landing but the excitement of the success led to the loss of the airship that had taken 20 years to design and build at a cost of £4,000 (Donoghue, Simon and Tait, Don 2013, *Harold Hill & Noak Hill – a history*).

In 1915 a later Royal Navy **airship** broke free of its moorings in West Thurrock toppling the pilot into the Thames mud, but the crew of the Training Ship Exmouth managed to recover the airship with grappling hooks and take it in tow.

In his online *UK Airfields & Airports Guide,* Dick Flute reveals much detail of local **airfields** and their history. Henry and Edward Petre of Ingatestone built their own aircraft which, after much redesign and rebuilding with Handley Page at Fairlop, Edward Petre flew from Fairlop in 1912 via Rainham along the Thames to Brooklands in Surrey making the first 'heavier that air flight across London'. During WWI Fairlop was a Military Landing Ground and it appears that close by were WWI Hainault Farm (Romford) Military aerodrome, Chigwell airfield (1938-1939) and Fairlop WW2 RAF Military airfield, a satellite to RAF Hornchurch, and later a barrage balloon centre (1941-1946); this area would eventually become Fairlop Waters Country Park.

During WWI there were local Military landing grounds at North Ockendon, Horndon-on-the-Hill and at Orsett and Barking Military Kite Balloon Station at Longbridge Farm. Dagenham Experimental Ground operated during 1909-1910 and at Goodmayes Park 1932-1933. This inter-war period was the era of the **Flying Circus** and with joy rides at places like Gidea Park in around 1923 and East Horndon during the 1930s; Havering Park Farm and Hog Hill were gliding sites for a few months in 1930 and Dagenham Common near Castle Green operated in 1938.

From 1931 Hillman Airlines operated a commercial airport from the landing strip at Maylands Farm, Harold Park that would become one of the best-known airline operators in the UK. At first it was another joyriding, taxi and charter service flying to Clacton initially, but it launched commercially in 1932 with an impressive *Essex Air Pageant*, at which time **Amy Mollison (nee Johnson)** flew as a star for the airline for a short period. Following the early death of Ted Hillman, in 1935 the business was merged with others to become British Airways Ltd (*Harold Hill and Noak Hill: A History*).

During the interwar period the Barking to Upminster **railway line** of 1885 was electrified in 1932 becoming the District line in 1933. New intermediate stations were opened as expansion of the built-up areas occurred between the Wars increasing local demand for rail travel. Named after the historic crossing point between Chafford Hundred and the Liberty, the new station at Upminster Bridge was opened in 1934 in a plain Art Deco[3] style it controversially includes the originally Eurasian reversed swastika-style design in the entrance hall. The original station forecourt lighting columns were removed to the Upminster Tithe Barn Museum of Nostalgia.

In his youth Philip Conrad Vincent, inventor and designer of the legendary **Vincent motorcycle** lived for a time with his uncle at High House (grade II*) Horndon-on-the-Hill, which now displays a Thurrock Heritage Plaque to his memory. Vincent designs influenced the development of motorcycles around the world and the 1948 Vincent Black Shadow was at the time the world's fastest production motorcycle. Philip Vincent is buried with his parents in the family plot at the overflow churchyard of St. Peter and St. Paul (grade I) and Vincent Avenue commemorates his two uncles.

Architecture There were new building designs based on the revival of traditional styles and often incorporating new materials such as concrete, and new methods, some more successful than others. For example, the listed Upminster Court in the Ingrebourne Valley (on the Thames Chase Walk 6b in the northern loop via Upminster town centre), was built in 1905/7 in Queen Anne Revival style using bricks from the local brick fields and apparently incorporating an experimental fire protection material between floors (Local Authority Building Control observation). The house was designed by local architect Sir Charles Reilly for businessman Arthur Williams, and continues the house design into the garden with the creation of *garden rooms*. Socially, at this early 20th century date, through the clever use of architectural design and detailing both house and garden were arranged so as to separate servants from the family and guests, and also to provide separate social spaces for male family members and guests from females.

Arthur Williams was the son of Samuel Williams of Dagenham Dock, and the inventor of the concrete piling system that made possible the deep-water Dock and other building on the marsh land (*A company's Story in its setting, Samuel Williams & Sons Ltd 1855-1955* pub. the Trinity Press, info. supplied by Lisa D. Lock, LBH).

The philosophy of Sir Ebenezer Howard's utopian *Garden City*[4] ideals and Henrietta Barnet's **Garden Suburbs**[5] for housing developments became popular with local builders. In Upminster (Thames Chase Walk No.6b) the first of the house building phases began in 1906 when W.P. Griggs & Co. acquired 61 ha (150 acres) of land from the Branfill trustees to develop Upminster Garden Suburb. Development

---

[3] Art Deco (Arts Decoratifs) is a style of the visual Arts, architecture and design popular particularly during the interwar period. It is characterised by sleek geometric, zigzag or stylised forms such as sunrise motifs, with bold outlines and in man-made materials.

[4] Garden Cities are planned and compact communities with residential and industry and ready access to a wide rural 'green' belt for agriculture and recreation.

[5] Garden Suburbs are outlying districts of an established town designed according to garden city ideals.

progressed according to the changing economic situation even through WWI until 1938 with more development in the 1950s and '60s.

In Gidea Park, Sir Herbert Raphael purchased the Gidea Park Estate in 1897 and donated the Canal and 6 ha (15 acres) of gardens, probably by Richard Woods, for Havering's first public park. More of the land was added later and the park opened in 1904 and a century after the occasion was celebrated by local people under the auspices of local group 'Havering Heritage'; some features and listed garden structures survive in the park and adjoining housing estate. For at least a century public parks had become important and increasingly popular politically for physical health and the good of *social morality*, they also helped to safeguard some older landscapes, as here in Gidea Park.

Raphael developed the adjacent land as the Romford Garden Suburb with the *House and Cottage Exhibition* held in 1910/11 for 'The Hundred Best Houses'. The preface to the Exhibition catalogue records the President of the Local Government Board speaking in the Garden Suburb in 1910 saying that 'Fifteen thousand Families move every year from Inner to Outer London'. The objectives of the Exhibition were to raise housing standards by demonstrating improvements to modern housing and building through the Garden City Movement and advances in scientific knowledge and the revival of the Arts and craftsmanship.

Following WWI during the interwar years of the 1920s and 1930s, a new **International Modern style** was briefly popular typified by the use of concrete with flat roofs. A *Modern Homes Exhibition* was now held on the Gidea Park Estate this time in Art Deco and International Modern style. The winning House being 64 Heath Drive (grade II listed) by the pioneering modernist firm of Tecton under Berthold Lubetkin, it still included servant accommodation. This was the *Sunshine House* built to take best advantage of the sun and incorporating a sun terrace in tune with the times that emphasized ventilation, hygiene and the health benefits of sunshine. Typically the facilities of the adjacent new Sports Ground were a key feature in the 1920s and 1930s (Havering Library-Local Studies). Both the Competition and Exhibition sites are within the Gidea Park and Railway Station conservation areas.

64 Heath Drive, The 'Sunshine House' by Tecton.
Courtesy of Architectural Press Archive/RIBA Collections ref. RIBA 23898

Council Housing (more usually *social housing* today) was common after the Housing Act 1919. In 1923 the London County Council (LCC) acquired over 10 square kilometres (4 square miles) of the old mid 13th century Parsloes manor in Dagenham stretching to Barking and Ilford to erect the huge **Becontree Cottage Garden Estate** is response to widespread slum clearance in the East End of London. Some 26,000 'homes fit for heroes' from WWI accommodating around 100,000 people were developed on the market gardens between 1921 and 1935 with another 1,000 houses added later. During this inter-war period the population of Dagenham increased by more than three-fold and many residents were employed by the Ford factory. A Council blue plaque[6] marks the first houses completed in Chittys Lane, Becontree. Another Council blue plaque on the estate at 122 Dagenham Avenue marks the house where Major the Rt Hon Sir Tasker Watkins VC, GBE, The Welch Regiment, lived for 15 years from 1931, he married in Dagenham parish church in 1941 and finally returned home to Wales on demobilisation.

Many of the rural farmsteads and manor houses were lost in the development including the then derelict Parsloes house. However, the parkland was retained as a centrepiece and opened as **Parsloes Park** to celebrate the completion of the estate in 1935. The park is now a Local Nature Reserve and in part a Nature Conservation Area and a proposed Tier 2 APA, and the Fanshawe family portraits are held at Valence House Museum. Lasting from the 17th century, the Fanshawe ownership finally ceased by the early 20th century when Parsloes became well known when leased by the National Trotting Horse Breeders Association. After WW2 the Heath Park Estate was built between 1949-1951 east of Heathway (O'Leary 1966).

At the Four Wantz crossroads leading to the estate the Eastbrook Public House is a suburban landmark building. Built in 1937-8 it survives as a grade II* neo-Georgian style roadhouse with original high-quality interiors. Elsewhere local authorities built Council Housing in large or small developments, and in Brentwood for example the London Borough of Newham built its East Ham Estate to provide overspill accommodation for its own 'bombed out' people. In its 'drive against slums' Romford's first batch of Council Houses were opened in 1935 (Romford Times).

Many people sought their own solution to the post-war housing crisis. The area became well known and popular during the Depression of the 1920s and '30s when many East Enders bought £5 agricultural plots from intermediary Land Agents selling off farmland in this manner. This came about in the face of competition from cheap American wheat imports, and as tinned and frozen foods were increasingly available making seasonal local foods less in demand. In Rainham on the Berwick and Parsonage Estate, at Havering-atte-Bower, at Dunton and Langdon Hills the self-sufficient weekend **plotlands** were developed with cabins or summerhouses. Developed from the *Homes for Hero's* ethos, plots were used as refuges from wartime bombardment of London. At first they were not much more than camping sites with no gas, electricity, telephones, main drainage or refuse collection and no pavements or street lighting; water was to be had from occasional standpipes in the unmade roads. But people gave their properties happy names like *Bonhomie, Joyville, Rosegarden, Sunshine Lodge, Floral* and *Happiness* evocative of the spirit of the age, or perhaps showing their political leanings with *Lansbury* for example.

---

[6] The national Blue Plaque scheme was introduced in 1866, at present the scheme for London is operated by English Heritage, occasionally with some variety in design. Local authorities and other bodies are also allowed to run their own commemorative plaque schemes also using different criteria.

The **Langdon Living Landscape** (Langdon Ridge SSSI) sites extend along Langdon Ridge from Dunton and Horndon to Basildon and Vange Heights. These sites are designed to take a strategic landscape-scale approach to connecting and developing habitats. The 186 ha (461 acres) of **Langdon Nature Reserve** of meadows, farmland, modern and ancient woodlands has an abundance of wildlife and also covers some 200 abandoned Plotland gardens, an area of significant cultural landscape. Here a surviving 1930s bungalow, now **The Haven Plotlands Museum**, is opened to the public in addition to the wildlife Visitors Centre.[7] Against the highly urbanised backdrop of Basildon this area provides an opportunity for people to reconnect with nature and has been described as '…a wildlife-rich landscape that deserves to be recognised as one of the most important for nature conservation in England (Aiden Lonergan, Natural England Area Manager, West Anglia).

The Haven' Plotlands bungalow, Museum

At Havering-atte-Bower the Italianate Havering House mansion that had been built on the Havering Palace site, was itself demolished in 1925 and the Park sold off in 0.4 ha (1 acre) plots between the Wars as smallholdings. Patrick Abercrombie's **Greater London Plan** of 1944 led in time to the compulsory purchase of the Havering plots in the *green belt* and in 1976 Havering Country Park was opened across the area.

At Rainham the smallholdings of pig and chicken farms, the orchards and summer shelters were redeveloped, often by self-builders during the interwar and the 1950s with permanent bungalows and housing now with perhaps more settled or composite family names or favourite holiday destinations that might perhaps be *DunRomin, Homeleigh, Rodann, Barnaby Lodge* or *Marazion*. The interwar optimistic sunray motif was commonplace and together such clues leave an intangible sense of people's interwar and early post war self-reliance and hope.[8]

---

[7] Design a sales poster for a Plotlands site.

[8] Design and colour a sunray motif for a house gable, window, door or gate, why do you think the *sunray* was a popular symbol at the time?

Typical sunray motifs on the gables of houses and bungalows

As the century moved along in Havering for example, sub Arts & Crafts estates were developed emerging from the Garden City ideals in Emerson Park and at Collier Row, Rise Park and the 'Elm Park Garden City' that opened in 1935 – and where the developers, Costain, negotiated for a railway station so the estate residents could easily commute to work (Hipperson, Chris; Donoghue, Simon and Brandon, Ingrid (2009) *The Elm Park Story – from Garden City to London Suburb*). There was a surge in speculative developments particularly where sites were close to the new railway stations, also ribbon developments[9] of housing along main roads.

Philanthropy In 1892 working-class politician and social reformer George Lansbury was elected as a guardian to the Poplar Board and helped bring new ideas to the operation of Workhouses for the poor. Amongst these ideas in 1904 Sumpners Farm just north of the railway line in Dunton, became an experimental **Farm Colony** to retrain unemployed men from Poplar in farm work. It was set up by the Jewish American millionaire philanthropist Joseph Fels with George Lansbury (who later became Leader of the Labour Party from 1932-35). This was England's first Poor Law labour colony and for a time it served the Plotlands with an abundance of farm produce until the site closed in 1935 (see Laindon & District Community Archive). In 1905 Little Mollands in South Ockendon was similarly set up as a farm colony by West Ham County Borough Council.

The **Poplar Training Schools**, Hutton were erected in 1906/7 as a training school for around 700 destitute children from Poplar and based on the 'cottage homes' village arrangement. It included orchards and a 16 ha (40 acre) farm where the children worked, boys were also taught trades and to play musical instruments, girls learned domestic duties. Queen Mary and her daughter Princess Mary visited in 1919. Eventually the Home was closed with the last child leaving in 1982 (Peter Higginbotham). The Hall and the 'Lansbury Suite' are now civil ceremony wedding venues.

---

[9] Ribbon development refers to building houses spreading out along roads leading from settlements and is considered to be a cause for concern as the process is unplanned leading to urban sprawl. In Britain the post-war Planning system developed green belt policies, new towns, planned suburbs and garden cities.

Women's Suffrage

After the closure of The George Inn in Corbets Tey (qv) it became known as the Old Cottage and from about 1905 it was the home of Henria Williams, a 'rather eccentric lady' and local leading light in the movement for Women's Suffrage. In 1907 a meeting organised at Upminster Boys School House attracted an overflowing audience to hear prominent suffragettes. In 1908 Miss Williams chaired a rally in Upminster with women arriving in open-top busses and with speakers from the Women's Freedom League (WFL). She went on to attend protests calling for women to be given the vote on the same terms as men. In 1909 Henria was amongst 120 arrested when she took part in a deputation led by Emmeline Pankhurst and a few days later was amongst a crowd that detained the Liberal Prime Minister Herbert Asquith. Amongst this information on his Upminster History site, Tony Benton goes on to describe Miss Williams activity at the appalling original 'Black Friday' event in November 1910. Determined suffragettes were treated cruelly and her death that New Year was publicly linked to the events of Black Friday recording that she had 'been used with great brutality, and was aware at the time of the effect upon her heart, which was weak.'[10]

In 1913 a peaceful, countrywide pilgrimage took place, originating from Great Yarmouth, nineteen suffragists made their way here through Brentwood to overnight at Romford. With banners aloft they held a well-attended meeting attracting local people at Romford market, then attended church and met again before rallying with up to 40,000 others in London's Hyde Park. As reported in the Romford Recorder: A local Councillor marked the occasion 'for general suffrage' in 2013 by a photoshoot outside Havering Town Hall of women wearing the suffragettes' colours of purple for loyalty and dignity, white for purity and green for hope.[11]

Religion Lying outside of Great Warley conservation area to the south-east there are more listed and other historic buildings including a grade I church erected 1902-4 in **Art Nouveau style**[12] by Charles Harrison Townsend an exponent of the **Arts & Crafts** movement. The church interior is by the eminent Sir William Reynolds-Stephens and features astonishing mother-of-pearl inlay. The building has been described as 'an orgy of the English Arts and Crafts variety of the International Art-Nouveau' (The Buildings of England: Pevsner N. pub.1965). This exceptional church together with access to the Nature Reserve at Warley Place direct from the village centre, make this village a tourist hot-spot, although only outside the busy rush hour Brentwood commuter traffic.

In a striking design reflecting contemporary trends, the Cemetery Chapel in Whalebone Lane North together with its entrance gates, piers and railings, are now listed. They were designed by

---

 [10] Compare and consider what can be learned from the handling of Henria Williams and others at the time with the controversy over the treatment of minority groups in official hands today.

[11] Design and colour a suffragette brooch or other piece of jewellery.

[12] Art Nouveau is an international style of art, architecture and decoration inspired by natural plant forms using long, flowing, organic lines.

the Borough Surveyor T.P. Francis and built in 1933-4 just as the vast Becontree Housing Estate was bringing a population explosion to Dagenham. More central to the estate is the listed Church of St. Mary, in Grafton Road, one of five built to serve the estate. It was designed by the noted partnership of Modernist architects Welch, Cachemaille-Day and Lander in rendered concrete with brick dressings and erected in 1930-5.

During this time, following the mass influx of refugees to London's East End from the terror in Imperial Russia, the Federation of Synagogues had been established in 1887 to improve integration. By 1937 there were 68 affiliated synagogues across London which purchased land for a walled **Federation cemetery** in Rainham that was consecrated in 1938. Some 40 per cent of the land remains in agricultural use and the site is on the local list of Historic Parks and Gardens.

The Parish church of **St. Alban, Protomartyr**,[13] Romford was built c.1890 and with a new stone alter installed in 1948 as a War Memorial. The building remains unlisted but under the guidance of Father S.P. Hingley underwent reordering and a major refurbishment of the church and Garden of Remembrance in the late 20th century. By introducing a 'number of significant works of art by leading contemporary artists' this has become 'a centre of excellence in terms of Ecclesiastical Art.'[14]

ECONOMY *'This area is justly famous for trade, commerce and industry: these have been important here for many centuries.'* (TellTale working with the public 2018)

Trade With increased demand on the river the **Port of London Authority** (PLA) trust was set up in 1908/9 to promote **river trade and travel**, to ensure navigational safety along the tidal Thames and to protect the river's unique marine environment.

East End charabanc outing

The inn at Rainham Ferry had become the Three Crowns from 1868 and still attracted **day-trippers** for a time over the turn of the century. Visitors arrived from the East End of London by charabanc or steam train – with watering stops for the engine and swift track-side ales for the passengers (pers. rec. by Old 'Pop' Hansford as a 17-year-old *dandy* or smart young man about town).[15] These excursions

---

[13] A Protomartyr is a cause's first martyr. St. Alban is the first recorded British Christian martyr, traditionally said to have been beheaded at Verulamium/St. Albans in early Roman Britain.

[14] Organise a family or school trip to study the modern Ecclesiastical art at this 'centre of excellence.'

[15] Design and write a postcard from your imagined day trip to Rainham Beach or Purfleet-on-Sea.

were curtailed as the hamlet became increasingly industrialised with the inn then serving the local workforce until it closed in 1951 (dem.1972). However, at Grays Town the Grays Beach Riverside Park survives even now with visitor facilities and attractions.

• • • • • • • • • • •

A more comfortable **retail** experience was introduced with the new covered shopping arcades in towns like Brentwood and Broad Street Market (dem.) in Dagenham (1930), in Romford the Romford Arcade and later Quadrant Arcade (1935) and the Romford Shopping Hall.

• • • • • • • • • • •

Cinemas now became a popular leisure option with plush interiors and some exceptional internal decorative plasterwork, like the Tower Cinema Hornchurch (dem.) they were designed to attract women and middle class families. Examples survive as listed buildings in Grays town centre where The State Cinema (II*) was built in a simple, austere Moderne[16] style. It is one of the late 1930s palatial *super cinemas* seating over 2,000 for stage shows or films, and the interior has been used in music videos and television productions and in 2000 for the film *Who Shot Roger Rabbit*. Nearby the Ritz Cinema was built in 1939-40 also in the streamlined Moderne style. This was 'one of the last cinemas to have opened from the classical era of cinema construction of the 1920s – 1930s' (Historic England list description).

• • • • • • • • • • •

Dagenham Girl Pipers were a professional organisation originally founded from the Congregational Sunday School on the Becontree Estate in 1930. Only two years later at the Lord Mayor's show they were described as '...portraying the spirit of the age...' and '...like a fresh breeze from the mountains.' They toured extensively in Britain and abroad performing in more than 45 countries. During WW2 some members performed for British armed forces personnel with the Entertainments National Service Association (ENSA), and some senior members performed in America for the First Lady, Eleanor Roosevelt. They are now an amateur organisation under pipe major Sheila Hatcher.

Commerce In the Agricultural hinterland the rich farmland of this area remained well known for its **agriculture and market gardening** for many generations and this historic use is often reflected in local road names like Bull Street and Barley, Pike, Pea, Bramble, Lambs and Cherry Tree Lanes, the Cauliflower, the Harrow and at one time the Plough, the Cherry Tree and the Bull public houses, and places like Cornsland and Warren, Orchard and Cherry Orchard Farms. Indeed in places like the lowland hills of Orsett remnants of orchards survive.

---

[16] *Moderne* was a development of Art Deco in the 1930s and 1940s, influenced by streamlined industrial design with curved surfaces, tubular chrome work, inlaid woods, bright colours and geometric shapes.

At the end of the 19th century farm-labouring households had still been relying on family gleaning wheat for flour to bake their own bread. Through the century the farming society and its culture here, as elsewhere in the countryside, gradually changed. The agricultural landscape did begin to produce new signs of prosperity at the turn of the 20th century but the individual family vegetable plots and allotments still provided essential supplies for local families. Gradually as income and choice increased so people preferred to buy provisions from local shops and they became less self-sufficient and this change was coupled with the introduction of agricultural mechanisation. The better mechanical harvesters left little usable wheat for gleaning and milling became threatened. During the early years of WWI, Orsett and Aveley mills had ceased working and by this time the country was no longer self-sufficient in food production. In this desperate situation, the Government acted by guaranteeing farm prices, with a fixed minimum wage and regular hours for farm workers.

The wartime Government support for farming changed after the War and by 1921 a slump had settled again and in 1923 South Ockendon mill also shut. Some Government assistance was again introduced from the mid 1920s and agricultural wages rose at that time, but farming suffered from a lack of national agricultural policy and in 1934 Upminster Windmill finally followed the others and closed.[17] After the War, Royal Flying Corps (RFC) Suttons Farm had been returned to the farmer for agricultural use, although bi-planes were soon flown from there again.

• • • • • • • • • • • •

Commercial shipping berths and jetties became well established along Thameside with clusters in this area at Dagenham Dock, Rainham, Purfleet, South Stifford and West Thurrock. At Purfleet for example, the old quarry sites and Thames riverside access gave opportunity for commercial development and between 1906 and 1917 coal was landed at the coal sidings at Cory's Wharf and by 1962 there was a new 244m (800 ft) jetty and oil storage tanks. The Yara Purfleet Terminal jetty for bulk liquid CO_2 storage and a distribution depot was nearby but these wharfs later became derelict. After WW2 containerisation of freight transport became common and led to many of the docks closing with the bulk of transactions moving from London downstream to the banks of Thurrock and north Kent and adding considerably to the strategic commercial road, rail and river transportation systems here.

As the London Loop finishes at Purfleet railway station (Section 24) so Public Footpath (f. p.) 141 runs through this area from the station to the Thames foreshore and eastwards along the riverside across West Thurrock marshes and via f. p. 171 to Grays taking in the dramatic and changing commercial and riverside views.

• • • • • • • • • • • •

In the matter of **public utilities**, Romford was early on supplied with water from Havering Well famed for a time as a medicinal spring; the site is now commemorated by a plaque at Havering Well Garden near Roneo Corner. A listed 19th century disused roadside water pump stands by the borough boundary

---

[17] Upminster Windmill (II*) is being restored to working order and mill open days with visitor centre and education room, are organised by the Friends of Upminster Windmill

Chapter 13 Early 20th century: Edwardian era

at High Road, Chadwell Heath, with another *curtilage listed*[18] neighbourhood pump at Blacks Bridge (the bridge designed by James Wyatt in the late 18th century and referenced in *Copperplate Magazine No. 33*, 1794) in Gidea Park, and one of local heritage interest further along Main Road in Gidea Park.

In 1860 the owner's offer of excess potable water from Grays quarries led in 1861 to the South Essex Waterworks company supplying drinking water to an area here of some 270 km² (103 sq. miles) obtained from boreholes sunk into the chalk aquifer. On the east side of the Beam Bridge stands the listed Italianate Dagenham Pumping Station built in c.1910 as a substation of the South Essex Waterworks Company. The pumping engines have been removed and the building converted to offices. At Davy Down the **Stifford Pumping Station** buildings were erected in 1926-7 to house large diesel engines to provide power to extract water from a 42m (138ft) deep borehole in the chalk below. Here water extraction continues today by using a modern electric pump and supplies the Thurrock area working in partnership with Essex & Suffolk Water. The building is at times open to the public to view the now disused original diesel engines.

Year 10 students discovering the Stifford Pump House
(Photograph courtesy Debbie Brady, Heritage Engagement Officer LotF, 2017)

Industry New industries and processes continued to develop along the rivers and creeks during the first half of the 20th century in response to the War effort at that time. As industry developed it attracted more workers and brought more people out of London leading to new settlement patterns fitted in across the landscape and spreading ever eastwards and north-eastwards. By 1901 the population had spread towards here from London so that over half the county's population were settled in metropolitan Essex.

---

[18] Curtilage listed buildings are listed by virtue of being a building or other structure within the curtilage of a listed building before July 1948, and are afforded the same protection and restrictions.

The **Cranham Brick and Tile Company** were established near Franks Wood (Warley Franks). They developed the local brick earth backing the coastal marshes and operated from 1900 to 1920 supplying local areas and the London market. The company offered an alternative to agricultural employment for around 70 men. Part of the brickfields were used in the **'Dig for Victory'** campaign for growing wartime fruit and vegetables. It is now the site of the Cranham Brickfields LNR and a Grade I place of Borough Importance for Nature Conservation with a public right of way running through it.

• • • • • • • • • • •

In the west, the expanding Thames riverside industries included the vast **Ford Motor Company Works** that arrived at **Dagenham Riverside** in 1929, led to the later 1930s becoming more prosperous here with effects like the boom in the car industry, helped by the growing work force from the Becontree Estate and easy riverside access with deep water port. During WW2 the Dagenham plant produced over a quarter of a million Ford V-8 engines for powerboats, landing craft and armoured military vehicles, including 14,000 Bren Gun carriers (*Automotive News*). Business peaked with around 40,000 workers in 1953 and the Works closed in 2013.

By the turn of the century Salamon & Co. Ltd. chemical works were established along with Hempleman & Co. fish manure works at **Rainham Ferry.** On a rented site occupied since 1903 by J.C. and J. Field, wax tapers, soap and candles manufacturer, Rainham Chemical Works Ltd. was set up in 1916 in association with the Ministry of Munitions as a weapons factory manufacturing a TNT substitute. In September that year a major fire broke out on the cramped site killing seven men and injuring more than 80 people with local residents fleeing offshore in boats. The Romford Fire Brigade rescued 13 women workers moments before the building exploded. Not reported at the time as this was secret war work but seven fire fighters received OBE's four years later (pictured in the Romford Recorder 2014) and one medal has since been donated to the Essex Fire Museum.[19] In 2018 in memory of those that died, a memorial oak tree with plaque was planted at the village end of Ferry Lane by the local MP and Barking, Dagenham and Havering Trades Union Council.

For a short time poison gas was produced in part of the Chemical Works factory by Southern Metropolitan Gas Co. Ltd. (E.A. Bird, 1972, *The Vanished Hamlet*). There were other factories here including Tykpe & King who were also engaged in war work. Obscurely recorded but according to Rainham Parish Council minutes record, Salamans factory also suffered a fire attended by the Fire Brigade in 1917 (Great War Forum; Jane Finnett).

Better known was the **Silvertown** munitions factory explosion further upriver at the Brunner Mond & Co. TNT purification plant in West Ham in 1917 (Graces Guide). This 'remains London's largest ever explosion' and 'an humanitarian disaster' (Museum of London Docklands). The fire was visible for miles and the explosion heard up to 160 km (100 miles) away, while neighbours reported that 'their ears rang for days afterwards because of the noise of the bang' (Susan Yates).

 [19] Arrange a school group visit to the Essex Fire Museum, Grays.

Also in preparation for the Great War, in 1917 the young international **Murex** Magnetic Co. Ltd acquired Hempleman's site for their pioneering magnetic process for separating ores and they gradually expanded and developed as metallurgists. During WW2 the Murex Ltd. Works continued operating day and night in essential and secret war work and the factory became an identified target for enemy aircraft. After the War their research and practical developments continued with pioneering work to become the world's largest manufacturer of industrial alloys. Their main building was designed to look like a liner along the riverside with its 'prow' facing London and outside stood a long, sinuous 1930s design of bus stand for workers. Murex closed in 1967 the buildings demolished in 1997 and the site redeveloped. However a Murex token set in the paving outside Rainham rail station forms part of The Rainham Tokens trail project[20] recalling local trading and commerce (*The Rainham Tokens* Elaine Tribley and Amanda Westbury, Urbanstrata public art).

The Dutch firm of Jurgens manufactured margarine and soap, which were both vital wartime supplies with the oil and fat industry under government control producing glycerine as a by-product for explosives. Their Dutch neighbours Van den Bergh's opened a factory in England in 1917 as Jurgens established their factory in **Purfleet** manufacturing margarine. In 1927 the companies merged and then merged with Lever Brothers Ltd soap manufacturers in 1929 described by *The Economist* as 'one of the biggest industrial amalgamations in European history' and led to the creation of Unilever in 1930 by merging with the Margarine Union. Purfleet became home to the world's largest **margarine works**.

• • • • • • • • • • •

In 1887 Thames Paper Board Mills, Purfleet began making strawboard from straw waste from stables. For most of his life Tommy Mansfield worked at **Thames Board Mills** in West Thurrock, he was also Thurrock's first schoolboy international footballer having won caps playing for England against Scotland and against Wales in 1931-2. Some of his football memorabilia were loaned to Thurrock Museum. The works club and sports ground was opposite the factory site with access from Purfleet Road and is now in private hands. Some of the Works buildings by James Lomax Simpson FRIBA are of interest, particularly the timber warehouse of 1937-8 with enormous laminated Belfast roof trusses more commonly associated with WWI aircraft hangers.

During WW2 production was turned over to war work and 48 bombs were dropped on the site with one death and other casualties (Archaeological Solutions: historic building recording 2012). After the war the Mills were recycling wastepaper from nearly 300 local authorities when the Works were badly affected in the 1953 floods (see Chapter 14). Nearby factories lent support including two powerful pumps from Ford Motor Company, and HM Queen Elizabeth II visited the district including the Mills site and flooded houses soon after (Newsreel report). By 1964 the Thames Board factory had grown to be the country's largest of its kind and occupying 1.8 sq.km (45 acres) and with over 3,400 employees producing cardboard and fibreboard for packing. However production finally ceased in 2004.

• • • • • • • • • • •

---

[20] Try taking the short heritage trail around Rainham village that recalls past local trading and commerce by Urbanstrata public art entitled *The Rainham Tokens*, details are available on-line.

From 1874 the **Tunnel Portland Cement Company Ltd.**, at Tunnel Farm, **West Thurrock** were mining chalk at the site (now Lakeside Retail Park) and receiving alluvial clay by barge from Canvey Island and London Clay slurry from Aveley. Investment in 1911 quickly transformed the Tunnel Works into the largest British plant and a deep water jetty was installed in the 1930s. Tunnel Asbestos Cement Co. Ltd was established in 1936 and was apparently targeted during the war, receiving substantial bomb damage. By 1968 this was the largest cement works in Western Europe with 1,200 employees. The plant closed in 1976 and the site is now light industry and warehousing (*Cement Plants and Kilns in Britain and Ireland* Dylan Moore). The cement dust seemed all pervasive.

• • • • • • • • • • •

Further east between Stanford-le-Hope and Canvey Island were the extensive **oil storage and refineries** for many years at **Coryton, Thames Haven and Shell Haven** - and a wartime sitting target for air raids particularly during the Battle of Britain in 1940.

LANDFORM *'The Land of the Fanns is about land and water and the often shifting relationship between them'* **(TellTale working with the public 2018)**

During WWI, The Great War 1914-1918, through its particular location alongside the Thames on its approach to London, this area played an essential role in the defence forces and their strategic role in protecting Britain throughout history to modern times, and none more so than during the World Wars of the 20th century.

Army Various popular and autonomous **volunteer forces** that were set up during the latter 19th century and typically formed from local rifle sports clubs, became part of the British Army Territorial Force (TF) in 1908 joining the Essex Brigade with its headquarters at first at Warley Barracks. Belhus Park was a Volunteer TF Annual Camp operating during WWI and in WW2 became a D-Day Marshalling Area (MA) for follow up troops (qv). In 1914 troops, horses and guns were marshaled in Romford and shipped out from the rail station amidst a typically enthusiastic crowd of well-wishers (*Romford to Beirut* by Edwin Blackwell and Edwin C. Axe, pub 1926).

> In 1876 Col. Henry Holmes J.P. had built the castellated (battlemented) **Grey Towers** in 32 ha (80 acres) of Langtons grounds in Hornchurch owned by his new father-in-law John Wagener, from money he made as owner of the Hornchurch Brewery. Henry Holmes became fully involved in Hornchurch village life and community and had raised a battery of the **1st Essex Artillery Volunteers** (1882-1898). A poem in his memory is recorded in C.T. Perfect's *Our Village* 1912.
>
> Following the death of Henry Holmes and his wife, Grey Towers was requisitioned in 1914 for billeting (and later an Officers Training Corps) the 23rd **(1st Sportsmen's)** Battalion Royal Fusiliers that included world-wide amateur sportsmen, big-game hunters and mountaineers. Sir Herbert Raphael, who helped found Romford Garden Suburb, and who raised the **Arts and Crafts Battalion** of the King's Royal Rifles, had enlisted in the **2nd Sportsmen's**

Chapter 13 Early 20th century: Edwardian era

Battalion[21] which was stationed at Hare Hall (q.v.) in 1915 and he generously provided additional accommodation for the Battalion at Gidea Hall and Balgores House. Both Battalions prepared to leave for the *Front* amidst rousing local support in 1915. That same year the 26th Middlesex regiment **(the Navvies' or 3rd Public Works Pioneers' Battalion)** moved into Grey Towers.

In 1916 Grey Towers became the first Command Depot for the **New Zealand Contingent** in England. From July 1916-1919 Grey Towers was a convalescent hospital for New Zealand troops (Lisa Lock, Langtons Gardens Activity Officer) and then briefly No.2 Transfer Centre for demobilisation. Several recreation buildings and huts were erected nearby including a chapel (origin of Holy Cross church, Hornchurch) and the *Te Whare Puni* (The Meeting House) in Butts Green Road where a commemorative plaque was unveiled in 2005 through 'Havering Heritage'. Grey Towers was redeveloped in 1931 for housing leaving only the giant fountain in front of the house extant in a back garden in Grey Towers Avenue. The churchyard of St. Andrews, Hornchurch contains Commonwealth war graves from both World Wars.

The **ANZAC**'s (Australian and New Zealand Army Corps) gave their name to the ten roads on the residential Dovers Farm Estate at Rainham developed after WW2, and in 2017 the estate Community Group organised the unveiling of a memorial plaque on the green in New Zealand Way with the Deputy New Zealand High Commissioner, prospective Parliamentary candidates and Havering Councilors in attendance (Romford Recorder, 2020).

In 1908 Francis Whitmore of Orsett Hall was a founder member of the Essex Territorial Army Association. He commanded officers and men of the **Essex Yeomanry,** fighting in the Boer War and WWI and was Commanding Officer of the **10th Royal Hussars** during WWI. Of his experiences he wrote *The 10th (P.W.O.) Royal Hussars and the Essex Yeomanry during the European War 1914-1918*. As Sir Francis he had become Lord Lieutenant of Essex serving the county from 1936 and all through the War years. After the War there were many royal visitors to Orsett Hall including King George VI on several occasions, and both the Queen Mother and Princess Margaret stayed at Orsett Hall. Thurrock Borough Council have erected a plaque in memory of Sir Francis Whitmore at Orsett Hall.

• • • • • • • • • • •

Between 1906 and 1915 the government had set up **rifle ranges** on Purfleet, Aveley and Wennington marshes to form one of the largest military training centres in rifles and small arms. Some of the buildings and features survive including a range of shooting butts and an anti-aircraft gun tower converted from an anti-submarine blockhouse (built 1905), now on the Royal Society for the Protection of Birds (RSPB) reserve. The location of a secondanti-aircraft gun site is said to have been on the remains of Purfleet lighthouse that had been used for testing oil lamps and reflectors in the mid 19th century. During WWI the military camp at Purfleet was used for army training, a military hospital and as a transit camp for soldiers shipping abroad from Tilbury docks, and in South Ockendon German prisoners-of-war were held at Little Mollands Farm site.

---

[21] Some early issues of the Sportsman's Gazette can be viewed by appointment at Havering Libraries – Local Studies, email: LocalStudies@havering.gov.uk

Surviving rifle butts on Rainham marshes RSPB Reserve

Also at the turn of the 20th century, Warley Camp became part of the *London Defence Scheme* and earth works were constructed. During WWI **Rudyard Kipling's** son John was one of the officer cadets at Warley, this is where he trained for military service and gave us Kipling's moving poem *My Boy Jack*. By his time at outbreak of the War the barracks were said to be wholly unfit, and the tenement married quarters were notorious even through to the 1960s. The War poet **Edward Thomas** (1878-1917) is commemorated in Poet's Corner in Westminster Abbey. The first of his *Household Poems* was addressed to his eldest daughter and makes reference to this area at Childerditch and Pyrgo and in *If I were to own* he includes Gooshays, Cockerells, Wingle Tye, Lillyputs and Rochetts. Thomas enlisted as a private in a Territorial corps, the Artists Rifles, another War Poet **Wilfred Owen,** and engineer **Sir Barnes Wallis** inventor of the *Dambusters Bouncing Bomb* were also members of the regiment. The officer training camp was at Hare Hall, Gidea Park and at the original entrance site in Main Road a commemorative war memorial was raised by public subscription in 2020.

• • • • • • • • • • •

In common with Florence Nightingale, the rare **Royal Red Cross** medal 1st class and bar were awarded to Kate Luard of Aveley who, after serving in the Boer War, was twice mentioned in dispatches for gallant and distinguished service in the field during WWI. She was a nurse, enlisted in the Queen Alexander Imperial Military Nursing Reserve Service working close to the front line. Her books *The Diary of a Nursing Sister on the Western Front 1914-1915* and *Unknown Warriors 1914- 1918* (pub. 1930, re published 2014) are based on her many wartime letters exchanged with her family back home (Susan Yates, Chair, Thurrock Local History Society).[22]

To cope with the huge numbers of WWI casualties returning to Britain, hospitals, private houses, public buildings and others were offered as **auxiliary hospitals**. These included Highwood, Purfleet Military and Warley Military Hospitals, Marshalls Park house and Coombe Lodge; St. Laurence Hall, VAD (Voluntary Aid Detachment – civilians nursing military) Hospital is now used for community events; Weald Hall was a military hospital and a secret training centre (*Brentwood in 50 Buildings* Sylvia Kemp) and Stifford Lodge became a WW2 Canadian military hospital.

---

[22] How could we best remember Kate Luard?

Chapter 13 Early 20th century: Edwardian era

Air force The **Royal Flying Corps** (RFC) operated a Night Landing Ground used by No. 39 Squadron near Orsett during WWI, but it is now partly developed for housing. Innovation in the development of powered flight remained a continuous process, and by 1915 enemy airships were terrorizing Londoners. The London Air Defense Area (LADA) was set up with a number of airfields, including RFC Sutton's Farm airfield (now Hornchurch Country Park), constructed around London for its defence. Finally in March 1916 the first **Zeppelin (LZ15)** was shot down from machine-guns mounted on the anti-submarine blockhouse on the Purfleet marshes, the crew were rescued and imprisoned. The gunners Captain J. Harris of the Purfleet garrison and others received medallions from the Lord Mayor of London in recognition of their action but there was little public adulation. However there is a Thurrock Heritage plaque on Woodlands Pre-school in Purfleet and in 2016 Thurrock Council also placed a Green Heritage plaque in memory in Tank Hill road near Purfleet Heritage & Military Centre (see *Well Hit* by Jonathan Catton, reprinted from Panorama, the Journal of the Thurrock Local History Society, no. 39, December 1999).

Zeppelin and attacking biplanes, artist's impression

Three of the next four zeppelins were downed by three fighter aces from RFC Suttons Farm with public acclaim going to the flying ace Flight Commander **William Leefe Robinson**. He had at last found a way for the biplane pilots to down the zeppelins for which he became a national hero. He received the Victoria Cross and public adulation including a gift presented to him at the children's Cottage Homes of St. Leonards in Hornchurch and recorded by Pathe News (now British Pathe). In 2014 *Paper Planes* the story of William Leefe Robinson VC became the subject of a very well received local community play as part of the celebratory commemoration events of the ending of WWI.

Having found the way in which to conquer the airships two of the next three were then brought down by two of Robinson's squadron, Second Lieutenant **Frederick Sowrey** on 23 September 1916 and Second Lieutenant **Wulstan Joseph Tempest** on October 1st. Both men were based at RFC Suttons Farm and both received the Distinguished Service Order (DSO). Silver cups were awarded to the three pilots at Grey Towers by the people of Hornchurch and again filmed by Pathe News.

The burning wreckage from Sowrey's efforts came down at Great Burstead just beyond the Brentwood and Langdon hills, the relief and spectacle drew enormous crowds for the following week with local people walking and cycling from all around. Harry, local man as previously mentioned, had re-enlisted by this time but his wife Rosa, now billeted in Warley, pushed her pram with baby and her four older kiddies from home to Burstead to see this long-awaited achievement. Many others arrived blocking the lane with 'motor cars, motor-cycles, bicycles, traps, tradesmen's carts, and pedestrians, all jammed together'.

On the 24th Sept. Lt. Brandon flying from Hainault Farm airfield brought down the third airship and its remains were invaluable to British designers in working on their own airship the R23 used for training. While Second Lieutenant Tempest, like the others of the 39th Home Defence Squadron flying a biplane essentially made of wood and paper, brought down the fourth airship. When the fuel pump on his engine failed, in order to keep flying he had to hand-prime it at the same time as flying his plane and firing his machine gun!

The Land During WWI women were needed to work on the land and in industry including at the cement works. In 1916 Lady Petre set up a milking school for children and women at Thorndon Hall to learn the art of milking, and in 1918 she organised a recruiting rally in Brentwood for the Woman's Land Army – or 'Land Girls' as they were popularly known. As men's football mostly ceased through the War, so the women's game became popular and included Brock's Ladies Football Team in Romford during 1916/1917. Women's football had become really popular by 1920 but in 1921 the Football Association banned women from playing its club grounds, saying it was inappropriate (Havering Libraries – Local Studies) and not changing their minds until towards the end of the 1960s.

• • • • • • • • • • • •

Following WWI, **War memorials** were set up in parishes in memory of the local people who lost their lives, sadly with more names added after WW2. At Rainham the War Memorial & Clock Tower is now a listed building. It was erected in 1920 on what was then a village green outside the parish church. The H.E. Brooks Memorial Rest Garden in Grays was opened in 1933 and today also contains a Holocaust memorial (Thurrock Local History Society).

The Thames Tilbury Fort and Coalhouse Fort played an important part once again during WWI in helping to protect shipping on the Thames and its entry to London, and Coalhouse was also a forward holding area for embarking troops. Tilbury docks had been constructed and operational by 1886 for trading goods and world-wide passenger services. Tilbury Docks became part of the Port of London Authority in 1909 and provided significant employment during the Great War period. It was

Chapter 13 Early 20th century: Edwardian era

also the place where the **spy**[23] **Augusto Roggen** arrived on board the SS Batavia from Rotterdam in Holland. He was captured and executed at the Tower of London in 1915. That same year, and after extraordinary exploits abroad, **Gunther Pluschow** escaped form a POW camp in Leicestershire and by hiding aboard one of the Tilbury vessels he was the only POW to escape from mainland Britain back to Germany in WWI (*Grays in the Great War* by Porter & Wynn). In 2015 Thurrock Council installed a Heritage Plaque at Tilbury recording the escape.

• • • • • • • • • • • •

Despite the terrible loss of the Training Ship Goliath in 1875, **Training Ships** continued to be used for teaching seamanship to poor or troublesome 12-16 year old boys from a wide area, and leading to a career in the Merchant or the Royal Navy. A Thurrock Council Heritage Plaque on the churchyard wall of the grade I listed St. Clements Church, West Thurrock records the loss of 16 cadets and an officer in a sailing accident from the T.S. Cornwall in 1915.

Another plaque records the T.S. Exmouth at Grays Beach moored there from 1876-1905, Sydney Chaplin, elder half-brother of Charlie Chaplin was a trainee (he was later taken on by Fred Karno[24] and achieved success as a comic and in the field of private domestic aviation in America). The ship was replaced by a second T.S. Exmouth until 1939, Eric Morley, creator of the Miss World contest, was an orphan trainee onboard. In 1915 the Exmouth crew found themselves throwing out grappling hooks to successfully take in tow a Royal Navel airship that broke loose from its moorings, while the pilot was thrown out into the West Thurrock river mud.

T.S. Exmouth was moved to the quieter river at Burnham-on-Crouch when war broke out and replaced after the War by the T.S. Joseph Hertz, named after Britain's chief Rabbi. It was moored off Grays for a year in 1947 as a training ship for Jewish orphans including some who had survived Belsen concentration camp (Burnham Library *WW2 Peoples War*).

Places to visit near and far:

- Havering Museum, High Street, Romford is housed in the early 20th century old Brewery office buildings
- Davy Down Urban Riverside Park, North Stifford and Stifford Pumping Station built in 1928 with a 40m borehole down into the chalk and still in use today; the two massive diesel engines once used to drive the pumps although no longer operational are on display in the visitor centre on open days; the impressive railway viaduct across the Mardyke Valley dates from 1892; from here the Mardyke Way links to Aveley and to Bulphan
- The Haven Plotlands Museum, a surviving Plotlands bungalow at Langdon Hills Country Park & Nature Reserve. The bungalow is now used as a museum entirely fitted out in original 1930s and 1940s style. The surrounding Plotlands are now a Nature Reserve and an excellent habitat for reptiles

 [23] Try to devise a code for a spy to use.
[24] Fred Karno was a slapstick comedian and producer of music-hall sketches.

- Purfleet Heritage & Military Centre in Magazine No. 5 of the Royal Magazine of Gunpowder
- Essex Fire Museum, Grays Fire Station, Hogg Lane, Grays
- Cater Museum, High Street, Billericay
- Essex Houses & Gardens are a group of historic buildings and gardens independently opening to the public and include the early 20th century The Gibberd Garden and the modern Beth Chatto Gardens and the Royal Horticultural Society (RHS) Garden at Hyde Hall
- Museum of London Docklands, West India Quay, Canary Wharf, E14 4AL
- Victorian & Albert Museum British Galleries for style, taste and innovation of the times

Ideas for future projects:

- Study of the history and development of local Plotland developments at Dunton, Havering-atte-Bower and Rainham
- Research into the story of the fens being drained
- A study on the impact that 20th development has had on this landscape
- A study into the role of the Ingrebourne Valley over the millennia as pre-historic routes and as a Saxon, medieval and modern administrative boundary and strategic corridor for the national motor-way network
- A study of vernacular building types in the landscape such as moated houses (13th C–16th C); lobby-entry dwellings (16th-19th C); commercial buildings (historic wind and water mills to 20th C commercial and industrial building types/areas); religious buildings etc.

References for further research:

More information on this historical period can be found through:

- See Section C: History Introduction, p. 99
- Bata Reminiscence and Resource Centre, East Tilbury Library, Princess Avenue, East Tilbury
- The 20th Century Society (C20 Society) is the National Amenity Society for buildings and artefacts that characterise 20th century Britain
- The Society for the Protection of Ancient Buildings (SPAB) is the National Amenity Society for all periods of historic buildings and is concerned with the care and protection of old buildings for the future. They offer free and independent advice on caring for historic and traditionally constructed buildings https://www.spab.org.uk/advice
- English Heritage Trust manages the London Blue Plaque scheme and maintains a register of similar schemes
- The Arts Council England
- Museum of London and Museum of London Docklands
- Council for British Archaeology (CBA) for *Home Front Legacy 1914-18* records
- Historic Environment Records (HERS) and Sites & Monuments Records (SAMs)
- Brentwood Museum, Lorne Road, Brentwood is the original Sexton's cottage now housing social and domestic objects from around 1840-1950. Outside is the closed cemetery, once the sexton's responsibility, some graves are maintained by the War Graves Commission and are testament to the First World War military camp in Warley, the grounds are now a Nature Reserve

Further Reading:

- Bird, E.A. (1971) *Rainham Village & its Ferry*
- Bird, Ernie (1979) *Murex – the history of a Company and its people* (ref. Havering Libraries – Local Studies)
- Doyle, Neville (2002) *The Triple Alliance – the Predecessors of the First British Airways* ISBN 10:0851302866/ ISBN 13: 9780851302867
- Eastside Community Heritage and Partners (2011) *Working Lives of the Thames Gateway* ISBN 0-9542697-7-2
- Everson, Gordon R. (2001) *East & West Horndon – A View of the Parish & it's Surroundings Today & Yesterday* Wednesday Press Ltd
- Higginbotham, Peter (2019) *Workhouses of London and the South East* pub. The History Press ISBN 978 0 7509 8777 6
- Hipperson, Chris; Donoghue, Simon & Brandon, Ingrid (2009) *The Elm Park Story – From Garden City to London Suburb* pub. LBH Library Service ISBN 978 0956327208
- Perfect, C.T. (first pub. 1920) *Hornchurch During the Great War*
- Porters, Ken & Wynn, Stephen (2015) *Grays (Thurrock) in the Great War* pub. Pen and Sword Books Ltd ISBN:978 1 47382 310 5
- Smith, Eric (2000) *First Things First RAF Hornchurch & RFC Suttons Farm* pub. Ian Henry Publications ISBN 0 86025 498 4
- Smith, Graham (2007) *Essex and its race for the skies 1900-1939* ISBN 978 1 84674 054 1 pub. Countryside
- Smith, Richard C. (2014) *Hornchurch's Air Heroes of the First World War* pub. Mitor Publications ISBN 978-0-9557180-4-5
- Young, Allan (2005) *Down the Line – Memories of the Dunton Bungalow Estate, Laindon 1935-1953*

Chapter 14
Mid 20th century: House of Windsor

'...George VI, then Liz instead.'

NATIONAL CURRICULUM Key Stage 3 hints

The history of the 20th century begins to be within living memory, which can make events fresher, more raw and personal than those of earlier periods. Now grandparents and great grandparents tell their own stories that add a real sensitivity to sad, amusing and desperate events making our intangible heritage so much more *alive* to us. They also give insight to life today and pointers to how we may face the future.

Throughout the post WWI period international unrest rumbled on until war in Europe finally exploded once again in 1939 with the ghastly WW2; after which came the birth of the welfare state, and the Cold War of the 1950s and 1960s. These all brought enormous social, cultural and technological change to post-war British society.

SURPRISE *'The Land of the Fanns is an intricate landscape, full of surprises and 'hidden gems' and rewards exploring.'* **(TellTale working with the public 2018)**

During the 20th century, this Thameside landscape was once again a key location in the defence of London and of Britain. Thameside became a 'bomb alley' as it lies on the direct route for enemy planes plotting a course along the river Thames to London. Later on this area comprised part of the military build-up location in preparation for the D-Day landings in northern France.

Subsequently, as pressure for the outward expansion of London developed, aided by improvements to transport systems for people and goods, north-east London relentlessly expanded into historic south-west Essex, bringing new scientific, cultural and business ideas. As a result, over the century of the many notable people born, residing, visiting, working or taking their inspiration locally, some in particular whether social thinkers and improvers or others, have affected the landscape of this area, its people, their character or culture through the Arts, architecture, science, engineering, religion or agricultural developments.

LANDFORM *'The Land of the Fanns is about land and water and the often shifting relationship between them'* **(TellTale working with the public 2018)**

WW2 and the Defence of London During the latter interwar period the Suttons Farm land was retaken from the farmer for use as RFC Suttons Airfield and just five years later in 1928 it became the much larger Royal Air Force (RAF) Hornchurch fighter station. From 1934 Empire Day air displays were very popular here with money raised for RAF charities, until imminent War brought celebrations to a close in 1939. The all-round entertainer and local lad Max Bygraves volunteered for the RAF and was a Spitfire fitter, he first met his wife, who served in the WAAF, at a concert at RAF Hornchurch in 1941.

This RAF base was once again an important site for air defence being located in *bomb alley* covering both London and the Thames corridor from air attack. It played a dramatic role during WW2 when squadrons of Spitfires were stationed here and played an essential role protecting London during the Battle of Britain and the Battle of France.

The 50 WW2 lines of Britain's defence in anticipation of invasion included The Eastern Command Line, The General Headquarters Line (GHQ line) and The Outer London Defence Ring – the most important of these three and today the M25 motorway follows a similar route

Many of the airfield's heroes are commemorated in local street names including Robinson and Bouchier (WWI) and Bader, Finucane, Tuck, Deere, Leathart, Broadhurst, Stephen and Malan (WW2) as well as R. J. Mitchell School built on the old Parade Ground and with a memorial facing the South End Road. Surviving historic military buildings include the Officers Mess (Astra House), Officers Quarters (Astra Court) and Warrant Officers (WO) Quarters (89-99 odd nos. Wood Lane), all now within the RAF Hornchurch Conservation Area. Some military structures survive in Hornchurch Country Park such as an aircraft dispersal pen ('E pen' now car park), air raid shelter, pillboxes and the unusual tett turrets. Tank traps survive below the bridge outside Hornchurch railway station and gun emplacement sites remain here and are marked in the footpath in Station Lane, Hornchurch, and elsewhere.[1]

---

 [1] Discover the relationship of your journey from home to school and its historic surroundings.

Life nearby was hair-raising at this time. Local farmers, Mr and Mrs Rippingale, just across the river Ingrebourne at Rainham Lodge Farm, could hear the airfield tannoy address system announcing 'SCRAMBLE' and the family would count the planes out - and those that returned.

On one occasion when the family emerged from their air raid shelter the farmer found a shell had landed on his pillow! The shell remains an amazing memento of a shocking war-time near miss.

*A tett turret at RAF Hornchurch/Hornchurch Country Park
– Hornchurch has the country's largest concentration of tett turrets*

Adjoining Suttons Farm, Suttons Institution had been built in Classical architectural style in 1939 primarily as a Home for Elderly People – essentially a 'new workhouse, potentially the last one ever to be built in England.' (*London Archaeologist* Vol. 16, Supplement 2, 2021 *Fieldwork Round-up*). In 1940, during the Battle of Britain and in the run-up to D-Day in 1944 it housed RAF airman and it was a target of enemy bombing. It became auxiliary to Oldchurch Hospital as part of the 1939 London Emergency Medical Service and in 1948 it became part of St. George's Hospital used mainly for geriatric care. The buildings are an historical landmark for which it is held in great affection locally and part is now destined to become a local museum 'Sutton House' commemorating the airfield and its distinguished record (Havering Champion for the Historic Environment, 2019/20). Meanwhile, the Essex Wildlife Trust Visitor Centre at Hornchurch Country Park introduced a memories recording room with various artefacts on display (Hacton Parkway and Thames Chase Walk no.5).[2]

At Langdon Hills recent housing development has also taken the opportunity to name new estate roads near Dry Street after local veterans who gave up their lives in these conflicts during the 20th century and include Hammond Close and Siggers Crescent (WWI), Llewellyn Grove and Parker Drive (WW2) and Judge Drive (Korean Conflict of 1950-53).

---

 [2] Pay a visit to Hornchurch Country Park and take time to check out the memories recording room.

Defensive rings of anti-aircraft batteries were set up to defend RAF Hornchurch from aerial attack, including the Warren Farm anti-aircraft 8-gun site (grade II and conservation area) at Chadwell Heath in the Dagenham Corridor, and Bowaters Farm, now a Scheduled Ancient Monument (SAM) at East Tilbury. Warren Farm gun site (codenamed ZE1) is strategically located at a high point about 45 metres (c.147 ft) above sea-level. It is protected because of its considerable interest for the invaluable part it played in the Defence of London as part of the **Inner Artillery Zone** (IAZ) that surrounded and protected London, and seeing a great deal of action during the period 1940-41 (Michael Gilman, 1991) protecting Londoners during the Battle of Britain and the Blitz. Further buildings were erected here during the **Cold War** threat of the 1950s and 1960s. The site is supported by The Friends of ZE1 and also by the Chadwell Heath Historical Society and others.[3] From the site are clear views of Romford, the Queen Elizabeth II Bridge at the Dartford Crossing and across to Canary Wharf to the west. (Marks Warren is recommended for Tier 1 APA designation for its multiperiod archaeology from the Middle Stone Age to the gun site; the surrounding Marks Gate area is a recommended Tier 2 APA).

The RAF Hornchurch bombing decoy site at Doesgate Farm (SAM) in Bulphan was made to replicate the Fighter Station in order to attract bombing raids away from the essential airfield target. Through most of the War it operated by both day (a 'K' site erected in wood and canvas) (*East & West Horndon* by Gordon R. Everson) and night (a 'Q' site with lighting controlled from surviving night shelter bunkers), and was successful on at least one heavy night-time bombing raid (Historic England). Another successful site was at Wennington where decoy beacon fires were lit during WW2 air raids).

At Pilgrims Hatch, Imperial and International Communications Ltd. (later Cable & Wireless Ltd.) had built an important telegraph radio receiving station in 1921 protected during wartime by substantial air defenses. The administrator was Harry Smith and young women operators like Doreen, Joan and their pal Scottish volunteer Babs Hood, were employed in teams; the corresponding transmitting station was at North Weald.

> There are local stories telling of many **dog fights** in the sky over this landscape right across to the Langdon Hills during 1940 with a 'rag-tag army' of local lads and elderly people chasing any pilots shot to earth and watching out for V1 'doodlebug'[4] and 'butterfly' bombs, parachute mines, airburst and V2 rockets or else telling tales of eating at the Communal Feeding Centres called patriotically **British Restaurants** (Alan Davis Laindon & District Community Archive 2012).
>
> When his plane's engine cut out and went into a spin on takeoff from RAF Hornchurch in 1943, Flying Officer Sanders Draper, an American volunteer, deliberately crashed his Spitfire to avoid hitting Suttons School. The pilot died but the school and its 650 students were saved and the school bears the name *Sanders Draper* in the pilot's honour. One young lad tells

---

 [3] Consider joining a local heritage group.
    [4] The last V1 on Essex exploded close by the Brentwood Road near East Horndon village (*East & West Horndon* by Gordon R. Everson).

> how he was standing outside the headteachers study awaiting punishment at the time, and found himself and his misdemeanors forgotten in the horror and shock of the tragic incident.
>
> In February 1944, New Zealander, Wing Commander Reg Grant parachuted to his death near Orsett and as a flying ace he is commemorated in a brass plaque installed on the 60 years anniversary near to the crash site outside Orsett Fire Station (Thameside Aviation Museum, closed 2020). The terrible toll across this landscape and on its forces, its allies and its civilians is told most poignantly in many local history books such as *Hitler V Havering* and a multitude of books about RAF Hornchurch.

The military camp at Purfleet was used for army training and as a transit camp for soldiers shipping abroad from Tilbury docks and had a military hospital and after WWI until 1920 it was a Dispersal Unit for soldiers arriving on the Thames or at Folkstone or Dover. As Beacon Hill Park it then housed homeless families. In wartime as Beacon Field Camp 286, it became a tented **Prisoner of War Camp** for Italian prisoners, who worked on local farms. Later it was a hutted transit camp (ref.654 & 655) for German POWs being sent on to satellite camps. At Purfleet several roads around the Magazine are now named after WW2 tanks or other wartime associations.

There was another hutted camp (ref.266) for 800 personnel at Bentley Farm, Old Church Hill, Langdon Hills. There was also a nearby Army Camp at Langdon Hills that after WW2 became a transit camp for troops before being demobbed. As late as 1954 the popular BBC television quiz master Michael Miles recorded his programme from this 'Embarkation Establishment' (Ken Porter, Laindon & District Community Archive, 2014). These were amongst over 1,000 such camps countrywide. The names of Camps, their locations and reference numbers were secret and changed at times so that even today it is often hard to uncover exact details (Ken Porter, Laindon & District Community Archive).

In preparation for **Operation Overlord and the D-Day landings** in the Battle for Normandy, the southern coastal areas of England and Wales were divided into secretly set up Marshalling Areas with their headquarters (HQs) and Transit Camps. This area was part of Eastern Command and Force 'L' (follow-up), the driving force for the inland attack embarking from Tilbury and London Docks. By May 1944 this area held thousands of troops and secret locations of service installations such as the Field Bakery at South Ockendon Hospital, also local roads and bridges were strengthened and all camps sealed off from local people and the A127 and A13 roads became largely vehicle parks. The Tilbury to Brentwood area made up MA 'S', with its main HQ at Ford Place, North Stifford (ERO C/W3/4/9). It was divided into eight sub areas at: Orsett Heath, Tilbury, Purfleet Musketry Camp, Belhus Park, Thorndon Hall, Little Warley, Warley Barracks and Weald Park. Further west, MA 'T' were sites closer to the London docks such as Canning Town, Plaistow and West Ham. HQ's and camps were afterwards disbanded and dismantled (theddaystory.com Portsmouth and Wartimes.ca *Remembering and Researching Canadas's Military Contributions*).

Around sixteen **Ferro-concrete and steel-framed barges** are still moored in a bay on the Thames between Rainham and Purfleet marshes (London Loop Section 24). Around 200 of the barges played a crucial role in WW2 operations together with the Mulberry harbours. The barges were used for the transportation of petrol, munitions and so on, and as floating pontoons. This group is understood to have been held in the Thames Estuary as backup supply vessels during the D-Day landings. Today they are an important and rare habitat for certain bird species and have generated an important habitat for plants within the bay.⁵

The concrete barges of supplies/equipment were towed out by tug to support the D-day landings (Artist impression)

Cold War In the November 1949 *Housing (Military Camps)* debate in the House of Commons, Mr. Solley Member of Parliament for Thurrock raised the question of turning over local military camps to civilian accommodation to ease the housing crisis but government resistance hinged on possible requirements for what would become known as the *Cold War*.

Following WW2 and during the Cold War period, apart from the desperate need to house local people, the threat of an **Atomic bomb** attack caused concern over the supply of foods and especially tea noting in a secret government report in 1955 (Daily Mail, 2008) 'The tea position would be very serious with a loss of 75 per cent of stocks and substantial delays in imports and with no system of rationing it would be wrong to consider that even 1oz per head per week could be ensured. No satisfactory solution has yet been found.' Purfleet, along with 13 British cities, was identified as a sensitive target for an A-bomb attack affecting imports of tea and other essential foods.

During the 1950s and 1960s there was a secret bunker site off Launders Lane at the wartime Gun Battery site at Ayletts Farm in Rainham (Peter Watt *Hitler V Havering*). At Warley the Barracks became a training depot for National Service recruits until it closed in c.1960 and similarly RAF Hornchurch continued in use for training purposes until the mid 1960s with barrage balloons and mock infantry attacks occasionally startling local children still living in the lee of wartime. The popular Air Shows had also resumed at RAF Hornchurch from 1951 until 1960 with the airfield finally closing in 1962 and allowing South End Road, that had crossed a flight path, to be permanently opened to through traffic.

---

⁵ Carry out a schools project to research into the impact of WW2 on this area.

In 1953 Hornchurch Airfield became a centre for assisting service personnel and South Stifford became a **flood relief distribution centre** from Purfleet to West Thurrock when the Thames broke its banks by the inundation of the North Sea. The water swept devastatingly from Scotland to the Netherlands including far into the Thames estuary and reaching more than 5.6 m (18.4 ft) above mean sea level. The tide swept across the sea wall at several sites including at Purfleet and Tilbury – which was the worst affected place in Thurrock. At Canvey Island 58 people died and 37 more at Jaywick near Clacton leading in time to the erection of the Thames Flood Barrier in operation since 1982. The Barrier is now being closed ever more frequently amidst calls for further improvements to the Thames tidal defence system.

MIGRATION *'This is a crossroads landscape: because of its location on the Thames ... people have always travelled into, through and away from this area.'*
(TellTale working with the public 2018)

After the War, when the **Empire Windrush** troopship docked at Tilbury in 1948 its passengers included several hundred people from the West Indies. This event symbolized the immigration from Commonwealth countries to the United Kingdom at the time. Locally, nearly 60 years later the event was celebrated by the unveiling of a Thurrock Heritage commemorative plaque at the London Cruise Terminal at Tilbury - London's principle cruise and deep-water port.

• • • • • • • • • • •

Housing Following WW2 the Garden City ideals of the late 19th century were now employed in **Abercrombie's** New Neighbourhoods (1944), as at Harold Hill (named after Harold Hill Farm in 1947) that brought 25,000 people to new homes and critically new work in a purpose-designed self-contained estate on the southern slopes of Havering Ridge. While at Basildon a New Town was developed close by Langdon Hills, designed for a cross-section of society to meet the needs of the many seeking new homes and work close to London. The new residential areas together with the construction of both self-build and volume builder housing estates like Belhus Housing Estate and Kenningtons Estate formed built-up hard edges to the rural landscape but were constructed to re-home people away from bomb damaged areas and for slum clearance. Eventually the old Havering Liberty area between the two river valleys, Beam and Ingrebourne, became built up forming an urban wedge of Romford, Hornchurch and Upminster towns.

Like its neighbours at Kenningtons and South Ockendon, Aveley expanded with post WW2 London population overspill and to house the workers in the factories at Purfleet and West Thurrock. Belhus was a 1950s planned London County Council (LCC) housing estate that lies on land previously forming part of Belhus parkland and contains some scattered listed buildings from the original country parkland. East of the Belhus estate and east of the railway line, the Flowers estate of 'Lecaplan' prefabricated concrete homes was erected during the 1960s and 1970s on the land between the railway and South Ockendon village previously accommodating emergency **prefabs**' erected here and elsewhere during 1946 and 1947 (a Uni-Seco prefab., as widely used in London and the south-east, is displayed at the Imperial War Museum, Duxford). The estates are connected to nearby towns of Grays, Upminster and Romford by bus (originally the distinctive 'Green Line' country buses) and train with connections by rail for commuting to London.

After WW2, Hornchurch Urban District Council made tiered mortgages available specially tailored for the resilient, post war families and their *baby-boomers* to become **self-builders** in places like Rainham. Such stories survive in local family memories adding a particular depth and relevance to mid-20th century history here and as recorded by local historian Frank Lewis in his history of Rainham Allotment Society (Havering Libraries – Local Studies).

The Scandinavian style of high-rise living set within masses of communal greenspace became popular, but in the event did not translate well to England producing social difficulties in places like the Mardyke Estate built at Rainham in 1964 but now redeveloped as Orchard Village. Similarly in 1969 Goresbrook Village was opened west of Dagenham, home to some 700 people, the bold use of colour on its three 16 storey tower blocks coined it the name of 'Legoland'. Although redeveloped in 2013 LBB&D Council with others funded a film by Verity-Jane Keefe to record the buildings, their demolition and redevelopment as **Castle Green Place New Neighbourhood**, together with the voices of past residents and concierge staff.[6]

Modern building materials were developed through the 20th century and old methods and materials universally abandoned and craftmanship forgotten or lost making the repair of historic properties difficult and ill-informed by the 1960s and 1970s. Archaeological recording also fared badly during this period through lack of funding, until *developer funding* was eventually introduced through the Planning process. Fabulous actual *finds* have famously been recorded from time to time such as the previously mentioned Aveley mammoth, the Dagenham idol, the Havering Bronze Age hoard, the rich Gerpins Farm hoard and the Roman lead coffins at Rainham sites, but this landscape is if anything even more important for the delicate *information* it can reveal about past lives and past environments of London's hinterland.

Leisure During the mid 20th century period, land reclamation sites have gradually been brought back into use, often as country parks providing leisure opportunities and nature reserves. Together with the success of the centrally located Thames Chase Community Forest with its extensive outreach, these areas well serve the many thousands of homes and families now pressing in onto this landscape so conveniently situated for London and the coast. Linkages are increasingly being secured and laid out and the regional London Loop long distance footpath and the Sustrans cycle network connect with local routes to take dedicated visitors both across this area and much farther afield around London.

Many fascinating sites with intriguing heritage or inspiring architecture have also been restored during the latter period and are open to visitors and, with lots of things to do are ideal for a day out. Many can be discovered through the **DiscoverMe** (Discover Metropolitan Essex) information hub online. Other sites include for example nature conservation at Beam Parklands wetland park by the Beam Bridge in Dagenham; Davy Downs at North Stifford on the River Mardyke with its water voles, marsh frogs and kingfishers[7] and Langdon Lake & Meadow nature reserve on lower Dunton Road which also has links to EWT Langdon Reserve. Also local museums have been established, often in historic buildings and providing linkages to the wider museums and archaeological community.

---

 [6] What can your grandparents or other older people tell you about life when they were young.

 [7] See the Davy Down Outdoor Learning Pack with curriculum linked activities emphasising self-led learning and support health and wellbeing.

In Hornchurch, Langtons House and Gardens were gifted to the town of Hornchurch in 1929 by the daughter of William Varco Williams. He was head of the haulage and collier firm of Samuel Williams, and brother of Arthur Williams of Upminster Court (see Edwardian Chapter 13). He began the tradition of Langtons summer Garden Parties that continues today as the Langtons Summer Concert. Now the buildings are listed, the house and 4.5 ha (11 acres) of gardens are restored and since 1976 this has been the home of Havering Registry Office. The grounds are open to the public and are poplar for summer events and a garden tea room was added in 2017.[8]

ECONOMY *'This area is justly famous for trade, commerce and industry: these have been important here for many centuries.'* **(TellTale working with the public 2018)**

Trade and Commerce As well as enabling flat roofs to be constructed, the experimental use of concrete also created opportunity for dramatic new forms of architectural design. Even so in **architecture**, only the very best of the generally early 20th century buildings are listed, including the Rom Skateboard Park in the Dagenham Corridor outside Romford. However later designs are otherwise at times found to be award-winning, such as the RSPB Visitor Centre (6 awards for sustainable design and an RIBA National Award) and the Thames Chase Visitor Centre (RIBA Eastern Region award for sustainable design), and bring distinction to this landscape.

Wildspace Rainham Warehouse refurbishment (5 standalone business units). Designed by Alison Brooks Architects for London Thames Gateway Development Corporation in 2011 responding to the building scale and its landscape setting on the edge of industrial land that is wedged between Rainham marshes and passing Eurostar trains alongside London commuter train services at Rainham (Photograph courtesy of Debbie Brady, Heritage Engagement Officer LotF, 2017)

• • • • • • • • • • • •

---

[8] See the Langtons website for activity worksheet and ideas for children.

Agriculture within this pressurised urban fringe landscape, is itself a story of marvellous resilience. WW2 reintroduced a national agricultural policy and austerity measures. During that time Tylers Common again became a contentious matter (see Victorian Chapter). The land had been ploughed for food in 1943 as it gradually eased out of Commons use. This led to a famous court case in 1951 won by the outrage and typical resilience of local campaigners over Essex County Councillors who aimed to retain the Common for the County Council. A memorial stone in a garden opposite the Common honours their victory. At its 150th anniversary in 2011 the event was commemorated by local people led by local heritage campaigner Laurie Ford ('Havering's Lone Rambler') and just shows how this landscape retains its significant importance to local people – these days for open air recreation activities here such as dog walking and for horse riding.

From 1945 a more flexible agricultural policy had been adopted more suited to peace-time and allowed farmers to plan ahead and invest. This area with its highly suitable soils continued developing in market gardening with for example advertisements for the 'Early Rainham Cabbage' still being supplied until 1957. Land at Davy Down was also used for market gardening, but this was abandoned and the Country Park formed when the construction of the new A13 split the land holding. Across Thurrock's reclaimed fens and fanns farmers kept their own small boats on the flooded ditches in order to get about and continue working during the frequent times of flood even into the late 1960s and bargemen used the fen ditches to bring in supplies and return with farm produce in times of flood.

During the 1950s and 1960s **agribusiness**[9] developed as agriculture became conducted on a strictly commercial basis. In this southern part of southwest Essex many local farms were destroyed mostly through gravel winning but a lead is shown in early agricultural land reclamation when attempts at agricultural **land restoration** were successful here in the late 1960s with a restoration to grade 3 agricultural land in Bramble Lane and Bush Farm that inspired further land restoration. From the 1970s the area was part of a nationally significant study into ground restoration to achieve at least grade 3 agricultural land. The methods used became a national model. Additionally, part of Bush Farm was retained as a 1.2 ha (4.5 acre) lake and carp fishery, and another area is now the Delta Force **Paintball centre** offering 'six massive battle arenas'.

Today farmers continue to feel pressurised as this agricultural landscape also has to accommodate new regional service needs such as roads and railways and urban growth that have divided up farming areas. Here the **Lower Thames Crossing proposals** cut across this south west corner of the fens turning south across Orsett Fen and a Green Lane to run beside the hamlet of Baker Street. The potential effect on the historic settlement and the fenland landscape and fen drainage implications would need to be carefully understood and considered to avoid or mitigate adverse impact in the area.

Local land managers and farmers have been ever prepared to adjust to outside pressures including flood management and woodland clearance and making best use of the mix of environments of the hills, the plain, the valleys and the marshlands; adjusting for competition of foreign imports; adapting to the subdivision of farming areas to accommodate new needs like transportation routes; over the millennia adjusting farming practices through fishing, fowling, wheat production, sheep grazing and wool industry, cattle rearing, market gardening with local chicken rearing and pig farms, and

---

[9] *Agribusiness* is defined as agriculture conducted on strictly commercial principles and their allied industries.

even yielding land for mineral extraction with some to be eventually reclaimed for farming; suffering desperate loss of jobs during the agricultural depressions and the converse influx of factory workers with the impact of heavy and chemical industries along the riverside areas; even being resilient against modern development pressures and vandalism borne of ignorance of the Country Code.

Creatives In addition to its built and natural form, the culture of the landscape includes its peoples and traditions and diversity, as well as the arts, and intellectual activity and achievement. Here those creative industries can be said to flourish.

In **art, music and literature,** personalities celebrated locally in modern times include the feminist painter Lady Edna Clarke-Hall (1879-1979) who lived at Great House, Upminster from 1902-1970s. She was a watercolourist, etcher, lithographer, draughtsman and poet, famed for her many illustrations of 'Wuthering Heights' by Emily Bronte for which she is said to have been inspired by *Great House* her home on Upminster Common including during the years 1901 to 1920 when she painted numerous pen, brush and sepia ink or pencil and watercolour or charcoal images in and around her home in Upminster. Together her father the philanthropist Benjamin Waugh, and her husband William Clarke Hall founded the National Society for the Prevention of Cruelty to Children (NSPCC). The same year that he died, her husband was knighted for his work towards reforming child law in 1932.

• • • • • • • • • • •

In respect of **popular culture,** Sandie Shaw MBE was born and brought up in Dagenham and went to work for Ford Motor Company before being 'spotted' by Adam Faith while singing at a charity contest in London. She was the epitome of the 'swinging sixties' and had two UK number 1 hit singles before she became the first British singer to win the Eurovision Song Contest with *Puppet on a String* in 1967 and she sang the theme song to the British film *Made in Dagenham*. Nearby, Mike Nolan grew up in Rainham, he was an original member of the group Bucks Fizz that won the Eurovision Song Contest in 1981 with the song *Making Your Mind Up*. While the pioneering electropop and alternative rock musician Imogen Heap grew up in Havering village. Her album project in 2011 included a single created as part of her work with charity Clear Village and Friends of Bedfords Park to restore the walled garden at Bedfords Park. Rochelle Humes the singer and television presenter was educated in Cranham. At Purfleet, the High House Production Park set around an historic, listed farmstead, is now an international centre of excellence for creative industries in association with the Royal Opera House and others.

• • • • • • • • • • •

In the summer of 2000 Mario Petrucci was the first **Poet in Residence** in Havering. During that year as part of the Year-of-the-Artist scheme he produced 21 poems inspired by the history and heritage of Havering, the Thames and across Essex. The book of poems with illustrations and photographs is entitled *The Stamina of Sheep* in reference to the ancient rule of locating markets towns one-day's sheep drive apart. For this proud achievement he remarkably won the Essex Book Awards 'Best Fiction' prize for 2000- 2002.[10]

• • • • • • • • • • •

---

 [10] Be inspired to write a poem or short story about life in the Land of the Fanns (see Future Projects list).

In **sport**, Weald Country Park had been chosen to host the 2012 Olympics Mountain Biking and preparations were being made when the course was found to be insufficiently testing. Brentwood does however host a number of Criterium Cycle Races that attract many of Britain's great cyclists. Barry Hearn lives in the area at Warley he is a sports event promotor of personalities including Steve Davis who lived for a time near Havering-atte-Bower, and Ronnie O'Sullivan previously of South Weald and a regular broadcaster on the Brentwood radio station Phoenix FM.

• • • • • • • • • • •

With international effect the **peace activist** Elizabeth Kucinich, wife of retired US congressman, grew up in North Ockendon and attended school in Cranham (*Mail online*, 2007).

• • • • • • • • • • •

At times various locations within this landscape are used for **filmmaking**, or as a backdrop or for inspiration. Amongst these, in 1927 Gibbs Pit, West Thurrock became a battlefield setting for the silent WWI film *The Guns of Loos* and in the 1960s the Tunnel Cement Pit featured in an instalment of the television programme *Dr. Who*. Several episodes of the late 1960s popular British television crime drama series *Softly, Softly* were filmed at the home and farm complex of the actor Victor Maddern in North Ockendon and in the early 1970s an episode of its revamp *Softly, Softly Task Force* was filmed at Murex Works at Rainham Ferry (Cllr. J.M. Holt). During 1970 the 'Saharan' launch television and cinema advertisements for the exciting Ford Mexico AVO car, was filmed in the sandy mineral extraction pits at Mollands Lane, South Ockendon that lent themselves to desert rally conditions.

In 1993 the romantic comedy film *Four Weddings and a Funeral* had scenes shot at St. Clement's Church (grade I), in West Thurrock. On a pre-Conquest site this distinctive, 13th century church was built for the support of pilgrims to the shrine of St. Thomas Becket (see Norman & Plantagenet Chapter). The church is now in the care of its neighbour Proctor & Gamble Company, who had restored the building for community, educational and cultural uses and is open to the public at times. The consecrated churchyard has been given over to nature but still holds many memorials, including to those tragically killed off Purfleet in 1915 from the Royal Naval Reformatory Ship 'Cornwall' (see Edwardian Chapter). The boys funeral was attended by several thousand people.

Other films include *Essex Boys*, based on drug-related murders in Essex, shots were filmed under the QE2 Bridge in 1999/2000; the riverside from Purfleet to Coalhouse Fort was filmed for *Walk over Heritage* in 2000. Lakeside Shopping Centre was the subject of a documentary television series in 1998 and had several times featured in *Fame Academy* in 2002. Garth Marenghi's *Darkplace* was filmed in Romford, and released in 2004. This landscape has also seen Harry Potter and Hagrid fly past on magical motorcycles via the Dartford Crossing in the 2010 film *Harry Potter and the Deathly Hallows*.

After the closure of Warley Barracks much of that site was acquired by the **Ford Motor Company** with their European Headquarters built on the old parade ground and drawing commuters and local people to its workforce. Many more local workers were based at the main plant in the area of the old Thames Breach at Dagenham (qv). The story of inequitable pay conditions for women workers that led to a strike at Ford Dagenham plant in 1968, was recorded in the 2010 film *Made in Dagenham* that portrayed the longsuffering but determined attitude of local people, which in this case resulted in widespread workers improvements in fairness for all, even then being taken to America. The listed White House in

Dagenham, once home to Hardy Amies, is now a Becontree Community hub for the Arts. The anniversary of the 1970 Equal Pay Act and the success of the Dagenham Ford machinists, is marked as part of a series of Radio Ballads part of New Town Culture in the Borough, supported by the Mayor Of London.

In 2015 the old, listed Warley Hospital was used by the local Queen's Theatre for the play *The Elephant Man*. *Death Walks* was filmed in the Mercury Shopping Mall with nearly 1,000 extras, many from the local area, and premiered at the Mall in 2016. American actors have filmed here in 2012 with *Welcome to Essex* with a local director it includes 800 'zombies' chasing along Brentwood High Street and a cameo role for Russell Brand; In 2017 Tom Cruise starred in *Mission Impossible - Fallout* with a scene filmed in Thorndon County Park and in 2019 Rainham Hall was used as the backdrop for a television film adaptation of Charles Dickens *A Christmas Carol* starring Guy Pearce.[11] [12]

Industry Although farming continues in the central eastern area of this urban fringe landscape, the major towns, Thameside and the M25 motorway junctions attract industry.

Clay, sand and gravel are used in the building industry and their quarrying degraded and blighted parts of this landscape for decades of the 20th century with extraction continuing in some places. However most modern development including mineral extraction provides opportunity for obtaining archaeological information and artefacts (e.g. the 'Havering Hoard' see Bronze Age Chapter), and for transforming pits into areas for geological research such as Chafford Gorges, or into wildlife and nature parks or leisure areas for fishing and sports activities like Kennington Park, Aveley or Eastbrookend Country Park and Beam Valley Country Park once worked-out gravel pits and landfill sites in Dagenham, or Stubbers Adventure Centre near Upminster and Grangewaters Outdoor Education Centre in South Ockendon.

• • • • • • • • • • • •

In **waste management**, pits filled with London's waste and rubbish conditioned local people to an acceptance of ever present lorry movements with rubbish and fill across the landscape, with copious amounts of fly-away litter, dust and dirt along roadsides. It is unsurprising that fly-tipping became common in places especially along rural lanes leading to a need for the provision and maintenance of excellent facilities for the disposal of rubbish and litter. Organised litter picking events can show a good example to others. Whilst completed landfill areas have been opened as low vantage point hills as at Rainham riverside. Other areas are planted with new Forestry Commission woodland walks as part of the Thames Chase Community Forest. At the newly emerging Little Belhus Country Park in South Ockendon, 86 ha (212 ac) of sand and gravel extraction took place on the farmland from the 1940s until the mid 1970s. The pits were then filled with household and commercial or industrial waste rendering it contaminated land. Rural Arisings have an ambitious project transforming it into a country park and Dilkes Academy pupils have named the lake *Wochaduna Waters* from the Saxon name for the area.

---

 [11] A schools' project with re-enactments or a film based on local history, perhaps shown at a local Visitor attraction/centre such as Thorndon Country Park Visitor Centre, the Millennium Centre at Eastbrookend Country Park, Bretons Sports & Social Club, Davy Down Country Park, Hornchurch Country Park Visitor Centre or Lakeside Shopping Centre.

 [12] Develop the stories of the history and heritage of the area through the Arts, literature and film to inform and capture the interest and imagination of local students of all ages and abilities, with potential for outputs such as cultural and natural heritage Arts installations in appropriate visitor locations.

• • • • • • • • • • •

Dagenham's huge, Victorian **May & Baker** chemical manufacturers continued to trade under that name, becoming firmly established at their site opposite Dagenham East Station although they were acquired in 1922 by the French firm that became Rhone-Poulenc Ltd. They discovered quinine to treat malaria and sulphapyridine (commonly *M&B 693*) in 1939. This was credited for saving many servicemen including those evacuated from Dunkirk in 1941 and used to treat bacterial pneumonia in a very poorly **Winston Churchill** in 1942. There were many social provisions for staff with clubs and sports facilities and children's parties for example. The Canteen in the Modern movement style by Edward David Mills was built in 1934/5 and extended to provided executive dining in 1953 - where waiting service was smartly provided by staff like local lady Mrs Elsie Hopkins. The Canteen is now a listed building, an early and elegant example of a concrete shell structure barrel vaulted roof, similar perhaps to Romford Brewery (dem.) at the time.

• • • • • • • • • • •

Many warships were decommissioned after WWI and broken up by scrap metal shipbreakers including two Royal Navy 'Admiralty M Class' destroyers by pioneering recyclers Thomas W. Ward at **Frog Island** (Historic England 2014 referencing *Britain From Above: Home Front Legacy 1914-18* group). From 1946 – 1989 the Phoenix Timber Co. for softwoods, hardwoods and building boards, operated on this tongue of land called Frog Island on the west bank of Rainham Creek. Here they made use of two ex-wartime PLUTO sheds[13] for timber storage. From 1948 they also acquired a section of a wartime **Mulberry harbour** (Getty Images), to bring in large cargos of timber by river to Phoenix Wharf from across the world. These were originally built as floating harbours for Allied D-Day landings at Arromanches (Sue Copeman, Port of London, 1985) and here linked to the 'Island' by a Bailey Bridge.[14]

Industry continued here along Ferry Lane despite the closure of the Creek to tidal flow as part of the Thames flood defences in around 1982. Today, against a backdrop of wildlife on ancient marshes, commercial docks, wharfs and jetties at Dagnam Dock, Rainham including Frog Island, Purfleet, West Thurrock, Grays and London Gateway operate a world-class port infrastructure in this area and continues to exploit the age-old economy of trade with Europe that goes back in this area to prehistory.

Container shipping at Purfleet in the early 21st century

---

[13] Pipeline Under The Ocean operation, and here used for pipe storage.
[14] A portable, prefabricated, truss bridge developed in 1940-41 for the British military.

CONCLUDING

Through the latter half of the 20th century to today this landscape has continued to provide convenient **national service corridors** for major road and rail networks and infrastructure such as the National Grid and even Wind Turbines, all as a kind of incongruous response in monumental building form to a monumental but by definition, flat marshes landscape. Major developments continued to press ahead across the landscape, disorientating the urban structure and at times obscuring the underlying historic fabric and its story, and the Lower Thames Crossing scheme demonstrates the continued demand on this area as a nationally significant crossroads location. The regional transport routes are heavily trafficked and the area suffers frequent traffic congestion. A proliferation of road 'improvements' with signage, rural lane curbing, mini roundabouts and lighting has had a cumulative used effect in places.

The development of industry attracted more workers bringing people out of London and helping to develop the new settlement patterns overlying the landscape. In time improved commuter journeys became possible through the better road provision and rail services, enabling younger couples and older residents alike to continue to migrate ever further eastwards to find cheaper accommodation and retirement homes and continuing to support the close association between London and this area.

However, continued fragmentation through road and rail building, compounded by gravel extraction, urban sprawl and industry have resulted in this area becoming an increasingly forgotten landscape. As it has lost its sense of identity, development decisions have inevitably been taken against a backdrop of weak information about the sense and meaning of the landscape, further compounding the problem. What remains are communities that still feel instinctively allied to this place despite its form being no longer easily understood and with no overarching narrative to support a joined-up appreciation of this landscape.

The **north Thameside and local river marshes** that are so important for migratory birds and other wildlife, are here hemmed in with their wildlife and old settlements alike between the Thames and the major east/west road, rail and service corridors and divided by the motorway and motorway services. Here are the regional Lakeside Shopping Centre (opened by Princess Alexander in 1990), the Retail Park and Cliffside Trading Park on the floor of the former Tunnel Cement Works chalk quarry, juxtaposed with the adjacent local open space gorges and their interesting and rare geological formations (see Geology Chapter). Thameside is also visually dominated by the striking Queen Elizabeth II bridge at the Dartford Crossing to the east, and the distinctive high rise buildings of the London skyline to the west.

QEII bridge looking east from Purfleet-on-Thames

A passing Thames barge and the London skyline looking west from Purfleet-on-Thames

Here are also visitor attractions with walks and cycleways and Visitor centres and handy rail stations for accessibility at Rainham and Purfleet where there is the emerging national centre for culture and creative skills at High House (qv).

In itself the high landscape quality of the **central fanns area and low hills** with unspoiled villages like Bulphan, Stifford, Orsett and the Horndon's retain their sense of history and heritage of strong local vernacular developments and local traditions. Together with its **higher land**, this landscape, particularly with its many Country Parks offers opportunity for secure, open air activities and facilities for families seeking safe places to walk, to run and to roam, to explore and to picnic, for children to have adventures and to learn the Country Code, its meaning and intent; for retirees, of all ages and abilities, wanting to take exercise, to sit and reflect; also for those wanting to walk their dogs or to ride horses; for commuters and local workers seeking morning, evening or lunchtime open air exercise and walking for health, cycling or running; providing education opportunities for school parties and others wanting to learn about the heritage of the landscape's inter-relationship with London the capital city and the heritage of the countryside its plants, animals and insects; for bird watching or for wildlife and scenic photography; or for mums wanting safe play for kiddies with coffee and companionable chat.

Here in the face of the effects of so much change to the landscape over the last century, from 1990 some 9,800 ha (38 square miles) of surviving countryside has been managed as the Thames Chase Community Forest. The heritage of this area is about hard work and about people pulling together when there are difficulties and this shines through with the staunch support shown by local volunteers and the keen questioning interest local people have in the built and natural heritage here. Woodlands have been planted and managed, footpaths and cycleways opened, road crossings installed, heritage interpreted and a well-informed and coordinated partnership of national, regional and local organisations brought together.

The LotF partnership working over the long term to establish and share the significance of this landscape by engaging with local people, enabling interest groups, providing craft and traditional skills training for in-depth practical knowledge and by fund raising, is designed to ensure the heritage bounty here remains viable and vital through its Legacy. The Thames Chase Visitor Centre at its heart is set to regenerate the landscape for the future with a Vision to become 'an inspirational example of landscape regeneration' making 'a clear difference to wildlife and people's lives'.

Places to visit near and far:
- Thames Chase Forest Visitor Centre, Pike Lane, Cranham
- High House Production Park, Purfleet, is an historic farm setting for creative industries buildings that include tours of the Production Workshop of the scene-making facility for the Royal Opera House operas and ballets; 'The Backstage Centre' is here opened by Creative & Cultural skills and now houses their national headquarters; also situated here are 43 artist studios in the park opened by ACME Studios
- Hornchurch Aerodrome Historical Trust, RAF Hornchurch Heritage Centre, 119-121 Suttons Lane, Hornchurch RM12 6RU
- The former ROTOR station, (Cold War Secret Nuclear Bunker) Kelvedon Hatch built hidden beneath a bungalow, 100 feet underground to house up to 600 government personnel in the event of nuclear war
- London Open House is a free festival of London's architecture, engineering and urban landscape from the medieval to the thoroughly modern, held annually over one weekend in September
- Brentwood Cathedral by Quinlan Terry architect specialising in high quality new buildings in a classical and traditional style. Here the design builds onto the original Gothic style Victorian parish church in Italianate Classical style to create opportunity for worship 'in the round' following modern liturgical fashion
- Rom Skateboard Park, Romford (grade II listed) and Documentary *40 Years of RAD*
- Walk Section 24 of the London Loop that runs alongside the river Thames between Rainham and Purfleet and overlooks the RSPB Reserve which has also preserved an Anti-Submarine Blockhouse and a section of the Firing Ranges, the Cordite Store and an Anti-Aircraft Ammunition Magazine on the marshes. 'The Diver: Regeneration' sculpture by John Kaufman stands near to the concrete barges in the Thames and was erected in 2002, shortly before the artist's death. The sculpture is made of galvanised steel bands on a steel frame and stands 4.6m (15ft.) tall and some 1.8m (6ft.) wide and at the time it was the only sculpture in the Thames. It is partly-submerged every high tide and totally submerged by spring and neap tides;
- Thames Chase Walks 1; 2; 3; 4; 5; 6a; 6b; 7; 8; 9; 10; 11; 12 and Broadfields Tree Trail begin from the modern and award-winning Thames Chase Forest Centre at Broadfields Farm
- Thames Chase Walks D1; D2; D3; D4; D5 are Destination walks

- Other walks include the Gruffalo Walk at Thorndon Country Park; Belhus Country Park Walk; the London Loop sections 20; 21; 22; 23; 24 and the Thames Estuary Path 1; 2; 3; 4; 5
- The Building Centre, Store Street, London is a not-for-profit organisation that promotes innovation in the built environment and is dedicated to education, information and inspiration, including for the general public, in architecture and construction
- The D-Day Story, Portsmouth, PO5 3NT

Ideas for future projects:

- See *New Mythologies – short stories about Havering past and present* edited by Ben Musgrave, Havering's Writer in Residence 2004 and *The Stamina of Sheep – the Havering poems* (ISBN 0-9539939-1-4) and the *Havering Poetry Study Pack* (ISBN 0-9539939-2-2) by Mario Petrucci for ideas about writing new stories and poems inspired by local history tales and events
- Consider the significant response of this landscape to the many demands of national transportation systems with their ancillary and support services and networks providing enhanced economic trade and visitor links with Continental Europe against adverse impact upon this landscape, the potential effect on it and particularly on the fen ditch landscape and the historic settlements of the Mardyke river valley. The listed buildings in this area and the archaeology and SAM's, would also need to be carefully understood and considered to avoid or mitigate adverse impact of schemes such as the proposed Lower Thames Crossing alignment in the area for example and with informed consideration given to the likely impact of new strategic proposals on this landscape

References for further research:

More information on this historical period can be found through:
- Thurrock Local History Society online
- Laindon & District Community Archive online
- Museum of London and Museum of London Docklands
- Historic Environment Records (HERS) and Sites & Monuments Records (SAMs)
- *Chadwell Heath Anti-aircraft Gun Site Conservation Area Appraisal,* LBB&D 2009
- Central and Local Government policies include:
  - National Planning Policy Framework
  - National Planning Practice Guidance
  - Individual Local Authority *Local Plans*

Further Reading:

- Fox, Michael (2014) *Chelmsford Diocese – the first 100 years* pub. Chelmsford Diocesan Board of Finance
- Deere, Group Captain Alan, DSO OBE DFC (1959) *Nine Lives* pub. Goodall Publications 1999 ISBN 10: 0907579825 ISBN 13: 9780907579823
- Jackson, Sophie, *Churchill's Unexpected Guests* pub. The History Press ISBN 10: 0752455656/ ISBN 13: 9780752455655

- Kemp, Sylvie (2019) *Brentwood in 50 Buildings* ISBN 9781445692135
- Pollard, Tony & Oliver, Neill (2003) *Two Men in a Trench II: Uncovering the Secrets of British Battlefields* pub. Michael Joseph ISBN 978-0-7181-4594-1;
- Porter, Ken & Wynn, Stephen (2012) *German P.O.W. Camp 266 Langdon Hills* pub. UK Unpublished ISBN: 978-1-84944-173-5
- Quin, Robin (2015) *Hitler's Last Army* ISBN: 9780752483313 pub. The History Press Ltd.
- Smith, Richard C. (2005) *Second To None*, pub. Grub Street ISBN 1-904010-78-4
- Thurrock Local History Society (2018) *Celebrating Thurrock's Rich Heritage* 2nd ed.
- Watt, Peter (1994) *Hitler V Havering* pub. Carlton Armitage Press 1994 ISBN 0 9524032 0 X

Legacy

By gathering together the history and heritage of this landscape as a whole entity for the first time, researchers, students and the general public have access to an immediate understanding and opportunity for interpretation of the local heritage and its place in history. By exploring the sense and meaning of this landscape through written records and taking opportunity to provide an outlet for local knowledge local people, visitors, and those on the ancestry trail alike may have a conduit for their local interest and discover or renew their enthusiasm for this landscape and its cultural and natural heritage.

An understanding of the heritage of this landscape may be achieved by drawing together the details of its natural formation through its geological evolution and the resultant geography; and the prehistory story of human impact and influence on the landscape told through the archaeology of the area and the historical events that have all come naturally out of its geological origins, and by considering the current trends and pressures and their mitigation. This can lead to improved and better informed and coordinated use of the area for all by revealing the significance of the landscape through understanding its historic legacy and what it has to offer through its cultural and natural heritage. The objectives can be achieved by sharing this information and by uniting sites through physical linkages and publicising information and by working together for cohesiveness and inclusivity and through partnership working.

Local people, visitors and decision-makers deserve access to a good understanding of the identity and significance of the landscape so that balanced planning, design and development decisions can be made and with well-informed mitigating solutions where necessary. This also provides a basis for better connecting the often isolated visitor attractions and revealing their significance, their offer and their physical and historical links that are crucially needed to help re-establish linkages and a *sense of place* to this historic landscape.

DiscoverMe (Discover Metropolitan Essex) aids in bringing together many fascinating local heritage sites to assist in exploring historical treasures of Metropolitan Essex on day-out or half-day linked visits to more than a dozen attractions that are, as they say 'intriguing heritage and inspiring architecture and things to do for all the family' (http://discoverme.london).

DiscoverMe exhibiting in the Elm Barn at an event at Thames Chase Visitor Centre

There are also nine **Visitor Centres** across this landscape (see Chapter 1 map) with at least another planned at Rainham Riverside. They provide access to nature, wildlife, history and heritage, and opportunities for friends to meet, clubs and societies to be formed and events organised, with activities and play opportunities for children and very often refreshments and a welcome loo break, also sport and leisure provision and opportunity through leaflets and posters for example to learn so much more about visitor opportunity across the LotF landscape.

In fact **Thames Chase Trust** is perfectly positioned at the heart of this landscape to lead partnership working in organising, providing and managing these objectives in order to help ease the current pressure and to make improved, and better informed and coordinated use of this landscape. Even more than this, local people can have fun at local Fairs such as R.A.V.E. (Rainham Events & Fayres) summer and winter events in Rainham Village, or the traditional Horseman's Sunday at Havering-atte-Bower.

Rainham R.A.V.E. Fayre in summer

Rainham Village School pupils singing at Christmas to Santa, to Havering's Mayor and the public

They can get involved with Community Plays through local theatres like the Queen's Theatre in Hornchurch or otherwise come together through membership of local heritage groups like HABCOS in Havering-atte-Bower or a Community Forum (C.F.) such as Bulphan C.F. Local people can volunteer time and learn new skills for example through Thames Chase, EWT or the RSPB at Rainham Marshes, in order to be actively involved in reading, serving and protecting the local natural and built heritage for all.

Ideas for future projects:

For a schools project, advertise or market the Land of the Fanns by designing a poster or leaflet or write a magazine or newspaper article or social media post, or compose a jingle or radio advertisement or plan out a draft video promoting the LotF. Your target audience might be families, day-trippers, retirees, business owners, London commuters, foreign business investors or housing developers for example. Encourage them to take pride in the LotF as much as you do. Say where the LotF is, what is here, what you love about it and any other things you would like people to know about this landscape like its history and wildlife, its busy, working landscape or its vulnerability to development pressure (National Curriculum link to English, art, music, Design & Technology Key Stages 2-4)

- See the online LotF Learning Resource www.landofthefannslearning.org
- Find out more about current local activities on the Thames Chase or the DiscoverMe websites as well as individual visitor attraction websites and through local history societies across this Land of the Fanns landscape

Appendix

Abbreviations used in the text and references for further research:

INTRODUCTION
LotF Land of the Fanns
GCSE General Certificate of Secondary Education
KS1, 2, 3, 4, 5: Key Stages for Education
 Bright ideas and projects for kids

NATURE CONSERVATION
BAP Biodiversity Action Plan
BHS (British Horse Society)
CoWS County Wildlife Sites
EWT Essex Wildlife Trust
fp public footpath
LNR Local Nature Reserve
NCA National Character Area
NIA Nature Improvement Area
RSPB Royal Society for the Protection of Birds
SINC Site of Importance for Nature Conservation

GEOLOGY
kya thousand years ago
mya million years ago
MIS marine isotope stage
RIGS Regionally Important Geological Site

ARCHEOLOGY
AD *Anno Domini* – in Latin *the year of our Lord* – running forwards from AD1
BC *Before Christ* running backwards from 1BC
BP: *Before the Present*
APA Archaeological Priority Area: Designated area of known, or particular potential for new archaeological discoveries. May also be called Archaeological Priority Zones (APZ) or Areas of Archaeological Significance/Importance/Interest or Areas of High Archaeological Potential for example
GLAAS Greater London Archaeological Advisory Service
GLSMR Greater London Sites & Monuments Record
MOL Museum of London
MOLAS Museum of London Archaeology Service
SAM Scheduled Ancient Monument
SSSI Site of Special Scientific Interest
UNESCO World Heritage site: United Nations Educational, Scientific and Cultural Organisation

BUILT HERITAGE

CTRL Channel Tunnel Rail Link
D-Day term used in military planning for a Day set for launching a wartime operation
EHER Essex Historic Environment Record
ERO Essex Record Office
EH English Heritage
HE Historic England
HER Historic Environment Record: Heritage Gateway provides access to county and Unitary Authority HER's
ILNCA Inner London National Character Area
MGB Metropolitan Green Belt
MCC Marylebone Cricket Club – the guardian of the laws of cricket
MA wartime Marshalling Area
NHLE National Heritage List for England
NMR National Monuments Record
NPPF National Planning Policy Framework
RAF Royal Air Force
RAVE Rainham Association for Village Events
RCHME Royal Commission on Historic Monuments of England volumes
TF British Army Territorial Force
UEP Unlocking Essex Past
WAAF Women's Auxiliary Air Force
WWI World War 1 (The Great War)
WW2 World War 2 (The Second World War)
VCH Victoria County History of Essex volumes

LOCAL AUTHORITIES

PLU Poor Law Union
USD Urban Sanitary District
RSD Rural Sanitary District
UD Urban District
RD Rural District
BBC Brentwood Borough Council
LBH London Borough of Havering
LBB&D London Borough of Barking & Dagenham
TBC Thurrock Borough Council
LCC London County Council

NATIONAL AMENITY SOCIETIES

AMS Ancient Monument Society (now Historic Buildings and Places) together with the Friends of Friendless Churches
CBA Council for British Archaeology; CBA(L): CBA London Branch; CBA East: CBA East of England; YAC: Young Archaeologists Club
GG Georgian Group: Objectives are to save Georgian buildings, monuments, parks and gardens, from destruction or disfigurement and to stimulate public knowledge and appreciation for them for the period 1700-1840
VicSoc Victorian Society covers the period 1837-1914 (Victorian and Edwardian)
20th C. Soc. Twentieth Century Society (buildings from 1914 onwards)
SPAB Society for the Protection of Ancient Buildings and includes a Mills Section
GHS The Garden History Society regarding registered historic parks and gardens

Acknowledgements and thanks

My most grateful thanks are extended to all who encouraged, helped produce or checked the contents of this Book, however any opinions expressed belong to the author alone and any errors or omissions are my own.

My most particular thanks go to:

My husband Ian, who patiently read the drafts and generously produced many of the photographs and illustrations, and family Alan and Sarah, and to Settle & Green Architects for their unwavering support and unlimited use of office time and equipment; also to Simon Donoghue, Paul Sainsbury, Susan Yates, Adam Single, Ian and Ros Mercer, Lisa Lock, Geoff Hodges, Paul Dennis, Mike Hansford, Mick Greenslade, Andrew Curtin, Lesley Davis, Ken Hill, Ken Worpole, Yvonne Evans, Sylvia Bates, Tony Gunton and Don Tait; the HLF LotF Team: Benj. Sanderson, Debbie Brady, Aisling Woodhead and Joanne Dungate; the LotF Partner organisations and members of the LotF Heritage Working Group, the Heritage Lottery Fund and other grant givers including those organisations that kindly permitted the reproduction of images.

Also, for generously sharing their memories: Bill Hansford Snr. and Barbara Hansford, Mrs E.J. Hopkins, Babs & Jack Smith, Tony Whitmarsh, Gill Livingston, Olive and Marion Jacobs and Mr J. Hardes.

I gratefully acknowledge the work of TellTale and of Kinetica, Alison Farmer Associates and Scott Sullivan for their part in interpreting the landscape. Also to Mary Wright at Thames Chase for helping me to see the landscape as a whole and especially to Bob Flindall for giving me the opportunity to compile the book.

P.S. here are the answers to the picture clues... The rushes are derived from the Bulphan and Orsett fens and marshy fanns central to this area; across this is drawn an outline of the shape of the Land of the Fanns landscape with red brickwork for the historic built heritage here; the architectural fanlight window is a play on words, it is divided into stained glass window panes, the coloured glass is white for the chalk with its fossils, blue for the rivers and the shipping, green for the woodlands, yellow for the fields and agriculture and grey for the Thameside industry. Well done if you got all the clues and answers correct – you certainly know your Land of the Fanns!

Notes

Notes

Notes

Notes